# Indians

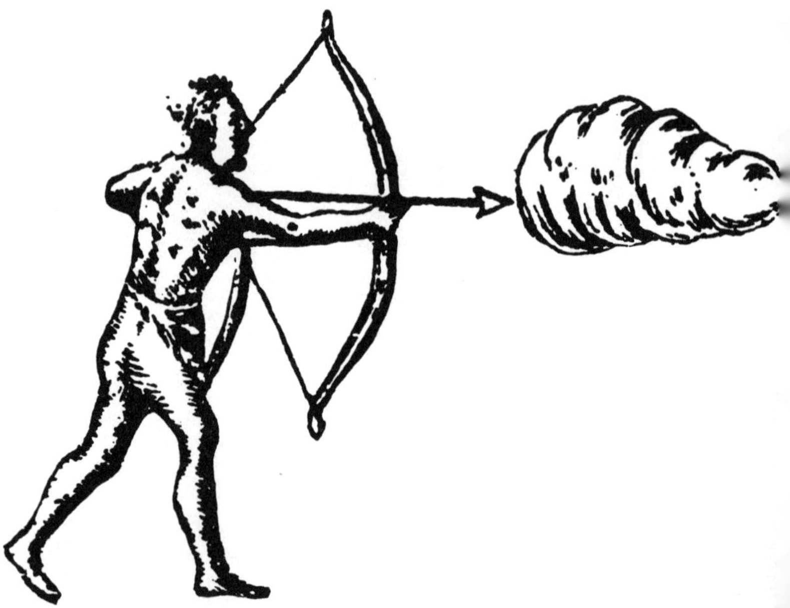

# Indians

William Brandon

HOUGHTON MIFFLIN COMPANY
BOSTON • NEW YORK

An American Heritage Book



Visit our Web site: www.houghtonmifflinbooks.com.



Library of Congress Cataloging-in-Publication
Data is available.

ISBN 0-618-16732-3

Printed in the United States of America

QUM 10 9 8 7 6 5 4 3 2 1

# Table of Contents

# I

# People of the Dawn

**This male figure was carved about 800 to 400 B.C. by the Olmecs, reknowned for their fat-lipped, baby-faced sculpture and their preoccupation with the monstrous.**

In the first days of men the world was new, and it really was. It seems to be sober scientific fact that the world was veritably remade in the geologic era preceding the coming of man. Flowers appeared, and songbirds, and hardwood trees. The marsh and mud landscape over which the giant reptiles had crawled was transformed into mountains, lakes, streams, flower-strewn meadows, and forests that turned from green to golden with each passing summer. The earth was bejeweled with colors, grandeurs, and beauties great and small it had never known before. Into this setting mankind was born.

The half of this new-made Eden waiting in the Western Hemisphere remained untouched for hundreds of thousands of years, according to present evidence, while thousands of generations of the earliest ape men and men of the Old Stone Age roamed the other continents.

No race of these earliest men seems to have originated in the Americas. Fossil forms of anthropoid apes or of the superapes which apparently set the stage for the emergence of man in Europe, Asia, and Africa have never been found in the New World. No American skeletal remains of archaic human forms ("no Pithecanthropi, no Sinanthropi, and no Neanderthaloids," in the words of one authority) have yet been discovered. The most ancient human bones brought to light in the Americas have been certified those of man in his present form, Homo sapiens.

Homo sapiens' precursors, the heavy-handed people of the Old Stone Age, are estimated to have begun fashioning their earliest fist-axes more than half a million years ago. But the first appearance of Homo sapiens himself is usually estimated to date back less—and possibly considerably less—than 100,000 years ago.

At some unknown time and place after the development of Homo sapiens, the forebears of the American Indians entered the still untouched New World.

The where and when of that entrance has excited a good deal of guesswork. In a more innocent age, when Archbishop Ussher's date for the creation of the earth (4004 B.C., at 9 o'clock of a Friday morning) was still printed as a learned footnote in Bible margins, the American Indians were suspected of being Egyptians, Phoenicians, Greeks, Romans, Chinese, Japanese, Welsh,

Irish, or descendants of the Lost Ten Tribes of Israel, or of having made their way hither via a lost continent of Atlantis or a lost continent of Mu, or both.

Modern science has shown that the American Indians are far more ancient than any of these candidates. Finds have been made proving the presence of man in America at the time of such Ice Age big game as camels, mammoths, giant ground sloths, and primitive horses—in other words during the last of the Pleistocene glaciations, the last great Ice Age, which drew to a close some 10,000 years ago. Even that remote date is being pushed back much farther into the past.

These dates can be given with a fair amount of assurance, long ago as they are, due to the technique of carbon 14 dating, a system of archaeological dating that can often provide almost calendar accuracy. This method uses laboratory tests of organic substances to compute the residue of a radioactive isotope of carbon designated as carbon 14. Carbon 14 is present in fixed proportions in most living organisms, and disintegrates at a constant measurable rate after the death of its host. It thus acts as an atomic clock of sorts, pinpointing the age of the substance tested with a precision only limited by the exactness of the measurement. The precision attained is quite remarkable, leaving an almost inconsequential margin of error of a few hundred years out of several thousand years.

These radiocarbon dates are not always infallible, but enough have accumulated, in conjunction with other archaeologic and geologic evidence, to place man unshakably in America well before 10,000 years ago, and probably before 20,000 years ago; certainly before the end of the last glacial period. A recent discovery near Puebla, Mexico (of which more later), may push back the horizon to well before 30,000 years ago.

And the wind blows steadily toward a still more distant dawn. Blood-group studies of living Indians have recorded the purest type-A groups in the world, as well as the only known populations entirely lacking A; the purest O groups in the world; and the purest B group in the world. An eminent geographer concludes that the basic peopling of the Americas may have taken place "before the primordial blood streams of man became mingled."

One thing is obvious: if the American Indians can claim direct descent from those early people of 15,000 or 20,000 years ago, and some undoubtedly can, then they are by far the oldest known race on earth. There is no evidence of the identifiable appearance of any of the other modern races, Mongolian, white, or Negro, until much later.

Time is the tonic chord in the story of the Indian.

With this sort of antiquity, it is clear the first Indians must have arrived long before there were boats anywhere capable of ocean crossings. The only place of entry more or less accessible by land from the Old World was Alaska at Bering Strait, separated from northeastern Asia by less than sixty miles. Two stepping-stone islands, the Diomedes, break the water distance into still shorter stages, the longest only twenty-five miles. At times, furthermore, the Strait is frozen over and can be crossed on the ice; and at times in the geologic past it has been dry land—more often than has the Isthmus of Panama. Mongolian characteristics of some Indians, implying an origin in Asia, corroborate the proposition of a long-used Bering Strait entry, which is so universally agreed upon by the experts today that it is scarcely regarded as a theory any longer, but as a well-established fact.

But entrance via the North, before 10,000 years ago, collides with those Pleistocene glaciations which sheathed the shoulders of the earth in ice and presumably barred any migrations. Either the first people came between glaciations or a way must be found for them through the ice. Both are feasible.

There were four major Pleistocene glaciations, each enduring for many thousands of years, separated by interglacial periods that lasted even longer when the climate probably became much as it is today—we are supposedly living in one such interglacial period now. Dates for the duration of the last great glacial advance, known in America as the Wisconsin glaciation, are in a state of flux. It used to be thought of as existing for more than 100,000 years before it retreated nearly 10,000 years ago, but the latest fashion is to give its duration less than half that long.

The glacial periods may have been distinguished by unimaginable rains and snows rather than unimaginable cold. The seas were lowered many feet by the volume of water turned into snow and ice, and the weight of the ice warped and buckled the crust of the land. Beaches and islands existed that are now ocean floor. At times during this era the Bering Strait may well have been a broad grass-grown plain.

These tremendous changes drove animals and plants from one part of the world to another, and where there were people they must have been driven also, whether so slowly they knew not that they moved, or otherwise. Each such tremendous change took at least centuries and often millennia to come about, immemorial multitudes of generations to short-lived prehistoric man.

Most of Alaska was ice-free during the glacial epochs—the glaciers did not spread from the North Pole, but radiated in all directions from centers in the latitude of Hudson Bay. Most of Siberia was icebound, apparently, with the possible exception of occasional valleys and the farthest North.

Perhaps the first human beings to drift from Siberia into Alaska were thrust along by these conditions, ice imperceptibly smothering Siberia behind them, Alaska's sweeping valleys imperceptibly filling up with refugee game ahead of them. Or perhaps they first came during an iceless interglacial period, following only the ineluctable gradient of time. Time, enough time, can herd along people unaided; it doesn't need an assist from readily discernible motives of man.

Movement southward from Alaska during epochs of glacial flows would have been limited. Canada generally was covered with plateaus of ice as much as 10,000 feet high. But geologists suggest a number of possible routes. For a period of several thousand years, in the early middle of the Wisconsin, an ice-free corridor hundreds of miles wide ran along the east of the Rockies all the way from the Arctic to the open country south of Canada. Several thousand years later another passage was open for a time through the Alberta-Saskatchewan plains east of the Rockies. Wanderers from Alaska could have reached them by way of the Alaskan north coast and the Mackenzie River valley—these areas were never glaciated. Several thousand years after that, in the last stages of the Wisconsin, passable travel might have been managed via the Yukon and the Peace, and Liard River valleys of northwestern Canada.

With the present confusion of dates concerning the duration of the Wisconsin, it is not possible to make up a theoretical timetable out of these theoretical routes. However, the first passage mentioned appears to have been the only one open early enough to get the first man down into the continent in time to occupy the sites archaeologists are dating for him—if even that will do.

If not, we will be forced to assume that the first American appeared some time in the long ice-free period that preceded the Wisconsin.

After that, any Ice Age routes later open could have been and probably were used by later peoples. The gradual populating of the Americas apparently went on for a very long time and involved various groups of differing physical types. Mankind's dawdling and discursive march from the Bering Strait to Tierra del Fuego may have taken, as a German geographer has calculated, something like 25,000 years.

Probably the view back through time to the childhood of man can only be seen in distortion. The world becomes a still picture, when it was alive with motion; or it moves, when it was as still as eternity.

The ice sheets of the "glacial periods" did not come and go as far as men living among them were concerned—they had always been there, the white lands beyond and beyond, and the tumbling cliffs of rotting ice along the edges, snarled with sodden vegetation, they were as permanent as mountains. The mammoths had not "migrated" from Asia with their mastodont ancestors—they had always been there, filling the forests with giant screams; the horses and camels were not migrating from America but had always been there, racing in herds over the rain-swept tundra, and a man's mother's mother's mother could tell how they had always been there in her day.

There is no reason whatever to suppose that men of such times were consciously migrating; they were only living, and very likely this valley or that had always been home until eventually some families found themselves spending more time in the valley across the ridge, and that became in turn forever home.

"Anything seems possible that is not immediately necessary," wrote the philosopher J. H. Klaren, and the reverse is equally true: given enough time, anything is possible. Lands are remade, beasts become men, and men become strangers to their fathers.

The drift of the first population may have followed the Rockies and Andes as principal north-south axes down into the two continents. From the eastern flanks of the Rockies people may have moved westward through South Pass to the Great Basin, eastward along the rivers leading to the Mississippi, westward

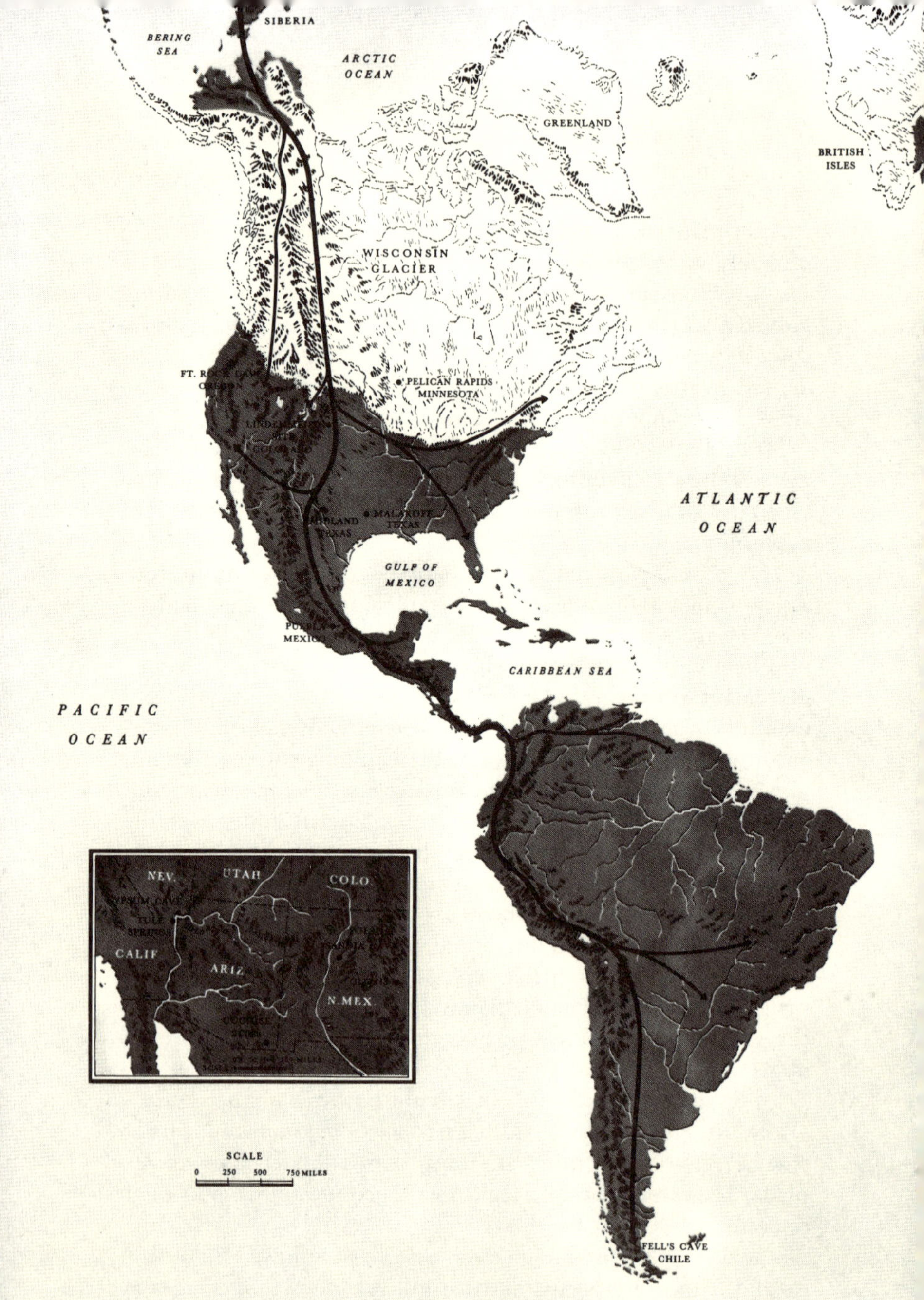


**This map shows the main routes used by early Americans as they populated the New World.**

around the southern heel of the Rockies to the pluvial lakes then watering what is now the desert of the lower Colorado, and on from this region to southern California, the Northwest Coast not being reached until much later.

In South America the hypothetical spread of the first population may have threaded down within the Andes from Venezuela to Bolivia, a center for subsequent penetration southward and eastward.

The coming of the people and the sagas of their ancient wanderings are only matters for speculation after all. A figure stirs behind the mists across the river of time, and all our piety and wit can make it nothing more. "The fogs of creation," goes a Zuñi legend, "the mists potent with growth."

But the story left in stone and bone is something else again. Wherever she came from, however she got there, a young woman died some 8,000 or 10,000 years ago in what is now west Texas near the New Mexico line at a site known as Midland; wind scoured the sand away from over her bones and they were found in the 1950s. Wherever they came from, men lived in a cave near the southern tip of South America (Fell's Cave) some 8,000 or 10,000 years or so ago, as men lived in a cave at about the same time 4,000 miles away in Nevada (Gypsum Cave), in both cases seemingly butchering twenty-foot ground sloths that may have sometimes been kept penned up like cattle, and in both cases leaving behind stone tools and spearheads that were found in the bottom layers of successions of floor levels indicating thousands of years of occupancy. Stone points made by men of the same approximate epoch have been found elsewhere on both continents.

Several thousand years earlier, at least more than 11,000 or 12,000 years ago, people hunting mammoths on the shores of Ice Age lakes near Clovis, New Mexico, left ivory spearheads as well as points of stone among the bones; and nearby in space but apparently far earlier still in time other people lugged a mammoth tusk into the New Mexico mountain cave (Sandia Cave) that was their home and left it there, together with spear points and the bones of camels, mastodons, and of the prehistoric American horses that have been long extinct. These things also were found in the lowest of several occupation levels. Many such dates are now regarded as fairly certain in their general range, and those quoted above are on the conservative side.

The mammoth tusk from Sandia Cave bears a carbon 14 age of more than 20,000 years, but it could have been several thousand years old when it was brought into the cave. Four samples of burned dwarf-mammoth bones from a "barbecue pit" on Santa Rosa Island off California produced radiocarbon dates averaging 29,650 (±2,500) years ago, but critics are not yet agreed that it was a man-made barbecue pit. Charcoal from a hearth beside a lake in what is now Nevada desert (Tule Springs) has provided carbon 14 dates far in excess of 20,000 years ago, but again there is as yet no absolute proof the charcoal came from a man-made fire.

Years ago, in 1870, deep-ditching work in the region of Tequixquiac, near Mexico City, uncovered at a depth of forty feet a llama bone, from an extinct species, carved to represent the face of a wild pig or coyote. A number of other artifacts and Pleistocene fossils have been found since in the same area, in two distinct geological formations, the younger dated at more than 11,000 years ago. Near Malakoff, Texas, not far from Dallas, gravel-pit workers found three heavy disks of sandstone roughly carved into human faces, veritable men of stone peering out to us from across the past. Geology dates them from long before the close of the Pleistocene. The gravel pits also yielded bones of mammoths and Ice Age horses.

And the aforementioned Puebla find: in the spring of 1959, at a site known as Tetela, southeast of Puebla, Mexico, four fragments of mammoth or mastodon bone were discovered on which were engraved feline heads, serpents, mastodons, and hunting scenes, all executed with an extraordinary artistic ability considering their probably antiquity. The find was kept secret for more than a year while Dr. Juan Armenta, in charge of the excavation, invited leading specialists to study what is perhaps an epoch-making discovery in the literal sense of the word, for a new epoch in the prehistory books will probably be coined from it. The belief at present, based on the geology of the site and the fossils found in association with these carvings, is that they may actually date back to the long ice-free period before the beginning of the Wisconsin glaciation. If so, they will prove to be of prime importance not only for the ancient history of America but for the entire world.

And so the people came. They came long before the invention

of the bow and arrow, before the domestication of the dog. They had fire, they roasted meat, they worked stone, horn, bone, and probably skins—skeletons of the extinct great-horned bison killed some 10,000 years ago are missing the tail bones, indicating the skins were taken. They made beads and used paint taken from a red iron oxide, and they drew pictures that are filled with exuberant action. And they were there. Scattered bands of new-made people watching through the interminable dawn of a new-made world, they were on hand when Niagara Falls came into being, and when Crater Lake in Oregon was exploded into existence.

"The Creator made the world—come and see it," says a Pima prayer.

Inference is probably a more hazardous game than pure speculation, but it might be inferred that some at least of these people practiced some at least of those rites thought to be nearly as old as humanity, rites practiced by Neanderthalers 100,000 years ago and perhaps even by ape men of the earliest times, rites involving fire and thunder and lightning; ceremonies involving physical demonstrations—dancing—of the entire family or band to show its wish to protect the individual member imperiled by such mysteries as birth, the rhythmic flow of woman's blood, and the dead. It might also be assumed that they lived with the world rather than in it, as much a part of the setting fashioned by nature around them as fingers are part of a hand, and it would follow as a matter of course that the beasts, trees, winds, and stars of that setting pondered and talked, aspired, feared, and desired as did anyone else. In fact, what was life but a conversation between all such beings, of whom man was only one? Pan had a long childhood.

The impressive thing about this world, after all, is time. The people can be imagined, and their thoughts and ways, everything but those limitless reaches of time, time so much longer than all the centuries of written history, while men leaned on their spears and dreamed and nothing really changed at all.

Such divisions of that time as exist are marked off for us principally by the changing forms for spear points and dart points and, later, arrowheads. These, and other weapons and utensils, are usually in stone. Time has consumed, for the most part, relics in other materials. There are some scraps of basketry (fragments of fine twined work were found in Fort Rock Cave,

Oregon, together with dozens of pairs of partly burned sandals made—and well made—of shredded sagebrush bark; the sandals produced a carbon 14 age of about 9,000 years), a few bits of wood, a number of pieces in horn and bone, and not much else as far as the earlier horizons are concerned.

The meager number of human bones from these times has a special reason all its own: the experts, until recently, were not looking for them. They were looking instead for an American Pithecanthropus, evidence that a separate branch of humanity might have originated in the New World. Otherwise, as was generally agreed, human beings could only have arrived a very few thousand years ago at the earliest, and the relative age of their bones was unimportant. Therefore, skulls and bones of claimed antiquity were examined, argued about, and judged on the basis of possible simian and other pre–Homo sapiens characteristics, and since no such characteristics were clearly established, they were all thrown out.

Nowadays some of them are being dusted off for another look, and the sites of their discovery reexplored. They range all the way from large finds of many burials to single bones, and geographically from South America through Mexico to Minnesota, and from Florida to California. "Minnesota Man," who was really a young girl, and Mexico's Tepexpan Man, both subjects of angry controversy, are among several that claim guess dates in excess of 10,000 years. Texas's female "Midland Man," mentioned earlier, is commonly regarded as having the most respectable proof of such great age.

The people who lived in Sandia Cave a possible 20,000 years ago left spear points of a distinctive silhouette: one-shouldered, heavy, long (up to four inches), roughly bayonet-shaped. Points of this type have since been found elsewhere in the Southwest and reported from other places as far apart as Alberta and Alabama.

The people who hunted mammoths on the shores of bygone lakes near Clovis, New Mexico, apparently several thousand years after the Sandia people, left stone spearheads of about the same size, but bullet-shaped and without the single shoulder, and grooved or "fluted" part way up the face. Clovis points have been found over the High Plains and the Southwest together with bones of musk ox, mammoths, and the rest of the usual Pleistocene cast of characters. Possible Clovises have turned up throughout the United States, sometimes in large numbers, and several have been reported from Mexico and from the Alberta-Saskatchewan plains of Canada.

Some thousands of years later still, perhaps 10,000 years ago, the famous Folsom point came into use. It is famous for having provided the first proof of the existence of American Glacial Man, with the discovery, in 1927, near Folsom, New Mexico, of one such point embedded between the ribs of an Ice Age buffalo. A great number of Folsoms have since been found over a wide area, but centering in the high Plains region and remaining pretty much east of the Rockies. A light, beautifully made point, distinguished by a long groove or fluting running up each face, it is smaller than either the Clovis or Sandia. The mammoth seems to have disappeared by this time, at any rate from the Southwest, and the giant ground sloth, an emigrant from South America, had spread from coast to coast, but the commonest kill for Folsom man was the colossal antique bison, whose hornspread could measure up to six feet.

Assortments of implements in chipped stone and occasionally worked bone have been found with all these various points, as well as rare beads and pendants. At a Folsom site in northeastern Colorado (Lindenmeier) some mysterious bone disks decorated with tiny incised lines have been turned up. There is a theory these might have been markers for a game of some kind. They look a little like poker chips.

With the Folsom people the glacial period suffered its final decline and became the geological Present, which embraces the past 8,000 or 9,000 years.

An early date of considerable interest comes from the Great Lakes area in and about Wisconsin, where the people of the Old Copper Culture made lance points (some of them socketed) and a profusion of other articles from the copper native to the region. Until very recently this culture was thought to date back 1,200 years or so, and it was "amazing to find a well-developed copper industry" so early, as a leading archaeologist wrote in 1947. Since then, carbon 14 tests and other evidence have dated it back to something between 5,000 and 7,000 years ago, a very early time for use of metal anywhere in the world, and incidentally the earliest definite date yet in hand for the presence of any people in the northeastern United States.

Another interesting early date comes from the site of a great bygone lake, given the posthumous name of Lake Cochise, in the now blazing desert country where Arizona, New Mexico, and Mexico meet. Here are signs of continuous habitation for many thousands of years by a people at least as ancient as the Folsom hunters, and yet quite different from them in their way of life. The chief items in all phases of this continuity are stones and pestles, known as "milling stones," obviously used for grinding or pounding some sort of food in the form of wild grains or seeds, and here again is an extremely early appearance anywhere in the world, for the oldest phase of the Cochise complex is dated at 9,000 years ago or more.

And still another comes from the maize found in a cave, Bat Cave, in western New Mexico. It is primitive maize, "pod corn," each kernel enclosed in a husk of its own (incidentally, it was also popcorn), but a hybridized form of the native wild corn and thus unquestionably cultivated by man, and it is some 5,000 to 6,000 years old (5,605 to 5,931 by carbon 14). Considering that this maize was a long way from the presumed first centers of beginning agriculture in the Americas (presumably agriculture first began far to the south, in the areas that later produced high civilizations), this age is venerable indeed. Villages of outright farmers were still to come, of course, but for comparison the earliest traces of one of the first farming villages in the Old World (Jarmo, in Iraq) have been dated by carbon 14 tests at between 5,000 and 7,000 years ago.

From end to end of the two Americas a people lived, many differing groups of many diverse kinds of people, strangers to each other, unknown to one another except at each little ripple of contact. The ripples transmitted ways of life and thought, sometimes with amazing fidelity and sometimes monstrously garbled, to the farthest points of the inhabited land, and then rebounded with as much force as before. They started from nowhere and they never ended. They crossed and recrossed each other at all angles, and their patterns changed at each new voice.

A man might live out his life and never leave his valley, a family might never have seen foreigners as long as could be remembered, and the cycle of the years might never have been disturbed in their land which they knew bush by bush and that never changed, and yet life was in constant motion. New people crossed the sill of the world in the distant north, and still another

This split-twig deer, one of many found since 1933 in almost inaccessible caves of Arizona's Grand Canyon, is probably more than 3,000 years old. It is believed to be a talisman used by prehistoric men to ensure successful hunts.

ripple was added, and another and another and another, at every fear or joy or thought encountered in its passage. Seen against a scale of centuries, the knots of people moved, merged, split, multiplied, died, appeared from every compass point.

We came from beneath the ground, the legends say, we came from the sunrise of the east, or the sunset of the west. We climbed up to the light from the bowels of our holy mountain, we climbed down from the sky by a ladder of arrows. At first there was only the god Coyote or Raven, Serpent or Jaguar. At first there was "only the calm water, the placid sea, alone and tranquil. Nothing existed," say the Mayas. And at first there was only the sea, say also the seafaring Haida of the Northwest Coast, and down at the volcanic tail of South America, not surprisingly, the Ona people have a tradition that "they came from the north and became isolated from their kin by a great cataclysm, which rent their island from the mainland."

In ancient times there were white men with long black beards, say people thousands of miles apart. A giant black man lives in the heavens, or the woods, or the mountains, and punishes those who do wrong. In ancient times women ruled, because they had the magic masks, or the magic flutes, but men spied on them and stole their magic away. In ancient times a beautiful girl had a lover who came each night but would not let her see who he was, so she painted her hands, or rubbed them in soot, and that night embraced her lover again, and the next day saw the marks of her hands on the back of her brother. She ran from him in horror and he ran after her, so she turned herself into the sun and he turned himself into the moon, and he still appears at night looking for her, but she has always gone away, and the marks of her hands are still on his back. In the first days men despaired and lost their repose, so the Creator gave them the tobacco and they chewed it and gained their repose, but it only lasted a short time and they despaired and lost their repose again, so the Creator gave them women.

All about them the world comprehended simply by being, and so did they. Of course there was meaning in the spring stars hanging in the silver branches of the spring forest, and the autumn stars hanging in the antlers of a tall silent beast, or the terror of a storm shouting in your ear, or the dread of hunger in black winter days.

With such comprehensions, the American Indians came into

existence, people of infinite differences and remarkable sameness. Some feared the world and placated its ferocity, and some worshiped with praise its goodness. Some apologized to animals they killed, and others insulted them. Some feared the dead—not so much death as the dead, with their unnatural sightless eyes and their ghosts that sprang up in the dark—and fled from the dead in panic, even while weeping with grief, to abandon them where they died; while others hung up the dead in a place of honor in the lodging and kept them there. One insistent tone is present in all these varying examples, an awareness of the harmony of things that can be struck out of balance at any moment, even by a man's own actions. (By a knife or a stone I can bring the abnormality of death; by careful and right behavior can I keep my normal world free of such abnormalities as death and sickness?) If time is the tonic note in the story of the Indians, this theme of the world's precarious harmony is the dominant.

It underlies one of the few traits that might be applied sweepingly to most American Indians, belief in a personally acquirable magic power. The widespread concept of ownership of land in common by a related group of people might be another such trait. These attitudes were overwhelmed in emerging societies elsewhere in the world by other sets of notions drawn from other primitive world views, but they gained the ascendancy in America. Operated upon by untroubled time, they became distinctively Indian.

By the dawn of the geological Present the giant beasts of the Pleistocene were gone—or nearly; some animals once thought long extinct may have survived here and there until much later times. But the usual game, about 8,000 years ago, had become modern, from the guanaco to the buffalo to the caribou. Native American horses had gone over the hill to extinction. It was still long before the bow; men hunted or fought with spears, clubs, slings, bolas—cords weighted at the ends with stones, flung to whip around the animal's legs and trip it up—or, like the heroes of the *Iliad*, with boulders.

Except for scattered fragments of weapons and tools, basketry and mats, jewels of shell or bone, and some knowledge or reasonable inferences as to their burial customs—naked in a pit or cremated, or the body tied huddled in a basket together with valuables, or the bones painted a bright red and laid out to point from the sunrise to the sunset—these people are as invisible today as the people of the long dawn before them.

Archaeology emphasizes weapon points, as it does later pottery, for the simple reason that these things offer a sequence of sorts and there's not much else to talk about anyway; but the making of the stone points could not have taken much of their time. Modern students have shown this by making very acceptable arrowheads and spear points, using the ancient flaking tools, in only a few minutes. Making them must have been as trivial a part of life as fixing a flat or washing the car today. But otherwise the people are voiceless and vanished. Projection of their shadows against the reality of how it must have been can only reveal further that they hunted or fished, built pitfalls and fish weirs, collected berries, and nuts, and roots that were good to eat, and that they traveled. Even though they stayed in a general area for thousands of years, they must have been always moving, incessantly following the seasons from the hills to the valleys, from the valleys to the hills.

Someplace, a people who doubtless had gathered wild seeds as part or most of their food since time immemorial found among the plants they came back to each year one with delicious seeds that became (we shall assume) especially famous among them. Perhaps they encouraged its growth, possibly weeding or digging around it, eventually replanted seeds from the best stalks, and at length were no longer dealing with a wild grass but cultivating a domestic plant, a plant the botanists now call *Zea mays*. When this first happened no one knows. The Bat Cave, New Mexico, instance and sites in the state of Tamaulipas, northeastern Mexico, revealing corn, primitive but domesticated, at a very early date, establish the presence and spread of its cultivation fairly securely in the area of 4,000 to 5,000 years ago.

The cultivation of squash, beans, or gourds may have preceded that of maize. The archaeologist who directed the excavations in Tamaulipas found evidence of the first haphazard motions toward farming 5,000 to 7,000 years ago, then a gradual increase in cultivated plants until, some 3,500 years ago, they amounted to about 15 percent of the food consumed—then an increase to about 40 percent during the next 1,500 years. Or the first plants worked with may have been still others, possibly some that no longer appear in the seed catalogues, such as cattails, cultivated at a very early date (4,044 ± 300 years ago) in

South America for their roots. Wherever they began, those that proved themselves worth the work all spread, slowly but surely, along the ripples of contact from valley to valley, from people to people.

Crops imply staying more or less close at hand to take care of them. By perhaps 4,000 years ago there were permanent villages in the Valley of Mexico and in the Guatemala region where the people raised both corn and cotton, and on the north coast of Peru where the people cultivated cattails, chili peppers, cotton, beans, although not yet corn, not for another 1,000 years or more. These people lived simply and their lives remained very much the same for generations. But in the course of the next 1,000 years pottery began to appear, and with it, at such early (1350–1100 B.C.) villages as El Arbolillo, Tlatilco, and Zacatenco in the Valley of Mexico, little clay figurines—and the people are faceless no longer.

They come marching into view tattooed, hung with ornaments, wearing turbans or string hats, otherwise usually naked. The majority of these figurines represent women with big hips, the age-old goddess of increase. If I model a fertile woman and show it to the world, will not the world become fertile in response? For all their archaic rigidity and the helpless clumsiness of the bits of clay stuck on them for eyes and mouths they are as animate with locked-in life as the springtime they symbolize. Some, originating in new villages a bit to the south, in Puebla and Morelos, are graceful, seductive, and young. They dance and run, doe-eyed, with bewitching smiles and beguiling bodies; they wear earrings and their elaborately coiled hair is sometimes streaked red and white, as the thatched mud-and-stick houses of the people were painted. They became understandably popular and were traded to all the villages of the Valley during many years; for in the beginning the goddess of love and the Earth Mother were one.

Now occurs an interesting parallel. New ways of doing things came to the Valley of Mexico and to the north coast of Peru at about the same time, give or take a few hundred years. A popular religious cult appeared with them, worshiping foreign gods perhaps brought from some tropical lowland region: a "feline" in Peru, a jaguar in Mexico. This began happening some 3,000 years ago, and for the next 500 to 1,000 years

**This delightful clay figurine representing a wide-hipped dancer dates from about 1,000 B.C. and is one of the earliest known portraitlike sculptures of people in the New World. It was found in an ancient pre–Classic-period Mexican grave beneath the site of a modern brickyard at Tlatilco, a suburb of Mexico City.**

the new styles, or the new peoples, remained in mastery of the loops and whorls of evolving little worlds in Peru and Mexico.

There is no suggestion they were the same people, or that the new styles reached each of these areas at exactly the same time. They may have been centuries apart, and while a few hundred years are not much in gross archaeological guesswork they can be all-important in real history, as for example the small matter of only 400 years separating the high point of Athens from the high point of Rome.

The place of earliest origin and development of these two styles is not yet pinned down; until it is, the early story of these little new worlds is rather like the story of early Greece (a contemporary) without Crete.

In Mexico, the strangers eventually became associated with the country later occupied by a people known as the Olmecs. Consequently, the early strangers have sometimes been called Olmecs too. Since 2,000 years separate them from the later, historic Olmecs, this has given rise to much confusion. To avoid this, the early people will be referred to here as the proto-Olmecs. Whoever they were, they made essentially the same figurines, and sorts of ornaments and pottery that had been made before them, but they did it a great deal better and they added their own particular designs. Their snarling jaguar's head or a peculiar "baby face," and a truly modern preoccupation with whatever was monstrous, deformed, disharmonic, appeared on all they touched.

And these people themselves come into view in their turn, fat little effeminate men with ornamentally deformed heads and ornamentally deformed teeth. They made some of the most charming of the seductive little figurines spoken of previously.

Through the years, through the centuries, they seemed to develop their most important centers in southern Veracruz, the rubber-producing country of ancient Mexico. Their island town of La Venta dates from about 800 B.C. They dragged multiton blocks of stone through the mangrove swamps to La Venta, to carve them into gigantic heads up to fourteen feet high, glorifying the typical fat-lipped "Olmec" baby face, and they worked jade with wizard skill into jewel-like representations of their half-human jaguars, deformed people, bearded men, and other monstrosities.

In the region next door, to the southeast, during the same

time, other maize-farming people were outgrowing the jaguar and baby-face cults of the proto-Olmecs to create a style of their own. In it they spring as resplendently to life as any people ever have in the art they left behind them. But they created more than a style; they created a civilization, one of the great civilizations of the ancient world. These were the Mayas.

Nearly everything is known about the Mayas (pronounced My-ahs, being a Spanish spelling) that any earnest archaeologist could want to know. We can follow every step in the techniques, each blow of every stone chisel involved in the building and adorning of their temples. We can unravel all the intricacies of their calendric calculations, which are quite impressive—their calendar in general use was one ten-thousandth of a day per year more accurate than is ours now. We know how they lived, loved, worked, talked, slept, worshiped, died. We know what they ate and how they cooked it, how they dressed, and how they wore their hair (long).

We know nearly everything about them, really, except what they said. Without that we really don't know the Mayas at all. These people present the most profound enigma in American history.

Why this should be so is a point of some interest. The Mayas attained the highest civilization known in ancient America, and one of the highest known anyplace in the early world. They developed a genuine written language, or a near thing to it—hieroglyphic ideographs, that is, conventionalized symbols standing for certain words, as in Chinese writing, or possibly to some extent (scholars disagree) representing phonetically syllables or sounds, as in the use of our own alphabet. Fragments of their written records remain, and some numerical parts of them have been deciphered, although this is not much help in knowing the people—as if all we had of Greek literature were some disjointed scraps from farmers' almanacs.

And the people remain, two to three million who speak the various related Maya dialects, and in many cases are so similar in appearance to the muscular, delicately posed little men on the temple walls that they could be the stuccoed frescoes come to life. Other people achieved less, left less, and in many cases have vanished altogether. Why, then, should this Maya puzzle remain to outpuzzle all the rest? The reason lies precisely in the heights they reached and fell from.

The Mayas practiced a primitive form of agriculture known to other primitive peoples all over the world since agriculture began: hacking down and burning trees and brush, planting a cornfield in the rough clearing, and slashing out a new such clearing a few seasons later. In all the days of their greatness, this technology was never improved. This kind of farming, by its nature, prohibits the growth of cities. Every man's home is his outlying jungle clearing, in contrast to the close communities fostered by such group undertakings as irrigation. And so the Mayas, in the days of their greatness, never built cities.

With no metals, they developed no metallurgy, no metalworking, no metal tools. With no draft animals (and probably no domestic animals of any kind except dogs), they developed no use of the wheel, although they used rollers on the *sacbeob* (artificial roads)—the raised causeways that ran from place to place and radiated into the countryside from the temple clusters. It was not easy to get from place to place in the Maya country; it still is not easy today. Although their world stretched from mountains to open savannas, it had its glory in the lowland jungles.

There were social classes, and priests conducting a complex religion, but no evidence can be found of any organized political government, centralized or local. The Mayas never had an "empire" or anything approximating one, so far as can be determined.

In all these respects they differ from other early civilized worlds, both New and Old. They are the foremost exception to the apparent rules attending the birth of civilization.

They were painted savages, in the phrase of the good old non-cosmetic days, and throughout the ages of their greatness painted savages they remained. They tattooed their bodies and painted them red—priests were painted blue, warriors black and red, prisoners striped black and white. They occasionally filed their teeth. They distended their pierced ear lobes with barbaric ear plugs, and pierced the septum of the nose to insert carved "jewels." They flattened their foreheads, and made themselves, if they could, cross-eyed, cross-eyes being considered beautiful. They decorated themselves with feathers, breeding birds in aviaries for the most gorgeous plumes, and men wore brilliant little obsidian mirrors hanging in their long hair.

But the Maya world was something more: "the multitude,

**The stately ritual of a Maya court arraignment more than 1,000 years ago is preserved on murals at Bonampak, near the Mexico-Guatemala border. When archaeologists found them in 1947, the frescoes were partly obscured by crystallized calcium carbonate formed by rain seepage. This reproduction is a faithful copy by modern artists of the original.**

the grandeur and the beauty of its buildings... for they are so many in number and so many are the parts of the country where they are found, and so well built are they of cut stone in their fashion, that it fills one with astonishment... that except to those who have seen them, it will seem to be jesting to tell about them," so begins (with Bishop Diego de Landa's *Relación* of over 400 years ago) the testimony of awe—no other word will do—that has been repeated by students and artists ever since.

Their country extended over an area as large as modern Italy. Their Classic Age alone endured longer than the entire life of the Roman Empire from Julius Caesar to Romulus Augustulus—with which it was probably parallel in time. Their "cities," for want of a better term to describe their ceremonial centers, numbered at least 116 great and small, for that many are already known as archaeological sites, and more, perhaps, remain to be discovered.

Besides the great temple-topped pyramids, various of the centers contained bridges, aqueducts, "palaces," reviewing stands, vapor baths, monumental stairways, ceremonial plazas for public spectacles, and astronomical observatories. Some of the more important "cities" were made up of numbers of building clusters around separate plazas, covering many acres or even extending for miles.

These buildings are genuinely impressive to a technicians' culture such as our own, and yet they take only second place among the Maya ruins left to us. Far and away in front are the records of their achievements in more abstract intellectual zones. The art, astronomy, and mathematics are world renowned. The literature, except for a few mangled scraps and tatters, is lost. It included history, science, the lives of great men, astronomy, astrology, prophecy, theology, ritual, legends and fables, "cures of diseases, and antiquities, and how to read and write with letters and characters with which they wrote," as Bishop Landa was told in the 1560s, and seemingly "certain songs in meter," and "farces... and comedies for the pleasure of the public."

"The original book, written long ago, existed, but its sight is hidden to the searcher and the thinker," wrote, in the 16th century, the compiler of the *Popol Vuh*, book of the highland Quiche Mayas, striving from the depths of the long night to remember the long noon nine centuries before.

Another still more subtle accomplishment was discerned by

Sylvanus Griswold Morley, who spent a lifetime studying the ancient Mayas. He found the 600 years of the Classic Age marked by general tranquility, "a near absence of warfare," an absence of repressive government, and an absence of discernible strong rules, and summed up by quoting Lord Moulton's remark that "the measure of civilization is the extent of man's obedience to the unenforceable." To which Morley added, "The Maya must have measured high."

If all this sounds like a golden world, maybe it was. An early Maya ceremonial center in Guatemala (Kaminaljuyu) dates back by carbon 14 tests to 1182 B.C. (±240), and Maya agriculture may have begun someplace nearby, much earlier, there on the flanks of the Central American Cordillera, a region of great beauty. The people here were the highland Mayas, somewhat backward in the Classic Age in comparison with the lowland Mayas, the typical Classic Mayas, who expanded from the vicinity of Lake Peten in Guatemala to occupy all the rain-forest country of central Guatemala and adjacent areas of the Yucatan peninsula as well as the dry brush country of northernmost Yucatan. The land of the Mayas, excluding the Huasteca (a splinter group living far up the Gulf Coast, isolated from the main Maya world), crossed the borders of what are today Honduras, El Salvador, Guatemala, British Honduras, and the Mexican states of Quintana Roo, Yucatan, Campeche, Tabasco, and Chiapas.

How long it took the priests to work out their calendars and system of writing is anybody's guess. They might have borrowed the beginnings from someone else (possibly those proto-Olmecs), as the Greeks took their alphabet from the Phoenicians. In any case, all the essentials were established by the time a carved jade plaque now known as the Leyden Plate was inscribed with its date, probably at the great center of Tikal, fifty miles north of Lake Peten, and by the time the oldest known stone monument, or stela, was dated, at the smaller center of Uaxactun (Wah-shock-toon), eleven miles north of Tikal.

The Spinden correlation of Maya dates gives the date for the Leyden Plate as A.D. 61, and the date for the oldest dated stela as A.D. 68. A contending system, the Goodman–Martinez Hernandez–Thompson correlation (sometimes abbreviated to GMT) reads these dates 260 years later at this period.

Carbon 14 dates support the Spinden system for the early centuries of the Maya Classic Age. However, many modern references are based on the GMT system. Both dates, therefore, will be given here. In later post-Classic centuries the two systems draw closer together until they reach virtual agreement.

The period of the Leyden Plate and the oldest dated stela—circa A.D. 60 (Spinden) or A.D. 320 (GMT)—is generally regarded as the opening of the 600 years of the Maya Classic Age, although of course such early centers as Uaxactun and Tikal had been in operation for centuries before this time.

The calendar systems were corrected by startlingly accurate observations of the sun, moon, and Venus (*noh ek*, Great Star). They were noted down in a numbers system based on twenty (counting fingers and toes instead of only fingers, as in our system of tens) and using positional numbers and zero, two concepts unknown in Europe for another 1,000 years.

The *tzolkin*, or book of the days, a ceremonial round of 260 days, was the simplest unit of the various day counts; it may have been based originally on the period between autumn and spring, the other 105 days of the year being devoted to the planting and growing season. It involved a series of twenty different day names revolving through an endlessly repeated number series of 1 to 13. Thus the same conjunctions of numbers and names were repeated in 13 × 20 or 260 days.

The solar calendar used nineteen named months (eighteen of twenty days each and one of five days) and turned through a cycle of fifty-two years between recurring conjunctions—in principle somewhat as if our calendar were arranged so that certain weekdays always fell on certain dates at regular intervals of so many years.

Further systems, a lunar calendar brought into a fixed relation with the day count (with an error of less that five minutes a year), and a Venus calendar meshing five Venus years of a mean 584 days each with eight solar years of 365 days, were all more or less complex. They created whole galaxies of cycles, wheels within wheels, all turning like the perpetual works of an infinite clock, and the emphasis was always on that marvelous repetition of time. The dated stelae set up during the Classic Age commemorated various of these cycles, usually in the cycle of slightly less than twenty years called a *katun*.

The most striking thing about the Maya achievements is that they were never of any practical use, in our meaning of the term. Possibly the ceremonial calendars came into being in connection with times for preparing cornfields, planting, harvesting, and so on, but it is doubtful they could have been very good weather guides, which is the only way they could have been much actual help to the farmer.

The temples and the palaces, the "civic centers," as they have been called, were magnificently nonutilitarian. If anyone lived in the palaces, it was presumably for penance; they must have been very uncomfortable.

The people lived in houses of poles and thatch, and while the calendars turned through their inexorable rounds, the people made *maadz* (corn mush) and dangled bits of pitch between the baby's eyes to make him cross-eyed and trooped in to the ceremonies along the well-engineered, gun-barrel-straight roads, and the nobles nobled all day and sometimes raided each other on state occasions, and the priests gazed over their crossed sticks at the stars.

This entire world, with all its mathematical wonders, its art of life, and its gods who assumed the forms of an old man or maize, a bat or eagle, or a serpent with jaguar's teeth, was operated (so far as we can see) for the sole purpose of marking time.

The temple ceremonies were for men only, women not allowed—with rare exceptions; but at the ceremonies in the plazas the people would have marked the time together, in communion with the brilliantly arrayed priests and the revered *halach uinic* (True Man), the chief priest, in ecstasy, perhaps, from the music and the dancing and the pageantry, the colors and the beauty, and the meaning of the ritual that marked another gesture in the tableau of good gods versus bad, another passing point on the holy calendar. As has been remarked of the ancient Egyptians, only the changeless was truly significant.

Maybe we don't understand at all. Time has stopped for them and moved on for us, and the people on the sculptured walls evade us utterly. They left no Aeschylus to tell us what they felt, no Anaxagoras to tell us what they thought.

The fragments are only fragments, luminous with old light though they are. "Then there sprang up the five-leafed flower... the little flower..." from the Chilam Balam of Chumayel, the Book of the Prophet of Secrets, the Book of the Jaguar Priest, a post-Spanish collection of such fragments. "Then there sprang up the bouquet of the priest, the bouquet of the ruler, the bouquet of the captain; this was what the flower-king bore when he descended and nothing else, so they say. It was not bread that he bore. . . ."

And from the *Popol Vuh*: "He who gives breath and thought . . who watches over the happiness of the people, the happiness of the human race . . . who meditates on the goodness of all that exists in the sky, on the earth, in the lakes and in the sea. . . ."

And a dawn prayer: "Look at us, hear us! . . . Heart of Heaven, Heart of Earth! Give us our descendants, our succession, as long as the sun shall move and there shall be light. Let it dawn, let the day come! . . . May the people have peace, much peace, and may they be happy; and give us good life . . . grandmother of the sun, grandmother of the light, let there be dawn, and let the light come!"

Their annals are blank, of course. It appears that their prayers may have been heard and that they may really have been a happy people, and happy people have no history, as everybody knows.

They built new temples, they dated new monuments, the people walked to the centers wearing their Sunday sandals, and the priests and the nobles read and wrote and studied; and time turned round and round, never changing.

They had no history until the Classic Age ended, when the central Maya, the people in the heart of the country, abandoned their gleaming temple clusters and drifted away and out of the jungle, leaving no signs of war, invasion, or general unrest, and thus leaving the greatest mystery of all.

This was not the end of the Mayas. We shall hear of them again. But it was the end of the great days, the long noon. The exodus from the Classic sites began about A.D. 600 (Spinden), A.D. 800 (GMT). Within a century or two the towering cities of the Peten region were deserted. No one knows why.

The two foremost puzzles of the Maya civilization concern their form of government and the abandonment of the centers that had been their capital cities for so long. But these are only different views of the same face, of the total enigma that is the Maya Classic Age, primitive, wise, poetic, placid, the unique example in the history of the world of a people lost in thought.

"Go and read it and you will understand . . . ," says the Jaguar Priest.

But we can't. It's gone.

# II

# Feathered Gods and Priests

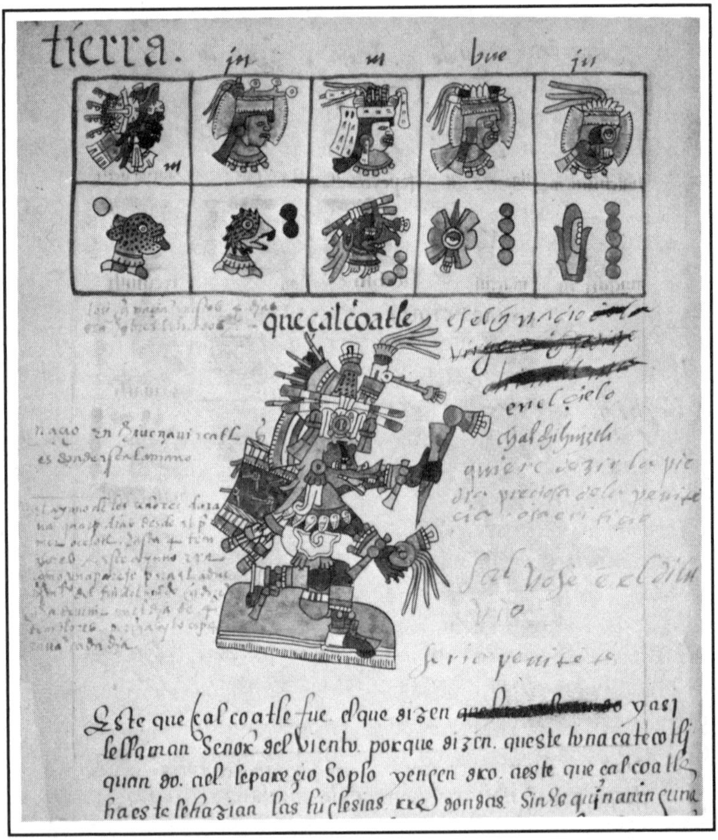


This portrait of Quetzalcoatl is from an Aztec manuscript.

The Mayas were not necessarily the first people in America to build pyramids and crown them with temples. Their art in carved wood and stone, stucco modeling and painting, is considered by common consent to include the finest such work in the New World and some of the finest anywhere, but they may not have been the first among their neighbors to practice it. The corbeled vault distinctive to their architecture, their use of zero, and some of the aspects of their written language seem to have been exclusively their own; but they may not necessarily have been the first to use the principles of their famous calendar mathematics. Somewhat as in the case of the proto-Olmecs, they did many of the same things that were done by others around them, only better. They were far from being alone in the growing world of their time, and ideas are no respecters of state lines. All of the middle zone of the Americas, from central Mexico south to Bolivia and Peru, was spawning varicolored little towns and cities. Corn farming, and the revolution in living that went with it—new gods, new wealth, new ways, new worries—had spread far beyond this sophisticated heartland.

A people who may have been descendants of émigrés from someplace in that heartland were farming in the Ohio Valley, far up in North America, and making pottery and building enormous burial mounds, several centuries before the beginning of the Maya Classic Age. Later, but still at least as early as A.D. 1, corn was established among the already ancient Cochise people in Arizona, and not long afterward was being grown by the incipient villagers of the Southwest we call the Basketmakers, ancestors of the modern Pueblo Indians. The potato, as much of a civilizer in South America as maize, was coming into use in the Andes region, and manioc, the third great South American staple, was cultivated still earlier. Tobacco was nearly every where.

While everywhere beyond the belts of little planted fields, everywhere throughout the boundless areas surrounding these few frontiers, the wandering tribes, untouched, lived as they always had.

"The people of the wood," the Mayas called them in the *Popol Vuh*. "There are generations in the world, there are country people, whose faces we do not see, who have no homes, they only wander through the small and large woodlands. . . . "

Some of these people then living in the Grand Canyon of Arizona were making tiny figurines, while the Mayas were building temples—little deer fashioned from twigs, with twig spears run through them: if this unnatural phenomenon is modeled and inserted in the world, might not the world produce it in response? (Archaeologists first discovered these, incidentally, for sale at a roadside curio stand in Arizona not too may years ago; they are more than 3,000 years old.)

Trading in more than ideas went on between the towns and cities—trading in everything from slaves to kitchenware. Articles of commerce found their way from town to town and covered astonishing distances.

West along the Gulf Coast from the Maya country were the fat-faced proto-Olmecs and their old, faded city of La Venta. The same people, or their cousins, known to us as Totonacs, may have built Tajin, the next town of importance up the coast, a town of a great pyramid and many temples.

Brilliantly painted mountaintop cities in the Oaxaca (Wah-hock-ah) area were inhabited by the Zapotecs, who traded their elaborate incense burners far and wide, and who may have originated the worship of Xipe (Sheepay), god of springtime, in whose honor the priest danced in the skin of a flayed sacrificial victim. The cult of this god also spread far and wide over Mexico.

At Cholula in the state of Puebla a pyramid was enlarged by successive additions until it eventually exceeded in volume Egypt's Pyramid of Cheops. A room inside it contained a mural of butterfly gods and a painting of Quetzalcoatl (Kate-zal-ko-attl), who, as the Plumed Serpent, God of the Morning, the Bearded Man, Lord of Life, Lord of the Wind, Bringer of Civilization, and in countless other guises, was known to all these differing peoples from the earliest times.

The southeastern end of the vast plateau in mid-Mexico is a high landlocked basin, wrinkled with networks of little valleys and ringed by smoking volcanoes. This, at an altitude of nearly a mile and a half, is the "Valley" of Mexico. Here there were numerous towns and villages and cities, most of them congregated around the great salt lake, Lake Texcoco, and its freshwater feeder lagoons, sizable lakes in themselves.

The Classic Age in central Mexico was in many respects uncultivated and immature compared to the same period in the realm of the Mayas, but its works made up in dimension what they lacked in elegance. From the Temple of the Moon to the Temple of Quetzalcoatl, Teotihuacan (Tay-oh-tee-wah-kon), the chief city of the Valley of Mexico's Classic Age, was a solid procession of majestic public buildings and religious barracks, decorated with the serpents, beasts, and feathered men of heaven, dominated in the center by the tremendous Pyramid of the Sun. A paved area more than three miles long and nearly two miles wide was occupied by these structures and their plazas, parks, and avenues.

This was less a city than a ceremonial center in the Maya sense. Long-continued drought in the time of the Classic Age brought large-scale irrigation to the Valley, and the organization of people required for this work resounded to the greater glory of Teotihuacan, making of it a place of worship to which the faithful thronged to join the black-robed priests in celebrating the mysteries that kept the world in balance—rain and fire, planting and harvesting, and the endless, mystical renewal of the holy days of the calendar.

Varying forms of the typical Maya calendar systems came into use among all the sprouting cities of Mexico—the calendar that swallowed itself, like the two-headed serpent, every 260 days and every fifty-two years, spinning out the revelation that everything came to an end and yet was reborn, everything changed and yet remained the same, and the circle revolved forever.

The sacrifice of human beings, dogs, birds, flowers, anything that lived, was an act in recognition and sustenance of this eternal process. The notion of sacrifice to appease angry gods is Mesopotamian, not Mesoamerican. Angry gods are shepherds' gods, living in the lightning, and the Indians kept no flocks. The gods of Teotihuacan were in the sunlight that buttered the Valley and brought growth, and in the stars that hung like volleys of javelins in the sharp brittle air and never failed in the ceaseless repetition of their flight. The American gods were hungry, not angry, hungry for the destruction of living things that was the bass-drum beat of the rhythm of life, the death that brought new life. Without constant death the life of the gods grew weak, for was not death the ultimate objective of life, and thus its food? The Teotihuacanos, in common with many other people before and since, ate the god to achieve divine communion, in ritual cannibalistic feasts.

Teotihuacan was twice rebuilt, the rooms filled in and the buildings covered with cut stone and adobe to provide platforms for new and larger buildings. Temples were customarily enlarged or rebuilt at the close of each fifty-two-year cycle, but this major reconstruction may have resulted from changes of political administration. Religion and politics were so entwined as to be one and the same thing; when the party of the old gods was overthrown, the party of the new gods raised new temples as well as a new society, and probably fed the new gods with any priests of the defeated opposition who could be caught. Such changes may or may not have meant invasion of new people. Sometimes they may have reflected a revolt of the masses.

The old gods, however, never really disappeared. Tlaloc, the Rain God, who was defeated at Teotihuacan, had the teeth of the long-ago proto-Olmec jaguar; and with new added attributes he reappeared and remained forever in the front rank of the pantheon. Quetzalcoatl, whose ornately sculptured temple was completely covered over and turned into the foundation for new construction, remained nevertheless a star actor in the march of the following centuries. The old gods melted into the new. The new gods became other faces for the old. The gods of good and the gods of evil, locked in their eternal embrace of combat were all, perhaps, only opposing manifestations of the same beings—even of the same single being, in some current scholarly opinion.

In the centuries following A.D. 600, turmoil became epidemic among the city-states of central and southern Mexico, and the Classic Age was pulled to pieces. The Olmecs (or whoever they were) and their relatives the Totonacs (if they were relatives) left their Veracruz coast and raged inland into the mountains of Puebla and Oaxaca, fighting anyone who got in their way. Monte Alban, the mountain-top city of the Zapotecs, was abandoned. (A long time later a neighboring mountain people called the Mixtecs used it as a cemetery; some of the richest treasures of ancient Mexico were found there in their tombs.)

A number of towns and cities throughout the civilized regions of Mexico were abandoned, as the Mayas were abandoning their jungle temples at about the same time. It seems a little easier to find reasons for the displacements outside the Maya borders, but still, the warmaking migrations that appear to have been their immediate cause were in turn set afoot by something, some prodigious motivation. Whatever these may have been, famine, disease, or signs and portents in the priest-watched skies, they—or at any rate the dislocations they set in motion—went on for centuries.

The people of the woods who invaded Mexico's cities during this age of chaos may have been driven by the general fever of unrest or may conceivably have been the germ of its beginning. However, that would not explain the preceding and following centuries of comparative stability. The wild tribes were in constant process of splitting and dividing, whenever they grew so large as to be unwieldy for their way of life. Probably these splits and divisions were seldom peaceful. Probably the exiles went forth in anger. Certainly they went forth in grief, condemned to separation and exile.

Long afterward, a thousand years afterward, the grandson of the last king in the Valley of Mexico compiled a set of annals from the records then still existing in books of picture-writing. Fable, myth, and legend mingle in them, evoking all the more movingly the distant shadows. Listen to the saga of the Toltecs, a nation of Nahua-speaking Indians who dwelt for ages in "the country toward what is now called California, in the Southern Sea" (i.e., Mexico's Pacific coast), who sent Mosquito to stab the sun in the rump and keep him moving when he stopped, who learned the calendar (strayed into the magnetic field of civilization and absorbed its beginnings), suffered earthquakes and eclipses of the moon and the sun, and who were then split by civil war.

The defeated rebels, driven away, sojourned for eight years in this place, three years in that, made slow, dragging marches of only 200 or 300 miles, "because of their great multitude," to new countries for new sojourns of four years, five years, and again marched on, always toward the east, stopped among islands on a seacoast for five years, crossed arms of the sea in "boats and canoes." They left families to populate this land or that and traveled on. They calculated the end of one fifty-two-year cycle since they had commenced the civil war that had ended in their expulsion, and at the end of a second cycle they

**This stirrup-shaped ceramic spout figure is typical of the Mochican pottery found in the Santa Valley of Peru. The Mochica were pre-Inca Indians of the North Coast and are known for their highly refined, very realistic pottery.**

were still moving on, stopping for seven years here, eight years there. After 122 years, and a series of thirteen temporary homelands, "they marched on, and founded . . . the city of Tula, which they were six years building."

The chant echoes from across that still river of time, perhaps truly the voice of the people of the wood moving so arduously into the light.

It may have been sometime in the eighth or ninth century A.D. that a horde of foreigners streamed down from the north into the Valley of Mexico, possibly Toltecs allied with the Otomi, residents of the northern end of the Mesa Central, the country just above the center of civilization around Lake Texcoco. It is believed they attacked, looted, and burned Teotihuacan the magnificent—somebody did. Bands of Teotihuacan refugees fled as far as Guatemala, others to a brother city west across Lake Texcoco, and others may have sold their skills (or spent them in slavery) to help the Toltecs build their capital city, Tula, north of the lake.

Most of the Otomi later returned to their own land; the Toltecs stayed to found the first real empire in the New World.

By the end of the tenth century they had extended their conquests as far as the heart of the Maya country, in Guatemala and northern Yucatan. The somewhat disorganized Mayas were reorganized and endured a long Indian-summer renaissance under Toltec domination, faithfully reflecting Toltec art and thought at such Yucatan Maya cities as the eloquent Chichen Itza and the rather dispirited Mayapan.

It would please our taste for sequence, probably, to think of the Toltecs as uncultured conquerors with the artistic sensibilities of rich used-car dealers, but this does not seem to have been the case. Mexican tradition has remembered the Toltecs as the Master Architects, the brilliant innovators, the ideal expression of the Mexican genius. For centuries after the Toltec empire had vanished, ruling families from Yucatan to Texcoco insisted on their Toltec descent. A pyramid recently excavated at Tula (it might be the site of the famous Temple of the Frog, the Sainte Chapelle of medieval Mexico) has excited rhapsodies over its delicacy, proportion, and decoration.

The scholars and the diggers have revealed a great deal of the New World's complex past, the least known and therefore the most intriguing of ancient histories, but there are so many things that are not yet understood and possibly never will be. The pattern is hopelessly elusive. It changes with each shifting wind that stirs the ashes. But here and there a coal is glowing yet, alive with a memory still warm to the touch. These bring the excitement of reality even though the cleverest of the specialists may be unsure—precisely the cleverest are the least sure—as to their exact place in the pattern. Such are the Mayas and such are the people called the Toltecs. Their magic still shines in the dark of the past, the Mayas with grace and profuse reflection, the Toltecs with grace and profuse power.

Tradition says the Toltecs introduced idolatry and human sacrifice to the Mayas. Tradition says they brought to Mexico the black god Tezcatlipoca, Lord of the Sky, the North, and the Night, to war with the white Quetzalcoatl, the Morning Star. Tradition says they introduced the sacred ball game, at which whole populaces, kings and commoners alike, bet and won and lost everything from their lip jewels to their lives. Tradition says that in the time of the Toltec king Iztaccaltzin a gracious lady of blessed memory named Xochitl (Sho-cheetl, the commonest Nahua girl's name, meaning Flower) invented *octli*, a booze made from the maguey plant, today called pulque and still the drink of the country.

But human sacrifice had been known before, although perhaps only rarely, among the Mayas as elsewhere in Middle America. No one can guess how long ago the practice began of sending dead souls to help the sun in his war against the stars, and feeding the rain with blood. What more could devotion offer, and who would not be glad to go? "Quickly slay me, trample me with thy feet!... May my body come to rest!" say the words of an ancient Mexican prayer. And Tezcatlipoca, whose symbol was a jaguar skin (and the jaguar of the proto-Olmecs had arrived 2,000 years before), had been fighting the sun on temple walls for centuries before Toltec times. And surely some of the ball courts in various cities were pre-Toltec; the origin of the Mexican ball game, in which players, without using their hands, tried to knock a solid rubber ball through the goal of a vertical ring set in the wall of the ball court, is believed to be very ancient indeed. The game was surrounded by ceremonies that seemed to be of a sacred character. And if the Maya wine, called *balche*, so much used in religious ritual, had not wafted its idea northward to Mexico proper in times long before, it would be surprising.

Tradition says the Toltecs' most glorious king, Topiltzin, being born on the day called in their calendar Ce Acatl (Say Ahcattl, One Reed), was given its name, after their custom, and that he was educated as a priest of Quetzalcoatl and therefore was given the god's name too, as was the custom, so that he was called in full Ce Acatl Topiltzin Quetzalcoatl. He was Hamlet in a feather crown; his wicked uncle, Lord of the Water Palace, murdered his father and stole the kingdom; and when Ce Acatl Topiltzin Quetzalcoatl reached manhood, he killed his uncle on the Hill of the Star (where the New Fire ceremony opened each fifty-two-year century) and took the kingdom back. He was a ruler of unparalleled goodness and wisdom.

But now tradition dissolves the priest into the godhead, and says the vengeful god Tezcatlipoca appeared on earth and drove Ce Acatl Topiltzin Quetzalcoatl from Tula to Cholula and then to Yucatan, and that everywhere "he was regarded as a saint. He taught them by his words and by his works the road of virtue.... After having taught... he departed by the way he had come, that is to say, to the East, and... told them that in time to come, in the year of Ce Acatl, he would return, and that his doctrine would be received...." So says Ixtlilxochitl, the previously mentioned grandson of the Valley's last king.

Other chroniclers say Topiltzin Quetzalcoatl burned himself in a funeral fire and his heart leapt into the sky as the morning star; his heart became a comet; the smoke from his pyre became green-feathered quetzal birds; his heart went into the underworld for four days and returned as the morning star; he parted the sea and walked away through it; he sailed away on a raft made of snakes. He says, in the translation of a manuscript in picture-writing known as the Codex Florentino, "I am called hence. The sun hath called me." Quetzalcoatl, Feathered Serpent, translated into the Maya language is Kukulcan, who was worshiped thereafter in the Maya country as a powerful god.

Quetzalcoatl taught and left behind him, they say, all the arts of peace, from metalworking to featherworking, from writing to weaving. He tried to abolish human sacrifice in Tula and limit worship to the burning of copal (resin) as incense and the sacrifice of flowers and butterflies; and as Kukulcan he demanded human sacrifice at Chichen Itza.

Possibly all this tangled welter of tradition is based on truth. The Toltecs seem to have brought a burst of energy, new ideas or a reformation of old ideas, new learning or a wider spread of old learning, in short a blazing rekindling of the cultural fires almost snuffed out in the collapse of the Classic Age. Every flying spark would have set off a different conflagration, leaving different memories in different places. These may very well have spread the religion of both white Quetzalcoatl and black Tezcatlipoca.

The Toltecs' greatest king may very well have been Topiltzin. His time is variously ascribed to the ninth or tenth centuries, which puts him fairly well in the company of Charlemagne, Harun al-Rashid of the Arabian Nights, and Alfred the Great—maybe there was something in the air.

Metalworking clearly was introduced during this period (about A.D. 900)—at last the sun could burst forth in the splendor of gold, "excrement of the gods"—and trade was enormously expanded. Cargoes of everything from macaw feathers and jaguar skins to drinking tubes and chewing gum traveled the roads in the tumpline packs (back packs held by a band passed around the forehead) of merchants and their slaves.

Certain areas exported products—salt, rubber, dogs fattened for the table, cacao for the delicious foaming chocolate so much in demand that cacao beans were used for currency. Other regions worked up manufacturing specialties—yarn, embroidered cotton cloth for mantles, loincloths, skirts, hair ribbons; war clubs with inset sword-blade edges of obsidian; rope, carved jade and turquoise, flutes and tobacco pipes of clay; pottery, paper, paints, and dyes.

Some trade went by sea—the Mayas imported at this time the famed Orange pottery from Veracruz, which had to be freighted more than 600 miles by seagoing canoe. The Maya dugouts, crewed by as many as twenty-five paddlers, carried for trade such building materials as lime, clay, and the metal-hard sapodilla wood, as well as corn and vanilla, wax and honey, stone cutlery from razors to hatchets, and chiefly (so wrote an early European explorer) "draperies and different articles of spun cotton in brilliant colors."

By circa A.D. 1000 the growing of corn and the other crops that followed (or sometimes preceded) it, such as squash and beans, and its accompanying art, the making of pottery, had seeped and trickled here and there throughout nearly all North America where the climate permitted, except the far west coast. The descendants of the Cochise people built ball courts for the sacred game in the Arizona desert, where their irrigation ditches had by this time already been carrying water for perhaps 200 years; and in the cottonwood canyons of the rainbow country where New Mexico, Arizona, Utah, and Colorado join, the Gold Age of the Pueblos was dawning (live parrots were brought here in trade, carried at least 1,200 miles from the markets of Mexico).

A corridor of maize-farming people extended from this Arizona–New Mexico outpost down the eastern slope of the Sierra Madre to the northwestern frontier of the Mexican civilization to the south, this frontier falling in the western marches of the land of the Zacatecas, nearly as far above the Valley of Mexico as the Maya country was below it. Pyramids, columns, and masonry buildings were constructed during Toltec times in these northwestern frontier regions.

Another corridor, a sea lane, apparently reached across the Gulf of Mexico to the Mississippi, and a long list of trade items, some markedly Mayanesque in style, went from hand to hand through what seems to have been a grand alliance of prosperous little nations, stretching from the Gulf Coast to Wisconsin, from New York to Kansas and Nebraska. Many of these people built earthwork walls and mounds, as burial monuments, ceremonial designs, or temple platforms.

The ripples of contact carried ideas, customs, fragments of holy ceremony, to the most distant peoples of the woods as well as to settled farmers—and brought back new ideas in return.

The bow was working its way down from the North, and in the northern forests moccasins were replacing bark sandals. A sporty small-caliber weapon, the blowgun, shooting little clay bullets to knock down birds and small game, had appeared in Classic Teotihuacan. But the universal arms in A.D. 1000 were still the mace, knife, spear, and spear-thrower.

Worked gold came to the Mayas from Panama and Costa Rica, presumably drifting northward from Peru and Colombia, where metallurgy had developed long before this time. The

Mayas never became metalworkers, but the Mexican city-states beyond them developed guilds of goldsmiths and silversmiths and poured forth lavish art in precious metals.

In this matter of metalworking, as in so many other respects, parallels with the Andean region of South America, evidences of some kind of communication or counterpoint of influence, seem to be obvious.

Each of these two separate centers of high civilization—Mexico and the South American Andes—practiced intensive farming, understood irrigation, shared some of the same basic crops, shared in their early ages even some identical pottery styles as well as the similar jaguar-feline cults; each built ceremonial centers and then towns and cities, temple mounds and step pyramids; each organized society into classes dominated by priests and then by priest-kings, and so on through an impressive inventory, including such details as Chichen Itza–style spindle whorls in Ecuador and the use in common of roller seals made of clay.

On the other hand, there are many equally impressive time lags and differences to be found between the South American and the Mexican high civilizations.

Metallurgy was known in the Andean region 1,000 years before it reached Mexican America. If there was any contact to speak of, what took so long? The widespread calendar of Mexican America never reached the Andes at all. Of course it is possible the Andeans would not have been particularly interested in the marvelous sacred calendar. The differences between the two civilizations of South America and Mexico seem to have been in some respects deeper and subtler than the similarities, as shall be seen.

Since the clearest resemblances between these two areas of high civilization fall in an early period and since the differences grow more pronounced as time goes on, quite a few experts have been tempted to the conclusion that both developed from a more or less common source and then grew apart. Other experts are inclined to take a cool view of anything approaching twinship, explaining the broad similarities as the natural result of similar levels of culture.

It is worth repeating that those levels of culture in South America and Mexico were not necessarily synchronized in time. It does appear that most of the specific parallels between them

**The Incas had many versions of the dawn of their dynasty, but all traced their origins to the demigod Manco Capac, shown in this sixteenth-century painting. He set out from Lake Titicaca, in the Andean highlands, guided by his sun-father, to bring civilization to the barbarians. After a journey filled with supernatural events, he settled near Cuzco.**

stem from a single period, the time of the feline cult on the Peruvian coast and the proto-Olmec jaguar cultists in Mexico, but whether one of these cults preceded the other in time, or they overlapped or were contemporaneous, the evidence sayeth not. Before and after this period any communication between the two worlds was indirect, haphazard, and hazy in the extreme. Maize reaching Peru at this time, after thousands of years of cultivation in the Mexico area, and after at least more than 1,000 years of a maizeless agriculture in Peru, certainly argues against any common source in the veriest beginnings.

Agriculture in Peru, in the era of the feline cultists (roughly, the 1,000 years preceding the Christian era), had squash, gourds, beans, cotton, manioc to work with, as well as newly introduced corn, peanuts, and avocados. The llama may have been domesticated at this time. Weaving and primitive metalwork in sheet gold was known. The Peruvian north coast and the adjacent highlands were apparently dotted with villages, more or less independent of each other, with here and there religious centers consisting of temple platforms and buildings of massive construction faced with dressed stone. Such a center was Chavin de Huantar, the type site of the age, located in a little valley near a little river, the Marañon—deceptively modest headwater of the Amazon.

During these many generations of this 1,000 years the fundamental principles of architecture, irrigation, and terracing were developed that remained essentially unchanged through all later Andean civilizations. The use of fertilizer (guano) was learned. Farming by digging-stick and hoe was established, never to change—the plow was unknown in the New World. Basic ceramic techniques were fixed, never to change—the potter's wheel never came into New World use.

Then, after its 1,000 years or so, from circa 1000 B.C. to circa A.D. 1, the Chavin style vanished. Revolution? Invasion? The same people remain (and even the recurring fashion of little conical hats). Possibly it was nothing more than too many centuries of singing the same hymns. The feline god sank from sight, and a half dozen or so "regional" styles of life laboriously built their way into view, to burst forth in the last few centuries of the following thousand years (circa A.D. 800–1000) in the Andean Classic Age.

The remains of this period, intricate mountainside terracing, systems of irrigation canals running for miles, wide roads, monumental fortresses and ceremonial centers, terraced houses of stone and adobe and underground stone-paneled galleries, skilled work in precious metals—but above all the pottery and the weaving—have been buried under so many superlatives that their creators have for the most part lost real-life identity, like the citizens of Renaissance Florence.

An exception is the case of the north coast people from the Moche, Viru, and neighboring valleys, known as the Mochica people, the makers of the Mochica pottery that reproduces with portrait-and-caricature realism every detail of their lives, from childbirth (women delivered on their knees) to sexual extravaganzas, war, and the resplendent songs and dances of religion. Helmeted warriors lope home carrying trophy heads, captives are sacrificed by being hurled from cliffs, impersonal executioners cut off a convict's lips; but strange and savage genres are only part of the program. These are, in effect, thousands of motion pictures modeled in ceramics with a rambunctious virtuosity that seizes on everything in life, and many scenes picture familiar, everyday subjects as recognizable to us as a TV comedy—a good deal more recognizable, in fact, since they do not have television's primmer restrictions. Comedy, incidentally, was given high billing, which ought to be considered indicative of something.

The uncanny plastic skill and a certain taste for the maimed and the monstrous hint faintly (maybe wrongly) at an echo of the proto-Olmec mind, dead these many lifetimes—but a feline returns to their pantheon, nevertheless, after an absence of centuries, in the cat fangs and whiskers of their monster god, Ai apaec. They may have had a sort of writing system, ideographs indented in lima beans.

The textiles made by the Paracas and Nazca people of the Peruvian south coast represent, in the opinion of connoisseurs, the greatest textile art ever produced anywhere. They were woven from cotton and the wool of llamas, alpacas, and vicuñas into every sort of cloth from gauze and lace to brocade and tapestry, in every sort of color—archaeologists have classified as many as 190 hues in seven color ranges. Apparently the finest were made as clothing for the dead, who were wrapped in huge mummy bundles of dazzling linens and richly embroidered brocades.

People all over the Andean areas added nose plugs and lip

plugs to the usual distending earrings and skull deformation, and possible body consciousness accounted for an extraordinary practice of the time—cutting baseball-sized holes in their skulls. This trepanning (it is not taken lightly by a modern surgeon) was fairly common, and clearly most patients survived: the edges of the cuts show later bone growth.

Medicine—surgical, herbal, and magical—was well-advanced. The white and sweet potato, quinoa, pineapple, and various other plants had been added to the fields; llamas, alpacas, ducks, and guinea pigs were raised. Cocoa had come into use, mixed—in the worldwide way of masticatories—with a touch of lime or ashes to release the narcotic. A beer, *chicha*, was fermented from corn or fruit. The permanent central Andean costume had evolved—loincloths, waistbands, knee-length shirts, various sorts of little hats, headbands, or turbans (Mochica aristocrats wore splendrous headdresses, with much gold). Balsa boats, large and small, traveled the oceans and lakes. The bladed club and spear-thrower were still the standard weapons. Feather masks and musical instruments from tambourines to coiled trumpets were used in the dances.

Everything, in fact, had been created that the Andean world was to have, except really widespread conquest and empire.

This came along in due course in the following centuries, creeping down in an almost all-enveloping tide from the central Andes. The capital and center may have been the city of Huari, although the style of this empire period is still customarily called Tiahuanaco, after a city on sky-high Lake Titicaca. Under whatever name, most of the little kingdoms from Nazca in the south to Moche in the north were united in its realm by about A.D. 1200.

At about this same time, in the mountain valley of Cuzco midway between Tiahuanaco and Huari, a backwoods tribe of Quechua-speaking people who called themselves the Inca were living in rough-stone villages, making bone tools, and, it may be, singing to the sunlit highlands the so-called Inca hymn:

*O Viracocha! Lord of the universe,*
*Let it not be*
*That I should tire,*
*That I should die.*

"The same mists that hang round the origin of the Incas continue to settle on their subsequent annals," wrote William Hickling Prescott in his *Conquest of Peru*, "and, so imperfect were the records employed by the Peruvians... that the historian finds no firm footing on which to stand till within a century of the Spanish conquest."

The origin of the Incas is of course no more mysterious than the origin of any of the scores of other Andean tribes—well over 100 have been identified; there were many more. Here as everywhere else on the two continents the knots of people had moved, merged, split, multiplied, appeared and disappeared from every compass point for untold thousands of years before history first caught them in its lens.

But extend the question, as Prescott intended, to inquire into the origin of this whole remarkable Andean civilization, or extend it even further, to inquire into the development of the entire civilization of the New World: as has been seen, the general outlines of this development show slow growth and accretion over immense periods of time.

The developing civilization of the Andes had witnessed Tiahuanacan warriors, coeval with Crusaders in the Old World, marching past stone felines of Chavin that were already as ancient, to them, as Cleopatra is now to us. It had seen the cat-cult priests of the Chavin period, coeval with the Druid priest-rulers of England, walking over farm fields that were already more ancient, to them, than the Crusaders are now to us.

There doesn't seem to be any scoring here for the sudden trombones of staggering mysteries.

But from the nineteenth century to our own day there has been no shortage of speculative antiquarians presenting evidence to prove that the civilizations of Peru or of Mexico were brought to the New World more or less ready-made from some Old World point of origin.

Efforts have been made to establish an Egyptian origin for New World civilization, or to show that civilization was transported to the New World by sailors of Alexander the Great, or that the civilization of the Incas was the creation of the troops of the "Grand Khan Kublai." Volumes have been filled with endless parallels (circumcision, for example), proving that the Aztec civilization was built by the Hebrews.

All unanswered questions and apparent parallels—and there are a great many—lend fuel to such speculation. One such question stems from botanical evidence that seems to show that New World cotton is a cross between Asiatic cotton and American wild cotton. If so, it would appear that the Asiatic plant must have been brought across the Pacific by the hand of man. It is generally agreed no one could have walked around with it by way of the Bering Strait. Bottle gourds, also common to Asia, are found with early appearances of New World cotton.

The earliest appearance of this cotton, at an exceedingly primitive pre-pottery site known as Huaca Prieta on the north Peruvian coast, produces carbon 14 dates close to 2300 B.C.

Fancy can play some pretty fine games with possible trans-Pacific communication at such a remote period (before there were ships anywhere that could cross any ocean, so far as we know), and the speculative antiquarians are unloading new theories by the bale.

With the proposed cotton crossing as a starter, theorists have ransacked Asia—India, China, and, later, Oceania (considerably later, obviously, since the Pacific islands were not inhabited, on the basis of present evidence, until after A.D. 500 to 1000 at the earliest)—searching for further connections or parallels between the ancient civilizations of the Old World and the New.

They have found a great many, almost as many as had previously been found proving a connection with the Hebrews. A few are based on generalized culture traits or occasional similarities in utensils, some are concerned with such matters as a ruler being carried in a litter, but by far the great majority deal with parallels in art motifs.

All are adduced to prove, again, an Old World "origin" for New World civilization. Some of the leading proponents show how the Old World transported this civilization across the Pacific piece by piece in a traffic continuing for thousands of years—one scholarly conjecture outlines a commerce of trans-Pacific sailing lasting until circa A.D. 1200.

But the civilizations of the Old World were based on sown cereals, the plow, the cow, and the wheel. The generations of supposed technicians sent to America left all those behind and brought cotton and countless cargoes of art motifs instead.

On the return voyages none of them bothered to carry back the New World products that after Columbus took the Old by storm: potatoes, tomatoes, corn, chocolate, all the list that now makes up three fifths of the world's agricultural items.

It does seem unlikely that trans-Pacific liners plied a regular trade. It also seems unlikely that all the reported parallels are derivations. Art motifs and culture traits can be made to prove anything, as the wildly divergent previous theories of this sort demonstrate. It is also unlikely that of the actual derivations all derived in one direction—the law of averages alone would argue that some at least originated in America and went the other way.

Nevertheless, the new waves of theorists are filling the Vales of Academe with clamors by day and alarms by night, insistent on proving, once again, that the early American civilizations were really created by the Old World.

It's a futile, Bacon-wrote-Shakespeare kind of argument. Or it has more kinship still with the who-influenced-whom books that the English professors write back and forth at each other (did Longfellow really influence Baudelaire?).

It's a pity only because the study of ancient America is side-tracked into this controversy and away from consideration of the American contributions themselves, in which, as a famous European anthropologist says, "Some general and fundamental laws in human development are certainly hiding. . . . " They deserve better.

For the important point is that the American high cultures differ basically from those of the Old World, as they differ also, in fact, from each other.

Pre-Columbian contacts with Old World civilizations must have been rare, chance, and of no great significance in the development of New World civilization. Undoubtedly there were such contacts, transoceanic, even trans-Pacific. There were myriads of years for them to be made in, and any craft, no matter how primitive, once launched on the bosomy deep can conceivably be carried to very strange and faraway places indeed. Probably some of the earliest contacts by sea came by way of the Aleutian Islands. Some scholars have also proposed an ancient passage by sea between Australia and the tail of South America, via Antarctica.

Appearances of Norsemen on the eastern coast of North America unquestionably took place. After the settlement of Polynesia, some trips back and forth (with a bow to *Kon-Tiki*) certainly occurred. That hybrid American cotton has been found in the islands of the South Seas, as well as several other items in common with the New World.

There were indubitable later contacts between Asia and the Northwest Coast; some of the results reached Hawaii and thence the far western Pacific, back to the doorstep of Asia, to create great confusion today.

Phoenicians, Egyptians, Greeks, Chinese, Britons, Irish—did a wandering boatload or a lunatic marooner ever stumble ashore on this land as strange as the moon in time incredibly long ago? Why not?

If the greatest epics were unsung, here they are.

The only high-society candidate conceivably old enough to serve as a point of departure for that Asiatic cotton—presuming a prosaic explanation doesn't come along involving a different world distribution of plants 4,000 years ago—is the very early Indus Valley civilization, inland from the Arabian Sea, as far away from the New World as it is possible to get, without any ships of any kind so far as is known, and flourishing a bare century or so (if that) before the cotton, hybridized and woven, was flourishing in America. The source of this civilization and the people who built it are not known. It existed only a few centuries, and fell to the barbaric Aryans sweeping down from southern Russia. It had trade ties with the early civilization of Mesopotamia, separated from it by the breadth of Persia. Sometime, perhaps even before its birth, there may have been, somehow, that cotton contact with South America, if the evidence of an Asiatic strain proves its case.

There is plenty of other matter for mystery in the origin of New World cultures. There are the Negroid characteristics some see, or imagine, in the proto-Olmecs. Or the white Indians, individuals here and there or whole bands, such as the highland Chachapoya of the Inca Empire, famous fighters. There is the sometimes white, sometimes bearded, sometimes bald Quetzalcoatl, much too ancient, alas, to be a Viking, as the old favorite theory had it. There are the black-boned, black-fleshed Araucanian chickens that lay blue eggs, and might be pre-Columbian, and might be related to the Silkies, a breed of Africa and Asia. There are the resemblances between Asiatic parcheesi (pachisi) and the Middle American game of patolli. And the resemblances some see, or imagine, between certain written ideographs from Ecuador and the so-called Easter Island script, from 2,000 miles out in the Pacific, and the far more incredible resemblances (separated not only by space but by 4,000 years) some see or imagine between the so-called Easter Island script, in use in the nineteenth century A.D., and the so-called Indus Valley script, in use in India in the twenty-fifth century B.C.

Some culture elements must have been exchanged to be sure, and it is interesting to guess what they were. More similarities, still a great many more, root back to the primitive Pleistocene soil out of which both the Old World and the New World grew. But the Old World civilizations turned one direction and the New World another. A society must be the product of its total time. Each impulse that enters or goes out from it, crosses over it or clashes with it, develops within it or is rejected by it, the thoughts that are not thought as well as the thoughts that become ideas, all must contribute to any society's complex pattern, a pattern infinitely too complex for glib dismemberment. In the New World, patterns were formed that were elaborately distinctive from those formed in the Old World, and distinctively Indian.

An impulse went forth (circa A.D. 1100) from the sprawling Andean city of Huari (if not from Tiahuanaco) that unified to some degree the people of the central Andes for the first time since the collapse of the ancient cat cult 1,000 years before. Nobody is sure this was a war-won empire; maybe everyone simply liked doing things the Tiahuanaco way.

Whatever it was it fell apart after a century or two or three, and the half dozen different Andean regions returned to an independence that took the shape of building large cities, more terraced farmlands, more irrigation systems, more roads and bridges—and conquering each other. The Mochica bounced back as the center of the little Chimu empire in the north. More goods of all kinds were made, and very skillfully, but the masterpieces of old were never again approached. The making of bronze was developed, and the casting of copper, and much more gold and silver was worked. In Ecuador even the fishhooks were of gold. The fashion for featherwork boomed. Priest-kings ruled, seemingly, and classes were divided into priests and farmers, warrior aristocrats and artisan workers.

The Incas in their Cuzco valley were one of the many little states only trying to survive, in the political atmosphere of devious alliances, treachery, ambitious conspiracy, and sudden

**At 8,400 feet the Inca fortress-city of Machu Picchu, in Peru, was hidden from the outside world until 1911. Now modern roads bring tourists to view the perfectly fitted stonework of its stepped terraces and walls. The Andes loom behind.**

death. They had done well at it: Cuzco was one of the few central Andean towns that had not been absorbed into the Tiahuanaco empire.

Viracocha Inca, eighth king in a line of insignificant local chiefs claiming direct descent from the legendary Manco Capac, son of the Sun, played for a long time a wily game of balancing powerful neighbors against each other, but eventually artful diplomacy and astute royal marriages were not enough—the kingdom of the Chanca to the northwest sent invading armies, and Viracocha fled with the heir apparent, Inca Urcon, to a mountain fort, abandoning his city.

In the high Andes, everything is larger than life. You could drop an ordinary mountain in any chasm, Baron Alexander von Humboldt said, and lose it there. The country cries out for Wagnerian music, and gods in the shape of heroes. At this moment it got one.

Yupanqui, a son of Viracocha, refused to run, led Cuzco in a hopeless defense, and at the critical moment the stones of the battlefield became warriors, so they say, and fought for the outnumbered Incas. The city was saved; the Chanca were utterly defeated.

When Viracocha died, he was given an emperor's usual deification (his women and servants would dance ceremonially at the funeral dance until they were ceremonially drunk on the ceremonial wine, when they would joyously surrender themselves to the strangler so they might accompany their lord; and living servant women would be assigned in perpetuity beside his mummy bundle to whisk the flies away), but Yupanqui casually set Inca Urcon aside and took for himself the strip of braid that was the Inca crown. He also took a new name, Pachacuti ("Cataclysm"), by which he was known forever afterward.

This was in the year 1438 (or thereabouts); within the next fifty-five years Pachacuti Inca Yupanqui and his son Topa Inca, by a process of adroit propaganda, diplomatic maneuvering, power politics, and the persuasive matter of eight major military campaigns, built and organized the Inca Empire, extending it for over 2,000 miles from north to south and ruling over an estimated six million subjects (other estimates have run from three and a half million to thirty-two million). The population of England at about the same time was some four million.

It has been mentioned that ideological differences between the

Andes and Mexico ran deep. The Mayas dreamed, the Mexicans worshiped, the Incas built.

The things the Incas built were copied from the older civilizations that they conquered. In their cities, fortresses, roads, terraces, temples, they did only what had been done before by the people around them, but a great deal more of it. The ornamentation, the woven fabrics, the work in gold they pursued so avidly as a symbol of the Sun, all were adopted from their predecessors. In general none of their art approached in quality the best work of earlier times, although in quantity it was truly inspired.

Totalitarian political organization may have been the Incas' own invention. They naturalized trustworthy subject peoples as honorary members of the Inca tribe and settled them among untrustworthy peoples, and if necessary transplanted whole populations of untrustworthy subjects to areas where they could be more easily controlled. Regimentation of all aspects of public life and even some aspects of private life and thought reached such Orwellian heights as attempts to obliterate pre-Inca history. The amazing Inca vigor was directed not toward timeless dreams or ageless gods but toward the fabrication of an Inca past and the creation of an Inca future.

Occasional human sacrifice, especially of children, existed among the Incas, and for that matter they also sometimes made the skull of a fallen enemy leader into a cup, in the age-old trophy of total vanquishment, or sewed his skin up as a drum. "Our emperor will conquer you and make you a drum," Inca ambassadors warned the hostile kings and chiefs. More commonly still, a state prisoner or an important criminal was disposed of privately, in the Cuzco dungeons furnished with snakes and wild beasts. Religion was of first importance, and certainly the Incas were divine (springing from the Sun), but they had no interest in the intellectual game of a complex world-devouring theogony. Public death as a daily bread for the gods was by no means the ultimate purpose of being; they had more practical things to do.

Their most reverent moment came with the simple offering of a chalice of wine to the Sun by the Emperor. Religion was rich with rites, administered by innumerable priests and priestesses housed in innumerable temples and convents; every act of life was adorned with religious ceremony; each day at sunrise priests cried out to the Sun to remember that we are thy children, and in the great public ceremonies before the gold-sheeted Temple of the Sun each step of the glittering dance, each drumbeat, and each note of a flute was exactly prescribed. And yet in essence religion was comparatively simple:one worshiped the creator Viracocha (who had made the world, taught all goodness and virtue, and then walked away on the water across the Pacific), the Sun, the Thunder, and observed the sacredness of the *huacas*—holy things, holy places, such as the tombs of ancestors, the extremely sacred bodies of dead emperors, the miraculous stones of Pachacuti's first battlefield. The Mayas sang

*The red wild bees are in the east. A large red blossom is their cup . . .*
*The white wild bees are in the north . . .*
*The black wild bees are in the west . . .*
*The yellow wild bees are in the south*

and to many American Indians, before and since, the Four Directions (or Five or Six, counting up-and-down by either one or two) have been the very cornerstones of religious faith—the symmetry of a universe in tune. But the Incas had no words in their language for north and south. They recognized only east and west, the rising and setting of the sun.

The Inca world of elegant gentlemen taking snuff, of engineers and sorcerers and busy city streets and the greatest collection of art in gold and silver the world has ever known, with everything meticulously organized from the careful education of the flawless girls chosen to be priestesses, imperial concubines, or sacrificial victims, down to the orderly rows of psalm-chanting farmers digging their fields in unison, brought nothing really new to Andean civilization except this rigid totalitarian organization. It touched only erratically the numerous peoples beyond its boundaries, so far as present study, which is pretty erratic here too, has shown.

Southward the Calchaqui, of northwestern Argentina, part of the larger nation called the Diaguita, were farmers and town dwellers similar in many ways to the North American Pueblo Indians. Eastern neighbors of the Diaguita were the Guaicuruan hunters of the Chaco region, some of whom, notably the Abipon, developed striking parallels to the hunting tribes of the North American plains.

Farther south still, in central Chile, the Araucanians, farmers and llama herdsmen and extraordinarily fond of freedom, lived in family villages, worked gold, grew the same crops (they may have been the first to domesticate the potato), but were otherwise thoroughly unlike the class-conscious, temple-building central Andeans and gave the Incas as little shrift as possible.

Below them only people of the wood roamed the storm-swept bush of Patagonia—some of them living in the same cave that had been the home of the giant-sloth hunters 8,000 or 10,000 years before. And some of them, incidentally—the towering Tehuelche of eastern Patagonia—were the tallest of all Indians and one of the tallest peoples in the world.

Except in a few rather isolated instances Andean ways, and the Incas, seem not to have penetrated very deeply into the entire continent east of the Andes. In the Amazon rain-forest country the common staff of life was flour made from the bitter manioc (modern tapioca comes from its juice), from which the poison had to be extracted by a tricky process worthy of a chemical laboratory. Fish were drugged; tobacco was rolled into cigars; signal drums sounded in the night; and God was most often made manifest in masks and skirts of shredded bark. Many Amazonian people knew that if a father did not take to his hammock and rest for a certain number of days after childbirth the baby would die. Here in uproariously stinking river villages lived the most jovially uninhibited cannibals on earth; some of the many bands of Tupian people bred their women to captives of war and raised the resultant children like veal calves for butchering.

To the north of the Inca Empire, in Colombia, Ecuador, Venezuela, and Central America, were various barbaric kingdoms and petty priest-ruled states, the best-known being the extensive domain of the Chibcha, centering in Colombia. Some of these had histories of more or less high culture as old as any in the Andes or Mexico.

Extravagant human sacrifice and a few other Mexican customs appeared in the northern reaches, but most of the people were clearly South American (Chibchan the commonest language) all the way to the southern Maya frontier in the region of the Ulua River in Honduras.

The islands of the Caribbean had been populated mainly by Arawak village people from South America (but some of them had learned the ceremonial ball game of Mexico), gentle, kindly, ridiculously inept at war. During Inca times or thereabouts raids and invasions began from a ferociously warlike set of cannibals along the South American coast, the Caribs, who gave their name to the sea as well as the word cannibal to the English language; the raids continued for generations, great sport to the Caribs.

Erratically, some Andean ways migrated during the centuries across the Gulf of Mexico to the melting pot at the mouth of the Mississippi; and even the farming forest people far to the north who were later called the Sioux learned someplace the word "wakan" (identical with the Inca word "huaca") for something holy, sacred, supernaturally inspired.

# III

# Empires of the Sun

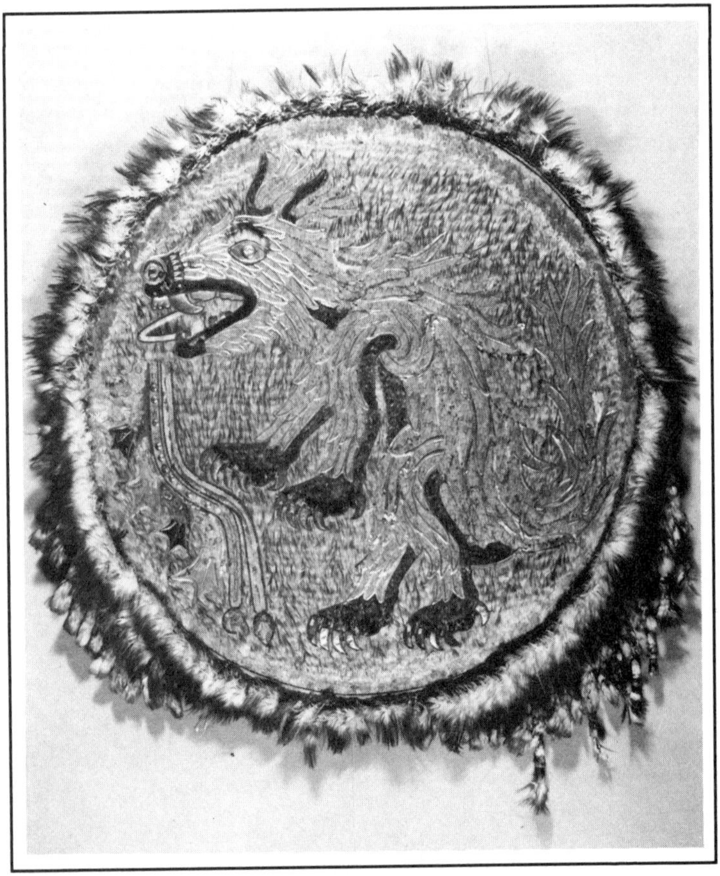

**Feather objects like this tufted shield were part of the sumptuous treasure given to Cortes by the emperor Moctezuma as a gift for Charles I of Spain.**

In Mexico drought, famine, and wars of the gods, which is to say revolution and foreign attacks, had long ago caved in the Toltec empire. Tula, that "very large city, and truly a marvel. . . . A great many powerful and wise men lived there...," had fallen in the year 1168, some say, and the same year is one of the traditional dates for the beginning of new barbarian migrations from the north, migrations of various tribes collectively called the Chichimecs (Dog People), tough, brutal, hungry, and armed with bows and arrows.

They crowded into the Valley of Mexico, probably over a period of many years, seized, sacked, and destroyed everything in sight, and emerged circa 1300 as rulers (usually claiming royal Toltec lineage) of some of the various city-states rebuilt, bigger and richer with gods than ever, about Lake Texcoco.

They were a fiercely pious people and brought a tremendous increase in the pattern of human sacrifice, and wars instigated at least partially for the purpose of capturing prisoners as sacrificial victims. They were also a supple people, and within a very few generations had become as aggressively cultured as they once had been savage—grand patrons of the arts, swooning esthetically over tastefully arranged bouquets and manipulating feather fans with a fine aristocratic grace. If they were not already Nahua-speaking people (some spoke Otomi or Pame) they became so, and forgot the tongue of their uncouth grandfathers.

However, they did not lose their muscles. Besides the wars customary to ducal states jostling for gain, power, dominance, there were the hungry gods, and that constant need for prisoners to feed to them; warriors and priests remained the highest castes of all. "Then the man dexterous in arms... such honor he won that no one anywhere might be adorned [like him]...," says the Florentine Codex. And the ascetic priests praying in the mountains ran skewers and cords through their own tongues, lips, ears, hands, genitals, to pour out their own blood in a thousand midnight fountains for the gods. One drew blood as penance from the part of the body that had sinned; as one wore magic charms at ears, nose, and lips—a hole pierced below the lower lip for the "lip plug"—so sin and sickness could not enter there.

Curiously, bows and arrows, after conquering the cities, largely gave way (except for the use of fire arrows in sieges) to the old standard arms of spear and spear-thrower and battle-axe, and of these it is the obsidian-bladed club that is most often pictured in the codices. It is hard to take prisoners with long-distance bows and arrows, of course, which may have been the reason.

Wars were battles royal, hand-to-hand; you either disarmed your opponent and made him surrender or beat him unconscious and then dragged him away. Battles were gorgeously costumed affairs, men in headdresses and shirts of yellow parrot feathers, sprays of costly quetzal feathers set off with gold, whole squadrons uniformed in jaguar skins or golden hoods with feather horns, carrying shields decorated with golden disks, butterflies, and serpents, wearing embroidered sandals with thongs of orange leather. And they raised a gorgeous din as well, with the two-toned drums, conch-shell trumpets, shrill clay whistles, screams full-voiced (so heaven could hear, and slyly designed besides to shock and terrify the enemy) calling on heaven for help and witness. The priests led the way to combat, carrying the gods, and then chanted promises of paradise and blew encouragement with piercing trumpet blasts while they waited with ready obsidian knives for the first prisoners to be dragged out from the battle for sacrifice on the spot, to be yanked spread-eagled on their backs, their chests slashed open, their hearts torn out and triumphantly raised "there toward where the sun came forth...." Decision gained, the victorious troops charged into the defeated town, burning the temple, butchering and capturing the noncombatants, until they finally deigned to listen to the losing leaders' supplications for peace and promises of tribute.

These were not, to be sure, the constant pleasures of all. While every able-bodied man was subject, if need be, to soldiering, the elite of the warriors tended to become more and more a professional class. Farmers, stonemasons, featherworkers, goldsmiths, silversmiths, singers, musicians, worked at their work as they always had. But even the everyday world was full of spectacle, excitement, terror, and joy, and why resent a famous warrior's glory? He didn't get there without sweat either; and for that matter anyone with courage and a lucky birthday and the help of the gods could become a ranking warrior or a priest. And anyway tortillas were yellow as sunlight or white as snow; green chocolate was tender, delicious, and foaming; and the girls, with their beautiful teeth and their blue-dyed hair, were always pretty.

The art of the featherworkers is gone, except for a rare time-tattered example, but the art in stone and gold and silver can still speak to us with passion, enthusiasm, and a dedication terrible in its intensity. Good work is hard work, usually, in art. They produced some wonderfully good work.

To the west of Lake Texcoco the city of Azcapotzalco, ruled by the Tepanecs, grew in dominion.

To the east of the lake the great city Texcoco, seat of the Acolhuas, had seventy towns paying it tribute.

To the south, where Lake Texcoco joined the freshwater Lake Xochimilco (Sho-chee-meel-ko), the Culhuas at Culhuacan (Cool-wah-kan) grew in power.

The Culhuas employed as mercenaries a landless tribe of spearmen, the Mexica, who had a heavy date with the future. They took the first step toward it when, wishing on a certain occasion to flatter the Culhua king with the highest honor they could think of, they sacrificed his daughter and invited the king to watch the solemn climax of a priest dancing in the girl's skin. To their amazement the king was enraged, sacrificed or enslaved the individuals responsible, and drove the rest of the Mexica people into exile. The dismayed fugitives founded a town on a miserable little group of islands in the lake, partway between Culhuacan and Azcapotzalco; they called their shantytown Tenochtitlan (Place of the Cactus in the Rock). This was, according to the traditional date, in 1325; the actual date was probably some years earlier.

The beggarly Mexica on their islands became auxiliaries of the Tepanecs at Azcapotzalco. Their quondam master-state, Culhuacan, was eventually destroyed by their new masters, under the voracious conqueror Tezozomoc, king of Azcapotzalco. The Mexica island town grew and took on airs; it wanted to be a city. Tezozomoc condescended to give his daughter in marriage to Huitzilhuitl II (Weet-seel-weetl), its chief, and Tenochtitlan thereupon assumed identity as a full-fledged city-state, and flourished to become Tezozomoc's stoutest and most worthy vassal.

With the constant help of the Mexicas (who were now beginning to call themselves Tenochcas, after the name of their new city), Tezozomoc extended his conquests for many miles beyond the Valley. Each new expansion of power tightened his rivalry with the only other remaining great power in the Valley of Mexico, Texcoco, across the lake.

At last, in the year 1416, when Tezozomoc was in his nineties and had to be wrapped in down and cotton and carried in a basket, he raised the curtain on the big war, and sent his troops of Azcapotzalco against Texcoco. Huitzilhuitl and his Tenochca Mexicas gave good service among the armies of subject warriors; Tezozomoc conducted the campaign with relentless craft; Texcoco was besieged, invaded, and finally taken. Its king, Ixtlilxochitl (Eesht-leel-sho-cheetle), tried to escape from the conquered city with his son Nezahualcoyotl (Nezza-wall-kee-otl, Hungry Coyote). The king was caught and died under the spears and battle-axes of Tezozomoc's soldiers. But the prince escaped, to become Mexico's most resplendent legend.

He hid in the forests and the mountains, or in disguise in cities; he wrote poetry, studied philosophy, discovered a personal religious faith to an Unknown God to whom sacrifice should not be made but only prayers; he was absolutely valorous, completely skilled in arms, he never did wrong, he always did right.

The followers who flocked to his secret standard (under the green oak greenwood tree) were loyal unto death: when he was once captured and put in a wooden cage to await execution, a guard released him and died in his place. The incredibly aged Tezozomoc—he was now past 100 years—could conquer the world but was powerless against the destiny of Nezahualcoyotl. A dozen times, according to the stories, Hungry Coyote miraculously eluded capture and certain death when Tezozomoc all but had him in his grasp.

"The goods of this life, its glories and its riches, are but lent to us. . . . Yet the remembrance of the just shall not pass away from the nations . . . ," so sang, more or less, the poet Nezahualcoyotl . . . while the soldiers of Tezozomoc went from house to house in vanquished Texcoco slaying out of hand all children who mistakenly answered "Nezahualcoyotl" when asked who was their king.

Huitzilhuitl II, ruler of Tenochtitlan, died, and the Mexica elders and chief priests and warriors elected his son Chimalpopoca (Tezozomoc's favorite grandson) as the new leader of their island city. And finally, in 1426, at the age of 106, old Tezozomoc went to his reward, at his all-powerful capital of Azcapotzalco.

But his empire crumbled immediately afterward: a disappointed son, Maxtla, conspired against the chosen heir, had him murdered, seized the crown, and to make his power secure then arranged for the assassination (by stranglers in the night, the stories say) of the king of Tenochtitlan, which had clearly become his strongest and most formidable subject state.

The Mexicas rose in revolt, elected a new leader, and formed an alliance with the exiled Nezahualcoyotl. Armies of the faithful sprang up from Texcoco to follow Hungry Coyote. A third member joined the alliance, the strategically situated town of Tlacopan, which provided a beachhead for the fleets of canoes sent across the lake from Texcoco. Maxtla was defeated and his city of Azcapotzalco taken in battle.

Nezahualcoyotl returned in triumph as the rightful monarch of Texcoco, married 100 wives, built a matchless palace at his summer place of Texcotzingo, and lived a long life of matchless wisdom and probity.

And Tenochtitlan, the island shantytown of a century before, suddenly found itself (with Texcoco) one of the two chief cities of the entire country.

As the Mexica people of Tenochtitlan had risen in power and eminence, they had given themselves a suitable family history, and taken as their own a suitable god, Huitzilopochtli (Wee-seel-o-poch-tlee), "omen of evil... creator of war."(Teoyaotlatohuehuitzilopochtli, "Divine Lord of War, Great Huitzilopochtli," to give him his formal epithet.)

They had originally come from someplace in the northwest of Mexico, a place they called in their legends Aztlan, and so they called themselves the People of Aztlan, or Aztecs.

Their god had told them to wander until they came to a cactus growing from a rock, on which an eagle would be perched, holding in his beak a serpent—the symbol of water and abundance; this promised land had been found, cactus, eagle, snake and all, exactly as predicted, at the site of Tenochtitlan. (The first Incas had been given a golden staff by the Sun, and told they would find their promised land where the staff should enter the ground—which had been at the site of Cuzco.)

Huitzilopochtli had also told the Aztecs they were his chosen people and would rule the world. Together with Texcoco, and with Tlacopan for a junior partner in a continuing triple alliance,

**This codex drawing depicts the founding of the Aztec capital at Tenochtitlan where, as the sun god Huitzilopochtli had said, an eagle coming to rest on a cactus would show them the end of their long search. The ideographs at bottom represent the subjugation of neighboring cities.**

they proceeded to do so, as far as Mexico was concerned.

Their conquests multiplied, extending far to the north and south. Tribute and captives poured into the city, and Tenochtitlan exploded in size. Swampland was reclaimed, its island was enlarged, blocks of new buildings were raised, a three-mile-long aqueduct (double-barreled so its channels could be closed alternately for cleaning) was built to bring fresh water from the mainland, and a second had to be built soon afterward. A thousand people, so they say, were employed each day in washing down the streets. There were in the city 60,000 hearths, so they say, or an estimated 300,000 white-mantled people. (The population of London at the same epoch was about 120,000.)

Texcoco became the artistic and intellectual capital of the Valley, but Tenochtitlan became the center of power and wealth for all Mexico. By constant intrigue as well as by constant conquests, the Aztecs gradually assumed leadership over Texcoco; Tlacopan was gradually forgotten as any kind of partner at all. After the death of Nezahualcoyotl in 1472—he left a reported sixty songs—the Aztec ascendancy over other Mexican peoples grew still more pronounced.

Sometime in the 1470s, in Peru, another renowned king died—Pachacuti; he also, incidentally, is credited with the authorship of many poems and psalms, including his own death song:

*I was born like a lily in the garden,*
*And so also was I brought up.*
*As my age came, I have grown up,*
*And, as I had to die, so I dried up*
*And I died.*

Pachacuti's son Topa Inca had been in command of military matters for some years while Pachacuti concerned himself with organizing administration; now Topa Inca campaigned to the south, where he and his father had previously driven toward the north. He marched his mace-men and peltists (who carried their slings wound like headbands in their hair) down into Chile, across the Atacama desert where rain has never been recorded, into the frontier zone of the country of the Araucanians, and set up, for all time, the southern boundary markers of the Empire on the banks of the River Maule. He spent his later years perfecting the Inca machinery of rule over this giant country, something more than eighty-five provinces (probably more than 100), far and away the largest political state yet known in the New World, and in the last year of his reign could see this creation trouble-free, perfectly functioning, magnificently complete.

This was in the year 1492.

The Aztecs conquered from sea to sea, from the Gulf Coast to the Pacific. They ran into setbacks with the Tarascans to the west, murderous bowmen who walloped them with a resounding defeat, and they never were able to crush the Tlaxcalans to the east, who used squadrons of Otomi archers as auxiliaries, although they surrounded Tlaxcala with satellite Aztec states that left its independence isolated and precarious, and its people deprived of the luxuries of commerce. Nearly all the rest of Mexico below Tampico and Guadalajara paid Aztec tribute—but with frequent defections requiring almost regular reconquests.

The Aztecs established no political empire in the Inca or Roman sense; they never thought of fighting wars for keeps in the modern sense. War remained at least partly a captive-catching game, its most notable feature the delayed-action battlefield casualties who played out their death roles later in ostentatious temple ceremonies rather than in the anonymous immediacy of battle. Occasionally some portion of conquered lands was placed under direct Aztec dominion, but in general defeated states were looted and then, in effect, left alone—as long as they continued to furnish the often heavy tribute assigned and recognize Aztec political hegemony.

Some peoples, theoretically subjugated, were in such a constant state of revolt that their names became almost synonymous among the Aztecs with the terms for captives, slaves, sacrificial victims—such were the Huastecs (the northern cousins of the Mayas) and the Totonacs (the relatives, if they were, of the Olmecs), both in the Veracruz region along the Gulf Coast. This area had first been conquered in 1462, the year also of a memorable earthquake.

Even so, there were still not enough wars to furnish enough prisoners to feed the gods with sacrifice, and so artificial wars, Wars of the Flowers they were called, were instituted between neighboring cities for the sole purpose of capturing victims from each other. These battles were formally arranged, each side fought until enough prisoners had been taken to satisfy its gods, and all parted friends, with no hard feelings. So they say.

As has been pointed out, the Aztecs did not introduce human sacrifice into Mexico. It had existed, at least to some degree, from the earliest times. They simply did the same things that had always been done, but, according to all accounts, much bigger and better.

Anyone or any group, a war captain or a trade guild, the merchants' association or someone ill with an itch, needing the intercession of a god, bought a slave and on the god's feast day had him (or her—goddesses, naturally, were fed with women and girls) ceremonially bathed and slain. The priests at the many temples needed slaves (or captives—all captives of war were slaves, although all slaves were not captives; one might sell himself or a family might sell its children into slavery and possible sacrifice, and many did when times were hard) for the established, official temple rites. Military organizations needed victims for their established religious observances. In the case of the Aztecs, the state needed slaves constantly as victims for the state god, Huitzilopochtli, who fought each day against the darkness of the night; without blood and human hearts the sun would fail.

Each of the eighteen twenty-day months of the year had its ceremonies and sacrifices. Hearts were torn out for Huitzilopochtli, and then, at Tenochtitlan, the heads of the victims were impaled on the towering skull rack in the central plaza. Captive warriors were given mock weapons and led by their celebrated keeper, Old Wolf ("He in whose care lay the captives, as if they had become his sons..."), to be tied to the gladiator's stone and killed in a pretense of combat by warriors armed with real weapons, and then the priests danced with the heads of the captives ("And Old Wolf wept at this; he wept for his sons who had died..."). Priests danced wrapped in the skins of victims, "stained, dripping, gleaming" with blood, "so that they terrified those whom they followed," in honor of Xipe Totec.

Victims were lashed up as targets and shot full of arrows and darts so their dripping blood would fertilize the earth; children were sacrificed to the rain god, Tlaloc; victims were burned alive to celebrate the August heat of harvest. In the ceremony of the Volador, four men costumed as birds swung down by ropes from a high platform, sailing round and round a tall pole to which the ropes were attached; at the top, perhaps 100 feet up, a fifth celebrant danced on a tiny platform that turned as the ropes of the flyers unwound; this may have been a calendar ceremony illustrating the years turning through the century, although one leading student of this rite believes it was (and still is, in the villages where it is still performed) a survival of a precipitation sacrifice, since the dancer at the top of the pole frequently fell. Crowds danced and sang hilariously around the slave girl dressed as the Earth Mother, laughing and joking to conceal from her her fate, and the young war captive chosen to represent Tezcatlipoca lived a full year as the god, amidst every comfort, pleasure, and delight, and at the end of the year climbed the temple pyramid, breaking at each step a flute symbolic of his joyous incarnation, to meet his death on the sacrificial stone at the summit.

The deep-voiced drum, the huehuetl, throbbed like an enormous pulse, and the people celebrated, "jostling, howling, roaring. They made the dust rise; they caused the ground to smoke. Like people possessed, they stamped upon the earth."

The Aztecs were full of contradictions: arrogant and yet prizing humility, implacable and yet emotionally affectionate and kind, and like the ancient Greeks devoted equally to law, order, and loot. A boisterous, ebullient, but intensely earnest people, with an absolute certainty of the superiority of their way of life, they were well organized, technically and psychologically, for the mastery and control of the less zealous world around them.

Tizoc, king of Tenochtitlan from 1479 to 1486, was poisoned by the clan councils (it is said) because he was weak in war, for all that he performed was the pious act of having a gigantic block of stone dragged to the city where it was carved into a monstrous bowl for burning human hearts.

Ahuitzotl (Ah-weet-zottl), his brother and successor, left a more satisfactory trail of terror up and down the land, conquering forty-five provinces. Together with Nezahualpilli, son of Nezahaulcoyotl and king of Texcoco, he campaigned for two years in Oaxaca to gather a fitting mass of captives for the dedication of the great new temple to Huitzilopochtli. Twenty thousand people were sacrificed on this occasion, so they say—or so some say; others say 80,000 (but more of this later).

Ahuitzotl also gave his niece to Nezahualpilli for wife, but this act of solidarity did not work out well; she not only took lovers with royal abandon in the court of Texcoco, but had statues made of them and worshiped them as her gods. Nezahualpilli, a true son of the just and austere Nezahualcoyotl, had her publicly judged, condemned, and executed in 1498. Her brother Moctezuma II (the familiar Montezuma of history, his name being Moctecucuma in Nahua; Moctezuma in modern Mexico; Angry Lord in English), who became king of Tenochtitlan five years later, never forgave him, and after several years of strained relations took some cold revenge by allowing the Texcocan force to be wiped out when the ostensible allies were attacking (unsuccessfully, again) the Tlaxcalans. When Nezahualpilli died in 1516, Moctezuma named his successor, as if Texcoco was a subject state instead of an equal ally; an opposing heir raised a party of revolt, and the alliance was, at last, totally broken.

But by this time there were other, even graver matters weighing on Moctezuma's mind. A temple burst into flame without cause and burned to the ground. In a school for musicians, a ceiling beam sang a prophecy of national doom. A temple was struck by lightning out of a clear sky. The waters of the lake suddenly rose up in a flood and destroyed some of the city's houses. A comet fell in broad daylight, in sunlight. In the year 1511 a column of fire appeared by night in the east, piercing the heavens; the people cried out in terror, striking their mouths with their hands, "all were frightened; all waited in dread." It appeared each night for four years. Cihuacoatl (See-wah-ko-attl), Serpent Woman, the Earth Goddess who wailed in the night streets to tell mothers when their children were to die, was heard weeping at night, crying out, "My beloved sons, whither shall I take you?" A marvelous bird was brought to Moctezuma, an ash-gray crane with a mirror in its head, and in the mirror could be seen people "coming massed, coming as conquerors, coming in war panoply. Deer bore them upon their backs." Moctezuma summoned his soothsayers and wise men, but the bird vanished before their eyes.

The New Fire ceremonies were held in 1507—the critical rites celebrating the end of a fifty-two-year cycle, their century. Temples were enlarged or rebuilt, old debts were paid, injuries forgiven, enmities reconciled. Sins were confessed (at any rate by those too old to sin any more) to the goddess Tlazolteotl, Eater of Filth. On the night of the New Fire all old fires were put out, and until midnight demons were free and the world hung in delicate balance—pregnant women were locked in windowless rooms so they could not be changed into animals, and children were kept forcibly awake so the demons could not eat them in their beds. The priests knew the world had been destroyed four times before, and would be destroyed again—this time by fire—in a divine rhythm that was inescapable. It would happen on such a night as this, when the New Fire would refuse to respond to the priests' control. But at midnight the fire priests succeeded in kindling the New Fire on the Hill of the Star, and raced with it along the miles of causeway to the city, and rejoicing burst forth. The sun would rise again, the world would continue; all would go on as before.

Cristoforo Colombo (Italian), Cristóbal Colón (Spanish), Christopher Columbus (Anglicized Latin), Christ-bearing Dove (as we would literally translate his name if it were Indian), wrote in his first report, while on his way home from his first voyage of discovery across the unknown western sea: "The lands... are all most beautiful... and full of trees of a thousand kinds, so lofty that they seem to reach the sky. And some of them were in flower, some in fruit, some in another stage according to their kind. And the nightingale was singing, and other birds of a thousand sorts, in the month of November.... The people of this island, and of all the others that I have found and seen... all go naked, men and women... they are artless and generous with what they have, to such a degree as no one would believe but he who had seen it. Of anything they have, if it be asked for, they never say no, but do rather invite the person to accept it, and show as much lovingness as though they would give their hearts... they believed very firmly that I, with these ships and crew, came from the sky; and in such opinion they received me at every place where I landed, after they had lost their terror. And this comes not because they are ignorant; on the contrary, they are men of very subtle wit, who navigate all those seas, and who give a marvellously good account of everything.... And as soon as I arrived in the Indies, in the first island that I found, I took some of them by force, to the intent that they should learn and give me information of what there was in these parts. And so it was, that very soon they understood and we them, what by speech or what by signs.... To this day I carry them who are still of the opinion that I come from heaven, from much conversation which they have had with me. And they were the first to proclaim it wherever I arrived; and the others went running from house to house and to the neighboring villages, with loud cries of "Come! Come to see the people from heaven!..."

Learned opinion favors Watling's Island in the Bahamas for the scene of the first landing, October 12; Columbus named the place San Salvador. Then, doubtless with the help of Arawak guides, he went to Cuba and then to Santo Domingo, which he named Española, where the *Santa Maria* was wrecked, and where he left a few dozen of his men to establish and hold a little fort, La Navidad. He sailed away to return to Europe on January 4, 1493, taking with him his six Indian interpreters, and returned to the Caribbean the following autumn with seventeen ships and 1,500 more people from heaven, most of them coming as colonists. He also brought horses, twenty stallions and mares surviving from thirty-four he had shipped aboard at the start of the voyage out.

Other islands in the Antilles were explored; a town was founded on Española and later moved to the south coast of the island (and called Santo Domingo) when gold was discovered there.

Christ-bearing Dove attacked the cannibal Caribs wherever they were found—a cargo of 600 of them were sent to Spain to be sold as slaves in 1498—but he did his best to enforce just treatment of the guileless and defenseless Tainos, as the Arawak island people called themselves. Two days after first encountering them on that October day in 1492 he had noted in his journal that "These people are very unskilled in arms... with fifty men they could all be subjected and made to do all that one wished...," but he also had written, "I knew that they were a people who could better be freed and converted to our Holy Faith by love than by force...they remained so much our friends that it was a marvel...."

But the Spanish settlers needed laborers for their plantations and mines, and the Indians were uninterested in work; the priests also protested that the Indians could not be taught and converted unless they were forced into congregations. More settlers came, 200 more in 1498, 2,500 in 1502, 1,000 to 2,000 a year thereafter. It became necessary, of course, to congregate the Indians in villages under Spanish jurisdiction and see that they stayed congregated, and worked and worshiped properly.

Some of the Tainos tried to rebel, more fled to the hills and other islands and the mainland, more still died in the epidemics of the strange new diseases that had come with the people from heaven. By 1513 there were seventeen chartered Spanish towns in Española, and 14,000 Tainos left out of an estimated original quarter million on the island.

And the invaders, hunting cannibals and hostile savages who could legally be made slaves, as well as following the incessant rumors of gold, were penetrating the other islands of the Caribbean, the coasts of Florida and South America, and Panama—where 1,500 Spanish settlers arrived in 1514 to reinforce a colony founded some five years before.

The first Indian children fathered by the people from heaven grew to manhood. The survivors, if there were any, of the first naked islanders who had ventured down to the beach to approach the hairy, shining strangers became old men, and their stories had long ago lost all their wonderful savor. Christ-bearing Dove, white-haired and bumbling among important newcomers who refused to obey him, sailed away for the last time. Some of the Tainos may have heard that he died a year or so later. They may have been too busy dying themselves, and running and hiding, to care.

Spanish shipyards came into being, and horse and cattle ranches to supply the settlers with livestock. Throughout these years the Spanish never heard, except in dream-sequence Indian tales describing golden cities in a gilded cloudland, of Aztec and Inca empires.

But in the year 1511 a Spanish ship, bound from Darien in Panama to Santo Domingo, struck a reef and sank in the Caribbean. Survivors reached the east coast of Yucatan where, ragged and starving, they were found by coastal Indians. Some were killed and ceremonially eaten, others died in slavery; eventually only two were left, two men named Aguilar and Guerrero, enslaved to Maya chieftains.

At about the same time, far up the Nahua coast of Mexico, a little girl named Malinal was stolen and sold into slavery. That this could happen is indicated by the existence of stringent Aztec laws against such kidnapers; but some say the little girl's father,

**The Aztecs were as ruthless in domestic ceremony as they were in conquering other tribes; indeed, many slaves and enemy captives were needed for the endless sacrifices to the state god. This vivid scene from the Codex Magliabecchiano shows priests atop a bloodstained Aztec temple, tearing out the hearts of victims in an offering to the insatiable Huitzilopochtli.**

chief and governor of the town of Paynala, had recently died, and her mother, remarried, had Malinal secretly sold to make secure the position of her new children. In any case, Malinal was owned by some people in Xicalingo, who in turn sold her to someone in Tabasco, on the frontier of the Maya country, in southeastern Mexico.

In the Maya country the ancient life of grandly marking time, the ancient days of solemn raptures, had ended long ago. The Toltecs had taught them the arts of pride and war, and the Mayas had learned exceedingly well. The cowering Maya warriors of the eleventh-century sculptures had become, by the sixteenth century, some of the harshest fighters in the New World.

The sacred center of Chichen Itza and the city of Mayapan—the first real city among the Mayas, in that it was an urban community rather than a ceremonial center for scattered farms—were no more, devastated and abandoned after centuries of intrigue and counterintrigue, treachery, murder for power, and civil war.

The family of the Itzas (who claimed Toltec descent) had been driven with its followers back into the jungles to Guatemala, to the Lake Peten region where the classic Maya world had centered 1,000 years before. Mayapan, long ruled by the Cocom family, had been destroyed in the middle 1400s, and all the Cocoms murdered except one son, who had been absent on a trading trip to Honduras at the time. The little Mayapan empire broke up into many quarreling city-states (at least eighteen), and the surviving Cocom, with what was left of his people, established a new city and carried on a smoldering cold war against the Xiu family, destroyers of Mayapan.

The Xiu (Shee-oo) claimed Toltec descent and had their name, a Nahua word meaning "fire," to prove it; on the other hand the name may be a Mexicanization of the Maya word *ciu* meaning "lord."After all but annihilating the Cocoms, the Xiu rulers and their supporters abandoned their old capital of Uxmal and built a new city at Mani ("It is passed"). Truly so, and the gods knew it; in 1464 a hurricane smashed Yucatan, in 1480 a pestilence decimated the people, and in the 1490s furious war became so general that the dead in the towns outnumbered the living.

In 1516 a terrible new pestilence swept over Yucatan, a disease never known before, with "great pustules that rotted the body," and the people died so quickly from it that the Mayas named it "the easy death." It was apparently smallpox, passed along on ripples of contact from Panama, perhaps, where a wildfire epidemic had followed the arrival of the colonists of 1514. It came like the first trumpet call announcing the people from heaven, for the next year a Spanish ship from Cuba hunting slaves touched on the Yucatan coast, not far from where the slave girl Malinal was living.

The Maya people there were unimpressed by the first white men they had ever seen, and drove the Spaniards away in a hot fight, in spite of gunfire. But the Spanish leader heard of cities and saw gold; he died of his arrow wounds not long after getting back to Cuba, but the next year four more Spanish ships came to cruise along the Yucatan coast. Again they were driven away, but again, a few months later, the Spanish returned, this time with eleven ships and 500 men. They also brought sixteen horses. Warriors gathered from the Maya towns along the coast and fought "face to face, most valiantly," and kept on fighting off and on for three days, until the Spanish were able to disembark their horses and field a little troop of barely over a dozen mounted lancers. The Indians, who had never seen horses before, fled in terror, and this time the Spanish stayed.

The new Spanish captain, a young man named Hernando Cortes, had heard of bearded men in the Maya towns and gotten a message through to Aguilar and ransomed him from his seven years of slavery. The other surviving Spaniard had become a Maya and would not leave. "Brother Aguilar, I am married and have three children and the Indians look upon me as a Cacique and captain in wartime—You go and God be with you, but I have my face tattooed and my ears pierced, what would the Spaniards say should they see me in this guise?" So reported Bernal Diaz del Castillo, a twenty-seven-year-old soldier with Cortes. And among other gifts of tribute the now subdued people of the Maya coast gave to Cortes were their choicest girls, and among these the slave girl Malinal.

Malinal had grown up to be not only pretty but bright ("good looking and intelligent and without embarrassment," said Bernal Diaz). She spoke Nahuatl as a birthright tongue, and in Tabasco she had learned the border Maya dialect known as Chontal, and also, possibly from merchants visiting the household where she lived, Maya proper, as spoken throughout Yucatan. She could talk to Aguilar in Yucatecan Maya, and Aguilar could then translate into Castilian for Cortes.

The Spanish called her, after she was baptized, Marina. She proved herself such a brilliant and valuable girl Friday that some historians are almost tempted to think of her as the real conqueror of Mexico.

"... and thus God," wrote Bishop Landa some forty years later, "provided Cortes with good and faithful interpreters, by means of whom he came to have intimate knowledge of the affairs of Mexico, of which Marina knew much.... "Alfred M. Tozzer, Landa's modern editor, adds, "God also provided Cortes with a mistress... she lived with Cortes and bore him a son." (Cortes at first allotted her to one of his lieutenants, but before long took her for himself.)

It was in March 1519 that the people of Tabasco gave the Lady Marina (as Bernal Diaz always speaks of her) to the strangers, and this was in the shadow-land country of the far frontier of the Aztec confederacy. That confederacy was a land larger in extent than all Spain, filled with towns and cities that astonished the Spaniards, who in a generation in the New World had not yet seen anything more than villages of thatched huts. Estimates of the population have run from three to fifteen million, with the best recent guesses, based on tribute rolls, hovering close to eleven million (Spain at the time had a population of four and a half million). And these were no timorous Arawaks or unorganized Caribs; city after city could produce at almost instant notice ranked and disciplined armies of thousands, war-loving soldiers whose courage and tenacity were never belittled by anyone who had fought them. Even on the remote Tabasco coast the great city of Tenochtitlan—sometimes called Mexico after the Aztecs' other name, the Mexica—was famous, the center of the world, and the omnipotent Moctezuma, who ruled there, was obeyed to the ends of the earth.

But by the end of the year the Spanish expedition, by then only some 400 men, held Moctezuma prisoner in the center of the city of Mexico, and through him commanded all the country.

The Spanish had superior weapons—but not that much superior. The quilted cotton armor of the Mexicans was superior, in fact, to the Spanish steel breastplates—and the Spaniards were quick to change. No more sudden decisions were won by the sight and sound of horses and cannon.

The important point is that throughout the first march on Mexico, after they were joined by Malinal, the Spanish were forced to fight in only one engagement—where only their immensely superior tactics saved their lives. Otherwise the road of their first penetration into the country—the perilous interval while they were still without important allies and could have been wiped out a dozen times over—was paved by a string of diplomatic victories as remarkable as so many straight passes at dice.

On the Veracruz coast, where the little Spanish army sailed from Tabasco, Cortes played a double game with the fat Totonacs, who lived there, encouraging them to rebel against their Aztec oppressors, and with the Aztec ambassadors from Moctezuma, convincing them that he was on their side against the treacherous Totonacs. The Totonacs gave him workmen, food, and warriors, and Moctezuma sent a solid gold disk as large as a cart wheel, carved to represent the sun; a larger silver disk carved to represent the moon; a helmet full of grains of gold; 100 bearers loaded with other gifts of richly embroidered mantles, gold ornaments, crests of feathers; declarations of friendship; and a polite refusal to permit the mysterious strangers to visit the city of Mexico.

But the refusal was evasive and halfhearted; for who, indeed, were the bearded white men?

Quetzalcoatl, the bearded white god (born, it will be remembered, in a year of Ce Acatl), had said, so the legends recorded, that in another year of Ce Acatl he would return from the sunrise to reclaim his kingdom, and by a coincidence out of grand opera the year 1519 was another year of Ce Acatl in the Aztec calendar. Was it possible?

It is reasonable that Malinal, fully aware of this stage setting of prophecy, would have intimated that it was truly very possible, when she talked for Cortes to the chief men of cities and to the chief priests of temples—the long-haired ones, the Nahua annals call them, their ears shredded from acts of penance and their waist-long hair matted with the blood of sacrifices.

Everywhere the troubled people flocked to the temples, and at every town the strangers entered they found sacrificed bodies on the altars, hearts before the idols, and the temple walls desperately splashed with blood. (One of the most memorable things about the temples, not surprisingly, was their overpowering stockyard smell.)

Deftly juggling Totonac allies and uncertain Aztec ambassadors, and with flowery expressions of the sincerest respect sent ahead to the great prince Moctezuma, the Spaniards marched inland for Mexico City.

The one instance of fighting was found in the independent city-state of Tlaxcala, where stubborn armies threw themselves against the strangers in a running engagement that went on for days. Javelins fell as thick as straw on a threshing floor (said the Spaniards), and the Tlaxcalans and their Otomi archers, far from panicking at the explosion of gunpowder, drowned its noise with their shrill whistles and threw dust in the air while they rushed the dead and wounded away, so no one could see the damage that the little cannons had done. They killed a mare, a good and handy mare belonging to Pedro de Moron, and almost captured her rider. Three times, by day and by night, the Spaniards only survived by the hottest of sword work while holding their ranks exactly intact ("We dared not charge them, unless we charged all together, lest they should break up our formation"). Bernal Diaz credits Doña Marina with wringing victory out of this equivocal and exceedingly dangerous situation (many of the Spaniards were for retreating to the coast, and "all of us were wounded and sick") by a combination of persuasion and threats delivered with "a courage passing that of woman" to the Tlaxcalan chiefs of council. Once decided on friendship the Tlaxcalans remained the firmest of allies, and the march was continued with an extra added ball to keep in the air—a large Tlaxcalan detachment trailing along, sworn enemies of the Aztecs and all their subject states.

At Cholula, of the great pyramid, and very much an Aztec subject state, Cortes tactfully encamped the Tlaxcalans outside the city, juggled exchanges of friendship again with the Aztec ambassadors, discovered a plot against him in the city, and arranged instead for the Tlaxcalans to rush into the town at a prearranged signal and join the Spaniards in a massacre to punish the Cholulans' planned treachery. The surprise massacre went off elegantly, except that Cortes had a hard time getting the Tlaxcalans to stop, once he thought the punishment had gone far enough. Cortes reported 3,000 of the city's inhabitants killed; others say 6,000 or more.

Evidently there really was a plot against the strangers, and the Cholulans and Moctezuma's agents were profoundly disconcerted by the strangers' ability to read their most secret thoughts, which is to say by the alertness of the Spaniards' intelligence service, which is to say the Lady Marina.

Cortes, through Malinal, blandly forgave everyone concerned, assured the Aztec ambassadors that he knew Moctezuma could have had no part in such an ungentlemanly plot, even succeeded in representing himself to the Cholulans as their protector against the Tlaxcalans, and marched on to the capital, the city of Mexico, Tenochtitlan.

There is no way of telling, of course, whether the extraordinarily effective cunning and guile displayed all the way along this march was due to the devious genius of Cortes or of the Lady Marina. Cortes, as he proved often enough in other situations, was one of the great non-losers of all time. Regardless of the odds or setbacks he seemingly could not lose, and until he tangled with lawyers he never did. Perhaps one reason was that he knew how to make true use of such loyal confederates as the Lady Marina. A modern historian writes, "Had it not been for her devotion to Cortes and his various and sundry captains, she could well have caused the total destruction of the small Spanish army.... Most great captains in history found their defeat in the arms of a tender morsel—not so Cortes, he conquered Malinche and thus the New World." The Nahua people called her Malinche, or so it sounded to Spanish ears (her supposed Nahua name of Malinal may have been only the Nahua pronunciation of Marina—where Christo became Quilisto—and Malinche could have been made by a suffix of some form of *cihuatl*, "lady"). Cortes was known to the Nahua people by the name of Malinche's Captain—or, for short, also as Malinche. Marina is given much importance in the Spanish chronicles, and it is even more striking that in such Indian chronicles as the Lienzo (picture history) of Tlaxcala, Marina not only appears in every important scene but is customarily drawn larger than any of the other actors, including Cortes.

All the wonders the Spaniards had seen had not prepared them for the numerous cities around Lake Texcoco, the towers and temples rising out of the waters of the lake, the long straight

**The Spanish army, led by Cortes and the Lady Marina (right) and accompanied by native porters, marches on Tenochtitlan in this sixteenth-century Indian drawing of the Mexican Conquest. Known as Malinche by the Indians, Lady Marina is thought to have been as important to the conquest as Cortes; she was certainly as revered by the Indians.**

causeways eight paces wide jammed with welcoming crowds, the dignitaries tall with the dazzling plumes of the scarlet spoonbill, hung with jewels of gold and jade and pearls, sent to greet them, and finally the capital, the city of Mexico; and the soldiers asked each other if they were dreaming, "for it is," Cortes wrote, "the most beautiful city in the world."

No doubt the strangers were of equal interest to the Aztec public, with their curious weapons and dress, the one black among them, the tired and scarred but caparisoned horses (there were fourteen or fifteen left, and one six-month-old foal), the two greyhounds, the loads of mysterious baggage borne by Indian servants from among all the allies they had so far made—Totonacs, Tlaxcalans (who had given Malinal alone 300 handmaidens, so some say), Cholulans, as well as a half dozen foreign Indian servants brought from Cuba.

Moctezuma himself was brought in his litter to meet them; all the people bowed their heads so as not to affront the chief-of-men by looking into his face; his priests fumigated Cortes with incense and presented him; and Moctezuma quartered the strangers and all their people in an immense house, with courtyards and many rooms and with walls of sculptured stone, the palace of his father Axayacatl (Ah-sha-yah-cattl), ruler (1469–1481), and conqueror of thirty-seven cities.

After a week or so of polite visits back and forth, during which Moctezuma showed the strangers his city, its temples, the market place greater than Rome's, so the soldiers said who had served in Italy—the vast market had been the center of a separate city, Tlatelolco, until Axayacatl had incorporated it by force in 1473—Cortes came calling one day with a handful of men, and the Lady Marina, and took Moctezuma prisoner. This was accomplished with no more than a flimsy pretext and "smooth speeches"; it took Malinal two hours of smooth speeches to convince Moctezuma it would be best for him to come along quietly. He went with the Spaniards to their quarters and remained from then on in their custody, although treated with the greatest respect, accompanied by his household, and free to carry on each day the business of state.

He swore fealty to the strangers' Don Carlos, king of Spain, and at the suggestion of Cortes got together a princely present for the lord across the sea—his family's heirlooms, and what he could raise from his empire; gold, Cortes wrote, such as no monarch in Europe possessed. The Aztecs regarded gold as of small value except when transformed by the goldsmith's art; jade was the precious stone. The Spanish preferred gold, and they like it in the raw; they had most of the worked pieces melted into ingots. Scholars disagree on the total value—Prescott made it some six million nineteenth-century dollars, exclusive of silver, carved ornaments, and some of the delicately worked gold figures left unbroken.

Only the royal fifth was set aside for the lord across the sea, of course. The rest was divided, with many bitter rows, among the company of the people from heaven. The Spanish captains had their shares made into heavy chains of gold, and wore them wound around their doubleted shoulders.

The war was still to come, but the conquest was accomplished. From the moment of the magic touch of so much gold so tamely taken, the strangers were masters and could never believe otherwise; the sumptuous people in their glorious cities were really only Indians after all.

This whole unbelievable interlude, 400 Spaniards coolly taking over a capital that could (and eventually did) raise an army of many thousands of fanatically determined warriors, has troubled historians ever since. Moctezuma had but to lift a finger, in the good old prose of Prescott, and the little band of strangers would be stormed under and destroyed.

Maybe the smooth speeches of the young Malinal were really enchantment. Maybe Moctezuma did believe the strangers were gods; maybe he reasoned that only gods would have their audacity. He seems to have been hopelessly uncertain, anxious to get the strangers to go away, but anxious not to anger them. It is possible that he did not quite realize a conquest was going on. Who knows the proper protocol for visitors from outer space?

And so months passed, and in the spring of 1520 a new Spanish army—a much bigger one—landed at Veracruz. This was a force of 1,400 men under the command of a red-bearded bully boy named Panfilo de Narvaez, come not to help but hijack; Narvaez had authority to make Cortes his captive, dead or alive.

Cortes took 250 or so of his men and 2,000 mountain Chinantecs as allies (he had his own men armed and trained with long Chinantec lances, as an improvement over Spanish arms for fighting from the ground against horsemen), and as much gold as could be carried, and went to deal with these interloping people from heaven. He left Pedro de Alvarado in charge in the city, where a highly touchy situation had developed: the Aztec priests were beginning to urge death or expulsion for the strangers. Moctezuma's scientists were reporting, in effect, that the visitors from outer space were radioactive and would melt the country's marrow.

Alvarado was blond and handsome (the Aztecs called him Tonatiuh, Sun God), chattery, edgy, covetous, and vicious. Apparently with some idea of terrorizing the Aztecs by a repetition of the Cholula massacre he ordered an insane attack on the people dancing at the feast of Huitzilopochtli, and the city, shocked and enraged, burst into violence.

Cortes returned, having whipped Narvaez handily (Narvaez lost an eye in the battle) and then bribed most of his defeated army into changing sides, and found a full-scale war in progress in the city of Mexico. He forced Moctezuma to try to calm his subjects (and the Great Moctezuma said with grief: "What more does Malinche want from me?"), and Moctezuma was killed in the attempt, some say by the infuriated Aztecs, some say by the desperate Spaniards.

The strangers had to fight their way out of the city and make for the safety of Tlaxcala. Cortes escaped, with Marina, but of his handsome new army (the 1,000 or so additional recruits from Narvaez's forces, and his 400 veterans) more than 800 were killed in the fighting, drowned in the canals by the weight of the gold they were trying to carry, or captured and sacrificed. The gods ate well on this midsummer Noche Triste, Cortes's Night of Sorrow.

It took a year to gather armies of Indian allies and return to attack Tenochtitlan again. The real war was fought during this time, a war for empire between the Aztecs and the invaders, a war of intrigue, deals, and ruthless force where it was needed. Tlaxcala and the Totonac towns and the anti-Aztec parties in many subject states, including Texcoco (Moctezuma's vengeance for his sister turned out to be costly), threw in enthusiastically with the Spaniards. States loyal to the Aztecs were put to fire and sword by Cortes and his insurgent allies, and their populations branded on the face and sold as slaves. Captured Spaniards were sacrificed; sometimes their faces were skinned (with the beards) for trophies to give to the gods. The heads of horses as well appeared on the skull rack in Tenochtitlan. Cortes's policy with prisoners of war was to free them, if there was any chance of making peace with their people; if not, he had their hands cut off and then sent them home. It was a long and bitter war, but the strangers pulled away more and more of the confederacy, and the Aztecs could never trap and destroy them—there was always Tlaxcala for refuge; and eventually it became clear that the invaders had won and the Aztecs had lost. When at length the strangers came back in massive strength to besiege the capital, the issue could not be in doubt.

The attack on the city was mounted from Texcoco, where the anti-Aztec leader, Ixtlilxochitl II, helped work out the same sort of operation that his grandfather Nezahualcoyotl had used with the Aztecs against the then capital of Azcapotzalco—heavy attacks by water and encirclement by land. The pincers closed and the island city was held under siege until fresh water and food became more precious than jade. Hundreds of thousands of allied warriors ("an infinite number," Cortes wrote) were supporting the Spanish.

But seemingly inexhaustible squadrons of Aztec spearmen fought like demons, from house to house, from temple to temple, along the canals that were the city's streets. Cuauhtemoc (Kwow-tay-mok), Moctezuma's nephew and the new Aztec ruler, had told his soldiers they would either be victorious or die fighting. They did, almost to a man—in the usual hyperbolic sense of the term. Losses of Aztecs and their allies in the city were put by Cortes at 117,000; survivors, excluding women and children, at 30,000. Losses of the Texcoco troops were estimated at 30,000.

"It was useless to tell them," Cortes reported, "that we would not raise the siege, and that the launches would not cease to fight them on the water, nor that we had already destroyed the people of Matalcingo and Malinalco, and that there was no one left in the land to bring them succour, and that there was nowhere whence they could procure maize, meat, fruit, water, or other necessaries, for the more we repeated this to them the less faintheartedness they showed. On the contrary, both in fighting and in stratagems we found them more undaunted than ever."

The battle lasted eighty-five days, and ended on the thirteenth of August, 1521, when the last few defenders in the northeast corner of the city were cut down.

"All through the Colonial era, and even up to now," the archaeologist Vaillant writes, "the northern district of Mexico [City] has found favour neither as a residential quarter nor as a business center. To-day there are railroad yards and slums where the Aztec civilization bled to death. The ghosts of its heroic defenders still haunt the place."

Nothing in all that has been written about the Aztecs tells as much about them as their song, their hymn, that runs like this:

*We only came to sleep*
*We only came to dream*
*It is not true, no, it is not true*
*That we came to live on the earth.*
*We are changed into the grass of springtime*
*Our hearts will grow green again*
*And they will open their petals*
*But our body is like a rose tree:*
*It puts forth flowers and then withers.*

In Peru at about the same time, sometime in the early 1520s, barbarians crossed the Andes from the east and raided the border provinces of the Inca Empire. They came from the wild bush country across the mountains called the Chaco, a Quechua word meaning hunting ground. They were the Guarani, bowmen and cannibals. This was not their first plundering appearance on the Inca frontiers nor their last—Huayna Capac the Inca, son of Topa Inca, built three fortresses to guard against them. But on this invasion they were accompanied by a few white men, shipwrecked survivors from an exploring fleet commanded by Juan de Solis, chief pilot of Spain. In 1515 and 1516 Solis had sailed down the east coast of South America as far south as the Rio de la Plata, where he had been killed and eaten by the inhabitants. Consequently the Europeans with the Guarani must have spent the intervening five or ten years wandering the length and breadth of interior South America, from the region of the present Buenos Aires to Peru, some of it country that is virtually unexplored yet today.

One of these Europeans, and the only name we have from among them, was Alejo Garcia, a Portuguese. Along with what may have been one of the most imposing lists of firsts in all exploration, he was the first European of record to see the wealth and civilization of the Incas. His name might be more than a footnote to history except that his Guarani friends killed him on the way back east.

The importance of this invasion to the Incas is in the sudden pestilence that followed it (maybe there was no connection, or maybe the Guarani and their guests had been carrying it wherever they went). For during the epidemic Huayna Capac died, so quickly and unexpectedly that he did not have time to make the usual formal announcement of his successor. He meant his son Huascar (Was-kar) to succeed him, who was duly crowned at Cuzco by the high priest. But Huayna Capac happened to die at Quito in the north, where he had a separate wife and a son by her named Atahualpa (Atta-wall-pa). Atahualpa assumed the governorship of Quito and the northern provinces, and command of the army that had been with Huayna Capac when he died.

The two veteran generals of that army, Quisquis and Challcuchima, gave Atahualpa their loyalty. They were the Empire's foremost generals, and their seasoned troops the Empire's best. In the civil war that followed, and lasted for five years, Quisquis and Challcuchima won a solid string of victories, ending in a decisive triumph north of Cuzco. Huascar was taken prisoner, his forces scattered, his lieutenants executed.

Huayna Capac died in 1527. In the same year word came of strange beings (perhaps gods, perhaps Viracocha returning?) at the far northern outposts of the Empire. The Viracochas went away, but five years later they returned. Atahualpa was at the town of Cajamarca in the north central highlands when he received the great news of the final victory over Huascar and, at the same time, a visit from the Viracochas. The Viracochas (164 Spaniards, 62 horses) were led by a hard-eyed old soldier named Francisco Pizarro, who sent his brother Hernando and a young captain named Hernando de Soto to invite Atahualpa to visit the Viracochas' quarters. The next day, November 16, 1532, Atahualpa came in his litter accompanied by several thousand soldiers. The Viracochas (who had been planning this expedition in search of the fabled Biru for years, and meanwhile listening attentively to tales of the way Cortes did things in Mexico) met him with a prepared ambush, blew the soldiers to pieces with cannon, rode down the remnants with cavalry, and took Atahualpa prisoner.

The story of the conquest of Peru contains no psychological

mysteries, no subtle and beautiful heroines, no heroics, and above all no heroes. It is a simple tale of unrelieved double-dealing and violent crime. Francisco Pizarro, illiterate, sixty-one years old, with a lifetime of blood on his hands, was a plain man with uncomplicated notions: blunt treachery, suspicious self-interest, and a sword thrust for persuasion.

With the sacred person of the Inca as hostage, the Spanish were immune from attack, and Atahualpa was now ordered to produce a ransom. Gold was gathered (in the process the gold plating was torn off the Temple of the Sun at Cuzco, and such objects of art were brought as a golden ear of corn sheathed in silver leaves with a tassel of silver threads) that amounted to a treasure considerably more than twice as large as Moctezuma's—Baron Humboldt made it twenty million nineteenth-century dollars.

Among the Inca people there was some feeling that the Viracochas may have appeared and seized Atahualpa in answer to the prayers of Huascar, who was still the prisoner of Atahualpa's generals and still claiming to be the true Inca. When the captive Huascar managed to get into communication with Pizarro, the captive Atahualpa smuggled out orders to his generals to put him to death. Tradition says Huascar was drowned by his jailors. A few months later, in August 1533, the gigantic ransom having been collected, melted down, and distributed among the enraptured Viracochas, Pizarro had Atahualpa publicly strangled.

And again a conquest was completed, although the war was still to come. In this case it was a savage, stubborn war that lasted forty years in the Inca Empire itself, and 300 years longer in the border country to the south. In the wild Chaco and Montaña to the east (where the first of the Viracochas appeared and disappeared, and where tribes still exist who have scarcely seen white men), it has not been completed yet.

# IV

# People of Peace

**Sheer cliffs rise almost 1,000 feet above the riverbed at Canyon de Chelly, Arizona, a refuge for the Anasazi people from A.D. 348. The dwellings date from the eleventh century.**

Columbus's great discovery had burst upon a Europe in full flower of Renaissance, and nothing would ever be the same again. But more to the point, it had burst upon a Spain in the first flower of nationhood, at the precise moment that Spain, newly united under Isabella of Castile and Ferdinand of Aragon, completed its seven centuries of reconquering the country from the Moors. The fall of Granada, marking the end of that 700 years of troubled enchantment where ceaseless war had seemed the natural order of life, came in 1492.

The first objective of Ferdinand and Isabella was to unify their raw, jangling, quarrelsome domains under the strict rule of an absolute monarchy. They made efforts to expel the Moors and the Jews, and among the many councils they established for various special tasks was the Council of the Inquisition. They extended royal sway over towns and castles with the help of their secret police and seized for the crown the grand commandership of the powerful orders of knights. They created a rigid dictatorship in which the king's word cut through any law and the king's hand covered every thread of the national existence.

The contract for his first voyage made Columbus governor-general of any new lands he might add to the Spanish crown, and gave him a cut (10 percent) of any net profits from trade or precious metals. With the establishment of the colonies in the New World a foreign trade office was set up in Seville and later placed under the supervision of a royal Council of the Indies. Through this council the crown controlled—and closely—all colonial matters. Multitudes of laws were placed on the books dealing with the welfare of overseas trade, exploration, mining, church colonists, and Indians (one of the earliest, instigated by a well-meaning Isabella, was a law to prohibit Indians from taking so many baths, as bound to be injurious to their health).

The governor distributed conquered lands to colonists, and, after the institution of the *encomienda* system in 1503, villages of Indians were "commended" to the care and protection of an *encomendero*, who could exact their labor, but as free men (technically) and for pay (technically). This resulted, in most cases, in virtual slavery. Encomenderos commonly spoke of owning their Indians.

Bartolomé de Las Casas, the first priest ordained in the New

World and son of a veteran of Columbus's first voyage, thundered against the practice, but it persisted. The encomenderos enjoyed being feudal lords; the Council of the Indies continued to hope abuses could be corrected; all agreed it was certainly vicious, but, after all, it was certainly practical.

Las Casas received his baptism of fire when Cuba was "reduced" by blood and terror. He tried in vain to stop the carnage, and at last was impelled to call down on reducer Panfilo de Narvaez a bitter, whole-souled, and formal curse. (One of Columbus's gentle Tainos, being burned at the stake, refused baptism for fear that in heaven he would find more Christians there.) From this time on Las Casas raged through the New World, and back and forth to Spain, swinging a propaganda sword of truly archangelical proportions on behalf of oppressed Indians.

Expedition after expedition received the royal commission and sailed forth, first from Española, then from Cuba. One after another hurled itself against Panama, in search of its storied gold and pearls and Southern Sea, only to be shattered by yellow fever and the poisoned arrows of the people of the little chiefdoms there, who were frequently friendly at first but usually alienated in short order by slaving, murder, torture, and extortion.

A number of questionable notions are widely held in regard to the early Spanish conquests, one being that the Spaniards merely walked in and took possession, frightening the simple Americans into fits of submission by their horses and godly cannon. As has been seen in the case of Mexico and Peru, it seldom worked that way. It was true that the strangers often gained a foothold with the help of a peaceful or even hospitable welcome, but the opening of hostilities brought man-sized fighting in which the Spaniards could lose as well as win. Plenty did.

The Spanish soldier was considered (after the Swiss) the best of his time, as the Spanish horse, sprung from the breedy Barbs and Arabs of the Moors, was the toast of Europe. Ingrown chivalry reached its most rococo luxuriance among the Spanish knights, but so far it had only made them unbelievably vain and valiant: lean, fanatical El Grecos not yet distorted into Don Quixotes. They habitually tackled matters that required more guts than sense, and more greed than either—they raised their war cry "Santiago!" (St. James!) in the face of any odds, if the smell of gold was in the offing. Above all, they were bounteously equipped with grand gestures—Cortes literally burned his boats behind him on the beach at Veracruz when he started inland to Mexico City, so there could be no turning back, and hanged a couple of men and cut off the feet of another who conspired to return to Cuba.

The driving forces of hot new nationalism, zealous religious solidarity, and capable armed strength under direct central authority eventually gorged Spain on New World winnings, but it was far from easy. The Conquistadors earned their name.

(The chief expansionist power in Europe at the time, the Ottoman Turks, conquered and held more territory in Europe during the first century after the discovery of America than the Spanish, with all their early conquests, managed to take in the same period from the Indians of the New World.)

But with all their boldness, it is of significance that those Conquistadors who won usually did so with some Indian help. As a rule those who lost, such as the leaders of the first two formal expeditions to Panama, who met utter disaster and left hundreds of Spaniards dead in the jungles and sand dunes, had none.

And so Vasco Nuñez de Balboa, a destitute ex-colonist from Española, too poor to outfit himself as a proper Conquistador (it was an expensive line of work), stowed away in a barrel on a ship bound for Panama, there successfully romanced the daughter of Careta, cacique of Coiba, made friends with Panciaco, son of Comogre, cacique of Comogra, and with God's grace and such allies became a leader of men and fought his way to the Pacific.

And now expeditions went forth from Panama as a base, from Mexico, and later from Peru, and from every little foothold in between, like hungry wolves plunging into a giant carcass in search of the fattest mouthfuls. The royal permission to explore continued to provide the explorers with a percentage of profits and governor-generalships of new lands found—powerful incentives for rapidly expanding exploration. But the geography of territory assigned was necessarily vague, leading to contest and conflict between rival would-be conquerors. And so when the expeditions bumped against each other, they fought, or sued, or preferred charges before the king. Superior courts, the

*Audiencias*, were set up in the New World to unsnarl such imbroglios.

Expeditions sent north from Panama by the governor there met and fought with expeditions sent south from Mexico by Cortes, and prospective Conquistadors from Española who had wangled new royal permissions met and fought with both.

The first to enter the country of a chief named Nicaragua brought back more than 30,000 recorded baptisms and gold trinkets and pearls in the amount of more than $100,000. In the next five years at least four more expeditions plundered up and down the Costa Rica–Nicaragua–Honduras region, usually accompanied by thousands of Indian allies happy to help the mighty strangers destroy their traditional enemies beyond the mountains.

The destroyed peoples were branded and sold as slaves; the ultimate fate of the allies was to be granted in encomiendas, although important men among them might be rewarded with fiefs of their own, to help hold their people in line. More commonly, persons of consequence sooner or later found themselves in the hands of the torture squad, for the Spaniards operated on the European model, knowing no other; and in Europe the velveteened burghers of a submitted town were as a matter of course given a touch of torture to make them cough up the last of their silver spoons. You got at the real marrow of truth by cracking joints. Were these people of the Indies any different, didn't they too have joints to pull apart?A few of the Spaniards, not many, had the wit to perceive that these people of the Indies were indeed different and that truly they treasured raw gold no more than clay, as Panciaco once contemptuously remarked to Balboa.

In Mexico, christened New Spain, the Spaniards laid out a new city on the site of Tenochtitlan—crushed Aztec gods were used in the foundation of the Cathedral of Saint Francis. Cuauhtemoc, the last Aztec king, who had been captured alive, was put to the torture to make him reveal the rest of the Aztec treasure; but there wasn't any left. (Cortes later had to answer for this indignity to a royal person in a formal trial before the royal Council.)

The people of Tlaxcala, as a reward for their faithful services, were specifically exempted from being distributed in encomiendas. Cortes wrote the king that he had wished to avoid the system altogether in New Spain, but that the Spaniards could not exist without it. The Council of the Indies, less and less encomienda-minded, decided they would have to exist without it and revoked the encomiendas, but the colonists, as usual, found ways to get around the Council's ruling.

Grants to Spaniards were given an appearance of legality either by being made from lands theoretically not under Indian use, or by being obtained by one means or another from Indian "lords."Many such lords and kings were maintained in their supposed offices by Spanish support, and a number of them, such as Ixtlilxochitl of Texcoco, were officially ennobled and became grandees of Spain.

The Spanish made a fundamental error in equating the society of the Aztecs and other nations of Mexico with European feudalism, somewhat like equating the Athens of Pericles with the France of Louis XIV. They have been excoriated for this ever since by anthropologists, who generally prefer to equate the Aztecs with the Iroquois or Pueblos, which is rather like equating the Athens of Pericles with North Danville, Vermont.

The Aztecs—to use them as a paradigm of the various Mexican peoples—were divided into twenty clans (known as *calpulli*), each of which elected officials roughly corresponding to our county clerk, treasurer, sheriff, and so on, although the correspondence is pretty rough, since the same person might hold widely varying posts at the same time. Each clan also elected a *tlatoani*, or "speaker," for membership in the top state council. This council in turn chose four executives for the four quarters of the state, into which the twenty clans were organized. In Tlaxcala this council of four seemed to rule jointly, which accounts for the Spaniards' usually referring to Tlaxcala as a republic (they were thinking of the Republic of Venice, not a republic as we think of it today). In Tenochtitlan a supreme ruler, *tlacatecuhtli*, chief-of-men, or also known as *hueytlatoani*, revered speaker, was chosen by the supreme council from among these four executives. The top job was for life, and was always filled from the same family, which accounts for the Spaniards' referring to such rulers as kings. Primogeniture was not followed, and the election appears to have been really an election ("they cast votes for . . . brave warriors . . . who knew not wine... the prudent, able, wise... who spoke well and were obedient, benevolent, discreet, and intelligent..."), but other-

The whimsical design of this tiny (1¾″) decorated pottery bowl is typical of Hohokam art of the Colonial period (A.D. 600–900). The Hohokam lived in southern Arizona near present-day Phoenix where the Gila meets the Salt River.

wise the tlacatecuihtli, by any other name, was a right royal figure, and heads could roll at his frown.

The nub of the Spanish error was not in calling the elected tlacatecuhtli a king—after all, their own Charles I, grandson of Ferdinand and Isabella, had just become Emperor Charles V of the Holy Roman Empire by election—but in assuming the existence of hereditary castes and private ownership of property, particularly land.

With a few exceptions land belonged to the clan, which apportioned its use to clan families. The same fundamental situation existed among the Incas, and, in fact, was as universal throughout all the New World as the concept of private property in the Old.

This ownership of things in common had been noticed from the first. Columbus wrote, "Nor have I been able to learn whether they held personal property, for it seemed to me that whatever one had, they all took shares of. . . . " Even the simmering pepper pot, Columbus noted, seemed to be free to any neighbor who wanted to fill a gourd, even—to his amazement—in starving times.

But it struck too deep a root of difference to be grasped. Europeans simply could not comprehend it. Likewise, the people of the New World were hopelessly bewildered by the European's spirit of competition for personal gain. For much more was at issue here than a difference of abstract ideologies: ramifications ran through every tissue of life. These two world views, each never dreaming of the other's existence, had really created two totally different worlds.

On the one hand the communal outlook produced attitudes toward cooperation and group identity that were reflected in some measure in every gesture of Indian existence, from practical jokery to religion. On the other hand the ingrained custom of personal acquisition at the expense of one's neighbors, of striving in constant competition against each other, colored every aspect of European life and thought.

In ancient Mexico "freedom of thought, individual liberty, personal fortunes, were non-existent," as Vaillant wrote, but ". . . an Aztec would have been horrified at the naked isolation of an individual's life in our Western world."

Since the only thing to be done with the incomprehensible is to pretend it does not exist, the Spaniards blithely designated council members "nobles" and owners of "estates," dealt with them as landed aristocrats, called on them to furnish feudal tribute and service from their peasants, and married their daughters, from whom descended some of the first families of a later Spain as well as of a later Mexico.

The Spanish gave deeper thought to Aztec religion, especially after the missionaries arrived and the whipping and burning of the so often "sullen" natives became the commonest topic of official correspondence.

The famous Aztec sacrifices have fascinated one and all to the exclusion, nearly, of the rest of Aztec history. The offering up of human lives—even their first-born sons—in the belief that this gravest of transactions would keep the shaky world upright and maintain their cherished way of life is again something inconceivable to our higher civilization, even though we fight wars today for precisely the same reason, offering up even our first-born sons.

Concrete facts and figures concerning the sacrifices are suspect, having been composed or interpreted after the Conquest by converts eager to please their new holy men. For example, the recorded 20,000 victims at the previously mentioned dedication of Huitzilopochtli's temple: four post-Conquest chroniclers speak of it, giving the number of victims all the way from 20,000 to 80,000. All agree that the victims stood in two long lines, extending far out on the causeways, that the two sponsoring kings themselves tore out the hearts of the first two victims, and that two teams of priests then took over, relieved by other teams when they tired. Some say the work took one day, others that it required up to four days, from sunrise to sunset.

Now the feast of Huitzilopochtli occurred in May, when the days between sunrise and sunset are about 12 hours. So we picture the four sacrificial assistants seizing a victim, throwing him on his back and holding him down on the convex altar stone, while the fifth man of the team gouges into his chest at the fork of the rib cage with an obsidian knife, finds the heart, saws and tears it loose, offers it to the sun, and deposits it in the Stone of Tizoc. The body is then hurled down the temple steps, and the next victim seized.

Even allowing for the most practiced dexterity on all hands, it is hard to imagine this being accomplished in less time than, say, one minute per victim. At that rate two teams could conceivably finish off 120 victims an hour, or 1,440 in a twelve-hour day, or 5,760 for the outside limit of four days.

Shaky or not, Spanish ideas of Indian theology and economics had far-reaching effects in the New World.

Racing each other for the fattest mouthfuls, the people from heaven scoured the seas and the shores, the mountains and valleys. Another Mexico, another Peru, might be just beyond—the pagans always said so. Mines of gold or silver might be anywhere, or spices or pearls, and there were sure to be slaves for the taking, and souls to be saved for Christ.

Fabulous mines were discovered in Peru and Mexico and worked with forced Indian labor. Tombs in Colombia and Ecuador were rifled of their incredibly ancient golden furnishings. Conquistadors rode with stirrups and scabbards of solid gold, and the Conquistador among the Araucanians was killed and his skull made into a cup.

The Huastecs, on the old northeastern frontier of the Aztec country, beat back a Spanish attack from the sea, were swamped by an invasion of 40,000 allied warriors under the leadership of Cortes, rose again against the strangers when Cortes turned to fight and defeat a new rival Spanish intrusion from the sea. An officer of Cortes subdued them in a manner recalling Aztec days—he rounded up 400 principal men and sacrificed them to the new gods by hanging.

Tangaxoan, a chief among the heretofore never conquered Tarascans to the west, was one of the many local caciques from all over Mexico who visted Cortes, made submission, was appointed a Spanish satrap, and gave the strangers a center in his territory. But many other Tarascans refused satellite status, and their country long remained a fighting frontier. A leader of the Otomis to the north was commissioned a captain-general of Spain by Charles V, made a Knight of the order of Santiago, given the Christian name of Nicolas de San Luis, and with the help of another noted Otomi satrap, Fernando de Tapia, held the northern frontier for Spain for thirty years.

The Mayas gave up hard, with wars and repeated invasions that went on for years. At one time five different Spanish adventurers were stalking each other in the highland Maya country—Cortes, as usual, came out the winner. Pedro de Alvarado, the febrile young Sun God, marched to Guatemala with 400 Spaniards and 20,000 Mexican allies and taught the obstinate Mayas a lesson by catching and hanging their women; babies were in turn hanged to their mothers' feet. Alvarado had recently married a bride from faithful Tlaxcala and proved how little interest he and his men had in the Maya women by picking out the most beautiful unmarried girls to be left scrupulously unraped while they were hanged or thrown to the packs of fighting dogs to be eaten alive.

Cortes, when he marched to Honduras himself to settle matters, found himself involved in one of the great epics of Central American exploration just getting there through the jungle. He took Cuauhtemoc, his captive Aztec king; crushed though the Aztecs where Cortes seems to have been wary of Cuauhtemoc, and when he so much as took a walk beyond his garden walls would demand that Cuauhtemoc come along to stay under his watchful eye. On this Maya campaign Cortes's nerve broke and he had Cuauhtemoc hanged, charging rumors of a conspiracy. Bernal Diaz was skeptical, and wrote that the killing was most unjust, "and was thought wrong by all of us who were along on that journey."

On this trip, Cortes married off the Lady Marina to Don Juan Xamarillo, one of his captains, and, so they say, she lived happily ever after.

Among the Mayas, the Xiu family occasionally made alliance with the Spaniards—most of the other Maya groups kept up an incessant guerrilla warfare that by 1536, after more than ten years of fighting against two major invasions, succeeded in driving the last Spaniard out of Yucatan. During the following interval of comparative peace, the Xiu people made a pilgrimage to the old abandoned center of Chichen Itza—the sacred pool there, scene of human sacrifice in the days of Toltec rule, was still regarded as a holy place. The Xiu had to pass through Cocom territory on the way, and the Cocoms had not forgotten the destruction of their city, Mayapan, and nearly all the Cocom family at the hands of the Xiu 100 years before. According to the stories, the Xiu dignitaries were invited to a banquet at the Cocom town of Otzmal, where in the course of the festivities Cocom warriors treacherously killed them all.

This act was, in effect, the final line of the long Maya history. The gods repaid it in kind with further calamities—plagues of locusts, famine, uncontrolled civil war. When the Spanish again invaded five years later, there was no strength left for resistance.

The last shreds of the Maya civilization went with their books: "As they contained nothing but superstition and lies of the devil, we burned them all, which the Indians regretted to an amazing degree and which caused them great anguish," wrote Bishop Landa from Yucatan. ("With rivers of tears we mourned our sacred writings among the delicate flowers of sorrow," wrote the unknown poet of the Book of Chilam Balam of Tizimin.)

Bishop Landa's zeal in torturing idolaters brought scandal, investigation, churchly rows, and left a persistent touch of sullenness in the air. The subjugation of some scattered Maya groups went on for generations longer—the important Itzas of Lake Peten held out for another century and a half, and the Lacandon Mayas of the Chiapas forests have held out into our own day, but they were Mayas no longer. They sank into the anonymity of "Indians."

With the conquest of Mexico and Peru the carcass of the hemisphere had lost its liver and lights. But the magnitude of early Spanish penetration is more evident in its extent of contact than of conquest. Early conquest was limited and insecure, but by the middle 1530s, when men who had sailed with Columbus were still living, the Spanish had already established contact with by far the largest population blocs in the New World.

Estimates of the total hemispherical population before white invasion scatter all the way from eight or nine million to seventy-five million. Middle-of-the-road guesses start from a floor of about sixteen million, assigning seven million or so for South America and another seven million or so for Mexico, the West Indies, and Central America. The chances are that these figures will be revised upward in years to come; two detailed studies of the first Spanish tribute rolls indicate an aboriginal population for Mexico alone of eleven to some fifteen million—reduced by disease and other disasters to about two million by the early 1600s.

Most experts agree that whatever the hypothetical population of the hemisphere may have totaled, three fourths or more of it was concentrated in the Mexican and Andean areas, the chief targets of early Spanish activity. In the enormous fringe area that was North America north of Mexico, population estimates allow only from one million to two million souls for all the pres-

**The ruins of Pueblo Bonito, including living quarters and circular kivas, cover more than three acres in Chaco Canyon, New Mexico. Built a millenium ago, it could house more than 1,000 people and was the world's biggest "apartment house" until a larger one was erected in New York late in the 1800s.**

ent United States, Canada, and Alaska.

Even so, the total body of the New World's nations had only been scratched. The number of separate tribes, bands, groups, then inhabiting the Americas is all but immeasurable; estimates here really run wild.

A greater variety of languages existed in North America than in all the Old World put together; and a greater variety in South America than in North America. The most conservative guesses put the number of mutually unintelligible languages in North America at from 500 to 1,000, and in South America to at least twice that.

But linguistic diversity is a poor scale for counting separate groups of people. Some peoples might be very closely related in everything except language—as the speakers of various provincial languages in modern France; or many completely independent societies widely differing culturally and racially might speak the same language—as in the varieties of English-speaking people over the world today.

In the time of the mid-1530s the great majority of the New World's nations and tribes had received no inkling of collision with another world. In North America north of Mexico very few of the many villages, tribes, kingdoms, confederacies, had heard of the people from heaven, and fewer still had seen any. Time went on as it always had.

Time is invisible unless we see it in relation to something in motion—a river standing still while life comes and goes on its banks. We tick off the life to measure the time, and a man stops the clock when he dies—we don't think of Shelley as older than George Bernard Shaw. There are not many other places on earth, perhaps none, where time in this sense, uninterrupted time, had gone on as long as it had in certain areas of what is now the Southwest of the United States.

The Papagos (pronounced Poppa-goes) and Pimas, close cousins, speaking dialects of the same language, the Papagos dwelling in the southern Arizona deserts and the Pimas in the nearby semiarid river valleys, are descendants of an earlier people who had lived in the same country in basically the same way, never catastrophically disturbed, for at least more than 9,000 years. So many archaeologists believe, studying what appears to be a continuously related sequence of artifacts and ruins stretching across this giant reach of time. While every conquering Ozymandias in all history rose and fell and was forgotten, these people, peaceful people, grinders of meal and singers of songs, endured, as natural as mountains.

They seem to have sprung from the western branch of the Cochise ancients, embryonic farmers living along the banks of Ice Age lakes and streams that then existed in their country, among cottonwoods and hickory trees and such roaming beasts as dire wolves and mammoths. Thousands of years later, the Ice Age lakes and animals long since vanished, the nearest hickories hundreds of miles away, their land a yellow desert of salt bush, mesquite, scarce water and rare rivers, and tall dust devils rising each noon to dance, they appear as a farming people who have been given the name Hohokam—a Pima word meaning "those who have gone."

While the Maya Classic Age flourished and withered, while the Toltecs came and went and the Aztecs rose to eminence, these people planted their corn and pumpkins, hunted the little desert deer, and squeezed some sort of use out of nearly every wild plant on their sun-dazzled horizon. They had many things familiar to the belt of farming villages that ran all the way south to the Valley of Mexico and beyond all the way to Central America—little clay figurines (sometimes turbaned, and with earrings, and often, of course, ripe and female), a snake and bird as the commonest religious motif, mirrors made of flakes of iron pyrite set like mosaic work in stone plaques, ball courts (after about A.D. 500) and the rubber balls to go with them, and the jingling copper dance bells that were traded so widely from Central America and Mexico. Around A.D. 1000 someone among the Hohokam seems to have developed a process of etching, using a weak acid possibly made from fermented cactus juice (the fruit of the saguaro, source of their ceremonial wine) to etch designs on seashells that had come by trade from the Pacific. After a century or two the practice ceased; it may have been a single family's magic secret. It is the first known use of etching in the world.

The Hohokam who lived in the river valleys, their center in the region where the Gila meets the Salt, the neighborhood of present-day Phoenix, built miles of irrigation canals, tremendous undertakings comparable to the city building in the Valley of Mexico, not only in their construction but in their constant maintenance. Scholars and modern farmers (and modern politicians) argue about how many thousand acres were under irrigation, but single ditches, some as large as twenty-five feet wide and fifteen feet deep, have been surveyed that ran as far as sixteen miles, and one network along the Salt River totaled 150 miles. The irrigation systems were well developed by A.D. 700 and reached their maximum size 600 or 700 years later. The first Europeans to see them wrongly supposed they had watered large cities; a Spanish priest wrote 200 years ago of "a very large canal, still open for the distance of some two leagues (six miles)... it appears to have supplied a city with water, and irrigated many leagues of the rich country of those beautiful plains."

But some things they had not at all in common with the mighty civilizations of far-off Mexico—these were an absolute democracy and a resolute peaceableness, an almost aggressive nonaggressiveness.

There was no division into classes, in spite of the organized labor the canals must have demanded; each family lived in the same sort of earth-and-pole house built over a dropped living-room floor, and even the house of the most respected elder, the house of the most holy priest who lived with august dream beings and gods, the "house, enveloped in white winds and white clouds, into which we went to perform our ceremonies" (in a Pima description), was only somewhat larger than the others, if different at all. The manner of government might have survived in the Papago council of four from whom was chosen one, the best and wisest, to be the principal leader—we seem to have heard of this before; but the spirit that made this government work is best revealed in a line from a Pima children's tale, a line expressing, in fact, a spirit typical of nearly all Indians, from the disciplined Aztecs to the wild Tupian cannibals: "I... went to consult a man of authority, to whom a boy should not have had the temerity to go...."

There are few indications of war, and none whatever of aggressiveness. Among the later Papagos and Pimas, when war was forced upon them and they discovered a taste for it and fought well and hard, like beasts of prey, like raptorial birds, so say their songs, a successful warrior returning (bringing the four hairs from his enemy's head that customarily served them as scalp or trophy) had to undergo the sixteen-day cure for insanity. Many Indian societies required purification ceremonies for warriors who had killed, but seldom quite this purifying. Ceremonial war speeches of the Pimas collected sixty years ago by Frank Russell all close with the ritual phrase: "You may think this over, my relatives. The taking of life brings serious thoughts of the waste; the celebration of victory may become unpleasantly riotous."

Studious individuals with their gaze fixed on the past sooner or later go a little nutty; every now and then someone springs up shouting he has found the secret of it all. But it is really very difficult to fit scientific theories of human behavior around ancient fears that the celebration of victory may become unpleasantly riotous. For the real stumbling block is that these attitudes of peace and quiet may be very ancient indeed, as ancient as any attitudes of savagery.

There has been a tendency for a long while to associate the most ancient instincts with the most savage, the underlying idea being that all men are ferocious by nature but that some (like us) have been steadily moving upward from their savage beginnings when they brained each other daily. But the peaceful Arawaks and the savage Caribs, both reasonably primitive, might be supposed to represent survivals of equally ancient instincts. For an extreme example of instinctive pacifism: the Arawakan Chane of the eastern slope of the Andes were conquered, enslaved, eventually destroyed as a separate entity, by the Guarani, all without fighting back—an early Spanish explorer reported 400 Guarani ruling a herd of 5,000 Chane, regularly rounding up a few to butcher and eat.

The peaceful people of the Southwest (although far from being this peaceful, and by no means particularly primitive) could trace their pedigree of nonaggressiveness back to a very early root, one of the deepest roots of their being. Maybe the sons of Abel have always been with us too.

Northeast of the Hohokam country was the land of another peaceful people, known to us by the name the Navahos give them when speaking of the ruins of their long-ago towns: the Anasazi, "Ancient Ones." Their early center was in the high, broken country where the four corners of New Mexico, Colorado, Utah, and Arizona come together: red-rock canyons and sagebrush flats, grasslands in the rolling foothills, juniper ridges and pine-clothed mountains.

The earliest Anasazi are called the Basketmakers, from the many examples of their extraordinary basketwork that have been found—some of them watertight for cooking vessels (hot rocks were tossed in until the mush boiled). They too lived in houses built over a dug-down floor until, about the seventh or eighth century A.D., they began building their houses entirely above ground, of log and adobe mortar and then of stone. At about the same time they acquired the art of making pottery, the cultivation of cotton and beans to add to their crops of corn and squash, and slowly changed their way of life. Clans—a mother and her married daughters and their families—joined their houses together in a single structure of a number of rooms, and eventually a whole village dwelt in the same many-roomed, multi-storied building.

The pit houses remained as religious centers for the men, subterranean chambers, usually circular, entered from the roof, with paintings of gods around the walls and the mystical hole in the floor, the *sipapu*, to remind the devout of the birth of their first ancestors from the belly of the earth. These chapels are known today as kivas, from their Hopi name, and we call the modern descendants of the Anasazi the Pueblo Indians.

It was for a long time believed that the Basketmakers and the Pueblos were separate races, representing two distinct "migrations," since the early Anasazi, the Basketmakers, seemed to be long-headed people, and the later Anasazi, the Pueblos, a round-headed people. It has since been found that in Europe as well as America most people's heads have been getting rounder down through the centuries, for reasons still unknown; it was also discovered that the later Anasazi had picked up the fashion of skull deformation, flattening the backs of their heads by strapping infants to cradle boards, which made their skulls look rounder than they were. It is now generally agreed that the Basketmakers were direct ancestors of the Pueblos, although there were many other intermixtures.

Seen in close focus, a given Anasazi pueblo (pronounced Pwebb-lo, Spanish "town") was a tight, closed little world, and years passed, sometimes a great many, while the people sang up the corn, called the rain with puffs of pipe smoke and clouds of eagle down, danced together with their mother the Earth, worked together, laughed together, gradually became grandparents and died and watched with their mountain mahogany faces through the unchanging masks of the dancing gods while their grandchildren gradually became grandparents—and nothing penetrated, nothing interrupted, nothing interfered.

House timbers from a single site in the Canyon de Chelly, now part of the Navaho country in Arizona, give tree-ring dates from A.D. 348 to 1284. Dates from the Mesa Verde, Colorado, complex of cliff pueblos, cave villages, and pueblos built in the open cover 1,000 years, A.D. 300 to 1273.

The mesa-top pueblo of Acoma, New Mexico, has been continuously occupied for more than 600 years to date. The Hopis (pronounced Hoe-pees) have lived on or about their same three mesas in Arizona for 1,500 years, and their modern village of Old Oraibi has been continuously inhabited for some 800 years.

But seen from a long view, the Anasazi moved, merged, split, built and abandoned towns, appeared and disappeared from every direction. Strangers entered, and sometimes learned Anasazi ways and themselves became Anasazi—and sometimes did not. In an early Anasazi burial there is a foreigner wearing moccasins, centuries before moccasins replaced the Anasazi sandals, and his body had been cut in two and then sewed together again; did the Basketmakers wonder what he was made of? But the Anasazi world seems to have offered a happier way of life than most of its neighbors knew, and it expanded willy-nilly, naturalizing many varied groups of people.

Nonaggressive though this movement generally appears to be, there must have been contentions, with each other as well as with wandering people of the wood such as the Utes of the Colorado Rockies; the communal buildings were sometimes made as defendable as fortresses. But the more usual motive that put people in motion seems to have been the death of old fields through drought or erosion—or other natural catastrophes such as a volcano eruption (it left a scar now called Sunset Crater near Flagstaff, Arizona) circa A.D. 1066 that sent a pre-Pueblo people fleeing from their surrounding homes; when they came back years later to fields now fertile with volcanic ash, Pueblos and the Hohokam came with them.

The square-shouldered figures of Basketmaker petroglyphs (pictures on rocks) range over a wide area. The Pan of the later Pueblos, a humpbacked ithyphallic love god usually shown leer-

**This miniature vessel and nine-inch-long sandstone effigy were photographed in a thirteenth- or fourteenth-century crypt near Vernon, Arizona, where they were recently discovered. The figure, possibly a kachina, or sacred spirit, is the first of its kind ever found.**

ingly playing a seductive flute, journeys into newer pastures green. By the time of the Classic Age of the Great Pueblos (c. 1100–1300) the way of life of the Pueblo world had grown offshoots and tendrils that reached from Nevada to Texas. These people spoke different tongues in different villages and were in no sense a single "tribe." They were related only in that they all followed a remarkably similar way of living.

The art and architecture of this way of living came to its finest hour in the time of the Great Pueblos. In the canyon of the Chaco River (northwestern New Mexico) are the ruins of at least a dozen giant community houses. The best known of these, Pueblo Bonito, rose to five terraced stories, had more than 800 rooms and could have housed well over 1,000 inhabitants, and, like a medieval cathedral, was 150 years building, from the year 919 to 1067 (by tree-ring dates).

The people made feather cloth and colored cotton cloth—high-style sashes, masterfully designed, have been found in burial caves where they had kept like new in the dry air of the Southwest; beautifully decorated pottery—although the finest, true works of art, come from a distinctly separate Pueblo-type people who lived far to the south, in the Mogollon mountains of southwestern New Mexico; and magnificent jewelry, particularly of turquoise—some necklaces contain thousands of worked stones.

Judging from the many ceremonial kivas and dance courts religion must have been a constant occupation, which is one of a number of indications that the congregations regarded it as fun as well as sacred duty. Constant sacred duty tends to become onerous, hence the usual necessity of high-powered high priests to keep enforcing it. But among the Pueblos as among the Hohokam democracy ruled and there were no distinguishable high priests—distinguishable, that is, by any upper-class attributes. The highest-ranking theocrats were simple farmers like everybody else.

During the thirteenth century the Pueblo world began to shrink in upon itself. The people drifted away from the great pueblos until many were left abandoned. Tree rings tell of a long and murderous drought, a period of twenty-three almost rainless years (1276–1299). This would seem to have been enough in itself to have filled the land with the dispossessed.

It is also probable that wolf packs of the nomads who were to become the Apaches and Navahos began to push their way in from the north at about that time, twanging their new and improved weapon, the sinew-backed bow (as against the flimsier oak or skunkwood bow of the Pueblos) with a new and improved arrow release (arrow held between first and middle fingers, pull on string with fingers) that pulled three times the power of the less sophisticated release (arrow held between thumb and first finger, pull on the arrow) then apparently in general use in the Southwest.

A notion popular among some anthropologists is that the great pueblos grew too large for the pure Pueblo democracy, and the Pueblo people simple chose to stick with democracy and small towns.

A Pueblan population in the Tonto Basin of Arizona moved gradually southward until eventually, during the thirteenth century, they began moving in with the Hohokam along the Salt and Gila rivers. There was no invasion, no fighting, no conquest physical or spiritual on either side. They lived mingled together for several generations, probably about a century, and each people followed its own customs—the Pueblos made tobacco pipes (the Hohokam smoke ceremonial cigarettes); the Hohokam got drunk once a year on their cactus juice, welcoming the green sun of summer (the Pueblos did not drink); the Pueblos buried their dead and the Hohokam practiced cremation; kitchenware and houses remained pretty much in their separate styles, which were considerably separate, with the single exception that in both cases house entrances faced the east, as did the house entrances of many other right-thinking Americans everywhere. Otherwise the houses of these Pueblans—the Casa Grande ruin in Arizona is an example, described in 1764 as "of four stories which are still standing; its ceiling is of the beams of cedar... the walls of a material very solid, which appears to be the best of mortar..."—were a far cry from the humble Hohokam dwellings.

About the year 1400 these Pueblan visitors among the Hohokam began moving on again, maybe south into what is now Mexico, maybe northeast to the Zuñi towns of western New Mexico, ending an instance of tolerance between strangers that has left archaeologists bedazzled, not to say bemused. The Hohokam people stayed where they were, eventually to become the Pimas and Papagos of today.

For the Pueblo world in general the center of things shifted a little southward, to the pueblos in the region of the upper Rio Grande River in New Mexico and scattered villages in the same latitude westward among the deserts and mesas into Arizona.

In the reeds along the rivers, in the willows on the creeks, in the dust-veiled, red-streaked canyons, the still wind of time never died. In their heaped-up earth-colored towns the Pueblos prospered, diverse and yet identical. Some said one name and some another, "Posoge," "Tséna," "Pajo," "Paslápaane," for the Big River, the Rio Grande, or "mowa," "piki," "hewe," for the paper-thin cornbread everybody made; everybody also made the sweetened dumplings—blue cornmeal mixed with ashes, sweetened by mouthfuls of chewed stale bread—that the old men traditionally filched from the pot, spearing them with splinters, as quickly as they cooked.

Among some, the people were divided into two birthright groups, the Summer People and the Winter People, each group taking turns at running the town for half a year. Among others, the head of a certain society automatically became the town leader. Among most, men grew the corn and women ground it, and among some the husband owned the house but among more the wife owned the house and everything in it, including the corn as soon as it was brought in from the field, and a man belonged more to his mother's house than to his wife's, and was more the preceptor of his sister's children than his own. Among some, membership in the various societies whose important activities filled the days was inherited; among others, one could choose what religious, warmaking, hunting, medical, or social clubs he might wish to join. Some wore cotton clothes and some, living too high in snow country to raise cotton, wore buckskin.

But the Milky Way was to all, with different words, the Backbone of the World, and all knew, under whatever names, the Corn Maidens, and the powerful gods, the kachinas, who had granted men the right to wear masks and represent them in dances of prayer. Most also knew the koshare, gods of sunshine and laughter and instruments of discipline by public ridicule, who had granted the same privilege of remembering them in masks when they had gone away long ago to their homes in the east. To most, in common with many other people all over the Americas, the first gods on earth had been two brothers, and men of authority were still called elder brother (the Aztec term for an army colonel).

All knew the fragility of the world's harmony and the danger of throwing it out of key by wickedness, ignorance, or accident. Evil magicians did so on purpose, and when one was caught (you could usually tell them by their harsh and aggressive nature; they also gave themselves away by such acts as peering in through a window at night), he might be hung by the thumbs until he died or his shoulders were crippled for life.

There were beasts, trees, snakes, birds, mountains, stars, of supernatural power, and a right way of living in concert with them, from presenting a newborn baby to the sun, to the wealth of pageantry surrounding the growing of the varicolored corn. Some of these rituals were complex and the formal property of specified organizations or priests, but some were not, such as cleaning up the pueblo for the arrival of the harvest (so "the corn will be glad we bring it in"). Anyone could pray anywhere, as long as it was done the heedful way, with a good heart, and votive offerings were also optional (a feathered prayer stick from a man, a sprinkle of cornmeal from a woman).

The first rule of this living, above all, was everything in moderation; nothing too much. None of the ecstatic religious visions of the Mexican eaters of the narcotic peyote or the narcotic mushroom, the *teonancatl*; although a powerful narcotic, Datura (Jimson weed), grew at hand. This was sometimes used as an anesthetic by Zuñi for putting a patient to sleep while the director of a curing society set a broken leg or, with an agate scalpel, cut out a tumor, but even then it was only given to women; men did not need such nonsense. The Pueblos knew and used at least seventy medicinal plants, some restricted by secret power-invoking, evil-averting ritual, some free to all—in moderation, and if used with a good heart. Plants too were living beings; one talked to them, and if the words were genuine the plants talked back.

There was none of the fearsome dread of sex so important to many other peoples, Indian and otherwise: he's a likeable fellow, he's always in trouble over women, ran a common, casual phrase in some pueblos. Puberty, menstruation, even childbirth, were not ringed around with supernatural terrors. There was little dread of the dead, and the dramatic, hysterical grief so common among many other peoples, Indian and otherwise. Grief was kept deep but decently within, and the most beautiful of pottery was broken in the grave. There was none of the ascetic self-torture, the gashes, the blood, the wild saintly suffering so important to many other deeply religious peoples, Indian and otherwise. The body was purified for certain rituals by induced vomiting, as among many Indians, but a yucca-suds shampoo was more usual. There was little of the dour, haughty exterior associated with such warrior people as the Aztecs; most of the Pueblos like a man who, as the saying still has it, talked easy and talked lots.

No excesses; industry, sobriety. But the women were expected to make a social bee of the never-ending community work of grinding corn, and the right way of doing things also demanded a man at the door of the grinding room, playing the grinding song on a flute.

Each gesture of living was an obeisance to living the right way, in unison with each other and with the past and with the rest of the living world, an acceptance of living, a reverence for living—in moderation. The Pueblos made a divinity of living, in moderation.

"I'm for the power of men... I strive toward joy," says the Politician to the Poet in Jean Giono's *Que Ma Joie Demeure*.

"I'm against the power of men... and I've found joy," says the Poet to the Politician. "It's all around us, as inexhaustible as the air... if instead of hounding it we accept it.... "

He might have been talking Hopi.

On a day in May in the year 1539 foreigners appeared at Hawikuh, the westernmost of the Zuñi towns; they were Indians from the land of the parrot traders to the south, probably Cahita-speaking people from Sinaloa, some 300 of them; but they were led by a man who was a new thing to Pueblo eyes, a man who was black. He was Estevanico (Stevie), from the west coast of Morocco, a Spanish slave, and the discoverer of New Mexico. He was a veteran at meeting strange Indians, but whatever it was he did at Hawikuh, it was not the right thing.

Some say, with a Zane Grey ring, that the medicine rattle he carried was recognized by the Zuñis as having been made by a people who were their traditional enemies. Some, leaning more to the adult Western, say the Aristotelian epistemologists of the Zuñi council were affronted by the black man's doubly fantastic claim that a white man was coming along three days behind him. Some say Estevanico made piratical demands of girls and turquoise. Perhaps some of Estevanico's Indian bearers happened to reveal that he represented a people who would come bringing war.

Whatever it was, the Zuñis, after along deliberation, took up their bows and killed him. Panicked fugitives from among Estevanico's Mexican Indians fled with the news to the party of the white man three days down the back trail, a Franciscan friar, who sprinted back for Mexico "with his gown gathered up to his waist." But in midsummer of the next year, when the corn was just beginning to ear, a terrifying army appeared from the south that really did contain white men, along with more Indians from Mexico, and hundreds of weird and gigantic beasts that were horses and mules.

The Zuñis collected at Hawikuh the warriors from all their six or seven towns, sent the women, children, and old people of Hawikuh to hideouts, probably high on the top of Corn Mountain, their sacred mesa, and telegraphed each movement of the approaching strangers with smoke signals from town to town. When the strangers arrived at Hawikuh, the Zuñis were unbendingly defiant. The Spaniards begged them repeatedly to submit without fighting, while the Zuñis came up to the very heels of their horses to shoot arrows at them and try to drive them away, until at last the "Santiago!" was raised and the town was stormed.

The Spanish leader, Don Francisco Vasquez de Coronado, was battered with so many rocks hurled down on his gilded helmet that he was knocked unconscious and carried from the field "as one dead," but the taking of the town was only the work of an hour.

An even larger army, the main force of the Coronado expedition, came up from the south in September, with more horses and mules and even odder animals—pigs, sheep, goats, cattle, and white women and children. The whole horde moved on to the pueblos of the Rio Grande for the winter.

The reports of the expedition list seventy-one pueblos, containing a total (at a broad guess, probably low) of some 20,000

An 1890 photograph from New Mexico's Sia pueblo shows a sick boy being treated ceremonially by medicine men in a kiva. These circular, semisubterranean structures once served as underground storage pits for the prehistoric Basketmakers.

to 30,000 people, stretching from the Hopi towns in the west, almost as far west as the Grand Canyon country, to metropolitan Pecos (with its five plazas and sixteen kivas) on the edge of the great plains to the east; and from Taos in the north to the Piro towns in the south, in the region of the present Socorro, New Mexico. The Zuñis spoke their own language, the Hopis a Shoshonean dialect, and the other towns a variety of languages gathered into two general groups, the Keres group and the Tano (including Tewa, Tiwa, Towa, Piro, and Tano) group, which does not mean—far from it—that all the speakers of each group could converse with each other, any more than an Englishman can talk Dutch.

But they were the same people by their way of life, as the Spaniards immediately realized, and what one of Coronado's private soldiers (Pedro de Castañeda) wrote of Zuñi he meant for all: "They do not have chiefs as in New Spain, but are ruled by a council of the oldest men. They have priests, who preach to them, whom they call *papas*. [The Zuñi word for 'elder brothers.'] These are the elders.... They tell them how they are to live, and I believe that they give certain commandments for them to keep, for there is no drunkenness among them nor sodomy nor sacrifices, neither do they eat human flesh nor steal, but they are usually at work.... "

During the winter of 1540–1541 they were usually at work for the Spaniards, who took their food, blankets, women, and houses, and when the people resisted took their lives by sword, fire, and rope—although with real regret. It comes through rather clearly that in spite of their disappointment at not finding riches, the Spaniards genuinely liked these brave and modest little people and were impressed by them. Coronado honestly did his utmost to avoid violence. But why wouldn't they submit? Unfortunately the Pueblos didn't have any history of submission. They didn't know how. Even the quiet Hopis insisted on a fight.

The Hopis' name, by the way, is their own word for themselves, from Hopitu, "peaceful ones."

In the summer of 1541 Coronado led his army eastward on the great plains looking for cities of gold, returned discouraged for another winter, and in the spring of 1542 all the strangers trailed away and went back to Mexico except two friars who stayed as missionaries. It was 1581 before any Spaniards returned, and then only a small party of friars and soldiers from the Chihuahua frontier. They learned the two missionaries of forty years before had been martyred; two more friars stayed, expecting the same fate, which they received, probably as soon as they tried to stop the dances of prayer. A few more small bands of the white strangers appeared in the next few years —some of them unauthorized, and Spanish soldiers came in pursuit and took them away under arrest—but in 1598 a whole population suddenly arrived, 400 men, women, and children, 7,000 head of stock, more than eighty wagons. The land of the Pueblos was being colonized.

Only the desert pueblo of Acoma, seemingly impregnable on the summit of its steep-walled mesa, made any serious resistance; strangers who tried to take blankets and food were shot down with arrows. Other Spaniards came and fought their way up to the town, impregnable or not, killed the warriors in their kivas, and took 500 women and children back to the Rio Grande for trial.

The few men over twenty-five years of age who had been captured were sentenced to the loss of one foot and "personal service" for twenty years; women, and children above the age of twelve, were given only the twenty years' slavery; children under twelve were put in the care of the priests. Two Hopis who happened to be visiting Acoma at the time were sent home with their right hands cut off, as a warning. The Spanish governor, Don Juan de Oñate, was later (fifteen years later) fined and stripped of his honors by a Spanish court for this mass enslavement, among other charges.

Oñate, son of one of the richest mine owners in Mexico and married to a great-granddaughter of Moctezuma, colonized the new province at his own expense, in the usual way of such affairs, and lost his shirt. The country was too poor. There was no gold or silver, and not even enough corn and cotton to feed and clothe the colonists—regular supply caravans had to be sent from New Spain, at the public charge. The tribute from the pueblos—a yard of cloth or leather and a bushel of corn a year from each house seems to have been standard, although firewood was a common substitute—was not enough for profit. The whole project would have been called off after a few years, except that the priests had by then baptized thousands of Pueblos, and insisted that these new converts could not be abandoned.

Succeeding governors, who bought the office and had to get their money back somehow, made desperate attempts to squeeze more return out of the Pueblos. The priests, outraged by the stubbornness of the Pueblos in clinging to their "devil-worshiping" dances, took increasingly stringent measures against them. The Pueblos, outraged by the public whippings (occasionally fatal) of their most respected elder brothers, now and then martyred a few more priests.

After fifty years of enduring, the Pueblos joined with their ancient enemies, the Apaches (who were, of course, subject to continual open season of outright slave raids, being unsettled infidels), and tried to raise a fight against the Spaniards. It was beaten down before it got started. Twenty years later disasters struck in clusters—there was a year of death-dealing famine, and the next year a sweeping plague, and the next year a furious onslaught of the Apaches, who "totally sacked" the entire province; and two years later, officials in Mexico stopped sending the supply caravans. The year after that a new governor, determined to put an end to the complaints of the priests, hauled forty-seven Pueblo "medicine-men" into custody, hanged three of them, and kept the others imprisoned in Santa Fe.

One of these was an elder brother named Popé, from the Tewa pueblo called by the Spaniards San Juan. He was released after several years, filled with bitterness over the punishments he had received, and went into hiding in Taos, where in the summer of 1680 he organized a real rebellion. Concerted action was very hard to achieve, due to the fairly strict Pueblo adherence to the unanimity rule—if the council of a given pueblo did not agree unanimously on the point at issue, no action was taken. But this time all the pueblos except those farthest down the Rio Grande, Isleta and the Piro villages, joined in, and this one worked.

Priests were murdered in their missions, and their bodies piled on the altars; families were slain in outlying haciendas; Santa Fe was held under siege for days, until the Spaniards broke out and fled down the river.

The Pueblos attacked "with shamelessness and daring," reported the governor, and of the total Spanish population of 2,500 or so in the province, nearly a fifth were wiped out. The rest, leaving their possessions and their homes of almost a century, made their way south along the blast-furnace desert trail the muleteers called Dead Man's Road, and did not stop until they reached El Paso del Norte, the present El Paso, Texas. The governor summed up, with infinite sadness, the Pueblo situation: "Today they are very happy without religious or Spaniards."

And the celebration of victory became unpleasantly riotous. Not only churches, church furniture, and Spanish houses were burned, but pigs, sheep, anything living or dead, that had been brought by the Metal People (Tewa for Spaniards). Popé, the Spaniards learned, "saw to it that they [the Indians] at once erected and rebuilt their houses of idolatry which they call estufas [kivas], and made very ugly masks in imitation of the devil in order to dance the dance of the cacina. . . . " The Indians sang, so the Spaniards were told, that "God, the father of the Spaniards, and Santa Maria, their mother, were dead." Popé ordered that nothing should ever again be used that the Spaniards had brought, including the plants they had introduced—watermelons, chilis, onions, peaches, wheat—but here he went too far for people who saw God in every flower and knew plants by their first names (generic words for tree, plant, bush, are usually lacking in Pueblo languages); the Pueblos "obeyed in everything except with regard to the seeds."

Popé was carried away by his success, and became, or tried to become, a dictator, demanding obedience from all, seizing whatever caught his eye, and ordering instant execution of any opponents. War broke out between the towns, Taos and Pecos and the Keres pueblos loyal to Popé, the other river pueblos insurgent against him. He was deposed (although eventually restored to power, eight years after the rebellion, shortly before his death).

But long before that, reaction had set in. The excesses, the civil wars, the bewildering despotism of a leader preaching freedom, were followed by repeated Spanish attempts at reconquest—four in eight years, and for a final nightmare touch the plague returned. Many people went away to the wild mountain canyons of the north, in the region of the present Colorado line, and hid out for years with Apaches and Utes, while thinking serious thoughts of the waste. Others went west to the country of other "traditional enemies," the Navahos. A couple of Rio Grande villages eventually moved all the way west to settle among the Hopis—one is there yet. The Hopis moved their villages to the tops of their mesas, and the Zuñis moved up to their sacred fortress-mesa, the gorgeously colored Corn Mountain that stands like a red and white banner in the desert, and stayed there for some ten years.

Twelve years after the revolt, in 1692, the Spaniards at last returned in sufficient force for a reconquest. It took four years of sporadic but heavy and brutal fighting. By an oversight the Hopis, so fanatically peaceful and stubborn, never were reinvaded, which was probably just as well for all concerned. When at last the people rebuilt their towns—most of them in new sites—they locked the years of war away and never, as a people, returned to them.

But neither did they submit. The dances and the old ways continued, secretly in the kivas if necessary. Spanish rule was never again as muscular as before the revolt; for Spain by then was a different Spain.

# V

# King of the World

**In this engraving from a sixteenth-century eyewitness drawing by Le Moyne, a Timucua chief in Florida consoles mourning widows.**

Spain, a nation on the move, met Zuñi, a nation that wasn't going anywhere, and conquered it with an almost casual Santiago! in a few minutes of a hot July desert afternoon. Zuñi wasn't going anywhere because Zuñi, in Zuñi's opinion, was already there. But Spain was on its way to building the greatest empire, as we say, that the world had ever known.

It was built of Indians—without the Indians there would be no Indies, said the Conquistadors, who were bristling believers in the power of men—and in this monstrous, sprawling edifice, burnished with blood and crowned with a cross of solid gold, the trifling conquest of Zuñi was surely one of the most insignificant of architectural details.

In one tremendous generation of incredibly widespread warmaking—with the massive support of native auxiliaries—the Spanish turned their first contacts into solid conquests over vast areas in South and Central America, Mexico, and the Caribbean. The probing contacts northward, into the great unknown continent above Mexico and Cuba, were (unless they should turn up another Mexico, another Peru) minor elements in that grand design. By the time of the fall of disappointingly minor Zuñi, other probes, far to the east, were reaching up into the northward mainland, into the country the Spanish knew as the Floridas.

Early and unsuccessful efforts to colonize Florida were made by Juan Ponce de Leon in 1521, by Lucas Vasquez de Ayllon in 1526, and by the red-bearded Panfilo de Narvaez, a one-eyed bully boy, in 1528. Narvaez landed on the Gulf Coast, near Tampa Bay, with some 400 men and 42 skeletal horses, to begin a saga of unrelieved calamities—both for the Spaniards and everyone they met. Gulf Coast villagers had also been visited by slavers for several years and were not inclined to be overly friendly, and without interpreters Narvaez could not persuade them with soft speeches. He tried to explore along the coast, hoping to travel westward to Mexico, and ran into the country of the Apalachee, at that time the most famous fighters in those parts. The expedition took to a fleet of homemade boats, all were wrecked on the coast of Texas, and four miserable survivors spent nearly seven years traveling across Texas, Coahuila, Chihuahua, and Sonora to reach the frontier of New Spain in

Sinaloa. One of these four was the black slave Estevanico; another was his Spanish owner; another was Alvar Nuñez Cabeza de Vaca, middle-aged treasurer of the expedition, who emerges as one of the most remarkable of the invaders the New World had yet seen, being, it seems, without guile of any kind.

All four were enslaved by wandering peoples of the Texas coast and shared, season after season, a poverty-stricken life of moving from the land of the pecan groves to the land of the prickly pears and back again and starving in between. During the starving times the famished people scrabbled for anything they could get, bark, bugs, dung, bones, or whatever could be bitten into, including on occasion each other. Wild was the rejoicing when by good fortune a deer was surrounded, driven into the ocean, caught, and clubbed.

Nuñez and his companions, after sundry adventures, became practicing shamans, or witch doctors, at which Nuñez particularly became famous. He says simply, and with unquestionable sincerity, that he prayed over sick people and they got well—even a man thought dead being brought back to life.

In the end Nuñez and his three fellow travelers were passed from band to band in a blaze of glory and reached the Mexican frontier accompanied by hundreds of faithful followers, whom Nuñez then had to save, at considerable effort, from enslavement by the welcoming Spaniards.

The stories the four men had heard of the wonderfully wealthy Pueblos (they seemed wonderfully wealthy, by report, to the underprivileged Mariame Indians of the Texas coast), and especially of the Zuñi towns (the Seven Cities of Cibola), were responsible not only for the Coronado expedition to New Mexico but also for another entry via the Floridas—a well-equipped army led by de Soto, Pizarro's dashing young captain of horse in Peru, and financed by de Soto's cut of the ransom of the Inca. From 1539 to 1542 this invasion force, led on by constant reports of riches just beyond, marched and fought its way from Tampa Bay to the mountains of North Carolina and westward across the Mississippi as far as present Oklahoma. Not surprisingly de Soto found more war than peace in Narvaez's legacy, and the venture was as much a total financial loss as the Coronado expedition.

But in spite of blind alleys, setbacks, and internecine feuds, Spain persisted in laboriously fulfilling her destiny of constructing, from the world of Indians, that greatest of empires. However, the people who were that empire were oddly ungrateful for their destiny. Their gods and homes were shattered, and from an enjoyment of living they were turned to working for it. They lost their subtle, mystic pride and forgot their very names, so that they called themselves by the Spanish names of Big Ears or Short Hairs. They died in massive numbers from measles, smallpox, cholera, and tuberculosis, from starvation, incredible overwork, from desperation, from sheer horror at inhumanities they could not believe even while they were happening. They died drunk, they died insane, they died by their own hands; they died, they said, because their souls were stolen. They vanished in such numbers that African blacks could not be shipped in fast enough to take their places. Their children were born dead, from syphilis; or their women, rotted with syphilis, became unable to bear children at all.

And so they went mad and rebelled and fought, fought and rebelled, escaped and fought, murdered and burned, and the *Indios bravos*, the wild Indians, filled with dread, became only wilder still.

There were outraged Spanish consciences, quite a few of them among the Conquistadors themselves. Cortes, in his will, questioned the right of Indian slavery. Some old Conquistadors not only inveighed against the oppression of the defeated peoples but rhapsodized over the civilizations they had helped destroy, where everything was "so administered that everyone had enough...," where "there was not a single thief, vicious or lazy man." But those who really got something done about saving the Indian populations from destruction were such men as the friar Las Casas, or Julian Garces, Bishop of Tlaxcala, or, in Spain, the eminent theologian and master of law, Francisco de Vitoria. There were many such. They were as much the Spain of the time as the Pizarros and Guzmans, and they were still more, when all was said and done, the spirit that formed the Spanish Indies.

One was Fray Bernadino de Minaya, who was with Pizarro in Peru (although as unauthorized personnel), and "when some Indians were sent to Panama to be sold as slaves... I notified Pizarro of Your Majesty's law against enslaving Indians even when they were aggressors. He proclaimed the law but at the same time stopped giving me and my companions maintenance.... "

The whole matter of Indian slavery in all its aspects was a hot issue at the time in the Council of the Indies, and Cardinal Loaysa of that Council, being informed that some Indians had thought the Ave Maria was something to eat, decided they were not capable of learning the Holy Faith ("no more than parrots") and so could be enslaved at will. Brother Bernadino begged his way to Spain, saw the puissant Cardinal but could not change his mind, upon which Brother Bernadino set his jaw and begged his way to Rome to see the Pope. "[A]lthough merely a poor friar, I should not fear to oppose a cardinal on this matter.... "

He saw the Pope (Paul III), and the bull *Sublimis deus* of 1537 resulted, accompanied by various papal briefs outlawing Indian slavery in any form. Unfortunately Brother Bernadino sent the glorious news direct to the Indies instead of through channels (the Royal Council), and a major international incident ensued. Charles V, feeling his sovereignty impugned, forced the Pope to call back the briefs, and had Brother Bernadino Minaya tossed in prison to reflect on diplomatic procedures while the affair was being settled—it took a couple of years. But *Sublimis deus* still stood.

Las Casas' monument, the *New Laws* for the Indies, was unveiled to the New World in 1544. They provided for the gradual abolition of encomiendas, at which the Spanish pioneers in Peru revolted, under Gonzalo Pizarro, who defeated and killed the viceroy, and, among other rampages, raided the royal treasury at the silver mines of Potosi—one of his lieutenants took 1,500 llama loads of silver bars in a single raid. But the king's long arm bore him down, and after four wild years Gonzalo was captured and executed.

The abolition of encomiendas simply could not be enforced and was delayed another half century, and Las Casas kept on battling until he died (he "has twenty-seven or thirty-seven Indian carriers with him—I do not remember the exact number—and the greatest part of what they were carrying was accusations and writings against the Spaniards, and other rubbish..." wrote an indignant opponent in 1555, when Las Casas was 81 years old). But inexorably reform won the day. Indian slaves in Mexican mines—160,000 of them—were to some degree actually, not only technically, freed from forced labor in 1551, and a special court for protection of Indian rights was established in Mexico the following year. Schools and colleges were opened in increasing numbers. The mission (often accompanied by a presidio with troops, just in case) began to replace the encomienda, and in Paraguay the Jesuits built, from the bravest of *Indios bravos*, a network of missions so prosperous and successful it became a glittering working model of a well-oiled, machine-tooled theocratic state.

The Conquistadors had been obliged by law (technically) to read a rather lengthy legal document to any Indians before making war on them—it explained the growth of humanity since Adam and Eve, the supremacy of the Pope, who had given the New World to the king of Spain, and ended by requiring the Indians to submit to said king. In the middle 1500s this was changed to a friendly, downright genial proclamation of greeting, rather as from one monarch to another, from the king of Spain to the "kings and republics of the mid-way and western lands." A few years later the very concept of conquest had become repugnant and the new *New Laws* of 1573 stated that even the word was not to be used; the word from now on was to be "pacification," in order not to furnish any possible color or cause for aggravation to the Indians.

Trials of Conquistadors accused rightly or wrongly of atrocities against Indians became almost standard procedure. Increasingly rigorous laws prohibited any punishment of Indians, even for refusing to become Christians—leaving a single loophole for punishment of those who "hindered the teaching" of Christianity, a clause much used by missionaries in commending troublesome elder brothers to the lash or gallows.

Indian wars and outbreaks continued, and many of them. For more than 200 years there was a major uprising about every ten years in the mine-and-mission frontier of northern Mexico, from Sinaloa and Sonora to the Pima country.

But an uneasy balance was ultimately achieved that made possible the comparatively stable colonial centuries, and that ultimately left traces of a Spanish stamp on the vast majority (90 percent, at a moderate guess) of all Indians who were to be much touched by any European culture.

From the first, outbreaks of Indian rebellion had been fought with the help, often substantial, of Indian allies. But by the end of the sixteenth century the Spaniards were beginning to find a

IN INDIIS PATRATÆ.

Quadam autem die, circa quartam noctis vigiliam in
multos Cacicos, Satrapas, & alios Indianos irruit, qui tamen ſe
ſatis tutos exiſtimabant (fides enim, & ſecuritas illis data erat, ſe
nullam iniuriam, aut damnum recepturos) qua fide nitentes, ex
mõtibus, in quibus latebant ad vrbes, ſine vlla ſuſpicione, aut ti-
more, reuertebantur, quos omnes cepit, & manus in terram ex-
tendere iubens, ipſemet enſe proprio illis abſcindebat, ſe eos
caſtigare

**This engraving from a 1598 book by Bartolomé de Las Casas, the "friend of the Indian," purports to show Spanish savagery to Indians in the Caribbean area. Las Casas worked tirelessly to end the ill-treatment and enslavement of natives by the Spaniards.**

new and even more urgent use for Indian alliances—as buffers against other European encroachment in the New World. This consideration was to become an increasingly important part of Indian policy as time went on, not only for the Spanish but for the other European encroachers as well.

Portugal, formally if reluctantly given a bite of the Indies by treaty with Spain, had ceased to be a threat for the time being, with the union of the two kingdoms in 1581. But France and England, Spain's blood enemies, and Holland, just breaking free of Spanish subjection, were interloping with growing insolence.

Francis of France, noted for his wit as much as his women, had remarked that he would like to see the will by which Adam had divided the world between Spain and Portugal—this while admiring part of Moctezuma's treasure, which had been intercepted by a French privateer on its way to Spain from Cortes.

Thereafter France had taken a piquant interest in the Americas from Canada to Rio de Janeiro, and French Huguenots by the 1560s were building Fort Caroline in the Carolinas to overlook the passing Spanish plate fleets, and finding "the natives... very kind to them out of hatred to the Spaniards.... "

Spain had just failed in still another attempt to colonize Florida, even though the colonists had been instructed to "settle and by good example, with good works and presents, to bring the natives to a knowledge of our Holy Faith and Catholic truth." But now a do-or-die Spanish effort founded St. Augustine, massacred the French colony at Fort Caroline, and installed a Spanish garrison. A private French vengeance party returned a couple of years later and with Indian help ("assisted by the kings of Homoloa and Servaratri," in an old account) massacred the Spanish garrison, hanging those who surrendered, but by then, at last, the Spaniards were firmly settled in Florida.

The Spanish governor, Menendez de Aviles, negotiated an alliance with Florida's most powerful nation, the Calusa, by marrying the sister of their chief, the renowned Carlos. Missions and presidios were planted up the Atlantic coast as far as South Carolina, and inland to western Georgia.

This period marked the high tide of the Spanish empire in reaching northward up the Atlantic coast.

As already intimated, a gaze fixed on the past becomes more and more untrustworthy (eventually even reporting that there is no past at all, only a boundless present), but one thing it does sometimes seem to see is that the seeds of greatness, as we call it, are also the seeds of self-destruction. The forces of hot new nationalism under total central authority, crusading religious passion, and the lure of quick riches that hewed out Spain's vast empire became the forces of its ruin.

The hot new nationalism, kept sealed in a vacuum of Spaniards only, cooled to stagnation. Central authority grew hard and rigid, and changed from a whip to a bar—nothing could be done without royal permission; every detail had to be reported, at officious length, through endless official channels. Oñate was kept marking time for several years, his army of colonists already assembled, while the king decided whether or not to let him colonize New Mexico. Alvar Nuñez Cabeza de Vaca, made governor of Buenos Aires and Asuncion in present Argentina-Paraguay, tried to protect the Indians and thus gained the enmity of the local slavers; it was the royal pleasure to throw both Nuñez and his principal opponents in prison, not being certain which side had the right of it.

Ecclesiastical zeal, solidly ensconced and grown unrecognizably fat, devoted itself to a chronic war with the miners and ranchers (and between rival religious orders) over Indian jurisdiction—it became customary for each faction to blame the other for every Indian upheaval, frequently with justice, and the spectacle of priests inciting Indians to murder settlers and settlers inciting Indians to murder priests was not unknown. Each courted the Indians with one eye and winked at subterfuge slavery with the other.

The king poured the wealth of the Indies into European adventures, and crusading religious passion put Spain in the forefront of the war against the Reformation. By 1596 Philip of Spain was broke, and abrogated a debt of fourteen and a half million ducats he owed to European moneylenders, thereby ruining Spain's credit.

Rivals shouldered their way into the New World, and weakening Spain, gorged and muscle-bound, was unable to hold them off.

The Spaniards centered in Florida, the English above them on the Atlantic coast, English and French pirates and later colonies below them on heretofore unoccupied West Indian islands, and by the start of the eighteenth century the French were west of them, toward the mouth of the Mississippi.

The American nations caught in the middle of these European advances took sides, often with gusto, for most of these people of the Southeast were lovers of war.

Some of them were also people with a long and notable history.

By present evidence, agriculture began to appear here and there in the Mississippi Valley well over 2,000 years ago. This was even before its earliest appearance among the Southwestern Hohokam and Anasazi. An elaborate society was slowly created in that long-ago time that appears to have had its focal point toward the north, in the valley of the Ohio. It spread down the Mississippi and very widely throughout the central regions of the present United States, culminating in an apparent great confederacy that reached from the Gulf to Wisconsin, from New York to Kansas.

This people of some 2,000 years ago built great burial mounds and extensive earthwork systems in their riverside towns or ceremonial centers, traded for raw materials (pipestone, seashells, metals) all over eastern North America from the Rockies to the Atlantic, and made objects of art of a high order in everything from wood and mica to copper. Their culture is usually given the name Hopewell, after a site in southern Ohio, and according to carbon 14 dates grew to its greatest development a very long time ago indeed—in the centuries from 400 B.C to A.D. 400.

At a later time a new and somewhat different order of things came into being toward the south, centering along the Mississippi from the present Cairo to the delta. This consisted of little city-states, stockaded villages built beside streams and bayous around ceremonial centers that featured flat-topped temple pyramids made of earth, sometimes quite large—70 or 80 or even 100 feet high, and covering acres of ground, and "the sides so upright," as a traveler wrote of one in 1790, "that the cattle cannot get upon it to feed."

This Temple Mound culture flourished for centuries, reaching a peak from about A.D. 1300 to 1500, and was still in some operation, although apparently on a remnant basis, when the first Europeans appeared in the Southeast.

The thatched houses sometimes resembled Mexican houses, the pyramids resemble the pyramids of Middle America and were topped by wooden temples in the manner of the earliest

Maya, and were built in successive layers, probably at periodic renewal ceremonies, as in Middle America; an eternal fire was kept burning in the temple, as in Mexico, and was renewed at a new-fire ceremony—although once a year, at least in the later times we know about, rather than every fifty-two years, as in Mexico.

Sacrifice of war captives was an enthusiastic community activity—occasionally the prisoner was tied spread-eagled in a wooden frame, much as in the ancient Mexican arrow-shooting sacrifice.

There are so many points in common, even to some specific pottery styles, with the Maya and other early civilizations of Mexico and Central America and even of South America that there must have been contacts.

It does not seem likely that the scattered gangs of emaciated indigents feeding among the cactus flats of Texas, as described by their sometime slave and physician Alvar Nuñez Cabeza de Vaca, would have handed on the torch of learning from Mexico by way of the Gulf Coast. In later Temple Mound times some fashions came across the plains from the Pueblos, but more often than not the most specific Mexican resemblances in the Southeast seem to be altogether different from those that reached the ancient Southwest, indicating quite separate trade routes.

So it would seem the connections must have been by sea, across the Gulf, possibly from the Yucatan peninsula, possibly from Toltec ports along the Mexican east coast. A few archaeologists suspect there may have been migrations of people themselves, not only ideas and fashions, from Middle America.

In the mid-1400s, further Mexican echoes reached the Southeast, accumulating until after a generation or two the whole area was seized for a time with what seems to have been a tremendous religious revival bearing Mexican overtones, the Death Cult. Skulls, weeping faces, feathered serpents abounded, as well as Eagle Warriors carrying trophy heads, and, a distant echo to roll ashore on the banks of the Mississippi, fat-lipped stone figures rather disquietingly reminiscent of the Olmecs and proto-Olmecs of so long, long ago.

Here as elsewhere populations had entered and vanished, merged and divided; only more so. Probably more than any place else north of Mexico, the lower Mississippi and environs had been a maelstrom of those ripples of contact. The loose Burial Mound confederacy, and the even looser Temple Mound confederacy—if they had been confederacies at all—had been composed of a tangled multiplicity of peoples, with varying customs and cultures, speaking different languages. The buzzard symbol of the Death Cult spread its wings over a medley of nations, from the numerous Caddo people west of the Mississippi, on the shore of the Great Plains, to the villagers of Georgia—probably ancestors of some of the later Creeks—who built the mound town of Etowah and crammed its graves with spectacular Death Cult ornaments.

In a general sense, all were hoe farmers growing the same crops; fishermen using the same tackle; hunters coursing the same piney woods, cypress swamps and canebrakes, and gaudy hardwood ridges where bears started up and ran like rolling drums. (Buffalo as well as deer were hunted on the Mississippi bluffs, and along the rivers a fearsome game was the "crocodile... it squashes people with its murdering tooth," as an early traveler reported.) All rode the winding rivers in the same model of dugout canoe or poled the swamps with the same cane raft. All boiled corn soup and hominy from the same recipes, and took the same extras and delicacies from the larder of wild nut trees and berry bushes. The village systems were more or less alike: a large town of perhaps 200 or 300 cabins, usually palisaded and moated for defense, serving as a center for a number of smaller communities.

But the underlying unity seems to have been one of a passionate and somewhat mystic endeavor. Living was on a high note. Death was the great crescendo. This traced back to an antiquity so remote that it was in another world (the world of the first elder and younger brother, or the first mother—made pregnant by a snake—who is a feature of so many widely separated New World genesis accounts).

A story told by the Alabama (who along with the Mobile had engaged de Soto's army in one of the largest Indian battles ever fought in the area of the present United States) deals with a familiar Indian theme, people descending from heaven "in a canoe singing and laughing," and a man on earth who catches and marries a girl from among them. But later she and their children sail back up to heaven, "singing and laughing, continually singing." In the Alabama ending to the story, the husband tries to follow in another canoe: "He went on for a while, singing, but looked down to the ground. Then he fell back and was killed."

There is a definite feeling that in later times the meaning of this music of passion and aspiration had been forgotten, and that it was only followed because it had always been followed. Or rather, that the theme was in a stage of change, modulating to a new key, as it must have done many times before down the years.

But the order of living remained: the engrossing game of sliding sticks and stones called *chenco* (English traders called it chunkey), on which great bets were made, and the ball game played at the harvest festival, in which arms and legs and sometimes necks were fractured; purification from the celebrated "black drink"—the purifying emetic of the Southeast, taken, says an early account, "until the blood comes"—and from physics that sometimes left the purified permanently crippled from violent convulsions; the taboos heaped on sex, which was charged with many perils (according to most reports, Creek women had to run and hide in a swamp, entirely alone and unattended, at time of childbirth); and the heart-springing excitement of battle and raid.

And there was the dramatic torture-sacrifice of captured enemy warriors, as good as a play. It is hard to escape an impression that simply the entertainment involved had become the main force behind the ritual torture of captives of war; with certain exceptions, religious significance is either absent or disguised out of recognition by the time European observers arrive.

In any case, this was no world of contentment but a world in search of rapture and excitement; this was no land for people of moderation.

When, in the seventeenth century, the Spanish, French, and English established the battlefronts of empire in the Southeast, the largest and most powerful Indian group was a loose confederation of some fifty towns (perhaps 30,000 people all told) in the area of present Georgia and Alabama dominated by a nucleus of associated tribes known as the Muskogee. Early English traders from South Carolina first met citizens of this confederacy living along a river the English called Ocheese Creek (now Ocmulgee River) and spoke of them as the Indians of the Creek,

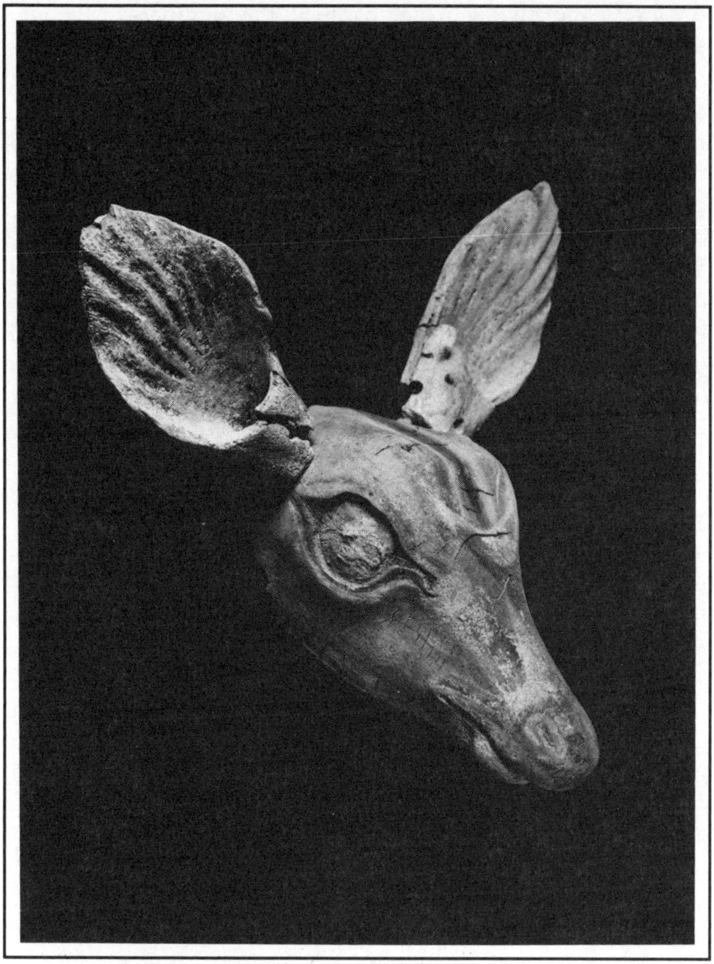

This wooden deer's head, found at Key Marco, Florida, is thought to be one of the finest expressions of prehistoric art. Carved in the fifteenth century by a Calusa Indian, it has ears that can be moved by strings. In addition to being used in ceremonies, it probably served as a magic lure for game.

the Creek Indians, by which name all the members of the confederacy have been known ever since.

Composed of a number of different peoples and fragments of many more, most of them related but some utter aliens (a half-dozen languages were spoken within it), the Creek confederacy was divided into two principal parts: the Upper Towns, and, in theory below them on the rivers, the Lower Towns, a division reflecting the widespread Indian arrangement of double government. The Summer and Winter people of the Pueblos became in the Southeast (and quite a few places elsewhere) the Peace and War people. Among the Creeks the Upper Towns (again only in theory, since in practice these matters got mixed up) were primarily the Peace Towns, the White Towns, controlling important civil ceremonies such as the *puskita*, the eight-day festival of the first corn, when new fire was made, grudges were forgiven, plazas were swept and sprinkled with new sand, and in general life was scrubbed, shined, and started afresh on another year. The principal chief of the confederacy was supposed to be chosen from a White Clan. The Lower Towns were the Red Towns, consecrated to ceremonies of war, and the elders of the council, the Beloved Men, were supposed to choose the confederacy's battle chief, the Great Warrior, from a Red Clan.

West of the Creeks were the people whose road to their landing place on the Big Muddy River, the Old Chickasaw Trail, first led English traders to the Mississippi. This traditional Chickasaw river port, more than 150 miles west of their central villages, was on the site of modern Memphis. Below the Chickasaw toward the Gulf Coast the most important nation was that of the Choctaw, who gave their name to a lingua franca used thereabouts in trade, the Choctaw Jargon—also called, depending on where one was trading at the moment, the Chickasaw Jargon or the Mobile Jargon, these languages all being much alike.

The Choctaw, Chickasaw, most of the Creeks, in fact most of the people over all this southern country from the Mississippi River eastward to the Atlantic, spoke languages related to various divisions of the Muskhogean language family. But to repeat: related languages did not necessarily mean related people. The Choctaw and Chickasaw, for example, with very similar languages, were considerably less similar physically and in their natures: the Chickasaw far-ranging, quarrelsome, aggressive; the

Choctaw close-mouthed farmers inclining to stay home and tend their gardens, which, in the rich bottom lands of southern Mississippi and Alabama, were some of the best in North America; the two were of course bitter enemies.

In this Southeastern sea of Muskhogean tongues there were islands of Siouan speech (notably, the Biloxi) and Algonquian (notably, bands of Shawnee). Up the Atlantic coast in North Carolina were the Iroquoian Tuscarora peoples, and north of the Creeks were the Cherokee, most populous single tribe in all the area (20,000 souls in sixty villages), speaking variant (the most variant known) Iroquoian dialects.

The main Siouan frontier of the seventeenth century, zigzagging northward up the west bank of the Mississippi, might be said to have begun in the south with the Quapaw (the name means "Downstream People"). Their territory lay generally westward of the Chickasaw country, most of it across the Mississippi, centering around the mouth of the Arkansas. Below the western range of the Quapaw, over an immense region centering in east Texas, were the principal Caddo confederacies.

The lower Mississippi, from the Yazoo to the delta, was controlled by a series of little riverine states, small in area compared with their surrounding neighbors but not necessarily always weaker in population or influence, the best known of these being the famous Natchez.

The Natchez (a French spelling, and therefore indicating a name pronounced something like Natchay) occupied nine or more villages, most of them on the east side of the present city of Natchez, and at the end of the seventeenth century may have numbered approximately 4,000 total population, including two villages of refugee foreigners they had taken under their wing (the Grigra and Tiou; the Tiou, at least, were refugees from Chickasaw aggression).

The celebrity of the Natchez comes from their position as a preeminent, if perhaps not typical, example of a Temple Mound state surviving into modern times.

They were ruled by a king, a descendant of the sun and called the Great Sun. Every deference was shown him, and his power over his individual subjects, their lives, labor, and property, was absolute and despotic; although in political decisions involving the nation as a whole the Great Sun in turn was controlled by the council of respected old men.

His residence, in the principal village, was a large cabin (forty-five by twenty-five feet) built on a long, flat-topped mound (some eight or ten feet high). Nearby on a similar mound was another large cabin, decorated with two carved birds perched at each end of the roof. This was the temple, in which two guardians watched the eternal fire, and in which were the sacred bones of previous Great Suns. No one but the Great Sun, who was high priest as well as king, and the few appointed temple officials, were permitted to enter the temple—whether its forbidding sanctity came primarily from the fire within it or from the bones interred there is uncertain; experts disagree.

The relatives of the Great Sun (with the exception of his children) were Little Suns; his mother or sister was the principal woman Sun and chose the successor from among her sons or brothers when the Great Sun died. The Great Sun appointed the two war chiefs of the nation, the two masters of ceremony for the public rites in the plaza before the temple, and other functionaries from among the Little Suns, all of whom were given slavish respect by the rest of the people.

Below the Suns in importance was a class of Nobles, and below the Nobles a class called Honored Men (to which anyone could aspire by distinction in war or piety), and lowest of all were the commoners, the masses, treated like dirt by the aristocrats, say the early accounts, and referred to as Stinkards, although the term was not used in the presence of the Stinkards themselves, as it offended them.

Suns could not intermarry—all Suns, male and female, including the Great Sun, had to take their wives or husbands from among the Stinkards. The children of male Suns were only Nobles, who again were obliged by law to marry Stinkards, and the children of male Nobles were reduced one more grade to Honored Men or Women, who also had to marry Stinkards. The children of Honored Men were Stinkards. Descent holding in the female line, the children of female Suns were Suns, the children of female Nobles were Nobles, the children of Honored Women were Honored People. The children of two Stinkard parents were of course absolute Stinkards.

This Gulliveresque system is unique, although its basis, descent through the mother, was and is very common among primitive societies all over the world.

Female Suns, naturally, must have held a decisive behind-the-scenes power, as well as living the life of a maiden's dream—at any rate the dream of a maiden of the gallant court of Louis XIV, whose Louisiana subjects recorded most of this; there would be a temptation to think their powdered wigs were getting in their eyes except that five reasonably dependable contemporary accounts all agree in essential facts. Anyway, the Stinkard husband of a woman Sun had to stand in her presence like a servant, shout his praise of her every remark, was not allowed to eat with her, and if he displeased her, particularly by any infidelity, she could "have his head cut off in an instant." Privilege of rank permitted her, of course, as many lovers as she pleased. She could also, if the whim struck her, have her base-born husband thrown out at a snap of her fingers, and pick another Stinkard in his place.

And yet this was a warrior state and in the usual Natchez home the husband "alone commands." Old men were held in such respect that "they are regarded as judges. Their counsels are judgments."

The Natchez may have been the people spoken of in a chronicle of the de Soto expedition as worshipers of the sun, to whom de Soto sent word that he was the Sun's younger brother. They replied that if he would dry up the Mississippi they would accept his credentials. Possibly they joined other Mississippians in merrily chasing the Spaniards down the river. But it was not until a century and a half later that their old life was definitively interrupted by Europeans who came to stay, when the French founded the colony of Louisiana, first established at Biloxi (1699) and then on Mobile Bay (1702).

The Natchez had seen Frenchmen occasionally for several years previously, leathern strangers who came floating down the river in canoes beautifully fashioned of bark, marvelously swift—the first of these (of record) had been a band led by a fretful trader named Robert Cavelier, Sieur de La Salle, an overnight guest with the Natchez in March 1682.

Now French missionaries began appearing and newcomers not only from Canada but direct from France, seamen in great boots, soldiers in steel breastplates, clerks from counting houses, farmers from Gascony—and three Carolina Englishmen came by way of the Chickasaws, already stout English allies, to visit the Natchez villages of White Apple, the Hickories, Grigra, and Tiou. The French would enslave the Natchez in their own country, the English traders said, and furthermore French guns and hatchets and knives were not as good as those made by the English, and furthermore the English would trade for a lower price in pelts.

The Englishmen fled back to the Chickasaws when a French trading post was opened at the Great Village of the Natchez in 1713. But some of the Natchez (from the villages of White Apple, the Hickories, and Grigra) murdered several Frenchmen and brief hostilities followed—armed parleys rather than a war—resulting in the execution of six village war chiefs, and delivery by the Natchez of the heads of three others: their heads, not their scalps, the French governor specified, "in order to recognize them by their tattoo marks." Another result was a garrisoned French stockade, Fort Rosalie, established in the Natchez country.

These first French colonies had been a business venture on the part of a rich French merchant who had obtained sole exploitation rights for all North America from the Illinois to the Gulf, from the Carolinas to New Mexico, but could not make his investment pay.

In 1717 a promoter took over his grant on speculation, formed a company that was given total power over this land and anyone in it, ransacked jails and hospitals or kidnaped people from the streets for colonists, sent out shiploads of black slaves to implement tobacco farming, exacted taxes from Indians in buckskins and bear oil, and in general went at things in a vigorous, businesslike way.

Agents of this company obtained large tracts among the Natchez towns for plantations, the region became the most flourishing department of the Louisiana colony, and seemingly every Frenchman there who could write recorded his observation on the remarkable Natchez—who are given more space in the literature of the period than all the other fourteen Indian states of the lower Mississippi put together.

The Natchez girls received much attention, due to their custom of extreme licentiousness before marriage and (Woman Suns presumably excepted) their extreme virtuousness after, the opposite of the European ideal of feminine behavior.

Natchez warriors are seen again and again, heads flattened to a mitred point, hair cut in whatever bizarre fashion the wearer likes—shaved on one side, left long on the other, or trimmed to a single scalp lock, or tonsured like a priest's. They stroll the plaza, tattooed (tattoos were, so to speak, war medals) from face to ankle, negligently waving fans, or recline on their mats while the women work the fields.

Homosexuals appear, male concubines as one French observer calls them, men who wear their hair woman-style, long and braided, wear skirts instead of loincloths, and work with the women. Many Indian societies gave transvestites some recognition, ranging from an embarrassed tolerance to a sort of priestly distinction—although Maya tradition says they had never heard of homosexuality before the Toltecs came, and the Aztecs and Inca punished it harshly by law.

The sensational torture scenes were painted by all. Male captives of war were brought back to dance and sing before the temple and then were scalped and lashed up naked in the wooden frames to be tortured and burned. Etiquette demanded that the victim sing his death song as long as life remained, and some, says Le Page du Pratz, the best of the Natchez reporters, "have been seen to suffer and sing continually during three days and three nights. . . . " Captive women and children had their hair cut short, badge of slavery, and were put to work pounding corn. As among most Indians, it was also possible for captives to be adopted into the nation, and even attain later eminence.

But it was the un-Indianlike caste system that made the Natchez remarkable to their French neighbors, who saw in hereditary aristocracy the surest proof that civilization's gentle step had once trod these woodlands rude, sometime or other. When it came to the Great Sun, his Louis Quinze admirers were downright charmed.

There were dissenters. The first French governor wrote of the Great Sun of his day (1700): "He appeared to me the most absolute savage I had seen, as beggarly . . . as his subjects." But other witnesses sing rhapsodies of the reverences of his subjects, his absolute authority, and his kingly demeanor. "When he gives the leavings (of his dinner) to his brothers or any of his relatives, he pushes the dishes to them with his feet. . . . The submissiveness of the savages to their chief, who commands them with the most despotic power, is extreme . . . if he demands the life of any

**These sketches by Le Page du Pratz were made for his 1758 account of the Natchez Indians. Above, the Great Sun is carried to the harvest festival; below, captives are scalped and fastened to execution frames where they will be burned and slowly tortured to death.**

one of them he comes himself to present his head."

Wearing his crown of swan feathers tasseled in scarlet, the Great Sun was carried in a litter to the festival of the new corn; his platform bed of state was furnished with a goose-feather bolster and heaped with the richest buffalo robes and bearskins, and he was wakened in the mornings by the most distinguished old men, who saluted him with respectful cries and bows that he did not deign to notice (a royal levee, to the life).

And "these people blindly obey the least wish of their great chief... for whatever labors he commands them to execute, they are forbidden to exact any wages. The French, who are often in need of hunters or of rowers for their long voyages, never apply to anyone but the great chief.... "

This last hints at a practical charm in addition to the regal romance of it all. One suspects the Natchez warriors did not spend too much time reclining on their mats after the French appeared.

This may have been a factor, along with constant English-Chickasaw agitation, for the fairly clear emergence of two political parties among the Natchez: pro-French and anti-French. There may have been some tendency for certain classes to cleave to one party or the other. The Great Sun and his brother, war chief of the nation, whose name was Tattooed Serpent, and their mother, the principal woman Sun, whose name was Tattooed Arm, were all strongly pro-French. The majority of the higher aristocracy seems to have followed them in pro-French leanings. The clearest division was among the villages (of which only six seem to exist after 1713): the Great Village and the Flour Village were pro-French centers, while the Hickories, White Apple, and the immigrant districts of the Grigra and Tiou seem to have been hotbeds of anti-French feeling, although here again some of the chiefs of these seditious villages, Suns all, appear to have maintained a sturdy pro-French loyalty as long as possible.

In the autumn of 1722 a young sergeant of the Fort Rosalie garrison had an argument with an aged Natchez warrior over a debt, "threatened to give the old man a cudgeling," at which the old man, riled, said they might see who was the stronger. "At this defiance, the soldier, crying 'murder,' summoned the guard to his assistance." The old man, walking toward his village "at an ordinary gait" was shot in the back. He died the next day of the wound. The commandant of Fort Rosalie reprimanded the young sergeant.

Some White Apple men a few nights later (drunk, the Tattooed Serpent said) shot and wounded one of the directors of the plantation (called "the concession of St. Catherine," giving the name it still bears to the creek running through the Natchez towns) neighboring their village, and killed and scalped a French soldier.

A detachment of troops was immediately sent up the river from the recently founded capital of New Orleans. Tattooed Serpent managed to make peace, and forced the villages of White Apple, the Hickories, and the Grigra to pay an indemnity to the French troops.

Not long afterward resentful individuals from these villages killed some cattle on the concession of St. Catherine, and this time a larger army, with Choctaw and Tunica allies, came up from New Orleans—the French after vengeance for the murdered cows, the Choctaw and Tunica along for incidental plunder. Again Tattooed Serpent made every effort for peace, but the French commander, this time the governor himself, was bent on blood, although he at length agreed to spare the Great Village and the Flour Village.

The expedition marched by stealth against White Apple, but on the way came in sight of three Natchez women pounding hominy in front of a lone cabin, and since the governor had inspired his troops, among whom were many New Orleans volunteers, by promising that they could keep as slaves any females they could catch, the whole army stormed the three women and the cabin with such an uproar and fusilade that the White Apple people were alerted and abandoned their village.

Thereafter the army found only empty villages to burn, although by chance an old woman was encountered, "who was perhaps more than 100 years old, since her hair was entirely white, a very rare thing among these savages.... The general... after having questioned her... abandoned her on the spot, as a useless encumbrance, to the discretion of a little slave he had, who took her scalp and killed her."

The Choctaw and Tunica managed to scare up four women and one man during several tiresome days of marching, and the governor, who wanted "blood worthy of being shed," summoned Tattooed Serpent and told him they were going to destroy the Great Village and the Flour Village after all, since they could not find anyone at home elsewhere. Tattooed Serpent, "who was really a friend of the French, made no other reply than to ask for peace."

The governor finally granted it, on condition that the head of the chief of White Apple be delivered to him. This was a Sun of great distinction named Old Hair, particularly respected by all the nation, and, very probably, the bulwark of the hard-pressed pro-French party in White Apple. Being a Sun, he was supposed to be exempt from capital punishment for any reason whatsoever, which made the request rather like asking the Pope to serve up the head of a cardinal.

But Tattooed Serpent submitted, and after two days for the necessary ceremonies and leave-takings, brought the head of Old Hair. The governor, rather as an afterthought, also demanded and got the head of a free black who had come to live with the Natchez—"It was justly feared that he would teach them the manner of attack and defense, and for that reason it was of the utmost importance... to get rid of him."

Some time later a Tiou malefactor cut the tail off a planter's mare (a trophy as good as a scalp). Tattooed Serpent bought peace this time with a tribute of corn from all the nation, "more than sufficient to pay an entire regiment of cavalry."

Tattooed Serpent died in 1725. The whole nation (and quite a few of his friends among the French) wept, for he was much beloved. His two wives, his chancellor, doctor, principal servant, pipe bearer, and various other followers, went joyously to the funeral rites, at which they were drugged and then, with their heads concealed in skin bags, strangled.

Several other volunteers insisted on being strangled to go along, one of them a Noble woman, a great beauty, a particular friend of Tattooed Serpent, and "intimate only with distinguished Frenchmen." The French called her *La Glorieuse*.

A Stinkard couple sacrificed their child and threw its body under the pallbearers' feet (a means of being raised to Honored rank), and the Great Sun himself, wildly grieving, had to be restrained from suicide.

One cashiered warrior marked for sacrifice did not want to go, and Tattooed Serpent's favorite wife sent him away: "it is not good that you come with us and that your heart remain behind you on the earth." To French friends who begged her not to die, she said "with a smiling air": "Do not grieve. We will be friends for a much longer time in the country of the spirits than in this, because one does not die there again. . . . Men do not make war there any more, because they make only one nation. I am going and leave my children without any father or mother. When you see them, Frenchmen, remember that you have loved the father and that you ought not to repulse the children of the one who has always been the true friend of the French." She was, it will be remembered, from the class of Stinkards.

The Great Sun died three years later, in 1728. The Great Sun who succeeded was young and less effective. The old queen mother, Tattooed Arm, was left as the sole mainstay of French support. The White Apple chief who had taken the place of Old Hair was hotly anti-French, and of growing influence. Pro-English Chickasaw, according to an English account, won the Natchez to their side in the year of the Great Sun's death: "But as the Indians are slow in their councils on things of great importance, though equally close and intent, it was the following year before they could put their grand scheme in execution."

For a final argument there came now as commandant at Natchez an unbelievably villainous ass (all accounts agree) named Chépart, who tyrannized over everyone in sight, French as well as Indian. The best plantation land being taken up, he commandeered the Great Village itself for his plantation, and ordered the youthful Great Sun to move his people away instantly. He granted a delay until harvest time (the first corn having just sprouted), on consideration of a rental paid in fowls, bear's oil, corn, and pelts—but at first frost (the year was 1729) the people would be gone or he would haul the Great Sun down to New Orleans in irons.

The old men met in secret councils. There could be no other decision than war. Messages were sent to the Choctaw, who agreed to join in and attack New Orleans. Tattooed Arm, in desperation, tried to warn the Sieur Chépart—he paid no attention to her messengers except to have them jailed.

At the first frost of 1729 the Natchez attacked the French everywhere in their country, killed more than 200 and made prisoners of several hundred women, children, and blacks. Natchez warriors refused to touch the Sieur Chépart with their weapons, but had a Stinkard beat him to death with a stick.

The Choctaw played a double game and sided with the French, so this was, of course, the end. Even so it was a long time coming, and required two full-scale comic-opera invasions from New Orleans, some savage fighting here and there, and a grand display of power politics up and down the river as each side tried to line up allies. In town after town the red-painted war posts were set up and hung with red feathers, red arrows, and red tomahawks, and after furious vomiting, warriors danced and struck the post (with their red-painted war clubs, with all their might) to signify their enlistment, and war chiefs anxiously consulted their dreams for guidance and good augur. The Yazoo Indians murdered the French living among them and one of them dressed himself in the clothes of their slain missionary to go to the Natchez and announce allegiance; the French secured the home front by sending blacks to exterminate thirty inoffensive Chaouacha, the nearest Indians to New Orleans.

But the defection of the Choctaw had been decisive, even though only the western villages of the colossal Choctaw nation were involved in the conspiracy and double cross: the Choctaw also were divided into two parties, pro-English in the east, pro-French in the west. These internal politics undoubtedly played their part in the devious course of Choctaw policy.

Eventually, after more than a year of maneuvering, the French managed to persuade a few dozen Natchez warriors and several hundred women and children to surrender. These included most of the leaders of the aristocratic pro-French party. Tattooed Arm refused to come along, but it is reasonable to suppose the children of Tattooed Serpent were among them. The French commander picked out a few men and women for public burning and sold the rest, including the Great Sun and his family, as slaves in Santo Domingo.

For a long while afterward bands of implacable Natchez harassed French *voyageurs* along the river, but the largest groups went into exile and established towns among the Chickasaw, Creeks, and Cherokee, where they acquired some reputation as mystics, possibly because of their antique religion.

In its small way the story of the Natchez is the story of the whole Southeast, where the three great Christian nations on the move, France, Spain, and England, all collided, boldly determined to fight to the last Indian.

# VI

# War in the Forest

**This portrait of Pocahontas was painted in 1616 by an unknown artist in London, where her husband, John Rolfe, had taken her and where she became a sensation in society.**

From the time of the Old Copper people on the shores of Lake Superior until the appearance of agriculture and pottery along the upper Mississippi was perhaps 4,000 years. From the time of the first cultivated corn until the high point of the Hopewell burial-mound-building states was perhaps half a thousand years, give or take a few centuries.

From the high point of the immense Hopewell confederacy (as it seemed to be) until the general invasion of Europeans along the Atlantic coast was perhaps another thousand years or more.

Beside the lakes and rivers, in the occasional park lands and in the long reaches of unbroken forest of the Northeast, a people lived, multitongued, of great diversities and many samenesses, who at the Europeans' arrival still traveled the worn paths of all these accumulated ages.

They hunted with the skill of Neolithics, and the Deer, Bear, Wolf, and Turtle were their brothers. They used wild plants with the magic incantations and racial memories of Cochise-type people who had gathered seeds, nuts, and berries in this country long before any knowledge of farming appeared. Trade networks moved obsidian from the Rockies to Ohio, tobacco from Virginia to the St. Lawrence, copper from the present Canadian border to North Carolina, flint and salt and pipestone everywhere. The political structure was the confederacy, a nucleus of associated bands in hegemony over other bands and fragments of bands, related or not, ex-enemies or ex-allies, ancient or recent acquaintances; immigration into the tribe was as a rule open to all.

They sought guidance in the supernatural dreams of the solitary hunter, and in the unison prayers of farmers. They raided each other for loot, glory, revenge, or for captives to sacrifice. They also warred at the drop of an arrow over territorial infringement. Sometimes captive killing was embroidered with tattered vestiges of sacrificial ceremony, including occasional ritual cannibalism, and often with frenzied excesses of public torture. Here and there over the spruce and fir of northern woods appeared Quetzalcoatl, disguised as the Morning Star.

Various gods were worshiped that were the same under the skin, from the solemn Master of Breath, the supreme being, to the deity straight out of a cartoon pantheon, the Great Rabbit, who went skipping about setting a chaotic world to rights, playing jokes, and getting himself into terrible trouble. Many of the Great Rabbit's jokes were quite obscene by European standards. The usual Indian attitude toward obscenity in general frequently seemed shameless and sinful to European eyes and ears, and still does; scholarly recorders of Indian folk tales still make occasional use of Latin paragraphs to veil the dirty passages. Conversely, Indians found many European attitudes—such as not isolating women during menstruation—not only grossly obscene but so wicked as to be terrifying.

Slash-and-burn cornfields were cultivated as far north as the climate permitted. Nearly all these forest-dwelling people were confirmed townsmen, although a few groups spent much time wandering and only touched base at a village during certain seasons. Many lived in long barrackslike multifamily houses, some in single family huts of pole-and-wattle "much like the wild Irish," observed a New Englander of the 1620s.

Some reckoned descent by the father, some by the mother; some organized society into clans that claimed descent from the spirit of an animal, Bear, perhaps, or Buffalo, some into special societies formed for specific purpose, such as war or healing.

Some, notably the Huron, north and east of Lake Ontario, practiced elaborate mass-burial ceremonies, when the collected bones of the dead of ten or twelve years were formally interred together with mountains of rich funeral gifts, from furs to beautifully worked tools and arms.

The Southern ball game, with racquets, was played: French traders called it *la crosse*. An East Coast innovation introduced in the centuries following the decline of the Hopewell world was in wide use: seashells strung on strings or beaded into belts, used almost like money, and exchanged between nations at diplomatic councils as guarantees of earnest intentions. English traders called it wampum, after an Algonquian word, *wampompeag*.

These Northeastern people enter our history to the cries of woodland battle. "The place where they fought was of great advantage to the savages, by means of the thick trees, behind which the savages through their nimbleness, defended themselves, and so offended our men with their arrows, that our men being some of them hurt, retired fighting to the water side where their boat lay, with which they fled towards Hatorask..." says an account from the year 1586.

Or, in a description of Indians fighting Indians published in 1634 by the trustworthy William Wood, a Plymouth settler, the Mohawks come "running, and fiercely crying out, *Hadree Hadree succomee succomee*, we come we come to sucke your blood, not fearing the feathered shafts of the strong-armed bow-men, but like unruly headstrong stallions beate them downe with their right hand Tamahaukes be staves of two foote and a halfe long, and a knob at one end as round and bigge as a footeball... one blow or thrust with these strange weapons, will not neede a second to hasten death, from a Mohackes arme.... "

The Indian story gives an impression of being writ larger in war whoops in the neighborhood of the English colonies along the Atlantic coast than elsewhere in the invaded Hemisphere.

It is important to realize that this is a distorted impression. The Indians of the Northeast were, most of them, warlike peoples, but no more so than many others Europeans had met, and less so than some. Their wars were of critical importance and cataclysmic dimension for all parties concerned, but they were fewer and smaller, even so, than the wars in a number of other areas of European colonization. The subtler turmoils of peace were of equal or greater importance, and there were more of them.

Will Wood's foregoing picture of charging Mohawks has been often quoted; another line in his 1634 survey has not received so much attention: "But to leave their warres, and to speake of their games in which they are more delighted and better experienced. . . . " Speaking of a New England tribe, he remarked, "Take these *Indians* in their own trimme and naturall disposition, and they be reported to be wide, lofty-spirited, constant in friendship to one another. . . . "

Thomas Morton, the merry trader of Merry Mount, Massachusetts, who probably knew the Indians of New England as intimately as any Englishman of his time, wrote of their festivals in the 1620s when "they exercise themselves in gaminge, and playing of juglinge trickes, and all manner of Revelles, which they are delighted in, that it is admirable to behould, what pastime they use, of severall kinds, every one striving to surpasse the other, after this manner they spend their time.... "

In the untouched Indian world, even among peoples of dreaded warlike reputation, there was a great deal more peace than war. War in the Old World definition was virtually unknown, and only approached by such highly organized states as those of the Aztecs and Incas. There is very little indication of whole countries being overrun by war. A meeting between strangers was more likely to be peaceful, even open and hospitable, than warlike. The raids that were called wars usually involved only a fraction of the available fighting men and those only briefly. Utterly defeated nations were assimilated rather than annihilated.

All this was to change somewhat under European tutelage, but the point is that the life lived by these woodland people in their stockaded bark-built towns, while it had its sudden storms of terror and violence, was by no means one of constant strife.

It was a life filled with discomfort, excitement, pageantry, color, emotion, uneasiness anent gods, ghosts, and goblins. It was made up of play taken seriously, and duties stylized into solemnity. But above all it was pervaded with the magical sense of rightness that inevitably settles on people who have lived a very long time in a very old house, and in this respect was underlain by a certain serenity.

The nations inhabiting the Northeast at about the time of the first European landings were for the most part divided among three large language stocks: Algonquian, Iroquoian, and Siouan.

What had so long ago been the Old Copper country, from Lake Michigan to Lake Superior and environs, was now the Wild Rice country, where, on the countless lakes and northern marshes, under a sky alive with waterfowl, people thrust their canoes and rafts, harvesting the rice. Judging from the reports of early European explorers this region was teeming with a surprisingly heavy population, the most important groups being the Siouan Winnebago, in the region of Lake Winnebago and Green Bay; the Kickapoo, Sauk, Menominee, and Foxes west and north of them, the Ojibwa west and north beyond, on the shores of Lake Superior—all these people speaking Algonquian languages; and various towns of the Siouan Dakota in the Wisconsin woods stretching westward to the Mississippi.

The Ojibwa (the last syllable is pronounced "way"; the name refers to the peculiar puckered seam of their moccasins; Europeans garbled it into Chippeway and stuck to it so persistently

**Trade between the Swedes and Delawares is shown in the context of the wars and daily life of the Indians in this late-seventeenth-century sketch by Peter Lindestrom. While the English seized what land they wanted, the Swedes and Dutch usually purchased it, cementing peaceful relations with the tribes. Buying land also helped guard their claims against their more numerous European competitors.**

that many Ojibwas today call themselves Chippeways) made up one of the largest nations north of Mexico, with a wild-guess population of 25,000 or more. North of them an almost identical people known as the Cree controlled the enormous spruce-fir country that ran all the way up to Hudson Bay. At the eastern end of Lake Superior, at the present Sault Ste. Marie, the Ojibwa joined with the Ottawa and Potawatomi in a loose confederacy known to white traders as the Three Fires. In the traditions of all three of these tribes they were originally one, and that not too many centuries ago.

The Ohio Valley, which had been the heart of the Hopewell burial-mound culture some hundreds of years before, had apparently become surprisingly sparse in population since that time. The Miami confederacy of Indiana and environs (one of their villages was called Chicago, meaning "Skunk Place") and the perhaps somewhat more populous Illinois confederacy to their west were not large in numbers, at any rate in historic times. These people too were of Algonquian speech. The Erie to their east, below Lake Erie, spoke an Iroquoian dialect.

Shawnee towns were south of the Miami country (the name Shawnee means "Southerners") and extended to the hills of the Chickasaw and the Great Smoky Mountains of the Cherokee, with their traditional center in the Cumberland Valley in present Tennessee, but the Shawnee appear to have been nearly everywhere throughout the Middle West and Middle South at various times. They were very closely related, in language, style, and race, with the Sauk and Foxes, Kickapoo, and the other Algonquian peoples on the Atlantic coast.

A sizable area embracing parts of present Kentucky, southern Ohio, and West Virginia was so thinly settled that portions of it were regarded as practically uninhabited, a sort of no man's land, a hunting ground and battlefield open to all. At least such seems to have been the case at the moment of the first European look. Since this was for so long the very epicenter of the ancient, thriving, town-dotted Hopewell world, some small riddle seems to be afoot, beyond those mists of time that hang like fogs of a frosty Indian summer over the beautiful Ohio.

Tidewater Virginia and adjacent beaches and backwoods, scene of some of the earliest European exploration and settlement along the Atlantic coast, was the home of a union of Algonquian nations called the Powhatan (accent on last syllable)

Confederacy. The name means Falls of the River and was specifically applied to the falls of the James River (present Richmond). The "king" whose home village was located there was called by the English colonists after the name of his town, and is in our folklore King Powhatan. His real name was Wahunsonacock. In accordance with a widespread Indian usage his real name was as much his own discreet private property as is a move star's real name today; the evil-intentioned, by pronouncing one's real name, could gain a handhold on one's soul; thus one was more customarily addressed by a title, Brother, Uncle, Warrior—as we might say Senator or General—or by a nickname.

The giant Powhatan Confederacy numbered some 200 villages and included quite a few separate tribes, or little states, each ruled (so it seemed to the English) by a minor king. It appears that the patriarchal Powhatan, at least sixty years old when the English first met him, had constructed this confederacy almost from scratch during his own lifetime.

Early reports of several other confederacies indicate they were in the process of being created by conquest and diplomacy—or dying from dissension—at the instant of European arrival. Since archaeological evidence hints at previous confederacies throughout much of the long past, it might be assumed that the centuries had seen a slow but incessant rise and fall, alignment and realignment, of such unions large and small, and that the confederacy was the normal American pattern.

Some at least of the confederacy provinces paid tribute to Powhatan, but quite a bit of autonomy was apparently enjoyed. This or that village could and did separately make war on the English settlers while the confederacy was nominally at peace. William Strachey, Gent., First Secretary of the Colony of Virginia, speaking of a "weroancqua, or queene," of one of the confederacy's towns, says, "Howbeyt, her towne we burnt, and killed some of her people, herself miscarieng with small shott in pursuit in the woods in winter 1610, for a treacherous massacre which she practized upon fourteen of our men. . . . " Similar incidents are far from uncommon in the early history of the Virginia colony.

Howbeit, peaceful coexistence was the general rule during the ghastly early years of the Virginia colony, when the settlers died

**John White's drawing of the town of Secotan is one of the most complete representations of the daily life of sixteenth-century Indians on the Atlantic seaboard. Ceremonial fire, feasting, and dancing were sketched on the spot by White. This engraving by De Bry from White's watercolor first appeared in a 1590 volume on the "new found land of Virginia."**

in batches in the miasmic Jamestown swamps (of the first 900 colonists landed during the first three years, 1607 to 1610, only 150 were still alive in 1610), and old Powhatan could have stamped it out or left it to starve with the greatest of ease.

There was distrust and blundering on each side in this meeting of worlds so disparate, quarrels between Indians and the German, Irish, French, Polish, and English artisans and would-be gentry who made up the colonists, and there was deliberate trouble stirred up by the Spaniards to the south—Spanish embassies to the Powhatans in 1609 are blamed for Indian attacks on Jamestown in 1610, and might have been responsible for the treacherous massacre practiced by the above-mentioned "weroancqua." Other such Spanish embassies followed.

But peace, even though ill-policed, persisted. There were two immediate reasons for this: the directors of the joint-stock company in London that owned and operated the Virginia colony voted, as the most profitable and least expensive course, to conciliate Powhatan as an independent sovereign rather than make war upon him as a savage—and sent him a copper crown to wear; and Powhatan himself earnestly desired peace, with an eye on the benefits of English trade.

He said to Captain John Smith, so Captain John Smith reported: "Why should you take by force from us that which you can obtain by love? Why should you destroy us who have provided you with food?... I am not so simple as not to know that it is better to eat good meat, be well, and sleep quietly with my women and children, to laugh and be merry with the English, and being their friend, to have copper hatchets and whatever else I want.... "

No king, but a kingly figure... "such majesty as he expresseth," said Strachey, Powhatan kept the peace.

The first settlers sometimes obtained Indian help by force or cajolery, but also, wrote Captain John Smith: "It pleased God (in our extremity) to move the Indians to bring us Corne, ere it was halfe ripe, to refresh us, when we rather expected... they would destroy us.... "

Later, "the Indians brought us great store both of Corne and bread ready made.... " And later the colonists traded for corn, an inch square of copper for a bushel.

Still later, when the shoe was on the other foot and the colonists had corn to sell to some starving Indian villages near

Jamestown, the English governor traded 400 bushels for "a mortgage on their whole countries."

It was impossible, of course, for businessmen not to feel contempt for such people, and once again a conquest was completed, in effect, although the war was still to come.

Peace was badly strained during the troubles of 1609 and 1610, but tranquility of a sort was restored by the tyrannical governor Sir Thomas Dale (1611–1616), who saved the colony by working colonists under the lash, burning captured runaways at the stake, and kidnaping and holding as a hostage Powhatan's beloved daughter, Pocahontas.

Pocahontas (a nickname meaning something like "Frisky"—her real name was Matowaka) is the most famous woman in early American history, and justly so, judging by subsequent events. "Blessed Pocahontas, the great King's daughter of Virginia, oft saved my life," wrote Captain John Smith, never a man to mince sonorities; and apparently she oft saved the colony as well, being "much at our fort," and a great friend of the English, supplying their wants and filling their jars with corn. "She, under God, was the instrument to preserve this colony from death, famine, and utter confusion," testified Captain John Smith.

At the time of her kidnaping she was seventeen years old and married to a warrior named Kocoum of whom nothing more is heard, for she married the next year one of the leading men of the colony, John Rolfe. An acquaintance wrote that Rolfe married her "for the good of the plantation." If so, it worked. Powhatan was pleased, and real peace resulted.

More significantly, John Rolfe forthwith learned, presumably with Indian help, the cultivation of tobacco. He became the colony's first tobacco planter, and the colony had what it needed, a fortune-founding cash crop.

John Rolfe took his bride to London, where she was a sensation and met everyone from the queen to drunk Ben Jonson (who later mentioned her in a play), and where she died of smallpox at the age of twenty-one, leaving a son from whom a whole hallful of illustrious Virginians have since claimed extraction.

But it was tobacco that fathered Virginia, and affected in turn the broader future of the English elsewhere in America. It had an even profounder effect on the future of Powhatan's people.

It was not a king, nor Christianity, nor knighthood gone adventuring, that muscled the conquest of the Atlantic seaboard north of Florida. It was the joint-stock company. The joint-stock company was organized and operated simply for profit and nothing but profit, and recognized no other purpose, higher, lower, or in between. This attitude was the foundation of colonial Indian policy in non-Spanish North America.

Bows were made in the direction of patriotism and piety, but for the most part they were frankly cynical. Said Sir Ferdinando Gorges, arch-genius of early English colonization efforts: "What can be more pleasing to a generous nature than to be exercised in doing publique good... and what more pious than advancing of Christian Religion amongst People, who have not known the excellency thereof, but seeing works of Piety and publique good, are in this age rather commended by all, then acted by any; let us come a little near to that which all harken unto and that forsooth is profit."

The earliest ventures into Virginia, from Raleigh onward, envisioned profits from gold mines, peltries, a passage to India, or such commodities as sassafras, believed at the time to be a specific for syphilis. William Strachey, Gent., proposed that the Virginia Company get a monopoly on sassafras, hold it until the price sky-rocketed, and then sell to all Europe "thereof at good rates."

Tobacco offered the first genuine indications of a profit breakthrough. Tobacco, introduced in Europe in the 1500s, had become the rage of fashion to Englishmen of 1600. No devout Indian offering tobacco to the gods of the four directions could have equalled English eulogies bestowed on "This pretious herbe, TABACCO most diuine.... " "The sweete and sole delight of mortall men.... " —to quote some laudatory verses of 1602. Tobacco quickly became the Virginia colony's only export, and Sir Thomas Dale had to force the colonists to give their time and land to the planting of grain, since they could not eat money.

Not only did the potential profit call for constantly expanding acreage, but tobacco used up the soil, and new fields had to be found every two or three years. It was usually easier to take fields from the Indians than to clear new land: early in the life of the colony Captain John Smith succeeded, by herculean efforts, in having forty acres of land cleared, but when not long afterward the village of Kecoughtan at the mouth of the James River was seized and its inhabitants driven away, its cornfields (according to Secretary Strachey) were 2,000 to 3,000 acres. Even allowing for a tenfold exaggeration on the part of the Honorable Secretary, it wouldn't take a canny eye long to see in this the birth of a pattern. The Americans loved their homes but they loved their lives (to say nothing of their peace and quiet) more. They wept but they moved.

It was easy to believe, each time, that the Coat-wearing People (the commonest Algonquian term for Englishmen) would now have all the land they could possibly want—but if the Indian mind grasped only dimly the European notion of land title, it grasped not at all the European notion of great personal estates. The principal officers of the Virginia Company were to be put in possession of personal estates of no less than 1,500 acres each—more, if they owned extra "great shares," which brought the estates of some officers to 5,000 acres. Junior executives were granted 500-acre estates. The company created a 12,000-acre estate for itself. Promoters who guaranteed to send out certain numbers of settlers were given large tracts of land.

Land encroachment was not the only cause for conflict on this first Virginia frontier. Livestock introduced by the settlers damaged the unfenced Indian gardens, hogs being the worst offenders. But if you damaged the hog, the hog's owner would damage you, and if your friends damaged the hog's owner, the English would then burn an Indian town and put a dozen people to the sword (the second more common Algonquian name for Englishmen was "cutthroats"), and another little war was afire that took all old Powhatan's influence to smother.

Trading, theft, rowdyism, liquor, women, and attempts at taxation brought contentions, and as the English grew more numerous and bolder, and the inevitable felons, toughs, and whores were swept over from London streets to fill colonist quotas, contentions grew more common.

Nothing personal was involved, and it is a mistake to think of Indians and settlers as making two hard and fast opposing camps; the "old settlers" of the colony often had closer ties among the neighboring Pamunkeys oı Appomattocs or others of the Powhatan league than among the johnny-come-lately new settlers. What was involved was the inexorable trending of basic official policy. Founded purely on economic considerations, this policy conciliated the Powhatan people while they were of use, and pressed them remorselessly, facelessly, mechanically, as innocent of conscious ill will as a turning wheel, when they became of less value than their land.

Old Powhatan died in 1618 (the year after Pocahontas's death in England). Some time passed, during which the councilors of the Powhatan Confederacy may have fought out a behind the scenes battle between pro- and anti-English factions. The aged Opechancanough, a brother of Powhatan's and an implacable English-hater ever since the days of 1607 and 1608 when he and Captain John Smith had taken turns capturing each other, came out the winner.

In the spring of 1622 the Powhatans at last exploded under the English pressure in a savage flash that left nearly 350 colonists dead and a number of settlements destroyed in the space of a few hours.

The English population just before Powhatan's death had been at this same figure, 350, scattered in a half-dozen villages. But in the five years since, the number of colonists had quadrupled, while the Indians had suffered disastrously from pestilence. Opechancanough was four short winters late.

The surviving English swore to scourge the Powhatans from the face of the earth, and did succeed in practically exterminating those along the lower James and York Rivers. Three punitive expeditions a year were carried out, year after year, giving the Powhatans no chance to plant corn or rebuild destroyed towns. Men, women, and children were slain without quarter; the English captains were under oath to make no peace on any terms whatsoever. The heaviest Indian losses were achieved when numbers of them were slyly persuaded to return to their villages, under promises of peace, and were then trapped and massacred. The greatest single victory came in 1625, with the defeat of 1,000 Pamunkeys and the burning of their town.

The campaign continued for fourteen years, and ended in mutual exhaustion. During this time, King James had secured an annulment of the Virginia Company's charter (for reasons having to do with European politics), and Virginia had become a Crown colony, but the Indian policy established by the original joint-stock company remained substantially unchanged.

In 1641, after five years of peace, land-grab pressures again rose past the danger point, and Opechancanough, now in his nineties and so feeble he had to be carried in a litter, struck once more. Again, hundreds of English lives were lost in a single flaming day, in a carefully coordinated sneak attack that took the settlers completely by surprise. But for some reason never made clear, the Indian soldiers seemed to slack away and did not follow up their advantage; one guess has it that they might have been frightened by an omen.

Opechancanough was eventually captured and shot, and the war came to an end; and this time the Powhatan Confederacy came to an end with it. The English broke up the league, made peace separately with the various tribes and assigned them to reservations which were subsequently whittled down at the colony's pleasure, and—within less than forty years after Jamestown's founding—the once mighty Powhatans turned their faces toward the oblivion of beggary.

At the time of the American Revolution there may have been perhaps a thousand persons left of all the "three or fower and thirty provinces," most of them moved by then to the more thinly settled eastern shore of Chesapeake Bay, with only a very few tribal societies, notably the Pamunkey, Chickahominy, and Mattapony, still functioning.

A traveler wrote of late Colonial Virginia (1759): ". . . Indians and negroes . . . they scarcely consider as of the human species; so that it is almost impossible, in cases of violence, or even murder, committed on those unhappy people by any of the planters, to have the delinquents brought to justice. . . . "

With local variations, this is the story of most of the nations of the Atlantic seaboard from the Carolinas to New England during the period of early European colonization.

Unlike the Spanish attitude, there was little official English interest in the Indians as a labor force or as souls to be saved. Here, where plantation exports rather than mines or Indian trade became the infant colony's main road to profits, and where other European rivalry was not imminent enough to be a commanding factor, dealings with the Americans followed a fairly simple and generally uniform course: initial friendship and cooperation, followed by dismissal of the Indians, so to speak, when their help was no longer needed. This dismissal usually took the dramatic form of growing hostility, massacre, war, and eviction, but in essence it was, as previously described, merely a matter of business. It was uncomplicated by any of the soul-searching agonies that beset the Spanish conscience; there was exceedingly little self-criticism of the Las Casas genre.

There was no body of law designed to protect the Indians from exploitation or deliberate extermination. The governor and council (corresponding to president and board of directors) of the parent joint-stock company were answerable to no one for any action against Indians, up to and including enslavement or annihilation. There was, in the beginning, little control by central authority, and an almost total lack of home-government concern with Indian welfare.

Some of this was to undergo considerable modification after the colonies were taken over by the crown—which customarily happened as soon as the parent colonization company had gotten the colony firmly established and more or less able to stand on its feet. Indian policy was to remain for generations a major problem in colonial politics. But at heart it was to remain what the hardheaded company directors in their paneled council rooms in Europe's capitals had first made it, a matter of business, basically a problem of economic expediency.

A local variation in the Powhatan story was the meager use of Indian allies by the Virginia colonists, when war came. More commonly, Indian auxiliaries made up the bulk of the little European armies, as in Spanish America.

The initial interlude of peace could vary considerably. The Nanticoke people of Maryland were destroyed almost at once by the Maryland colonists. But the Delawares, the leading people of all the eastern Algonquians, remained pretty much at peace with Europeans for more than a century.

The great Delaware confederacy—made up of large divisions—occupied an extensive territory in New Jersey, eastern Pennsylvania, and vicinity. Hollanders of the Dutch West India Company and Swedish colonists sent out by the New Sweden Company were the first Europeans to establish themselves in the Delaware country—the Dutch came primarily as fur traders and the Swedes were never numerous; consequently their relations with the Delawares were generally peaceful. Both Dutch and Swedes bought Indian land, perhaps in order to legalize their occupancy in the eyes of other Europeans. The prevailing English usage (with rare exceptions) at the time of earliest colonization was simply to seize what was wanted, claiming English ownership of all North America by right of prior discovery—even the Indians, in this view, could only clear title to their lands by grant of the English king.

In 1749 Old Nils Gustafson, at that time ninety-one years of age and the son of one of the original Swedish settlers, related, "At the time when the Swedes arrived, they bought land at a very inconsiderable price. For a piece of baize, or a pot full of brandy, or the like, they could get a piece of ground, which at present would be worth more than four hundred pounds, Pennsylvania currency."

Old Nils also recalled walking with an Indian and meeting a red-spotted snake on the road; Nils got a stick to kill it but the Indian begged him to let it live "because he adored it. . . . " On hearing that it was the Indian's deity, Old Nils killed it "in the presence of the Indian, saying: because thou believest in it, I think myself obliged to kill it."

The Delaware tradition of peace with the foreigners was maintained after the appearance of the English Quaker colonists in 1681 and the treaty meetings with William Penn in June of 1683. The most famous Delaware leader at these meetings was the councilor Tamanend, of whom a missionary wrote more than a century later, repeating Delaware yarns: "He was an ancient Delaware chief, who never had his equal. He was in the highest degree endowed with wisdom, virtue, prudence, charity, affability, meekness, hospitality, in short with every good and noble qualification. . . . " The English spelled his name Tammany.

People of the Delaware confederacy inhabited Staten Island and Long Island (a Delaware subtribe called the Canarsie sold Brooklyn to the Dutch), but the present Manhattan, the Bronx, and Westchester were occupied by members of another Algonquian-speaking union, the Wappinger confederacy. These were relatives of the Delawares and also of the people of the Mahican confederacy (Mohicans, they were called, in J. Fenimore Cooper's time) who lived north of them up the Hudson River. One of the Wappinger groups, with its central town at the site of modern Yonkers, participated in the famous sale to the Dutch of a woodland island that is now the center of New York City. This was the Manhattan group (the name—Manhattes in its earliest Dutch spelling—probably had something to do

Van Nieuw Engelandt. 21

op matjens aen malkanderen gewrocht van biesen/sommige op bladeren van boomen/ dragen altijts al haer goet met haer/ datse hebben/ als eten en groenen Toback/ welck sterck is en goet om nemen; schijnt vriendelijck Volck te zijn / dan is seer genegen tot stelen/en subtiel om wegh te halen alles 't gene haer aenstaet. Op de hoogte van veertig graden en acht-en-veertigh minuten / alwaer de Wilde seer schoone Oesters aen sijn Schip brachten/ getuygt de voor-noemde Hudson van 't landt aldus: Is soo schoonen landt als men met voeten betreden magh / overvloedigh van allerhande houdt / om Schepen te bouwen/ en om groote vaten van te maken; 't Volck hadde daer koperen Toback pijpen/ waer uyt ick vermoede dat daer Koper moet zijn / als oock Yser naer der Wilden beduydinge/ dan sy en hebben geen wetenschap om 't selve te bereyden. De selve getuygt mede/dat sy op de Rievier allerhande Rievier-visch met de Segen vongen/ oock jonge Salm en Steur. Op de hoogte van twee-en-veertigh graden en achtien minuten was dito Hudson aen landt; Ick voer (seght hy) met een van haer Prauwen aen landt/ met een out Man die daer Overste was/ van veertigh Mans en seventien Vrouwen / die ick daer sagh; in een Huys van basten van Eycken-boomen wel ge=maeckt/ en rontom soo gelijck of 't een verwelft hadde geweest / was overvloedig van Maiz en Boonen vant voor-gaende Iaer/ en daer lagh by het Huys wel soo veel te dro=gen/ als dry Schepen mochten voeren/ sonder dat noch stondt en wies; by het Huys komende werden twee matjens gesprept om op te sitten / en terstont eenige gerichten voort gebracht/ in roode houte backen wel gemaeckt / en sonden terstont twee Man=nen uyt met bogen om Wildt te schieten/ brochten twee Duyven die sy wel haest ge=schoten hadden/ sloegen terstont oock eenen vetten Hont / en kregen het vel af metter

B 3 haest

This earliest known view of New Amsterdam, published in 1651, features fur-laden Indian canoes as well as trade and protective war vessels of the Dutch West India Company. Relations between the Dutch and the Indians were not always amicable: eighty Indian heads were once brought back after a massacre to New Amsterdam, where they were used as kickballs in the streets.

with *munnoh* or *manah*: "island"). The much-quoted price of $24 may be based on a questionable exchange rate: a modern economist has estimated the 60 gulden worth of trinkets would have been closer in buying power to several thousand dollars today.

The Dutch traded for furs with people of inland regions, notably the Iroquois; the coastal people had supported the first *swannekins* (Algonquian for Dutchmen) with gifts of food, but now, hanging around the vicinity of the colony at New Amsterdam, they were of no use and became a nuisance. Incidents occurred, and multiplied. The half-naked natives were indolent, insolent, and as thievish as monkeys, but when a farmer caught and killed one of the women who was stealing peaches, her relatives or friends wantonly slew the farmer, and the tribes refused to turn these murderers over to the Dutch authorities.

In 1643 (seventeen years after the purchase of Manhattan Island) the Dutch governor, according to some accounts not only exasperated but inebriated, ordered the massacre of a number of Wappinger people who had run to the Dutch for protection from raiding Mohawks. The Indian refugees were lulled by friendly Dutch treatment for several days, and then were attacked by the Dutch while they slept (in a village on the Jersey side of the Hudson), and eighty heads of men, women, and children were brought back to Manhattan, to Fort Amsterdam, where a New Amsterdam dowager played kickball with them in the street. A captive Hackensack Indian was publicly tortured, charged a contemporary pamphleteer, by being skinned in strips and fed with his own flesh while the "poor, naked, simple creature" stubbornly tried to keep up his death song, until at last, flayed from his fingers to his knees, castrated, dragged through the streets, but still alive, he was placed on a millstone and his head beaten off by the soldiers. The Dutch governor looked on throughout and "laughed right heartily."

In the war that followed, the Wappinger villagers were stamped out by hundreds, but even so only some 1,500 of their total population of (maybe) 5,000 had been liquidated at the end of the year. And the war was expensive. The Dutch governor requested permission from the Dutch West India Company to keep on until "the Indians who waged war on us should... be utterly destroyed and exterminated..." but the company directors were far from pleased by the "bloody exploit" of the massacre that opened the war and had no intention of authorizing complete extermination, "since it would necessitate so heavy an expenditure on so uncertain an event and so little appearance of profit."

A wall built across lower Manhattan in the course of this war gave its name to Wall Street.

The New England coastal area, roughly from New York to Boston, is regarded as having been the most densely populated section of eastern North America in aboriginal times. East of the Wappinger country, in Connecticut, were the Mohegan, a separate, eastern branch of the Hudson River (the same name, of course, through different ears; it meant "wolves"); above the Mohegan, in the region of Rhode Island, the Narraganset Indians made up the principal nation; above the Narraganset the Wampanoag; and above the Wampanoag the Massachuset. All these were Algonquian-speakers, and generally similar peoples.

Dutch traders had been active in the Hudson River area since 1610, and European deep-sea fishermen had been visiting the New England coast since the early 1500s. English traders had been appearing there at least since 1602. English shipmasters had been pausing here to pick up an occasional slave or guide, either by kidnaping or smooth speeches, at least since 1605, when five New England Indians were brought into Plymouth in England; one of them, named Tasquantum, was "seized upon" by Sir Ferdinando Gorges, then governor of Plymouth.

The Plymouth (joint-stock) Company was actively interested in the New England coast a few years later when they employed the redoubtable Captain John Smith to explore it for them; Captain John Smith, exploring his way along in 1614, renamed a Wampanoag village in honor of his employers—the Indian name of the town was Patuxet, the new name bestowed by Captain John Smith was Plymouth.

In the next year (1615) an English slaver, one Captain Thomas Hunt, kidnaped a Patuxet citizen reportedly named Tisquantum and sold him into slavery in Malaga, whence he escaped to England. In 1616, the year after Captain Hunt's visit, an epidemic, probably smallpox, broke out among the people of the New England coast "with such a mortall stroake," wrote an English trader, "that they died on heapes. . . . " It raged for three years. The Wampanoag and their nearest neighbors, the Massachuset, who lived just north of them in the region of modern Boston, seemed to be in the center of this long storm of sudden death.

The Massachuset were slashed in population, according to some estimates, from 10,000 to 1,000 persons.

In 1620 a band of English colonists, organized into an unchartered joint-stock company financed by a group of businessmen independent of the Plymouth Company, left England for the northern reaches of the territory assigned to the Virginia Company. The Virginia Colony's new tobacco prosperity had influenced the choice of a destination; Guiana in South America had also been considered. But the Virginia Company's northern territory was within the sphere of Dutch trade, and the master of the colonists' ship landed them still farther up the coast, "having been bribed by the Hollanders to carry them and land farther to the northward," according to later London gossip.

These colonists were the Pilgrim Fathers of the schoolbooks, a sect of religious revolutionaries, a grim and bitter people, enormously industrious, and as mercenary as purses.

They found the forest clearings of their new country bespangled by the scattered bones of plague victims, and the village of Captain John Smith's Plymouth, née Patuxet, was a ghost town, the population dead in the houses or fled from the plague in horror and despair. The colonists made the village and its fields their own, fields so handsomely cleared, said a delighted colonist later, there was "scarce a bush or bramble, or any cumbersome underwood to be seene in the more champion ground. . . ."

And behold, a solitary survivor of Patuxet's people appeared and spoke to them marvelously in English. It was, says orthodox history, the ex-slave Tisquantum, kidnaped by Captain Hunt in 1616. But Sir Ferdinando Gorges said that his Tasquantum, brought to Plymouth in 1605, "must be acknowledged the meanes under God of putting on foote, and giving life to all our Plantations. . . . "

Whoever he was, to the Pilgrims he became "a spetiall instrument sent of God for their good beyond their expectation," wrote the historian of the colony. "He directed them how to set their corne, wher to take fish, and to procure other comodities, and was also their pilott to bring them to unknowne places for their profit. . . . " The English shortened his name to Squanto, and until he died of an "Indean feavor" in 1622 he was of inestimable use to the struggling colony.

A local sachem, or chief, named Samoset, who had picked up a few words of English from (presumably) previous traders, was even more the colonists' salvation by introducing them to the noble Massasoit, grand sachem of the Wampanoags. (Massasoit, again, was only a title of address; the grand sachem's real name was Wasamegin, meaning "Yellow Feather.") The noble Massasoit and his equally noble councilors remained fast friends of the English, notwithstanding repeated English "usurpations," as a nineteenth-century authority put it, upon Wampanoag lands and liberties.

Seven years after the founding of Plymouth, a combine of the colony's leading men bought out the stock of their financial backers and formed a joint-stock company of their own. The considerable debt from this purchase was paid off in six years from the profits of trade, primarily Indian trade.

And more colonists came, under the auspices of still other joint-stock companies, to found settlements from Connecticut to Maine. The joint-stock company of Massachusetts Bay, formed by Anglican Puritans, brought over more than 17,000 settlers between 1629 and 1642. They were lured by such promotional literature as the Rev. William Morrell's verse description of New England, published in 1625: "The fruitfull and well watered earth doth glad all hearts... And yeelds an hundred fold for one...

*O happie Planter if you knew the height*
*Of Planters honours where ther's such delight...*

The churchly colonists exulted over the epidemic of 1616 to 1619 that had cleared so many heathen from the path of the Chosen People. "The Wonderful Preparation the Lord Christ by His Providence Wrought for His People's Abode in this Western World," wrote a Puritan chronicler, pointing out with particular satisfaction that the plague had swept away "chiefly young men and children, the very seeds of increase." Even Thomas Morton of Merry Mount, who had more affection for the Indians than for the Puritans, observed that in "this, the wondrous wisedome and love of God, is shewne, by sending to the place his Minister, to sweepe away... the Salvages.... "

But there were still enough seeds of increase left to be troublesome, as happie planters multiplied, trade moved inland, and the nations near the coast became of no benefit whatever. In 1636, sixteen years after the beginning of colonization, the Massachusetts Bay Puritans sent a force to smite the

Indian nation that had become the strongest in New England, a division of the Mohegan known as the Pequot ("destroyers"). The Massachusetts Bay Puritans massacred a village, and having thus declared war went back home. (The Seal of the Massachusetts Bay Colony was the figure of an Indian with a label at his mouth saying, "Come over and help us.")

The Pequot had attacked no English settlements. The excuse for the war was a resurrected murder charge dating from an affray with two dissolute Virginia traders that had occurred four years earlier, and had presumably long since been settled and forgotten. Will Wood said of the Pequots, two years before the opening of hostilities, "The *Pequants* be a stately warlike people, of whom I never heard any misdemeanour; but that they were just and equall in their dealings; not treacherous either to their Countrymen, or *English*. . . . " The war against them was begun on the flimsiest of pretexts and was rather clearly a matter of political and economic expediency.

During the time of first English settlement the Pequot were busy conquering their weaker Indian neighbors, and by the middle 1630s their great sachem, Sassacus, ruled over more than two dozen subchiefs and claimed most of Connecticut and Long Island. Being on the border between the Dutch and the English, Sassacus had played shifty politics with both, growing more and more arrogant and independent with everyone in sight as Pequot power increased.

The Pequot were not only of no benefit to the colonies—they were powerful enough to be a definite threat. But these are cold reasons, and it takes hot blood to go forth and kill: in this case blood was heated by religious lust, a moving emotional force in the New England colonies.

The English settlements in Connecticut and at Plymouth were dragged into the war by the precipitate action of the Massachusetts Puritans. A splinter party of Sassacus's own people had broken under a malevolent leader named Uncas, and become the Pequot's bitter enemies; this small group retained the name of Mohegan. They entered the fray on the English side with pleasure.

The strongest English allies, and perhaps decisive in the conflict, were the Narraganset, obtained through the intercession of Roger Williams, who the year before had been banished from Massachusetts for advocating the eccentric heresies of religious tolerance and Indian land rights. He had been given shelter by the noble Canonicus, chief of the Narraganset.

In June 1637 the English army (240 colonists; 1,000 Narragansets; 70 Mohegans) made a stealthy night attack on a stockaded Pequot town near the Mystic River in Connecticut, burned the town, and slaughtered its 600 inhabitants. Wrote the Plymouth governor: "It was a fearful sight to see them frying in the fire... and horrible was the stink and stench thereof. But the victory seemed a sweet sacrifice and they gave praise thereof to God...." The only other engagement of the war was the surrender of a crowd of Pequots trapped in a swamp; the adult male captives were killed, boys sold to the West Indies, women and girls parceled out among the colonists as slaves.

The Pequot nation was broken. Refugees fled in all directions. Survivors were put under tribute and placed under the sovereignty of their old enemy, Uncas, and so sweet was the savor of his revenge thereof that the colonies mercifully took them back out of his jurisdiction a few years later. Sassacus escaped to the Mohawks and begged sanctuary; they deliberated, and put him to death.

The year following this war the New England colonies, pursuing the idea of united action that had worked so well against the Pequot, began negotiations that led to the federation in 1643 of the United Colonies of New England, the first union of English settlements in America.

The Pequot defeat left the Narraganset the strongest nation in New England. Uncas, commanding only a handful of warriors in comparison with the Narraganset military potential, was nevertheless able to maintain an Indian balance of power by the threat of help from the English. He boiled with ambitious plots, and ceaselessly stirred up English suspicion against the Narraganset and Wampanoag. The usual hostile incidents accumulated. But peace, of a sort, was sustained for a generation.

It must be pointed out again that many individual settlers and Indians were not only peaceful neighbors but close friends. It was from these various Algonquian people of New England that nearly all the common Indian words in the English language originated: squaw, papoose, moccasin, wigwam, succotash, and many more. The settlers adopted New England Indian cookery from clambakes to baked beans. The Indians adopted European designs in beadwork. A Colonial dancing match, or play party, was called a "cantico," from a word of Algonquian root, and many a time Indians and

**This picture by Seth Eastman after an Indian original depicts Atotarho, the Medusa-headed Onondaga chief who became the first ruler of the Iroquois. His conversion to the Great Peace of the late 1570s made possible the confederacy of five Indian nations: the League of the Iroquois. A warrior—red-coated, perhaps in honor of the long English-Iroquois peace—hands Atotarho the staff of sovereignty.**

settlers cut a cantico together, as the phrase had it.

The period's friendliest view of Indians comes from trader Thomas Morton, who so scandalized the Puritans with the Maypole he put up at Merry Mount (and by outsmarting them in the beaver trade) that Captain Miles Standish found an excuse to arrest him, and who said, "It was my chance to be landed in the parts of New England [in 1622], where I found two sortes of people, the one Christians, the other Infidels, these I found most full of humanity, and more friendly than the other. . . . "

John Eliot studied the Algonquian languages with a captive from the Pequot War, and after thirty years of labor published the Bible "translated into the Indian language." He founded at Natick on the Charles River the first of his villages of "praying Indians," and by 1674 had four congregations totaling 2,000 persons, mostly, alas, from the weaker Indian towns located between the proud and pagan Narraganset, Wampanoag, and Mohegan. The missionizing Mayhew family remained in business as missionaries there for a consecutive 116 years. At Providence (where church and state were impiously kept separate) Roger Williams continued to agitate for Indian land rights so successfully that purchase of Indian lands, on the Dutch model, gradually became accepted practice up and down the coast in the English colonies.

But the New England settlements grew in strength and property. The weighty, propertied men at the direction of affairs waxed inexorably weightier. The wheel of basic policy inexorably turned, to complete its inevitable full circle.

The noble Narraganset Canonicus, whose help had saved impetuous Massachusetts from disaster in the Pequot War, died in 1647, very old. The noble Wampanoag Massasoit, who had succoured Plymouth Colony in its first years, died in 1662. The proprietors of Plymouth Colony then began a campaign to place the Wampanoag under outright subjugation. Threatened by war if he refused, Massasoit's son Metacom, known to the English as King Philip, at last bowed to the yoke and acknowledged himself under Plymouth's rule, committing his nation to pay £100 a year tribute. This was in 1671.

Probably war was a certainty from this moment on, Philip very likely having only submitted to gain time. But English pressure increased, regardless. The drum blows of hostile incidents came at a faster tempo.

When war burst out, in 1675, the mighty Narraganset (helped by Massachusetts' high-handed bungling) threw in with Philip, as did nearly all the lesser tribes nearby. Uncas, delighted at the prospective ruin of his last American rivals, brought 500 Mohegan gunmen and bowmen in on the English side. The Praying Indians remained loyal to their missionaries—although they had to be moved to Boston for protection from the inflamed populace, after the war got rolling.

For it was the most devastating war New England has ever experienced, before or since, ancient or modern. Philip had been underrated. The Indians had not yet learned proper battle tactics, but they were better armed with muskets than had been expected, and they had made some progress in learning how to do their own gunsmithing—Indian forges in the forests became prime military objectives for the English. (And some Indian war chiefs were resplendent in English armor.) In matters of larger strategy Philip revealed another unexpected talent. Clearly the Wampanoag and Narraganset believed they could win. Their remarkable courage—apparently born of optimism as much as desperation—is mentioned as a prominent factor, in contemporary accounts.

The value of Mohegan and Praying Indians as English scouts and spies is mentioned by some later historians as a prominent if not decisive factor in the ultimate English victory. Perhaps they romanticize. There were now more than 50,000 European colonists in New England. The total population of the Indian states allied against them could not have exceeded 20,000, and was probably much less. English superiority in basic military ability was unquestioned. King Philip's "genius" notwithstanding, the final issue could not be in doubt. That is easy to say now, of course, toting up statistics out of books, but those on the scene at the time, both red and white, were a little too busy wiping the sweat (and fear) out of their eyes to see how simple and clear it was all going to look in books, later on. In the first few months of the war the outcome appears to have been felt in real doubt.

As before, the Puritans distinguished themselves by wholesale massacres of noncombatants that could scarcely be credited if not for the fact that it is the Puritans themselves who record them, with relish; and at each such instance Reverend

Increase Mather thundered rejoicing from his Boston pulpit. The people needed no blood-warming this time, with fifty-two of New England's ninety towns attacked, twelve or thirteen utterly destroyed and others heavily damaged, and 600 men—"the flower and strength of the country"—killed. But it was warmed again anyway by the divine leaders of the New England theocracies, who repeatedly proved by Biblical interpretations that it was the sacred duty of the Christian English to root out the godless Canaanites. Deliberate extermination of the independent Indian nations, discussed in Massachusetts ever since the Pequot War, was now to be carried out.

Canonchet, a Narraganset sachem, great-nephew of the noble Canonicus and Philip's most famous field general, was trapped by the English after six months of war and executed, technically by the Indian allies of the English although the technique employed, drawing and quartering, hath an English smack. Philip's wife and nine-year-old son were captured in the summer of 1676, at which Philip is reported to have cried out, "My heart breaks; now I am ready to die. . . . " while the Rev. Increase Mather said with gusto, "It must be bitter as death for him to lose his wife and only son, for the Indians are marvellously fond and affectionate towards their children."

In August 1676, Philip himself was killed, in the decisive battle of the war. The confederacy was shattered. Survivors, as usual, fled or were hunted down. Hundreds were sold as slaves, 500 being shipped from Plymouth alone.

Philip's wife and son, held prisoners in Plymouth, where Philip's head was exposed on a pole (along with others of the slain enemy, men and women), became the subject of high deliberations as the clergy decided their fate.

The Rev. John Cotton of Plymouth and the Rev. Samuel Arnold of Marshfield quoted Deuteronomy 24, 16 as authority for sparing the boy's life but the "scripture instances of *Saul, Achan, Haman,* the children of whom were cut off, by the sword of Justice for the transgressions of their parents," as deciding their vote for death to the child of him who had dared to attack the "whole nation, yea the whole Israel of God." The Rev. Increase Mather of Boston also voted for death, quoting the instance of "Hadad, who was a little child when his father (the chief sachem of the Edomites) was killed by Joab; and, had not others fled away with him, I am apt to think, that David would have taken a course, that Hadad should never have proved a scourge to the next generation. . . . " The Rev. James Keith of Bridgewater urged milder treatment, writing, "I know there is some difficulty in that Psalm, 137, 8, 9. . . . " but, "That law, Deut. 24, 16, compared with the commended example of Amasias, 2 Chron. 25,4, doth sway much with me. . . . " Mildness prevailed, and Philip's wife and the grandson of the noble Massasoit were sold as slaves to the West Indies.

Northward from New England, northward through the unbroken Maine woods, there lived other Algonquian peoples. Still others dwelt farther north, north as far as corn could grow and farther still, all the way to the freezing black spruce forests and the treeless sub-Arctic plains encircling Hudson Bay.

From the Abnaki of Maine through the Micmac of Nova Scotia and the Montagnais and Naskapi of Quebec and Labrador, hunger was increasingly a part of life and legend, in direct proportion as farming dwindled and hunting became the only gainful occupation. Even in a country teeming, as the saying goes, with game, the chase is bound to be a shaky provider, there being nothing stable about a supply of wild meat.

But through fat times and lean, snows and spring, meat had to be brought in. Inevitably there were strings of empty-handed days. Then starving times, always waiting, the veritable wendigo, the real embodiment of the mythical monster of the north woods, moving in to creep among the lodges. Especially at the end of the long winters there were weeks when the woods seemed to grow magically still and all game vanished, and the world sank into the semblance of death that preceded the first stirrings of spring. Famished people ate broth made of smoke, snow, and buckskin, and the rash of pellagra appeared like tattooed flowers on their emaciated bodies—the roses of starvation, in a French physician's description; and those who starved died covered with roses.

Naskapi and Montagnais are umbrella-names for a considerable number of related groups that roamed over their immense northern territory. The Micmac, remote in the Nova Scotia land's end country that sticks out like a thumb into the Atlantic, spoke an Algonquian dialect only remotely related to the Algonquian languages of their neighbors; some geographers have speculated that they may have been descendants of very early arrivals in the Americas, gradually pushed to the outermost

**Gustavus Hesselius painted this portrait of Lapowinsa, the Delaware chief who signed the Walking Purchase treaty in 1686. In this treaty, the Indians relinquished all the land between the Delaware and Lehigh rivers that could be traversed in a white man's leisurely day-and-a-half stroll. When the agreement was revised in 1737, the authorities used their fleetest runner and covered some sixty miles.**

fringes of the continent. Although not quite the last outermost fringe—the little-known Beothuk, a timid, primitive people who painted their unusually white skins red with ochre, were still beyond, on the island of Newfoundland.

The Abnaki of Maine were rather close kin, in language, with the Algonquian peoples hundreds of miles to the west, around the Great Lakes; the names Abnaki, Wampanoag, Wappinger, all stem from Algonquian words meaning "easterners."

But between the Algonquian-speaking nations of the Atlantic coast and those of the Great Lakes there stretched another world, the world of the Iroquois.

On archaeological evidence, Iroquoian people had lived in the region of the lower Great Lakes for at least two or three centuries before the time of Columbus. Their ancestors may have come up from the south, to mingle with mound-building populations in the areas of present New York and Pennsylvania.

During, perhaps, the century after the time of Columbus, five Iroquois nations inhabiting all of central New York, from the Genesee River to Lake Champlain, organized a confederacy. They were, reading from west to east, the Seneca, Cayuga, Onondaga, Oneida, and Mohawk. In the customary frame of reference, these five nations are regarded as the Iroquois proper. Other Iroquois nations and confederacies north, west, and south of them are usually fobbed off with the qualificative Iroquoian. The confederacy formed by these five New York nations was the far-famed League of the Iroquois.

North of the Five Nations were the Hurons, a populous confederacy made up of four aristocratic tribes, richest in tradition and ceremony of all the Iroquoian people, and a number of dependent tribal groups, one of these an Algonquian community.

West of the Five Nations were the Iroquoian state that came to be known as the Tobacco nation and the Iroquoian confederacy that came to be known as the Neutrals.

Southwest of the Five Nations were the Erie, also known as the Cat nation, from the meaning of their full name in Iroquois: "People of the Panther."

South of the Five Nations, in central Pennsylvania and adjacent regions, were the Susquehanna, also known as the Conestoga.

The Five Nations Iroquois were traditionally hostile toward most of these surrounding Iroquoian peoples, according to early reports. They were also traditionally hostile to surrounding Algonquian peoples. According to legend, the Five Nations were traditionally hostile even to each other before the founding of their League.

Legend says the League was organized by the saintly statesman Deganawidah (son of a virgin mother), assisted by the great and noble councilor Hiawatha, a Mohawk, to put an end to broils and wars between the Five Nations and to establish a universal peace based on harmony, justice, and a government of law.

From the earliest days of contact with Europeans, the various Iroquoian peoples were subjects of superlatives. Said Captain John Smith in speaking of the Susquehanna: "Such great and well-proportioned men are seldom seen.... "

Numerous French writers remarked on the exceptionally fine minds of the Huron. Other reports speak of the superior farms of Iroquoian people, the miles of fields of corn and beans and squash, and of their well-built multifamily "longhouses" and their log forts (their "castles" as the English called them)—and still other reports emphasize the dirt, the dogs, and the eternal racket of laughter, horseplay, and constant multifamily chatter.

But for the Five Nations the choicest superlatives, in early accounts, are reserved for their ferocity; and of the Five Nations the Mohawk in this repute led all the rest (the name "Mohawk" came from an Algonquian term meaning "man-eaters"). One reason the Mohawk in this repute led all the rest was their geographical location: the most easterly of the Five Nations, they were the nearest to the frontiers of the first European colonies, and so better known to the first European reporters. Some early records refer to all the Five Nations Iroquois indiscriminately as Mohawk, thus giving the Mohawk credit for all the rip-roaring deeds of the whole confederacy.

Iroquois cruelty in torturing captives was notorious. In general tales of Iroquois cruelty were told simply to raise the listener's hair, and any underlying religious significance, if present, was not mentioned.

One account speaks of prisoners being hamstrung, cords drawn through slits gashed at the tendons of their heels, and thus roped together being forced to march over the lovely countryside to the town of their captors, there to be burned alive.

As among the people of the Southeast, a captive was supposed to continue singing his defiant death song while the jubilant, screaming women and children burned him with torches, gouged out bits of his flesh with jagged pieces of seashell, or while a warrior tore off his scalp and poured red-hot coals over his bleeding skull, all this cunningly managed so as to delay as long as possible the moment when the last glint of life, like a melting snowflake, died from the body.

Maybe Iroquois torture was a trifle too notorious, considering that most of their neighbors indulged in similar delights. Also considering that the Iroquois were particularly noted for adopting captives into their nations, to the point that at various periods naturalized Iroquois may even have outnumbered the native-born, it seems reasonable that such wholesale adoptions must have cut into the torture supply.

In later accounts and subsequent history superlatives have been lavished on another aspect of the Five Nations Iroquois—their political sophistication. The League of the Iroquois is usually said to have been the best organized of any of the many confederacies north of Mexico.

It was operated by a council of fifty, made up of the ruling councilors of each of the Five Nations. These sachems were chosen from specific families by the mothers of their clans (groups of related women and their families), and were appointed for life—although the matriarch of his clan could have a sachem deposed if he turned out to be a bad choice.

A second class of sachems existed, known as "the solitary pine trees," to which anyone could aspire by merit, rather than birth. These Pine Tree chiefs had the right to speak in council and made up a house of representatives, so to speak, as against the senate of the hereditary chiefs. The usual road to Pine Tree honor was, as might be expected, via fame in war.

Each of the Five Nations was left alone in its own domestic affairs, but theoretically they were to act together in matters international. They seldom did. Individual nations, or even factions within the individual nations, went their own jolly way again and again in making peace or war—except when it came to fighting each other. The League, or the Great Peace as its founders called it, did keep the peace among its members.

No doubt it was also of value as a shadowy bugaboo for use in power diplomacy—My tongue speaks for all the Iroquois, said the Mohawk ambassadors, when they did not even have authorization to speak with finality for their own nation.

One other value that perhaps should not be minimized was the spiritual sense of union. However often the League may have proved a fiction in actual political practice, it was a reality in the minds of the honored old men who composed the council, and doubtless in the mind of the general nonpolitical public.

The great council of the League held each summer at the principal Onondaga town (the Onondaga also furnished fourteen of the fifty councilors, and the council's presiding officer) was an impressive show that could not have helped but instill this sort of feeling, as it continued year after year, generation after generation.

A pooling of the religious power of the Five Nations—cooperation in prayer as well as in war—had been one of the main objectives of the League's founders. This objective was never achieved either. But to some degree the magic of friendship was established, the emotional (even if unsound) conviction that come what may one's country did not stand alone, that all the way from the Seneca to the Mohawk the west wind streamed over a forest of brothers.

# VII

# The Anvil of America

**This study of Joseph Brant by Wilhelm von M. Berczy is believed to be a realistic likeness of the brilliant Mohawk leader.**

The performance record of the Great League notwithstanding, the Five Nations Iroquois wrote a crucial chapter in the story of colonial North America. This came about in the following way.

North of Maine the first European colonies were French, and their reason for being was fur, primarily beaver. By 1608 when the first permanent colony, Quebec, was founded, French fur traders had already been active around the Gulf and the lower St. Lawrence for seventy years or more. Fur, primarily beaver, remained the grand preoccupation of the French in Canada.

Furs were obtained by trade with the Indians. French fur traders courted the Indians with whom they did business; they were partners. The Indian nations were essential to the enterprise. The Indians wanted the wonderful kettles and hatchets of the foreigners, but the French wanted even more the help and good will of the Indians, their woodland skills, their knowledge of winter snowshoe traveling, their birch-bark canoes (up to forty feet in length) and the paddlers to man them, their familiarity with the river-and-lake waterways to still more treasures of fur, and above all the French wanted to maintain in working condition the tribal channels of trade.

Where the English plantation colonies destroyed, as soon as possible, the Indian cocoon around them, the French supported and sustained the Indian world in which they found themselves, for out of that world came fur. Thus the Indians here were strengthened and enriched by white contact.

The first fur-trading partners of the French were the Huron and the Algonquian people of the lower St. Lawrence, principally the Montagnais and the numerous bands next above them on the river who were known collectively as the Algonquian proper—one of these bands, the Algonkin, being the original bearers of the name later applied by anthropologists to an enormous stock of related languages and peoples.

The Hurons and Algonkins had been friends of the French for some time when in 1609 Samuel de Champlain, founder of Quebec and lieutenant of the owner of the French fur-trade monopoly, went with a Huron and Algonkin war party on a long journey to the lake now known as Champlain. There he won a battle for them, singlehanded, against a little army of their hated enemies, who had never before met firearms. The foe were bold in arrowproof body armor made of plaited sticks, but Champlain killed two of their three war captains and wounded the third, and the bold foe broke and ran. And the thunder and lightning of his arquebus echoed for 150 years. The bold foe had been Mohawk. The Five Nations Iroquois nursed a dogged animosity toward the French, with only a few interludes of real peace, from that time onward.

In 1614, five years after this little battle with big consequences, Dutch fur traders built a trading post up the Hudson, near the present location of Albany, on the doorstep of the Mohawk country. The Dutch were also primarily in the beaver business, eager to uphold and sustain the forest nations who might act as district jobbers for them. Within twenty years or so, Iroquois fur salesmen were procuring guns from Dutch, English, and French traders.

As spheres of trade expanded, a clear area of conflict came into being between French, Dutch, English, and Swedes. Likewise a clear area of conflict came into being between Indian nations stimulated and aggrandized by trade with Europeans, yet far enough from white settlements to remain reasonably independent.

The earliest frontier did not move with westering European settlement but with the aggressive expansion of Indian nations who were in business with Europeans.

There were, in effect, two frontiers: one strictly Indian, the other, following years behind, European. Out of the hurricane belt of that Indian-versus-Indian frontier came winds that affected and sometimes determined the course of American history.

The Five Nations Iroquois became the determining force of this Indian-versus-Indian frontier in the Northeast. Perhaps favored by their strategic location, they were no colony's creature. They were from the beginning their own masters. They traded, when all the magnificent oratory of the councils was done, with whoever offered the best deal, all things considered. All the things considered made for a bewildering tangle of loyalties, emotions, and motives, as does any political action. But no European business partner could be confident of calling the tune, either for any of the separate Five Nations, who so often went their separate ways, or for the broad policy of the confederacy as a whole.

During the first half of the seventeenth century the Five Nations, singly or otherwise, were sometimes at war, sometimes at peace with the French and the "French Indians" to the north: Montagnais, Algonkin, Hurons, and the long-established river traders westward of the Hurons known as the Ottawa (from an Algonquian word meaning "he buys"—evidently the Ottawa were professional traders even in pre-European times).

There were several Iroquois attempts in this period to form a coalition with the powerful and populous Hurons. Their failure may not have been due to Mohawk and Seneca resistance among the Iroquois, and French machinations among the Hurons to keep them at odds with the Five Nations, but these things at least played a part.

The Hurons funneled through to New France whole canoe-flotilla loads of pelts taken in trade from the enormous country north and east of the Lakes, a limitless country sparkling with streams and beautiful with beaver. The French felt they had the Hurons, and this trade, in their pocket. They feared to lose them to the more independent Five Nations.

The Hurons had accepted missionaries, who from the times of Champlain had acted as the governor's agents in stirring up anti-Iroquois sentiment when needed. The Hurons themselves being an Iroquoian people, the priests distinguished between them and the Five Nations by calling the Hurons the "good Iroquois." Letters of missionaries published in France were loaded with extravagant praise of the Hurons (for all that the name Hurons, bestowed by the French, was an old French word with a meaning similar to "slobs"), and a continuous propaganda barrage against the Iroquois.

In the summer of 1639, the Hurons captured and burned a total of 113 Iroquois, some from roaming war parties, some casual Iroquois travelers. Nevertheless, the Hurons remained to the French the good Iroquois, while the Five Nations were those demons, those tigers, those wolves. When in the 1630s repeated epidemics swept over the Hurons, reducing their population from an estimated 30,000 to an estimated 10,000, French administrators, writing home for more money, sometimes forgetfully attributed these plague losses to battle deaths at the hands of the bad Iroquois. Some twenty years after this, a French governor mentioned, "It was politic to exaggerate more than ever the cruelties of the Iroquois," revealing more by the qualifying phrase than by the statement.

Spheres of power swelled. Guns became more common. Cardinal Richelieu's joint-stock company, which had taken over (and kept until 1645) the French fur-trade monopoly, permitted trade in guns to Christian Indians and there were thousands of baptized Hurons who could have qualified, but the French monopoly policy, with its attendant high prices, may have made them too dear a luxury. The traditional view has it that the Hurons were not so well armed as the Iroquois, who were made the possessors of some 400 muskets by information as of 1643. But the tensions rising on the Iroquois-Huron frontier seem to have come from equally aggressive pressure on each side.

In 1648 Mohawk and Seneca war parties deliberately broke a truce with the Hurons that had been made in the name of the League—their reasons for doing so are unfathomable, but may have had to do with intra-League politics. At this point Skandawati, statesmanlike Onondaga councilor who had pledged his word to the truce, invoked the ultimate diplomatic protest of killing himself. To no purpose. In the dead of the following winter, in March 1649, an overwhelming army of no fewer than 1,000 Mohawk and Seneca warriors suddenly invaded the heart of the Huron country in the area of Lake Simcoe and Georgian Bay, north of modern Toronto. Most of these troops are said to have wintered in Huron country, living off the snow-drifted land, without the Hurons suspecting their presence, while the massive strike was being prepared.

In two days of fighting they took and burned two Huron towns, were repulsed from a third, and vanished with many captives and much loot. The Huron losses could not have been ruinous; their casualties were perhaps 300 warriors killed as against 200 of the enemy. But panic followed. With no thought of provisions or shelter, the Huron people fled from their towns. Before the long northern winter ended, many had died from starvation and exposure. Survivors kept on fleeing, literally, for years. In those two days of invasion the mighty Huron confederacy, outnumbering the Five Nations in population by perhaps three to one, had been smashed. The ancient desultory war that had gone on so long between the Hurons and the Five Nations

Iroquois, those evil people (as the Hurons described them) all armed even to their fingers' ends, was over.

Some Huron refugees went to join their conquerors, occupying a town to themselves among the Seneca, and identifiable Huron groups turned up among the Mohawk and Onondaga tribes. Others emigrated to the Iroquoian nations of the tobacco-growing people, the Neutral people, or the Erie. Others scattered to the four winds, sometimes calling themselves by what had been their own name for their confederacy—Wendat (the name became Wyandot in white literature).

The sense of utter defeat when there had been no defeat, the nightmare demoralization that so suddenly destroyed the Huron confederacy, is inexplicable. Maybe it was the roll of thunder in the air, for from now on the Iroquois frontier was alive with lightning. Neighbors of the Hurons were thrown into panic, and the Iroquois interpreted their panic as hostility and anti-Iroquois agitation, as no doubt it sometimes was.

The Tobacco people living at the western door of the Huron country were blasted by the Iroquois thunderbolt in December of 1649. These people appear to have been Hurons in everything but name, and were famous for cultivating, besides tobacco, immense fields of corn and large quantities of hemp, used for making fish nets. They seem to have been a larger nation, in population, than all the Five Nations put together. Each of the opponents the Iroquois demolished, one after the other, was a Goliath in size compared to the Five Nations, whose combined population at this time probably did not exceed 12,000.

The next great Iroquoian confederacy to the southwest of the Hurons, called the Neutral confederacy by the French because of its neutrality in Iroquois-Huron troubles, was broken by the Iroquois in 1651, with mopping up continuing for several years more.

The next people to the south, the People of the Panther, the Erie, another powerful Iroquoian nation, struck first at the Five Nations in 1653. An Iroquois counteroffensive the following summer won a desperate battle in taking by storm an important Erie town located near the present Erie, Pennsylvania.

Here 3,000 to 4,000 Erie warriors were defeated by an army of 1,800 Iroquois in a victory that should have won the war on the spot, but this time the enemy re-formed and fought back again and again, and two more years of fighting were required

**Catherine Tekakwitha, a Mohawk girl converted by Jesuits, was persecuted by her people because of her new faith. Later, as the first Indian nun among the Iroquois, she was called the Lily of the Mohawks. In 1681, a year after her death, Father Claude Chauchetière painted this portrait of her.**

before the Erie, too, were finally vanquished.

One of the temporary Iroquois-French friendship pacts was in effect during the Erie war; a couple of the Iroquois war chiefs even wore French uniforms, and a French Jesuit mission was attempted, very briefly, among the Five Nations. This peace ended in war and in 1666 the French made a full-scale, organized military invasion of the Iroquois country, burning towns and cutting a swath of devastation that should have been enough to destroy any nation. The Iroquois, furthermore, were in a disastrously weakened condition. There had been too much war. The Iroquois were bled white by war. In the expert opinion of the Jesuits the native-born Iroquois were by now reduced to a minority in their own towns, outnumbered by the immigrants they had adopted. They were still further reduced by a death-dealing epidemic in the 1660s. But they made their enforced peace with the French, and somehow the Great League still stayed on its feet.

It faced continual wolf-pack attacks from remnants of the shattered nations to the north and west, and now a new major threat appeared from a new direction: from the south. The Susquehanna, armed with the best guns and tall from easy conquests among their unarmed eastern neighbors, the Delawares, gave a humiliating beating to the Seneca and Cayuga and very obviously prepared to sweep the Five Nations from the face of the earth.

Something intervened—perhaps fate, perhaps Tahiawagi, Holder of the Heavens, the Iroquois national deity. The Susquehanna lost staggering percentages of their people in a sudden epidemic. Europeans along the borders of the Maryland and Virginia settlements took the opportunity to attack the crippled nation—in contravention of the policy of their colonial governors, who valued the Susquehanna as a frontier buffer.

The Five Nations Iroquois destroyed or dispersed or took over whatever remained of the Susquehanna without even the necessity of a major battle. This took place in the middle 1670s.

And with this their Indian-versus-Indian wars, the big ones at any rate, ended, and the Iroquois were king of the hill. From their worn-down low point of the 1660s they bounced back with astonishing rapidity, strong with immigrant blood: some twenty immigrant tribes were represented among the Onondaga alone, including a little colony of French residents who had chosen to become demons and wolves.

In the paramount area of conflict between rival European invaders the Great League now stood alone, the ruling power, holding the key to the entire interior of the continent.

During the 1680s and the 1690s the French, with Indian allies, smashed again and again at this Iroquois barrier, sending invasions that again and again should have broken forever the confederacy of the Five Nations, but did not. Iroquois crops and towns were laid waste but the Iroquois state remained, frequently still capable of delivering heavy reprisals. ("Men make a state," Thucydides wrote, "not walls nor empty ships.")

The Tree of Peace (as the Iroquois orators like to refer to their Great League) remained unshaken.

It was from this point on that the League really began to function as a more or less unified force. At no time in the thirty years of great wars had the Five Nations all worked together. But now, it seems, they began to realize the strength of their position and made the most of it.

Swedes and Dutch were gone, as official entrants among the European invaders; English and French remained. The Iroquois learned to play them off, one against the other, with a certain amount of artistry.

They could never be true friends of the French. "Between us and them there is no more good faith than between the most ferocious animals," said an astute French administrator. At bottom, Iroquois sympathies were with the English, as they had been previously with the Dutch.

But they fashioned a broad policy of independent neutrality that kept the balance of power in their hands for nearly a century.

We are born free," a French governor was told in 1684 by La Grande Gueule ("Big Mouth"), renowned Onondaga orator. And he spelled out what he meant: the Iroquois would go where they wished, allow passage through their country only to "those who seem to us good," buy and sell with whom they pleased. They wore no muzzle, neither French nor English. The French governor retired to his tent to rage and curse (so a witness reported), and a long line of French and English empire builders raged and cursed, threatened, wheedled, conspired.

The Iroquois, those "subtle, adroit, and arrant knaves" (in the accolade of a French Jesuit), remained blandly independent and in command.

Their country lay athwart the one good water-level route to the interior (as a modern railroad advertises) and was a centrally located gun turret that could cover the St. Lawrence and Ottawa River trade routes, the lower Great Lakes, the Ohio country, and the wilderness thresholds of New York, Pennsylvania, Maryland, and Virginia. In every plot and plan of French or English expansion, in every scheme to penetrate the interior or secure the alliance of the interior tribes, in every move of intricate fur-trade politics, the position the Iroquois would take had to be considered, often as the problem of foremost importance.

There was no help for it. Neither side could afford to let the other take possession of the Iroquois and their country, highroad to the center of the continent. Neither side could afford to let the other become the Iroquois' one and only friend.

And so the latest decisions from the council of the Great League of the Iroquois became matters of moment to the busy strategists of St. James's and Versailles. A French frontiersman was elevated to the peerage for his valuable work as interpreter to the Iroquois. Thirty-six Iroquois councilors, seized during a wartime parley and sent in chains to the galleys of Marseilles, as a means of cutting their arrogance down to size, were apologetically freed, dusted off, and returned in state to the dignity of their senatorial mats. In even more state, four Iroquois councilors were escorted to London to visit the Queen—Queen Anne, this was, in 1710, and they were showered with gracious attentions and official favors, for, it was said, they were about to sign an important treaty with their friends, the English. The governor of New York, at about this same time, spoke glowingly of the Iroquois as the "bulwark between us and the French." The New York Indian commissioners at Albany reported that the Iroquois held "the balance of the continent of North America," and a French missionary in Canada recorded the same thing in almost the same words. The secretary of the Pennsylvania colony wrote to William Penn, "If we lose the Iroquois we are gone."

Colonial delegates from New York, Massachusetts, Virginia, Maryland, Pennsylvania, and the Carolinas traveled to Albany to meet with the Iroquois. The Iroquois themselves are said to have urged the concerted participation in these assemblies, expressing wonder that the colonies did not meet together over common interests, as did the Five Nations. Such irregular meetings had gone on for seventy years when, in 1754, the first great intercolonial conference (outside New England) was held to work out a design of colonial union; it took place, as a matter of course, at Albany.

The Tuscarora, driven from North Carolina in the years following 1712, were an Iroquoian people: "They were of us and went from us long ago, and now are returned..." said the Five Nations, who gave them land for a new home, and made a place for them in the council of the Great League. Thereafter, the Five Nations were the Six Nations. The event caused concern among the colonies, for fear that it would embroil the Iroquois in southern Indian troubles. To prevent this, the governors of Virginia and Pennsylvania together with Indian ambassadors from the South went to Albany in 1722 and persuaded the Six Nations to agree to a dividing line between North and South. The line was laid down from the high ridge of the Alleghenies to the Potomac—forty-five years before the portentous Mason and Dixon survey to establish a Pennsylvania-Maryland boundary in the same area.

Iroquois power and glory during the eighteenth century reached the highest point attained (so far as history knows) by any Indian nation north of Mexico. An English chronicler writing in 1727 draws a picture of an Iroquois tribute collector at an Algonquian village on the New England coast ("An old Mohawk sachem, in a poor blanket and dirty shirt... issuing his orders with as arbitrary an authority as a Roman dictator") that calls up Aztec memories. Although the impressive old Iroquois councilors, sincerely respected by the generations of Europeans who dealt with them, had no magnificence to display other than their simple presence: "The chiefs are generally the poorest among them," wrote a Dutch pastor at Albany in the 1640s, "for instead of their receiving from the common people... they are obliged to give."

For the people in general, there was prosperity: calico dresses and hickory shirts, log houses with fireplaces, barns filled with farm produce, extensive orchards. There were sometimes luxuries of such things as livestock and brandy from the French and English, and such things as sleek, all-white canoes from the northerly Indians of the birch-bark country (the usual Iroquois canoe was of elm bark, as clumsy as a boot).

Vainglorious young men could and did go forth on war parties, sometimes to very distant lands, and the gaudy round of ceremonies and councils continued as before, but the old days of incessant war, of furiously painted soldiers with high-roached scalp locks, receded into the past. The old, old men recited their deeds against the Erie or against the French, and taught the young men how to dream a proper death song; but why should the young men take them seriously? Sometimes the old men wept when they heard recited each year the rite of the Great League's founding: "You see the footmarks of our forefathers... all but perceptible is the smoke where they used to smoke the pipe together.... "

The union lived, triumphant. The hurricane belt had subsided to soft showers and golden days. But the disturbances of its years of storm had sent repercussions bounding across the lakes and forests of the wilderness as far as there were missionaries or traders to record them. There is no reason to suppose they did not roll on farther still, toppling ancient societies, uprooting peoples, tumbling together fugitives and invaders, littering the whole middle of the continent with wreckage left by the tumultuous winds of change.

Bands of Hurons and Ottawas straggled westward to the upper Mississippi, quarreled with the forest Sioux, and were driven back eastward. They joined with other Huron and Tobacco people calling themselves Wyandot, and with Algonquian groups from the eastern St. Lawrence who had adopted themselves into the loose nationality of the Ottawa; they joined and divided again and again. Some planted villages near the French trading posts of the far Lakes: Michilimackinac, Sault Ste. Marie, Detroit. More and more these dislocated peoples tended to coagulate around French forest forts or end-of-the-world French trading towns, little settlements that were Indian in everything but the language.

The aloof people known as the Foxes were an exception and fought off French foreigners, but the Ojibwa pushed them southward to settle with their brothers, the Sauk, in the rich, gorgeous country of lower Wisconsin. The Ojibwa, armed with trade guns, then began a 100-year war against the Sioux, eventually forcing them westward clear across the Mississippi and out into the plains of Minnesota and the Dakotas. The Cree of the northern forests, armed with trade guns and hunger for all the beaver country in the world, assaulted and dispersed the wandering people of the woods to the north and west of Hudson Bay.

The fierce Winnebago west of Lake Michigan were crushed by pestilence and by a war they provoked with the Illinois. The Illinois, Potawatomi, and Miami, jostled here and there below the Lakes, were subject to Iroquois onslaughts in the 1680s. For many years afterward displaced persons from the broken eastern nations drifted into the Miami and Illinois country, sometimes settling, sometimes gathering around the French posts that were springing up along the Mississippi, sometimes traveling away southward down the Warrior Trail, while displaced persons from the South moved past them traveling hopefully to the North.

The land was filled with Ishmaels. They transmitted their restlessness wherever they went; they brought strange ways with them and learned strange ways as they wandered. But they found new homes and settled among nations where they could live in brotherhood, and, in the words of a French observer, tried "to forget what was past for their own preservation."

East, south, and north of the Iroquois the turbulence of the Indian-versus-Indian frontier coincided with the frontiers of European settlement. French frontiers were directly affected by the Indian organization of the fur trade. But events and attitudes within the Indian world also had much to do with the subsequent movements of the English colonial frontiers.

The usual picture of land-hungry white settlers irresistibly pushing the Indians back, "clearing the Indians out," is naïvely oversimplified for any period, and basically wrong for the decisive years before 1800. That something is lacking in the picture is indicated at once by a comparison with Africa, where the same invading white races were propelled by the same impulses but where frontiers of colonial settlement remained virtually motionless for centuries.

In its early phases the progress of the North American frontier was at least as much a creation of Indian politics and attitudes as white pressures. Many forces within the Indian world operated on this far from inexorable advance, sometimes in such ob-

**Thomas Davies's watercolor, entitled *A View Near Point Levy Opposite Quebec*, typifies the everyday life of nomadic Indians living in the Northeast. Home to these hunters was a cluster of bark wigwams, preferably by a body of water and tended by women.**

vious ways as an Indian nation's encouraging white settlement in order to gain European support and auxiliaries, or storms among Indian states leaving a shattered borderland that invited occupation. It was no accident that the first frontiers of English settlement to move westward across the Alleghenies, in the mid-1700s, happened to move into the country south of the Ohio, centering in Kentucky, that was, as previously noted, uninhabited by any Indian nation.

The first tendrils of the white frontiers, Dutch *boschlopers*, English traders and "long hunters," French *coureurs de bois*, were directed from here to there not only via devious Indian trails but for devious Indian purposes. With rare, if any, exceptions no white frontier before 1800 was initiated in the face of opposition from an intact Indian nation being pushed back from it. The first frontiers in Virginia and New England, for example, were the original colonies; and their founding was not only tolerated by the Indian nations at hand but, as has been seen, given some Indian assistance. By the time Indian opposition developed, these frontiers were too strongly established to be dislodged.

For after the initial invited penetration, the story, as a rule, quickly changed. But in the subsequent destruction of such penetrated Indian nations, Indian politics continued to play a large part, both for the whites and for the Indians allied (for reasons of their own) with the whites.

The white frontiers moved where these factors existed. White population pressure was a minor force in determining their direction or first setting them in motion.

But once begun in any area, the seepage of settlement over the border into Indian country became a clamorous factor all its own, unimportant at first but ultimately to become the most explosive ingredient of all, both for the Indian and white worlds.

Most often these frontier outposts were settled by newly arrived immigrants from Europe too poor to afford a place within the recognized boundaries of the colony. The frontier was the low-rent district, the slums of colonial days. From the beginning the frontier also attracted outlaws, runaways, malcontents, freethinkers, and other such undesirables.

The border jumpers brought trouble with them, and the region into which they intruded was frequently a troubled, unstable sector of the Indian world to begin with. When they and their troubles had sufficiently multiplied, a policy of clearing the Indians out came into being automatically. This was primarily a vocal policy, a matter of political agitation: they wanted, of course, the government militia to come and do the clearing out for them.

But their desires were quite often at variance with the policy of the colony's government or of His Majesty's government across the sea, who with their sights set on grander strategy had more often than not done everything possible to keep the settlers from settling in the frontier country in the first place.

If the borderers resented the Indians' presence on what they regarded their land, they resented fully as much the rich, bloated, unfeeling, profiteering, tyrannical colonial governors back yonder in their brick colonial mansions, and the blood-sucking Lords of Trade in their lordly London halls. These fine gentry, lolling safe in their lace and powdered wigs, refused to give white men sufficient protection against the bloody savages because they did not want to hurt their trade with the savage nations or endanger their dangling war schemes against the distant French, accusations which were usually true.

Not surprisingly, these pioneers were more inclined to be vicious than brave, and as far as they themselves were concerned their policy of clearing the Indians out was only exercised against tame Indians or the remains of previously broken Indian nations among which the frontiersmen so often settled. Making a dent in an unbroken Indian nation was a job for the troops (with Indian auxiliaries), then and later. The frontiersmen's direct effectiveness in advancing the frontier, in a sense of Indian conquest, was never important.

But their indirect effectiveness, in the truly inexorable expansion of their influence in official government policy, was something else again. And their spirit of hatred for the established order, the citified and pompous central government that spurned their needs and arrogantly repressed their demands, springing from however small a source was a spirit that grew into a large and rushing river. It became the traditional spirit of the border, the spirit of the West, and the left wing of the angel of the American Revolution.

An early example of this feeling showed itself in Virginia in what has been known since as Bacon's Rebellion, its leader being one Nathaniel Bacon, a young American cousin of Francis

Bacon. It was touched off by border clashes with invading Susquehanna Indians, who had left their Pennsylvania homes to dodge a visit from the Iroquois. Virginia frontiersmen got even with the tough Susquehanna by forming an unofficial army and slaughtering remnants of the peaceable Powhatans, and the frontier army then went on to take over the colony, chasing out the governor and burning Jamestown before the frontier dander simmered down. The year was 1676. An authoritative figure from another year of '76, Thomas Jefferson, putting his finger on not the Indian policy involved but the resultant spirit of protest against centralized, disdainful rule, suggested more than a century later that Nathaniel Bacon would "no longer be regarded as a rebel, but as a patriot.... "

In sum, white frontiers were set in motion with the considerable assistance, voluntary and involuntary, of forces within the Indian world. Once in motion, any frontier developed a growing force of its own, exerted primarily to impose its policy upon its own reluctant government. One desired feature of that policy was to clear the Indians out. This process formed the pattern of the Indian story on the white frontier. Sufficiently repeated, this process helped eradicate European government, along with eradicating Indian nations.

Frontiersmen sometimes became genuinely industrious about cleaning out the debris of demolished Indian societies caught in the tide of this process—I've shot and chopped and drowned the critters, I've fried 'em by the houseful and roasted 'taters in their grease, ran the Davy Crockett school of stories—but their efforts only amounted to casual rape as against the total score.

Drink and the devil did for the rest, a devil crowned with the three heavy horns of degradation, prostitution, and disease. Religion helped by providing the circumstances for point-blank epidemics among converts crowded in squalid imitation-white housing. (There were exceptions, such as the thriving Indian villages founded in Pennsylvania by Moravian missionaries; the villages were destroyed one after another by indignant white frontiersmen or equally indignant non-Christian Indians.)

Descendants of friend and foe alike shared the common Indian fate within the white world: by about 1800 neighboring Connecticut villages were occupied by the few forlorn survivors of the anti-English Pequot tribe, fewer than 100 strong, and the few forlorn survivors of their tribal brothers, the pro-English Mohegan, also fewer than 100 strong.

Some, maybe many, escaped from the long nightmare to the intact tribes beyond the borders; the Narraganset went to Maine and turned into Abnaki by the hundreds, maybe thousands, after King Philip's War; and the parade of Tuscarora plodding north to the Iroquois took 100 years to pass.

But one after another of the intact tribes marched to destruction in their turn in the major colonial wars from 1689 to 1763, echoes for the most part of European wars between France and England, but in America fought on the American plan, with as much use as possible of Indian allies. The brunt of these wars was felt on the frontiers, with enough wanton hatcheting of settlers and burning of farms and villages, enough wives and children carried away into captivity, to madden a people with far less motive for madness than property-minded frontiersmen. The stories can still communicate the reality of agony behind the archaic phrases. Wrote a mother, of parting from her six-year-old son, both made captives by "French" Indians at Charlestown, New Hampshire, in 1754: "The inexorable savage... forced him away: the last words I heard, intermingled with his cries, were 'Ma'am, I shall never see you again.' The keenness of my pangs almost obliged me to wish that I had never been a mother. 'Farewell, Sylvanus,' said I; 'God will preserve you....' " It is good to note that God did, and Sylvanus, although by then as Indian as English, came back when grown to live near his mother in Charlestown.

Typically, though, much of the understandable fury of the frontier elements was turned inward against their own governments, their grievances used as levers to secure various official concessions. One of these was the scalp bounty, frequently extracted by the radical frontier bloc as a sop for damages claimed from Indian depredations. Scalp bounties had been used first by the Dutch, and were adopted at one time or other by most of the colonies. It was an expensive business—Massachusetts paid £12 per scalp in 1703, which was a lot of money, and £100 in 1722, which was a lot more—but effective. Of course, no one could be sure the scalps brought in were scalps of whatever Indians happened to be enemies at the moment. Missionaries had to keep a frantic guard over their Indian flocks during bounty years—when you could collect hair worth $1500, as did some militant Pennsylvania frontier settlers in 1763, simply by hatcheting three old Indian men, two women, and a boy, who plied the basket-making trade in a nearby town.

The French used the scalp bounty to have the inoffensive Beothuk of Newfoundland Island cut off, as the phraseology of the time had it, by the Micmac of Nova Scotia. The Beothuk were a minor nuisance to the French, who offered the Micmac a bounty for Beothuk scalps. After a generation or so not a single Beothuk was left alive; some may have escaped across the Strait to join the Naskapi of Labrador.

Those Indian nations left in shambles by the stress of colonial wars were, if within reach, swallowed up and digested by the European frontiers—at an accelerated rate, as the frontiers and the shambles spread. In each instance the cycle of disorder, decay, and fitful extermination was scrupulously repeated, only faster.

The fissures opened in intact Indian nations by the disruptive influences of Indian-versus-Indian wars and European colonial wars are seen in white history as the "opening to settlement" of the trans-Appalachian country, the Ohio country, and the country northwest of the Ohio known as the Old Northwest.

Previous Iroquois conquests in this back country made possible the first tentative entry of English traders and settlers. The principal avenue of the march of settlement was through the Delaware confederacy, cracked open by Susquehanna wars of conquest in the middle 1600s.

The Iroquois, after their conquest of the Susquehanna in the 1670s, claimed sovereignty over the Delawares and by the 1730s were freely selling Delaware lands to the proprietors of Pennsylvania. The Delawares objected but Pennsylvania, not surprisingly, sided with the Iroquois claims.

Many outraged Delawares drifted westward to the region of the upper Ohio, accompanied by their brothers the Shawnee and remnants of other dispossessed peoples, and there became the nucleus of bitter anti-English (and anti-Iroquois) feeling.

In the 1740s the Iroquois granted control of the upper Ohio area to the English, and several land-promotion companies were formed to subdivide tracts there and sell them off to settlers. Christopher Gist, a fur trader exploring for a combine of wealthy Virginia land promoters known as the Ohio Company, was at the falls of the Ohio (present Louisville) in 1750.

Some of this country, as previously noted, had been regarded by the various Indian nations for a long while as a sort of no man's land, owned by no one—not even the Iroquois. Refugees from the Iroquois and the English were plentiful in the surrounding regions. Naturally they encouraged French resistance to the English occupation of their country. The French and Indian War resulted, the final titanic struggle between France and England in the New World.

The immediate cause of this war was conflict between Virginia and France for control of the upper Ohio, specifically the key point at the forks of the Ohio where the French, at the opening of hostilities in 1754, built Fort Duquesne (now Pittsburgh). Two British forces sent against this point, Frye's in 1754 and Braddock's in 1755, were cut to pieces by the French and their Indian allies.

Perhaps the most influential of these allies were exiled Delawares from Pennsylvania (in the scalp bounties General Braddock offered his troops, the scalp of the Delaware leader Shinngass rated by far the highest price, £200, forty times the price for an ordinary French soldier's hair, and even twice as much as was offered for the scalp of the Jesuit missionary among the Ohio Indians). After Braddock's defeat the entire western border of Pennsylvania, Maryland, and Virginia was laid bare to these Delawares and their allies, who skinned it alive with pleasure. Outposts and settlements were abandoned, and the English frontier recoiled, on the average, 100 miles.

The exiled Delawares were eventually appeased by the desperate diplomacy of Conrad Weiser, Pennsylvania's wily interpreter and ambassador extraordinary to the Indians, who managed to win the cooperation of Tedyuskung, leader of the peaceful Delawares still living in Pennsylvania. In 1758 Tedyuskung and the governor of Pennsylvania sent Christian Post, a Moravian missionary, on an urgent journey to the western Indians in the vicinity of Fort Duquesne bearing Tedyuskung's plea for peace and Pennsylvania's guarantee that fraudulent land sales would be corrected. Post succeeded, not only in his long trip on foot through hostile forests and snowy passes, but in winning enough support from the western Indians to break the French alliance. Post returned to the Indian council at Easton, Pennsylvania, in October 1758, and in November of that same year Fort

**This resolute Indian dressed in white man's clothes is believed to be Tecumseh, the great Shawnee chief who conceived of a vast Indian confederacy stretching from Wisconsin to Florida. This portrait by an unknown artist was obtained by the Chicago Natural History Museum in 1894 from the grandniece of William Clark, the explorer, and General George Rogers Clark, both of whom fought against Tecumseh in the Ohio Valley.**

Duquesne fell to a new English expedition without a shot being fired.

Some Indian nations who had not used themselves up by 1763 were drawn into further debilitating hostilities by the grand Indian alliance on the western border under the Ottawa leader Pontiac, who fought a hopeless last-ditch campaign for France and the French beaver trade—hopeless because it came after the defeat of France in the French and Indian War—and the French support Pontiac had been promised naturally failed to materialize. The Pontiac alliance was not composed of intact nations but of bits and pieces of many tribes. The Illinois country seized by the alliance had been open as a frontier—and a center for white settlement—for more than sixty years. Even so, the Pontiac war stood off the British for three years from the Illinois country and the Great Lakes, sustained at Detroit one of the longer sieges in American military history (nearly a year), and was finally settled only by bribes, conciliation, and unkeepable promises on the part of the English.

The unkeepable promises guaranteed to restrain English settlement if Pontiac would demobilize his allies and leave the restraining up to the English. This conciliation and the genuine efforts by the English government to keep its promises enraged the frontier West, which, as usual, had suffered the most from the war, to the point that the border became openly seditious toward the Crown, and was a noisy and obvious factor in the outbreak of revolution ten years later.

The Iroquois, as steadily neutral as their subtle, adroit, and arrant knavery could manage, had avoided serious involvement in most of the colonial wars. In 1754 at the start of the French and Indian War, the French made desperate efforts to win Iroquois alliance. Quebec and Louisiana were like two stones at either end of a 2,000-mile string, a string that had to make a wide, difficult detour by way of the Great Lakes around the Iroquois country. With Iroquois help, the French could have used the waterways of present New York State not only to shorten and straighten and reinforce that impossibly long front, but also to drive a wedge into the heart of the English colonies. The Iroquois stuck to official neutrality, a neutrality that in itself was of consequence in deciding the outcome of the French and Indian War. Worse, they gave some unofficial help to the English.

An English fur trader named William Johnson had settled in the Mohawk Valley and become such a friend of the Iroquois that the English had commissioned him "Colonel of the Six Nations" in 1746. He was later placed in charge of all northern Indian affairs for the English crown, and was given so many bosomy grants of their beauteous land by the Six Nations that he became one of the largest landowners in all colonial America. The last two of his three wives were Mohawk girls, the last being Molly Brant, whose younger brother, Joseph, became Johnson's special protégé. The most renowned Pine Tree of the Mohawk at the time of the French and Indian War, Hendrick (son of a Mohegan), was also related to Colonel Johnson by marriage.

In 1755, the year that Braddock's defeat threw most of the wavering Indian nations into the French and Indian War on the side of France, Colonel Johnson flung a painted war belt among the Six Nations council, in the manner of a war chief, and asked for some of their briskest men as unofficial allies. Hendrick himself volunteered, and several hundred warriors came with him. Their effect in the battle of Lake George which followed has perhaps sometimes been overestimated—there were 2,000 or 3,000 English militiamen in Colonel Johnson's command as well as the 200 or 300 brisk Iroquois—but the propaganda value of their presence was certainly important.

At this battle Hendrick, then an old man of about seventy, is supposed to have made one of those battlefield remarks that have a way of reappearing down through the ages: "If they [his warriors] are to fight they are too few; if they are to die they are too many."

They fought and they died. Hendrick was killed, and the Iroquois casualties were exceedingly heavy. But the battle was won, English America was saved, the war could go on to ultimate victory and the finish of France in the New World. Two months after the crucial Lake George action, Colonel Johnson was elevated to a baronetcy.

The finish of France in the New World was also the finish of the Iroquois as a determining weight in the balance of power, there being only one great power left—England. But the friendship of Sir William Johnson and that of his son-in-law and successor, Colonel Guy Johnson, could cut both ways, and the Iroquois (most of them) enjoyed an amiable hour of prosperity and peace after the close of the French and Indian War in 1763, in spite of continuing cessions of land to Sir William for white settlement.

Sir William placed his youthful brother-in-law Joseph Brant (who had been at Lake George as a thirteen-year-old warrior) in Moor's Indian Charity School, recently opened in Connecticut by the Reverend Eleazar Wheelock. The young man came forth with an education and a religious bent, and assisted various missionaries in revising the Mohawk prayer book and in translating the Acts of the Apostles into the Mohawk tongue.

During the French and Indian War the British Crown took exclusively unto itself the management of Indian affairs. It also reserved to itself the right to purchase or treat for Indian lands, forbidding these dealings in the future to colonies, land companies, or individuals—the United States was later to continue this same policy. In the late 1760s, after the French and Indian War, the British government secured permission from such intact Indian nations as the Iroquois, Cherokee, and Creeks, and expanded settlement once again into the Ohio country of broken tribes.

New land-promotion companies were formed, some getting charters and grants from the British Crown, some evading the law by privately "leasing" Indian lands. One such group of speculators, the Transylvania Company of North Carolina, employed a land prospector named Daniel Boone, who spent six years "in quest of the country of Kentucky" before he bought it for the company in 1775, paying £10,000 to the Cherokee for what was at best an extremely doubtful title.

The various Indian bands in the Ohio country, under such leaders as the Shawnee Cornstalk and the expatriate Iroquois Logan, son of a famous Iroquois sachem, made occasional resistance to the fairly frequent discourtesies of the incoming settlers. Lord Dunmore, governor of Virginia, defeated these Indians in a formal war in 1774, thereby incidentally strengthening Virginia's claim to the newly opened country—which may have been the real reason for Lord Dunmore's formal war in the first place.

Prices asked by the land speculators were often so high that poorer settlers were prompted to cross the legal line and take their chances as squatters on Indian lands—the Transylvania Company's prices ranged from \$2.50 to \$40 the hundred acres, a substantial piece of change in 1775, in backwoods country where a man received 33 cents for a day's work. Numbers of emigrants crossed the Ohio into the territories of the broken nations northwest of the river, and the pattern for further Indian "wars" was once more established.

There is a poetic symmetry of a sort in the fact that the American Revolution, the genesis of which the Iroquois had for so long been indirectly and directly involved with, should have brought about the death of the Great League. Joseph Brant, who had become a leading young chief of the Mohawk (his proper Mohawk name was Thayendanegea), insisted on alliance with the English. Sir William had died, but the Johnson influence was still strong: Colonel Guy Johnson and the Brants, Joseph and Sir William's widow, Molly, succeeded in bringing most of the Mohawk, Onondaga, Cayuga, and Seneca into the war on the English side.

The Tuscarora and the Oneida sided with the Colonies. Thus, finally, the Iroquois were divided against themselves in war. It was the end of the Great League.

Joseph Brant led his Mohawks in border raids that were seized upon and magnified, according to his biographer, by the "public writers," until his "name was terrible in every ear... associated with every thing bloody, ferocious, and hateful...," the idea being that "accounts of such deeds of ferocity and blood" would keep "alive the strongest feelings of indignation against the parent country, and likewise induce the people to take the field for revenge, if not driven thither by the nobler impulse of patriotism." "The Monster Brandt," wrote the world-famous English poet Thomas Campbell, "with all his howling desolating band. . . ." "A banditti of robbers, murderers, and traitors," stated a military proclamation of 1777 signed "B. Arnold, M.G.," in command of American forces at the time on the Mohawk River.

The most resounding of the Revolutionary War deeds attributed to the Monster Brant were the Cherry Valley, New York, raid and massacre; the full-fledged Battle of Oriskany, New York; and above all the frightful Wyoming, Pennsylvania, massacre of 1778. However, it appears that Joseph Brant was not present at this last event, the Indians who accompanied the British on this attack being principally of the Seneca and Cayuga tribes, not the Mohawks.

Also, the Wyoming battle and subsequent slaughter were by no means prompted only by Revolutionary War considerations: the causes were deep in the ancient conflicts of the Indian-versus-Indian frontier. Since 1728 the Wyoming valley on the Susquehanna River had been a point of bitter contention between the Delawares, who claimed it as a permanent home, and the Iroquois, who claimed the right to sell it to white land speculators.

Pennsylvania complicated matters in the early 1770s by trying to eject the white settlers who arrived in the wake of fraudulent land sales. But in the summer of 1778 white squatters and Delawares alike sallied forth from their principal settlement (site of the present Wilkes-Barre) to give fight to the invading British and Iroquois. They were defeated, and the rout and massacre that followed were given top atrocity billing in border song and story for a long time to come.

American troops in reprisal laid waste the Iroquois towns, as the French had done so often 100 years before; although now there was much more in the way of corn, barns, farms, livestock, and orchards to lay waste.

After the war, Joseph Brant and the Tory Iroquois were given lands on the Grand River, Ontario, and the fearsome Brant returned to his occasional hobby of translating the Scriptures into Mohawk. He also made a return visit to England, where he had been at the start of the Revolution, and where he was a lion of society; he was taken up this time as an intimate friend of the Prince of Wales.

The fragments of the Six Nations who had given their loyalty to the Colonies remained in New York.

The rites commemorating the founding of the League of the Iroquois repeat in their closing lines: "Now listen, ye who established the Great League. Now there is nothing but wilderness. Ye are in your graves who established it. Ye have taken it with you, and have placed it under you, and there is nothing left but a desert. There ye have taken your intellects with you. Ye have placed under your heads what ye established—the Great League."

The Indian wars of the Old Northwest broke out after the close of the American Revolution, with secret encouragement from British fur traders. Little Turtle, a Miami, in command of combined Indian forces, won victories over two American armies in 1790 and 1791 but met the inevitable shattering defeat in 1794 against a third American army, under Mad Anthony Wayne.

A long series of land-ceding treaties was wrung from a dozen crushed tribes in the Old Northwest between 1794 and the great final Indian convulsion in the region, the abortive war raised by the Shawnee Tecumseh in 1811. Tecumseh made an effort to engage every border nation or remnant thereof from the deep south of Florida to the far north of the upper Missouri River, his object being to hold the Ohio River as a permanent Indian border.

His plans were wrecked by premature military action undertaken by his brother, Tenskwatawa, called the Prophet (one of the many messiahs springing up among a people beginning to sense the numbing odor of genocide). Tecumseh, in four short years, had made amazing progress in forming the basis of a genuine pan-Indian union. "He is," wrote William Henry Harrison, territorial governor of Indiana, "one of those uncommon geniuses which spring up occasionally to produce revolutions and overturn the established order of things. . . . " Harrison chose a time of Tecumseh's absence to lead troops against his headquarters, the large Indian village of Tippecanoe on the banks of the Wabash. The Prophet ordered an overhasty attack, instead of playing for time until Tecumseh's return. Losses were about even on both sides, but the Indians were forced to retreat. The Prophet was utterly discredited and Tecumseh's union, from this moment on, steadily crumbled away.

But it did not really matter. For by the time of Tecumseh, the frontiersman's policy—clear the Indians out—was at last triumphing to become the national policy of the United States, thinly disguised behind a screen of enforced treaties, and by this time there were few tribes left intact, from the Great Lakes eastward, to resist it.

Other such treaties followed for many years, but they became more and more hollow formalities, signed by treaty chiefs without authority in the name of nations that had become little more than memories. The paper storm of these treaties moved all the way west to the Mississippi, driving the scattered survivors of the nations before it or leaving them here and there as islands of paupers, and rarely meeting resistance.

A string of treaties negotiated by Keokuk as chief of the Sauk Indians (which he was not) giving up the Rock River country of the Sauk and Foxes did bring a show of something the authorities construed as resistance from Black Hawk, the legitimate leader of the Sauk. (When Keokuk announced in council that the United States government had made him supreme chief of the Sauk, Black Hawk, so they say, struck him across the face with his breechclout.) In any case, Black Hawk's reluctance to keep his village west of the Mississippi in obedience to the terms of Keokuk's treaties brought on some excitement and the shooting up of Black Hawk's fleeing people by the military. This holiday excursion of the frontier militia took place in 1832. It is embalmed in the history books as the Black Hawk War, a rather unfortunate example to serve as the last of the Indian wars of the Old Northwest.

# VIII

# The Dispossessed

**Driven off their lands, Cherokee migrants take with them the few possessions they can carry in this detail from Robert Lindneux's dramatic rendering of the Trail of Tears.**

In 1790 the government of the brand-new United States of America succeeded in negotiating a treaty with the Creek Indians of the Southeast. This treaty was much desired to assure the peace and safety of the southern border against the machinations of the Spanish then in Louisiana and Florida. The Creeks ceded certain lands north of the Thirty-first Parallel, and the United States government took its solemn oath to guarantee the remaining boundaries of the Creek nation.

In 1791 an Indian agent newly appointed by the American Secretary of War traveled through the territory of the Creeks (highland Georgia and environs) and reported that it "must, in process of time, become a most delectable part of the United States."

The territory was large, some 84,000 square miles, and "remarkably healthy.... The constant breezes, which are probably occasioned by the high hills and numerous rapid water-courses, render the heat of summer very temperate; and towards autumn they are delightfully perfumed by the ripening aromatic shrubbery, which abounds throughout the country.... The winters are soft and mild, and the summers sweet and wholesome.... The country possesses every species of wood and clay proper for building, and the soil and climate seem well suited to the culture of corn, wine, oil, silk, hemp, rice, wheat, tobacco, indigo, every species of fruit trees, and English grass.... "

But this warm and charming land might give pain to a traveler at present, he reported, since its many resources and natural beauties were "only rendered unpleasant by being in possession of the jealous natives." In the 1790s that possession was still strong and secure, after generations of high living in the fast company of Europeans.

The position of the Creek confederacy in the Southeast was somewhat similar to that of the League of the Iroquois in the Northeast: a ranking Indian power strategically located in an area of conflict between European rivals.

The heart of the Creek country was near enough to early European settlements for trade but not near enough for serious trouble; the center of the Creek world was 300 miles inland from the nearest early settlements along the coast. The loose confederacy seldom acted with unity, and there was sometimes serious hostility between the two main divisions of the Upper and Lower Towns, but in general the various Creek towns threw themselves into active, on occasion enthusiastic, alliances with Europeans, more often pro-English than otherwise.

Studies of the relations with Europeans of such tribal nations as the Iroquois and Creeks and the Creeks' northern neighbors, the Cherokee, native American states that were of importance in colonial history, have at times made much of the trade motive, the obvious enrichment to be gained in cornering as much of the European trade as possible.

Motives of all kinds were no doubt present in the making of Indian alliances with Europeans and in Indian efforts to open European trade, even in Indian requests for European missionaries. But the motive most commonly advanced by early Indian orators for wanting to establish relations with Europeans was that of learning the Europeans' higher wisdom. The tall and turbaned Creeks as well as the tall and strong-armed Iroquois were, by most accounts, superior people, and it seems reasonable that some of them may have been sincerely motivated by nothing more than a wish to sit at the feet of the people from heaven and learn better things.

Said Yahou-Lakee, Micco ("king" in the English interpretation) of Coweta, principal town of the Lower Creeks, when the Creeks visited James Oglethorpe on the site of Savannah in 1732: "We are come 25 days' journey to see you... when I heard you were come, and that you were good men, I knew you were sent by HIM who lives in heaven, to teach us *Indians* wisdom. I therefore came down, that I might hear good things:—for I knew, that if I died in the way, I should die in doing good; and what was said, would be carried back to the nation, and our Children would reap the benefit of it.... "

And said, on the same occasion, the very tall old Honored Man the English called Long King: "that though they [the Creeks] were poor and ignorant, HE, who had given the English breath, had given them breath also. That HE, who had made both, had given more wisdom to the white men. That they were firmly persuaded, that the GREAT POWER which dwelt in heaven, and all around, (and then he spread out his hands, and lengthened the sound of his words) and which hath given breath to all men, had sent the English thither for the instruction of them, their wives, and children.... "

This was the reason stated by the Creeks for giving land along the coast and the Savannah River ("where the Savannah bends like a sickle before rolling to the sea") for the founding of the colony of Georgia.

The Creeks had first come in tenuous contact with Europeans in the 1500s, with the Spanish explorations and the early Spanish and French attempts to establish beachheads along the coast of the Carolinas and Florida. In the first half of the 1600s Spanish missions prospered sporadically, between outbreaks of pestilence and uprisings of the catechumens, among the Timucua and Apalachee of northern Florida, and among the Guale of the Georgia coast: perhaps 30,000 Christian Indians were by 1635 gathered around more than forty mission stations, missions reportedly as rich, gracious, and idyllic as the later and better known Spanish missions of California.

It seems likely the Creeks would have known Spanish traders by this time—the Cherokee in the mountains north of them, when visited by Virginia traders in 1673, already possessed several dozen "Spanish flintlocks" as well as some Spanish wives. But English traders from Virginia must also have appeared early among the Creeks: the Creek word for white Americans was and still is *Watcina*, meaning Virginians.

After 1670, with the founding of the English colony of Carolina, more English traders and explorers probed into the Creek country toward the Spanish frontier of the Florida missions, and in 1680 Spanish missionaries responded by probing northward into the Creek country toward the English frontiers. In the military expeditions that naturally followed, a Spanish commander burned four Creek towns, including the important Lower Creek towns of Tuskegee and Coweta, and the Creeks drew back from the Spanish and resettled nearer English sources of trade.

During the next generation many Creeks, together with some neighbors known as the Yuchi, who spoke a language unrelated to any other and seemed to be absolutely devoted to fighting, happily joined English slavers in raid after raid on the Spanish missions.

The Spanish abandoned their missions on the Georgia coast before 1690 and moved what was left of the converts there to the region of St. Augustine in Florida. In 1704 the sadly tamed descendants of the Apalachee were rounded up like cattle in a crushing English-Creek (50 English; 1,000 Creeks) attack on the northern Florida missions: 6,000 head of livestock were butchered; 6,000 to 7,000 mission Indians were captured; three Franciscan missionaries were burned at the stake. The Creeks took the prisoners, the English bought some of them as slaves, and everyone was satisfied. The English wanted the slaves for the Carolina plantations, and they wanted to punish the Spanish not only for being Spanish but for providing in Florida a refuge for runaway slaves (by Spanish law, any foreign slave became free on reaching Florida).

In Florida the Spanish were attempting an experiment: a Christian Indian state. No colonies of Europeans were permitted. The tiny garrisons were only for protection of the missionaries and could not be used for conquest. Firearms were not allowed among the mission Indians. This last oversight made the Florida mission Indians sitting ducks for the English slavers and their Creek, Yuchi, and occasionally Cherokee auxiliaries, whom they not only armed but trained.

By 1745 the flourishing missions of northern Florida were in ruins, their thousands of converts wildly scattered, and immigrant bands of Yuchi and various peoples from the Lower Creek towns were moving into the country thus left vacant. They mixed with the few feral survivors of the mission Indians, with runaway slaves of all kinds who kept appearing from the colonies to the north, and with later immigrants from the Lower Creek towns. As the years passed an amalgamated society was formed by all these elements, a loose confederacy of many groups speaking many languages but with dialects of Muskhogean, the great language family of the Southeast, gradually becoming the basis of the common tongue. This new-made tribe spread on southward down the peninsula of Florida and came to be known as the Seminole (originally pronounced Seminolee), from a Creek word meaning something like "outlanders."

The English, French Protestants, and Scots who settled in the Carolinas had an unquenchable thirst for slaves. Blacks were expensive (even though plentiful), but anyone could snare an Indian or two or three. Many Indians were anxious to have tir children given an education by Europeans, and it was easy to take a child or two away and have the parents' grateful blessing into the bargain. The child or two duly sold, one later told the parents an affecting tale of a sudden illness, fatal in spite of all one could do, and with a few honest tears another child or two might be picked up on the same visit, to repeat the process.

Kidnaping of children was simpler and quicker, and deservedly more popular. The large Tuscarora confederation of North Carolina suffered from this industry for years and finally, in 1710, sent ambassadors to Pennsylvania asking for permission to emigrate there, for the safety of their children and the children yet to be born. The Pennsylvania commissioners regretted that it could not take them without a certificate of good behavior from the Carolina government.

In September of the next year, 1711, the Tuscarora solved their dilemma with a savage attack on the North Carolina colonists, opening the war, ironically enough, with the capture and execution of the Surveyor-General of North Carolina, the one Englishman of the region who knew the Indians best and felt the warmest affection for them. "We look upon them with disdain and scorn," he wrote, two years before his death, "and think them little better than beasts in human form; while with all our religion and education, we possess more moral deformities and vices than these people do." But ironically enough the Surveyor-General, at the very time he was writing, was selling an extensive tract of Tuscarora territory to a European promoter, without mentioning the transaction to the Tuscarora (the crime for which the Tuscarora condemned him to death). Swiss and Palatine colonists were settled on the land just before the Tuscarora uprising, and suffered grievously in death and destruction.

A military expedition of colonists and Indian allies brought the Tuscarora to terms, but as the expedition felt insufficiently rewarded by North Carolina for its efforts, the English commander violated the truce just made with the Tuscarora and trapped a large number who ingenuously responded to his invitation to a general friendship parley. These captives went to the slave ships and the Tuscarora went back to war, to be defeated by a second expedition the next year, 1713. By this time the Iroquois had offered the Tuscarora a new home in the Five Nations country, and the Tuscarora began migrating northward.

The numerous little coastal tribes who had joined with the Catawba, a South Carolina confederation of Siouan peoples, in helping the English against the Tuscarora had been promised certain trade preferences as a reward. That these trade matters were deadly serious to the Indians is indicated by the previous national disaster of the Sewee, a coastal tribe that undertook to open direct trade relations with England and lost most of its male population at sea in the attempt.

However, the promise of trade preferences was not kept. This led to the mass murder of several hundred settlers by the little coastal tribes, in the so-called Yamasee War of 1715, which was the finish of the little coastal tribes.

The defeated Yamasee, a people living just inland from the Georgia coast, emigrated to Spanish Florida and became Spanish allies (as they had been once before, until 1685, when they had migrated up from Florida to become English allies). The Catawba went back to being steadfast friends of the colonists and, being the largest nation left in the coastal region now that he Tuscarora had been dispersed, received many refugee bands from the shattered little coast tribes. The far eastern division of the Shawnee who lived on the Savannah River (the river's name was a variant of Shawnee), having driven away the Yuchi there about 1680, moved out in their turn, drifting northwestward.

All these turmoils operated rather to the benefit of the Creeks, safe in their secluded hills. Their population was enhanced by refugees, and their prosperity enhanced by the unhindered spread of European trade. The Catawba declined with astounding rapidity under the onslaught of drink, disease, and attacks by any gangs of Shawnee or Iroquois or other wild Indian juvenile delinquents who happened along, and for the frightened Catawba as well as the displaced persons who had taken shelter with them, there was no further escape except to the Creeks or Cherokee.

The Creeks waxed stronger, and the Carolina colonies grew in wealth and colonists. By the 1730s upward of 200 ships a year left Charleston "laden with the merchandize of the growth of the country. . . . "

It was natural that speculators in England would look with interest on the uncolonized territory just below the Carolinas, "the Most Delightful Country of the Universe," as it was called in a prospectus of 1717. In 1732 its colonization was successfully undertaken by General James Oglethorpe, a wealthy philanthropist, who established the colony of Georgia as a land of opportunity for imprisoned debtors. It would also serve as a buffer state for the rich Carolinas, and as an obstruction across that beaten path to freedom, which was still being taken by so many Carolina slaves running away to Florida. Slavery was prohibited in the new colony (at first), which fit in splendidly both with Oglethorpe's humanitarian sentiments and the idea of an all-white cordon to fence in Carolina's slaves.

The proprietors of Georgia and the statesmen of England had use for the Creek confederacy, as an instrument of trade and as a line of defense against the Spanish to the south and even more so against the French by now ensconced in Louisiana. The French, following their customary policy of vigorous Indian diplomacy, had kept Carolina, Virginia, and Maryland in a state of endemic alarm for thirty years, with recurring rumors of a general attack by "thousands" of French-allied warriors from the Mississippi River tribes.

Since 1703 the English had been endeavoring to form various anti-French combinations with the four great nations, Cherokee, Chickasaw, Creek, and Choctaw, located in the touchy Southeastern area between the Atlantic and the Mississippi. Their most enduring success was with the bellicose Chickasaw, who remained pro-English from first to last and were almost as valuable for the English cause in the Southeast as the Iroquois were in the Northeast.

Since Chickasaw country bordered on the Mississippi, the Chickasaw were a never-ending menace to French *voyageurs* going up and down the river; the French waged a total of five full-dress wars against the Chickasaw from 1736 to 1753 and were soundly whipped each time. For good measure the Chickasaw also handed thundering defeats to the Creeks and Cherokee at various times in major wars, although both these nations had the Chickasaw ridiculously outnumbered. As far as known history is concerned the Chickasaw, by far the smallest of the four Civilized Tribes of Cherokee, Chickasaw, Creek, and Choctaw, never lost a first-class battle, starting with a whirlwind attack that hastened the de Soto expedition's march in 1541, and including the destruction of an Iroquois war party in 1732.

But the Chickasaw, although a most useful salient in French territory, were far from the English colonies; the Choctaw (hereditary Chickasaw enemies) were generally more friendly to the French than to the English; the mighty Cherokee, in their

**The Creek pictured here in a sketch by John Trumbull visited George Washington in 1790 to discuss land cessions. Because the Indians feared his "magic," Trumbull worked surreptitiously, describing them as having "a dignity . . . worthy of a Roman senator."**

mountain fastnesses of northern Georgia and the Carolinas, were off on the northern edge of the theater of conflict and were inscrutable to boot, in the way of mountaineers. If the southern English colonies were to stay healthy and grow, and above all if the new colony of Georgia was to survive at all, the continued friendship of the powerful next-door neighbors, the Creeks, was needed.

The Creeks, as previously noted, were delighted to give it, and to give land as well for the establishment of the new colony. More, a dozen important men from the Creek confederacy, and a Yuchi chief, went to England in 1734 with General Oglethorpe to publicize the new colony, at which they were a huge success. Costumed in scarlet and gold and furs, wearing moccasins, and with feathers hanging in their hair, they went to court in royal six-horse coaches for a state visit with George II and his Queen Caroline. Seven Cherokee Indians of doubtful rank had been brought to England in 1730 by a private individual, and had supposedly agreed to a "treaty" that no other Cherokee ever bothered to take seriously. Moreover, their trip had been clouded by a dubious carnival air. The Creeks, now that they too had a European colony of their own, showed their ancient Cherokee enemies how such matters should be handled, solemn protocol preceding every step. The only interruption for a commercial was a dignified address by the doyen of the Creek delegation, Tomochichi, said to be more than ninety years old, who asked "a fair and substantial basis for trade; standard weights and measures; standardized prices; favored-nation treatment; free repair of firearms; and the prohibition of rum." He also asked for missionaries. With the Indian's comical blindness to property he also observed that the English houses were built to last too long for the short lives of the people who lived in them.

Tomochichi's modest and sensible requests for fair trade practices could not be met, of course, even by colonial administrations genuinely willing to try (most did try to effect some kind of controlled system, but efforts and results alike were so spotty as to be all but imperceptible). The only really workable trade regulation was that enforced by the Indian towns themselves; since the Indians were ignorant of the finer trimmings of civilized misconduct, this regulation was usually confined to the immediately apparent evil of rum-running. ("Brandy goes off incomparably well," concluded a typical eighteenth-century list of "goods that are proper for the savages.")

English traders swarmed into the Creek country. They were not ideal preceptors of that higher wisdom the simple Indians sought, but good and bad, French and English, they brought new ideas. In the main, the intact nations of the Southeast prospered during the eighteenth century. They acquired livestock, improved farming methods, and many took to European clothes and houses. The Chickasaw developed the locally famous Chickasaw horse, a breedy and nervy strain apparently based on a superior stock imported from New Mexico in the Santa Fe trade. The Choctaw (in keeping with the sturdy, down to earth Choctaw character) developed the Choctaw pony, claimed by its admirers to have more bottom to the hand of height than any other horse on earth. The old ceremonies, the black drink, the busk or green-corn festival, the eternal games of chunkey and ball play, went on as ever. The red-painted war post still called men to battle, and if the battles were fought more and more in the interests of European politics—why not? Obviously the Europeans were on hand to stay, an important part of the future. All in all, that future looked good.

Not that the century was a placid one. The world cracked with change and opened many rifts of unrest. The Cherokee ceded a large amount of territory to the English in 1755, but four years after that a war flared up between them and the English that continued off and on for a generation. The Creeks in 1752 had been within a hair's breadth of a major war with the Savannah colony, brought on by the intrigues of a South Carolinian, the Reverend Thomas Bosomworth, who had married a highborn Creek woman and attempted to use her political position as a lever to extort money from the Georgia English.

A great many Europeans married into the Indian nations of the Southeast, principally Englishmen everywhere except in the western Choctaw towns, which were strongly pro-French. Traders who were reasonably honorable or able, or both, won the absolute trust of the Indians, married into leading families, amassed political power as well as wealth; and the rise of an oligarchy composed in large part of such families created an invisible revolution in both Creek and Cherokee societies.

The half-English princes who evolved lived by Indian customs, but their ambitions were frequently European; many became personally wealthy in livestock, slaves, and goods; some became petty tyrants, manipulating Indian law for their own purposes; some became tribal statesmen of the first rank, of the greatest value to their nations, and of note in American history.

The ascendancy of the chief was a phenomenon that accompanied European invasion everywhere. The Europeans needed some one responsible official to deal with in Indian negotiations, and if no real chief existed, as was usually the case, they invented one. Sometimes the fictitious power thus invested in these "treaty chiefs" was accepted by the other Indians and became actual. More often it led to discord.

Among the Creeks, favored by their key location ("they have the French and Spaniards to apply to in Case you won't supply them," as a Cherokee reminded the English in the 1750s), personal diplomacy became a constant necessity, with a consequent accretion of real authority around those Beloved Men who were of influence with Europeans. This emergence of strong political leaders brought on a struggle for ultimate power between various "chiefs" of the two divisions of the Upper and Lower Creek towns, which at times had an effect on Indian politics throughout the whole region. To a lesser degree, a conflict came into being between full-blood conservative tribal members and mixed-blood progressives, particularly over the incessant question of land cessions to the white. Similar problems, but with variations, beset the Cherokee and the Choctaw. The Chickasaw, their smaller population unified by unswerving loyalty to the English and persistent wars with the French, were perhaps a little less disturbed by such dissensions.

The French, English, and Spanish were constantly busy with agitation for this or that course of Indian policy, and with wrangle-making bribes and payoffs to the chiefs. However, the overriding exigencies of trade and empire demanded that the European colonies do their utmost to sustain "their" Indians, and so through it all the four nations not only survived but flourished. In the interaction of these many forces the New World took shape in the delectable land of the Creeks and their neighbors.

The close of the French and Indian War in 1763 brought vast changes to the Southeast. French Louisiana was divided between England and Spain: New Orleans and the Louisiana territory west of the Mississippi to Spain, and the Louisiana country east of the Mississippi to England. Florida went (temporarily) from Spanish to English control. French settlers here and there up and down the Mississippi crossed to the west side of the river to avoid English domination, and crowds of Indians went with them: Kaskaskia and Peoria from the Illinois country; Alabama, Biloxi, ancient refugee Apalachee, and many others from the smaller nations along the lower Mississippi. Spain was rejuvenated as a colonized power under the aroused administration of the Bourbon Charles III and brought more prosperity to Louisiana than it had known under France. The Indian nations were skillfully wooed, maneuvered, and deployed and became more valuable than ever to the colonial contenders.

Majority parties in the Creeks and Cherokee stood loyal to England in the Revolutionary War, although Little Carpenter, a Cherokee chief, raised 500 gunmen for service on the American side. Spain regained Florida at the end of the American Revolution and carried forward an accelerated and increasingly successful campaign to win Indian friends, helped by Indian reaction to the upsurge in American frontiering that came with the defeat of the Lords across the Sea. Important pro-Spanish factions appeared among the Creeks and Shawnee and even among the Cherokee and Chickasaw, and for that matter even among some of the American frontier settlers in the south and west.

But a new and weaker king came to the throne of Spain, and the brief, brilliant Spanish renaissance was over. Napoleon set foot on his star-wagon; France took Louisiana back and sold it to the new United States. Spain faded into empty Florida. The few Spaniards left there, pursuing small-time intrigues with the Seminole and the Lower Creeks, were no longer El Greco knights or even Velasquez dwarfs but desolate, sun-dazzled, spiritually enchained little figures out of Goya.

With the influx of new settlement into the southern states (colonies no longer) the world of change spun faster for the Civilized Tribes, who turned still more to the ways, fashions, and ideas of their white neighbors.

Among those who did not change to European clothes, quite a few took to wearing a long shirt in the manner of a flowing tunic, which, with the customary headband or turban, was curiously like a costume prevalent in ancient Mexico. Cherokee women, however, were said to dress "almost universally" in European style, "in gowns manufactured by themselves, from cotton which they have raised on their own plantations."

The Cherokee built roads, schools, churches, and adopted a system of government modeled on that of the United States; and a Cherokee warrior crippled in a hunting accident devoted himself to perfecting a system of writing the Cherokee language. His name was Sequoya, since famous far beyond the Indian nations. He had no education, and neither spoke nor wrote English, but after twelve years of work produced in 1821 a workable alphabet of Cherokee characters; the Cherokee studied it with such enthusiasm that within a matter of months thousands could read and write. A printing press was obtained, and in 1828 the Cherokee began the publication of a weekly newspaper. But in the meantime more than a fourth of the Cherokee, some 6,000 persons, highly displeased with all the radical changes and new-fangled innovations, had migrated west of the Mississippi.

Among the Creeks, Alexander McGillivray, son of a Scotch trader and a half-French Creek mother (a famous beauty named Sehoy, of aristocratic lineage from both parents), had become undisputed leader of the Creeks and Seminoles as well, with 10,000 warriors, so they said, under his command, and at the time of his death in 1793 was one of the wealthiest men in the entire South. He negotiated in 1790, amid much fanfare, the aforementioned treaty with the new American government in which the United States, in return for concessions, gave its solemn guarantee to the adjusted boundaries of the Creek nation.

Pro- and anti-American parties in the Creek towns, aided and abetted by American and English politicians, squatters, vagabonds, and traders, split the nation into open civil strife at the time of the War of 1812. An anti-American war party under the half-Scot chief, Weatherford, descended on Fort Mims, about forty miles north of present Mobile, and massacred most of the 350 or so people there—troops of the Mississippi militia and families of settlers with their slaves. The principal pro-American leader, William MacIntosh, son of a Scotch trader and a Creek mother, who had climbed ruthlessly to the office of head chief of the Lower Creeks, led his followers in a massacre of 200 of the anti-American party.

Another mixed-blood war captain, Menewa, celebrated for

the exploits of his wild and reckless youth when his name had been Hothlepoya (Crazy War Hunter), was one of the ranking commanders of the "Red Sticks," or anti-American faction. The so-called Creek War, in the closing days of the War of 1812, was in part a personal struggle between Menewa and William MacIntosh.

Surrounding states organized militia to march against the anti-American Creeks, and five separate volunteer generals took the field, one of these being an obscure backwoods politician from west Tennessee named Andrew Jackson. Tennessee's Governor Blount "bawled for permission to exterminate the Creeks," in General Jackson's words, and General Jackson's command won the race to exterminate a pretty fair passel of them in the battle of Horseshoe Bend, Alabama, which polished off the Creek War.

Menewa had dug in some 900 Red Stick warriors on a tongue of land surrounded by the Tallapoosa River, except for a narrow neck fortified by a breastwork of logs. A number of women and children were in a village at the river's edge. Indian auxiliaries with General Jackson's Tennessee militiamen were several hundred Creeks under William MacIntosh and Timpoochee Barnard, chief of the Yuchi then united with the Creeks, and perhaps 600 Cherokee—and with them a long young white man who had been living with the Cherokee up in Tennessee, Sam Houston.

Before the battle started, General Jackson's Indian guides and "spies" were able to place his 2,000 men so as to surround the Red Stick position on both sides of the river. The artillery—two cannon—were placed to enfilade the breastwork at a range of eighty yards, and opened the engagement with a two-hour barrage. The Cherokee and American Creeks then attacked repeatedly from across the river, burning the Red Stick village in one of the first attacks.

When it was clear the Indian auxiliaries would not be able to overcome the Red Sticks alone, the main body of militia stormed the breastwork. The remaining Red Sticks were driven to a thicket in the center of the peninsula, and the cannon brought up to finish them off in another barrage of several hours. At length the battered thicket was fired, and the few survivors shot down as the flames drove them out.

More than 300 women and children were taken prisoner, all

**Sequoya, shown in this 1828 portrait with the printed Cherokee alphabet he invented, left his tribe and disappeared into the Southwest when the Cherokee were removed to Oklahoma. News of his death in exile was sent on May 15, 1845, the letter written in the Cherokee script he had created.**

captured by the Indian auxiliaries. Of the 900 Red Stick soldiers, only seventy were left alive, and of the seventy only one escaped unwounded—he jumped into the river and escaped at the first shot. General Jackson lost forty-nine killed (twenty-three of these Indian auxiliaries) and 154 wounded (forty-seven Indians). One of the American casualties was Sam Houston, whose wounds from this battle plagued him the rest of his life.

The Red Stick chief Menewa fell, hit seven times by rifle fire. He recovered consciousness some time after the battle was over, shot a soldier passing nearby, and was in return shot through the head, the bullet going in one side of his face and out the other and tearing away several teeth. He came to again in the night, crawled to the river, found a canoe, and floated downstream to a swamp where other Red Stick wives and children had remained hidden. By the time his wounds were healed the Creek War was long ended, and the Red Sticks' land had been opened to white settlement. Menewa's store, 1,000 head of cattle, and hundreds of horses and hogs, at his town of Okfuskee, had vanished: William MacIntosh had won the contest between them, for the time being. But Menewa was still alive, and still very rugged, and as far as he was concerned the polls were not yet closed.

The brilliant victory brought General Jackson wide recognition and an appointment as major-general in the regular army, which opened the way for his triumph in the battle of New Orleans the following winter that made him a national hero.

Anti-American Creeks escaped to Florida in such numbers that the Seminole population was doubled or tripled, and mounting disturbances there brought an invasion of Spanish Florida in 1817 by General Jackson that in turn caused enfeebled Spain to cede Florida to the United States.

This was the end of Spain in the Southeast, the end of all foreign menace in the Southeast. And finally the Indian nations of the Southeast were not needed any more.

They were no longer of use as buffer states; there were no rival European nations left to buff against. White settlers were all over the back country; Indian trade and Indian middlemen east of the Mississippi were of no further importance. The spirit of the frontier—clear the Indians out—had already outgrown opposition to become the prime moving force behind American policy when in 1828 it took over the government completely with the election of Andrew Jackson, the embodiment of the frontier spirit, as President.

One of the first pieces of business for the new administration was the passage of what was known as the Indian Removal bill, which became law in the spring of 1830 after Congressional debate of exceptionally hot-tempered style, even for those hot-tempered Congressional times. This bill did not authorize enforced removal of any Indians, but merely gave the President power to initiate land exchanges with Indian nations residing within the states or territories—aimed particularly at the powerful intact nations of the Southeast: Choctaw, Chickasaw, Cherokee, and Creeks.

However, force was necessary since these nations did not want to remove.

The states principally involved, Georgia, Alabama (created in 1819 mainly from Creek and Cherokee country), and Mississippi (created in 1817 mainly from Choctaw and Chickasaw country), passed legislation outlawing tribal governments and placing the Indian nations under the jurisdiction of state laws. This was in violation of securities granted the Indian nations by treaties with the United States, and the Indians appealed to the federal government for protection. General Jackson and General John H. Eaton, his Secretary of War, told them the federal government was simply unable to comply with its treaty pledges, and redoubled efforts to obtain new treaties in which the Civilized Tribes would agree to removal beyond the Mississippi River.

State law prevailing within the Indian nations, the Indian lands were wide open for trespass by anyone, including liquor dealers. This too was in violation of federal law as well as tribal regulations, but again General Jackson and General Eaton said they simply could not enforce the federal law. Bootleggers crowded into the nations, grog shops bloomed like the blossoms of spring, and large numbers of Indian citizens went on a drunk that didn't quit until they found themselves either removed or dead.

Actions could now be brought against Indians in the state courts, and their goods attached for debt by sheriffs and constables. State laws were enacted prohibiting a court from accepting the testimony of an Indian against a white man, so that a claim, no matter how fraudulent, brought by a white man against an Indian could not legally be protested.

As the tribal leaders began to accept treaties providing for eventual allotment of their lands and removal to the West, white squatters and land speculators moved in by the swarm to jump the gun on the land allotments, stripping the Indians of their lands and properties by fraud, liquor, or force. Large numbers of Indians, many of whom had been comfortable or prosperous, took to the woods or the swamps in terror, divested of their possessions and driven from their homes. Occasionally they were divested of the clothes they were wearing by frolicking white men armed with writs or rifles.

Drunkenness, panic, privations, starvation, brought an increase of Indian-versus-Indian violence. Crimes of violence by whites against Indians did not ordinarily go to court and so are not recorded; but under the circumstances there may have been a few. A renowned Chickasaw warrior and councilor, Emubby, who had served with General Jackson in many campaigns, was killed rather casually by a white man named Jones; the incident got into the papers because of Emubby's prominence: "He had been murdered without any provocation. . . . When Jones presented his rifle at him, he leaped from his horse, opened his breast, and said, 'Shoot! Emubby is not afraid to die.' The wretch did shoot and the Indian fell. . . ."

Appeal after appeal to General Jackson and General Eaton and General Lewis Cass, General Eaton's successor as Secretary of War, brought the fixed reply that the federal government was simply not able to restrain either the squatters or the state legislators, even though it had bound itself to do so by definite and enforceable guaranties in previous treaties. All appeals were referred to a statement of General Jackson's that the matter was not one of right but of remedy. The remedy was removal of the Indian nations to the West, where they would be given land grants that would endure, said General Jackson, "as long as the grass grows, or water runs."

Choctaw chiefs accepted a provisional treaty of removal in 1830. This was preceded by much inside finagling as to who were to be chiefs, since the treaty chiefs received substantial favors and gratuities. The majority of the Choctaw nation appeared to oppose the treaty, but lack of organization and leadership left them helpless. The Senate added to the confusion by refusing to ratify a Whereas in the treaty wherein the President avowed the United States could not protect the Choctaw in previous treaty rights against the state of Mississippi. Difficulties were smoothed over, more or less, and in November of 1831 the first official Choctaw emigrants, 4,000 people, started for the new lands they had selected in the western part of Arkansas territory. Other parties followed the same winter.

It happened to be an unusually hard winter. The Mississippi at Memphis was so choked with ice as to be impassable for days at a time for flatboats and most steamboats. There was zero-degree weather and heavy snow in the Great Arkansas Swamp through which the emigrants, many of whom had left their homes destitute, barefoot, and nearly naked, had to struggle.

Matters were complicated by lack of funds. Congress had appropriated money to pay the expenses of Indian removal; this was to be disbursed through white agents and contractors who signed to "conduct" so many emigrants to the new Indian Territory for so much money, and of course expected to make a profit; some of these contracts, at least, were given as political plums. Major Francis W. Armstrong, of General Jackson's home town of Nashville, Tennessee, was appointed Choctaw agent in the autumn of 1831 and left Washington in November with $50,000 in cash to meet the expenses of that first desperate winter of Choctaw removal. The Choctaw and their conductors were obliged to make their chaotic journey without funds, however, since Major Armstrong did not arrive with the money in Arkansas until the end of February. He had spent the worst of the winter at home in Nashville because it had been too cold, he said, for him to travel. Major Armstrong was put in charge of the rest of the Choctaw removal in the following years and was the subject of angry, albeit futile complaints from the young Army officers sent along with the emigrants to see that treaty provisions were fulfilled.

And so removal began. It went on for years, and it developed that the experiences of this first winter were the easiest of all—with the single exception of the Chickasaw migration; the Chickasaw could not be entirely defeated, even in this.

Cholera appeared in the summer of 1831, centering around Vicksburg, and came back each summer until 1836, setting up a belt of death that halted most traffic, but through which the armies of Indian exiles had to be moved, the federal government and the states concerned being inflexibly opposed to any delays.

Pressures and harassments notwithstanding, the removed people left their homeland with the greatest of reluctance. They bore, be it remembered, the weight of time on their eyes; they were the descendants of the temple-mound people of this region long before, and perhaps of the burial-mound people of still longer before. They had lived for countless generations in this sweet and luxuriant land, and did not share the white frontiersman's restless passion to be always moving on. Likewise the whites could not comprehend the Indians' fanatical attachment to a particular part of the earth. "They cannot appreciate the feelings of a man that loves his country," so Washington Irving quoted the Creek chief Eneah Emathla. Some watching whites were moved and some amused when departing Indians went about touching leaves, trees, rocks, and streams in farewell.

Another sort of distress was added when the pressures and harassments and conspiratorial treaty politics tore the nations open with dissensions and set friend against friend and family against family, so that some groups went west in hostile divisions and carried on the quarrels for years in their new country.

More commonly the educated and the ignorant, the good and the bad, those used to high-style gracious living and those from huts in the wildest depths of the forest, were herded together, reduced to the lowest common denominator by corn likker, degradation, and despair, and driven like cattle, like wild animals, so they said: "We were drove off like wolves... and our peoples' feet were bleeding with long marches.... We are men... we have women and children, and why should we come like wild horses?"

Rotten boats were occasionally hired for river passages, being cheap, but being rotten as well as overcrowded they were unmanageable and occasionally sank, with most melancholy loss of life (to use the favorite term of the time). A number of emigrant parties lost many of their people, the aged and children first, always, from deaths on the march.

White heroes of removal were not plenty (in another favorite word of the time), but there were a few, principally young officers such as Lieutenant Joseph W. Harris of New Hampshire, an 1825 graduate of West Point, who wrote in 1834 in the midst of a cholera epidemic among his Cherokee emigrants (he had cholera himself at the time), "I am not much of a physician & feel that I am but a poor prop for these unfortunates to rest upon—but I have done and will do my best." Lieutenant Harris's best, in the whole story, was resplendent with humanity and valor, although not always according to regulations. He kept on giving his best in the work of Indian removal until his death in 1837 at the age of thirty-two, and may have received his Order of Merit from Higher Headquarters later.

The Chickasaw made removal treaties in 1832 and 1834, insisting on provisions by which the government would sell their lands and hold the money for their use, and by which a commission of Chickasaw councilors would pass on the competency of any tribal member making a private sale of property. Even with these safeguards the Chickasaw did not escape unscathed. But as a whole the nation appears to have gotten away with more wealth and in better order than any of the others.

When they moved west in 1837, they took along thousands of their horses, and got a fair percentage of them through—gangs of white horse thieves hanging on the flanks of Indian emigrant parties that had any horses at all were the chief livestock menace; the swamps were next. Their horse herds made for slow travel, and the superintendent in charge of Chickasaw removal wrote: "The Chickasaws have an immense quantity of baggage. A great many of them have fine wagons and teams. They have also some four or five thousand ponies. I have used all the influence that I had to get them to sell off their horses, but they would about as lieve part with their lives as part with a horse."

In 1821 and 1823, some years before the push for removal, William MacIntosh of the Creeks had made treaties with citizens of Georgia ceding fifteen million acres of Creek land. He had been supported in these treaties by twelve other Creek chiefs under his control, but opposed by thirty-six chiefs representing nine tenths of the Creeks. MacIntosh was in the pay of the Georgia commissioners, and in 1825, said emoluments being fattened, MacIntosh and his followers signed a treaty ceding the remaining Creek land—ten million acres—to Georgia. These treaties were in violation not only of Creek custom but of a specific Creek law that provided the death sentence for any Creek who sold land without the consent of the entire nation in council. Formal sentence was passed on MacIntosh after the

**In this Creek war scene, Indians armed with hatchets, rifles, and bows and arrows rush to defend their village against American soldiers. In 1836 the Secretary of War ordered the army into Alabama to "inaugurate an operation of war" against the Creeks to "subdue them and remove them to the West." Cherokee, Choctaw, Seminole, and Chickasaw tribes suffered similar fates.**

signing of the 1825 treaty and on the morning of May Day, 1825, a party of Creek soldiers went to his house and shot him to death, and his son-in-law as well for good measure. The appointed executioner who killed William MacIntosh was Menewa, the ex–Red Stick commander.

The illegal treaty of 1825 was annulled, and the following year Menewa went to Washington and signed a new treaty, securing the Creeks in the possession of their remaining territory, and promising his loyalty henceforth to the United States.

Governor George M. Troup of Georgia, William MacIntosh's cousin, was enraged by his murder and became one of the leaders in the subsequent large-scale and extralegal campaign to drive the Creeks out of the country regardless of treaty rights.

By 1831 this campaign had progressed to the point that the Creeks were reeling from the waves of white squatters, land speculators, and bootleggers who were invading their country under the protection of Georgia and Alabama state laws. There were 1,500 such intruders in December 1831, according to a protest made by Eneah Micco, principal chief of the Lower Towns. They included "horsethieves and other criminals" and also included men of heretofore respectable position.

The President and his Secretary of War openly stated that they had no intention of trying to keep the government's treaty promises and insisted on a treaty of removal to the West as the Creek's only hope of relief. In 1832 (two months short of the one-hundredth anniversary of their first cordial treaties with Oglethorpe) the Creeks, driven to desperation, finally accepted a removal treaty, with the provision that white intruders were to be removed from their lands for five years while the tribe prepared to depart.

But the treaty also contained a provision giving each tribal member the right to sell his individual selection (or remain on it, if he wished), each sale to be protected from fraud by being subject to approval by the President. Under the new state laws this could mean that the land and property of any individual Creek were now legally up for grabs to the first white man who might present a claim for it, no matter how plainly fraudulent—unless the federal government enforced these protective provisions it had just agreed to.

General Jackson and his Secretary of War did not enforce these provisions—while enforcing with rigor the provisions of cession by the Creeks. If the Creeks had been troubled before by intruders, now they were being overwhelmed.

Six months after the signing of the 1832 treaty, the Creek council said in a memorial to the Secretary of War: "Instead of our situation being relieved as was anticipated, we are distressed in a ten fold manner—we are surrounded by the whites with their fields and fences, our lives are in jeopardy, we are daily threatened.... We have for the last six months lived in fear, yet we have borne it with patience, believing our father, the President, would comply on his part with what he had pledged himself to do."

The Creeks were driven into the forests and swamps, their crops and homes were taken, and many were reduced to starvation. Said newspaper stories of the time: "To see a whole people destitute of food—the incessant cry of the emaciated creatures being *bread! bread!* is beyond description distressing. The existence of many of the Indians is prolonged by eating roots and the bark of trees... nothing that can afford nourishment is rejected however offensive it may be.... " "They beg their food from door to door... it is really painful to see the wretched creatures wandering about the streets, haggard and naked.... "

White speculators had their capital in Columbus, Georgia, across the Chattahoochee River from Coweta, the capital of the Lower Creeks. The leading business, of course, was fraudulent certification of land titles, but another thriving sideline was seizing title to the property of Creeks who died, since according to state laws only a white man could administer the estate of a deceased Indian. These businesses sometimes assumed the rather jolly air of a mass sports event, and while a United States marshal said they attracted "some of the most lawless and uncouth men I have ever seen," they also involved "men of every degree," as another investigator reported. A special agent wrote to the President: "A greater mass of corruption perhaps, has never been congregated in any part of the world.... "

The capital town of the Lower Creeks eventually taken over by these whites became the present Phenix City, Alabama.

Legal aspects of the situation received much national attention. Georgia claimed some technical justification for its aggressive actions by pointing to the Compact of 1802 between Georgia and the federal government in which the United States had agreed to buy title to Indian lands in Georgia at its own expense, as soon as reasonably possible—although this commitment seemed to conflict in certain legal particulars with the previous treaties dating back to 1790 between the United States and the Indian nations.

General Jackson's pronouncements occasionally seemed to invoke the principle of states' rights, although in 1830 he had announced himself opposed to that principle ("Our Federal Union, it must be preserved"); he also asserted that the federal government was simply too feeble to enforce federal law in the states of Georgia, Alabama, and Mississippi. But in the contemporary action of South Carolina in nullifying the federal tariff General Jackson reacted with promptness and vigor, sent General Winfield Scott and heavy troop reinforcements into South Carolina and sent a naval force to anchor off Charleston, and avowed that if need be he would execute upon a charge of high treason not only John C. Calhoun, leader of the South Carolina nullifiers, but every member of Congress from South Carolina who had taken part in the nullification proceedings.

Obviously General Jackson's administration only countenanced the open defiance of Georgia, Alabama, and Mississippi because in this case it was in sympathy with their objective—clear the Indians out. That objective was as much the baby of General Jackson's administration as of the various states involved, but the independent extralegal actions of the states were necessary both in pressuring the Indians and in furnishing an excuse of sorts to the administration, which after all needed some kind of pretext in asking the nation to wink at violations of the national word of honor and the President's oath of office.

Some aspects of this situation are of more than ordinary historical interest. For one example among many: an Alabama citizen named Hardiman Owen, a tough boy noted for his exceptional thoroughness in beating up Indians when chasing them off their lands, made an unsuccessful attempt to murder a United States marshal. Troops from Fort Mitchell, Alabama, ran Owen down and killed him when he fired on them. An Alabama grand jury then returned indictments against the soldier who shot Owen, the other soldiers and officers present, and the United States marshal who had called out the troops; and a court order was issued attaching the person of the army major commanding Fort Mitchell. Alabama's basic objection was to the molestation of white intruders in the Creek country by federal officers, some of whom had made a nuisance of themselves by individual efforts to enforce the protective provisions of the recent treaty. Alabama held, in effect, that its state jurisdiction took precedence over that of the federal officers.

General Jackson sent Francis Scott Key to Alabama to settle the trouble, and Alabama at length dropped the indictments in return for certain concessions: the terms are less important than the fact of the capitulation by which the Star-Spangled Banner refrained for the nonce from waving over the state of Alabama.

In spite of pressures and harassments the Creeks delayed their departure for four of the five years allowed them by the removal treaty, being unable to decide on the specific lands of destination. But in 1836, when a resistance movement against their sufferings spread among some of the Creeks under the general leadership of Eneah Emathla, the Secretary of War immediately gave orders to the military to remove the whole tribe at once as a military measure. An army was ordered into Alabama, to "inaugurate an operation of war" against the Creeks, "subdue them and remove them to the West."

Menewa, true to his promise of loyalty, joined this army in rounding up the rebellious Creeks, as did nearly 2,000 other Creek warriors.

The captured "hostiles" were started west in a double-file procession, manacled and chained together, eighty-four-year-old Eneah Emathla among them: "I was informed... that he never uttered a complaint," said a reporter in describing the first leg of the march.

And so the nations departed. The Cherokee resisted with incredible tenacity in the face of concerted oppression that mounted year by year. (It had its entertaining incidents—the extraordinary Cherokee leader John Ross, evicted from his beautiful Georgia mansion and living in a dirt-floored log cabin across the line in Tennessee, received as a guest there John Howard Payne, the author of "Home, Sweet Home." The Georgia State Guard happened to cross the border at that time to abduct Ross and kidnaped Payne too as a suspicious character; he was held in a Georgia jail for twelve days.) The Cherokee pushed a legal fight until they won their case in the United States Supreme Court, Chief Justice John Marshall delivering with the opinion a blazing denunciation of the wrongs perpetrated by the state of

Georgia upon the Indians. The Supreme Court found the acts of the state of Georgia unconstitutional and in violation of solemn treaty rights. The decision was wildly celebrated in the Cherokee nation.

However, President Jackson refused to execute the decision of the court.

Finally, with the excuse of a false treaty, the United States Army in 1838 and 1839 removed the Cherokee people by force, with the exception of a few hundred who hid in the mountains of North Carolina—where their descendants still live.

The Cherokee, having resisted longest, suffered most in the process of removal, nearly one fourth of their entire population dying on the way.

An effort was made to include the Seminole of Florida in the general removal from the Southeast—this brought on war, which lasted until 1842 and cost the lives of 1,500 American troops and $20,000,000 in military expenses. Its most publicized feature was the capture of the young Seminole chief Osceola by the American General T. S. Jesup. When the much-wanted Osceola at last set up a conference under a flag of truce, General Jesup sent an officer to the appointed place, seven or eight miles from St. Augustine, and while the conference was going on had the conference ground quietly surrounded by a body of troops, who at a signal made Osceola and his followers prisoners. This means of capturing prisoners was used repeatedly by General Jesup against the Seminoles—once with the inadvertent help of a well-intentioned Cherokee peace delegation. The shocked Cherokee chief John Ross wrote to the Secretary of War, "I do hereby most solemnly protest against this unprecedented violation of that sacred rule... of treating with all due respect those who had ever presented themselves under a flag of truce." But, unfortunately, it was the only means that worked. Wrote General Jesup, "No Seminole proves false to his country, nor has a single instance ever occurred of a first rate warrior having surrendered." Osceola died in a military prison three months after his capture. But the war went on.

Seminole women (as some of the women of the Creek resistance had done) killed their small children to free themselves to fight beside their men, and the war developed into a game of hide-and-seek in the swamps of the Florida Everglades; obviously it could never be won by either side.

Peace was finally made on quite honorable terms worked out by Army Colonel Ethan Allen Hitchcock, who during the war wrote, "Five years ago I came [to Florida] as a volunteer, willingly making every effort in my power to be of service in punishing as I thought, the Indians. I now come, with the persuasion that the Indians have been wronged. . . ." Most of the Seminole moved west to Indian Territory but several bands remained in the region of the Everglades and are still there, having resisted, down through the decades, inducements to emigrate such as have seldom been offered to any other tribe.

The old ever-faithful American allies among the Creeks and Cherokee, who had made possible the Horseshoe Bend victory that had launched General Jackson's national career, came off no better in the removal than the ancient hostiles. Ex-hostiles such as Menewa, who had become steadfast American allies (Menewa adopted the army uniform of an American general), fared no better than the implacable anti-Americans who remained implacable. Several hundred Creeks, including Major David Moniac, a Creek graduate of West Point, volunteered for service with General Jesup against the Seminole, with the understanding that their families would be protected until their service ended and they could emigrate to the West—but while they were fighting in Florida, citizen companies from Alabama and Georgia overpowered the defenseless federal agents assigned to protect the waiting families, seized whatever property was available, made a number of the families prisoners on various pretexts, and clubbed to death with their muskets a ninety-year-old Creek who foolishly tried to prevent the rape of a fifteen-year-old girl. The Creek volunteers returned from Florida to find the last of their possessions gone, and their families already started west.

The terms of the Creek treaty permitted individual Creeks to elect to stay in their native land (if they were willing to brave continued persecution by the States), and quite a few meant to do so. However, these provisions were abrogated by the government, and all the Creeks were forced to leave, including Menewa, who had received a personal promise from high authority to the contrary. On the night before he left for exile he went back to his town of Okfuskee and spent the night alone. He said to an old white friend the next morning, "Last evening

I saw the sun set for the last time, and its light shine upon the tree tops, and the land, and the water, that I am never to look upon again." Then he walked away. He was an old man, and had been many times wounded. But those who believe that Indians don't cry haven't looked over the official reports of the Great Removal.

And so the nations were gone from their warm and charming land. But something more had happened than the mere uprooting of 50,000 or so people from their homes. The frontier spirit had clearly paraded the black horse of its evils coupled to the white horse of its virtues. Natural resources—in this case, people—had been merrily exploited in an open conspiracy involving the President of the United States and large portions of the population. Young America, in short, had been told a most effective bedtime story of crime without punishment. The nation, in short, had been exposed to quite a spectacle of dirty business, and it is reasonable to suppose the sinuous folds of the young American mind had picked up a new wrinkle or two.

# IX

# The Image Makers

**This charming but unrealistic French lithograph shows a warrior, his weapons cast aside, wooing a maiden in the approved romantic style of the nineteenth century.**

The statement had been made in foregoing chapters that the Indian story is of considerable historical importance. It might be well to pause in the narrative and examine that point.

Christopher Columbus's first reports of the New World and its people were contained in two letters written in February and early March 1493, in the course of the return trip from his voyage of discovery. On his way to Spain he touched at Lisbon, where he was given a state welcome and a royal cross-questioning by King John of Portugal, and the two letters were transferred to a courier to be rushed overland to the Spanish court, then at Barcelona.

A foreign agent in Spain had the gist of the first letter on the way to his employer, the Duke of Ferrara, by March 8, and by April the letter was in print in the Italian states.

The second letter was put into Latin and sent in April to Rome, where it also was rushed into print, in at least eight different editions, and by June was being published in a verse paraphrase of sixty-eight metrical stanzas for the common reader. This also went through a number of popular editions. It was sung in the streets—the news magazine for the illiterate—while learned scholars met to discuss the official Latin text.

*Ego statim atque ad mare illud perueni prima insula quosdam Indos violenter arripui*: "As soon as I had landed on the first island that I encountered in that sea I had several Indians taken prisoner..." and the people of the New World were thenceforward Indians. Columbus had brought back six of those *quosdam Indos* with him; they were a "well-formed people and of fair stature... very comely" and created a sensation, especially among the Spanish ladies.

In Spain, holiday was declared wherever Columbus appeared. Business was suspended, bells were rung, the streets were illuminated with torches; and the Admiral of the Ocean Fleet, as he styled himself in the signature of the famous second letter, was granted the extravagant honor of being seated in the presence of the sovereigns; and his Indians ranked about his throne like wonder-bringing cherubim.

For wonders had arrived in the Old World from the New. From that time on, in a fairly real sense, they never ceased.

Much has been said about the prodigious changes brought to the New World by the Old. Something needs to be said about the changes, perhaps less immediately obvious but no less prodigiously effective, brought to the Old World by the New.

Within a matter of weeks after Columbus's return Portugal was locked in a diplomatic struggle with Spain over rights to the new Discovery. Portugal was the great seafaring nation, and the efforts of four kings, Prince Henry the Navigator, and many brave fleets had brought her various guarantees in the realms of the farther oceans that were supported by three papal bulls and the formal Treaty of Alcacovas. (Columbus dodged trouble over this treaty and gained time for Spain by discreetly falsifying, at first, the latitudes of his discoveries.)

But the Discovery was Spain's. And the newly elected Pope, the licentious Alexander VI, was also Spain's—he was the Borgia Pope (father of Cesare and Lucrezia Borgia), and the Borgias were an Aragonese family.

By the end of summer 1493, new papal bulls were cutting the ground from under Portugal's position, and Columbus was on his way back to the Indies with a hastily assembled expedition to seal the Spanish claim with commerce and colonies. The Pope established a line 100 leagues west and south of the Azores, preserving everything beyond for Spain and confining Portugal, in effect, to Africa.

This line (enforceable, of course, by the fact that any Christian who disregarded it might be excommunicated) was too drastic to be realistic, and was revised more to Portugal's liking the following year by the Treaty of Tordesillas, agreements between Spain and Portugal "for the Partition of the Ocean Sea" that moved the Pope's line considerably farther west, to 370 leagues west of the Cape Verdes—thus, as it turned out, giving Portugal the hump of Brazil.

This, the first of many American matters to occupy the chief statesmen of Europe, was America's entrance on the stage of world history. The script thereafter was ceaselessly and sometimes hectically rewritten to give the newcomer an ever-growing role. The New World and its innocent people so easy to plunder went straight to the Old World's heart and became a star overnight.

Rich America played a part of many sides in the Reformation;

in the expansion of the fur trade so important in the lives of England, France, and Russia; in the rise of English and Dutch mercantilism; and even in the foundation of modern international law, as laid down in the lectures of the learned Francisco de Vitoria at Salamanca in 1539, establishing the legal principle that any foreign people should be dealt with honorably even though they might differ in religion and culture from one's own people. All of Europe's plots and counterplots and the process of Europe's ideas after 1492 were in some wise altered and shifted by the New World and the peculiar character of the New World's people.

The point to be emphasized here is that the role of the New World's people was not entirely passive. It was active in the sense that they so often welcomed their conquerors, nursed fledgling European colonies, and to such a degree helped the European conquerors in their business of conquering that, as has been previously noticed, the conquest of the New World was principally one of European-directed Indians conquering other Indians. In this respect the peculiar character of the American Indians was of some import in world affairs almost from the moment of the Discovery.

In other obvious direct respects the impact of the world of the American Indians worked fairly rapid changes in the Old World, with the spread to Europe of such Indian crops and products as corn, tomatoes, rubber, white potatoes, tobacco (in all its Indian usages—pipe, cigar, cigarette, snuff, and chaw), a long list of medicinal drugs including quinine, and such essentials to modern living as peanuts, popcorn, and chewing gum. Chocolate, brought from Mexico, became so popular in Spain that church services were disturbed by worshipers sipping the chocolate they had brought along to Mass.

Some authorities believe that an influential item of another kind, syphilis, first came to Europe from the New World. Other authorities believe the opposite, that it was one more in the catalogue of disastrous diseases brought by the people from heaven from the Old World to the New; and perhaps the weightiest current evidence leans toward this view. But the controversy has jogged along for centuries and still goes on.

Indirectly, the peculiar character of the American Indians became profoundly operative upon the European soul, an operation which, in all its ramifications, also still goes on.

The smell of gold and spice and azure jewels filled the nostrils of the first Spaniards in the New World, but, curiously, it is the childlikeness of the lovely people that most fills the first Spanish reports. They could almost imagine that the beautiful (and nude) island girls who came forth dancing and singing to welcome them at Caribbean towns were the fabled dryads, the wood nymphs sung by ancient poets, so said (in 1530) Peter Martyr of Anghiera, first historian of the New World. Simple childlikeness was transfigured into unearthly poetry when the Spaniards broke their way into the marvel-filled civilizations of the mainland, and the Maya sang of their coming (in the *Book of the Jaguar Priest of Tizimin*): "They are agitated by the drums. The Bat is awakened by the drums. The four Bacabs ride to earth on the back of a green rainbow. One by one the stars fall. . . . " The bearded invaders thrust with their swords and were pierced in return by words: "The warrior will employ his prowess on nobody. When they are taught about the abundant life, they will have compassion on the fields. They will have compassion on the mountains. . . . "

The childlikeness and the poetry seized on the imagination of Europe and remained a living force long after the plunging swords had crumbled into rust.

"I wolde think their life moste happye of all men, if they might therwith enioye their aunciente libertie," to quote the language of Peter Martyr's first English translation (1577), speaking of the Indians. "Emonge these simple sowles, a fewe clothes serue the naked: weightes and measures are not needefull to such as can not skyll of crafte and deceyte and haue not the vse of pestiferous monye. . . . So that if we shall not be ashamed to confesse the truthe, they seeme to lyue in that goulden worlde of the whiche owlde wryters speake so much: wherein men lyued simply and innocentlye without inforcement of lawes, without quarrelingue Iudges and libelles, contente onely to satisfie nature. . . . "

The famous *Essays* of Michel Eyquem de Montaigne, published in France in the 1580s, contain in Chapter 30, Book I, a widely quoted dissertation on "the new world we have lately discovered. . . . " This essay was first translated into English in

1603, entitled "Of the Caniballes," and made to read in part as follows:

"I find (as farre as I have beene informed) there is nothing in that nation [the New World], that is either barbarous or savage, unlesse men call that barbarisme which is not common to them. . . . " Wishing that the Greek philosophers could have known of this people so "neere their originall naturalitie" and of a genuineness "so pure and simple" as an example of the ideal state sought by Plato, "It is a nation, would I answer Plato, that hath no kinde of traffike, no knowledge of Letters, no intelligence of numbers, no name of magistrate [which, incidentally, Montaigne was], nor of politike superioritie; no use of service, of riches or of povertie; no contracts, no successions, no partitions, no occupation but idle; no respect of kindred, but common, no apparell but naturall, no manuring of lands, no use of wine, corne, or mettle. The very words that import lying, falsehood, treason, dissimulations, covetousness, envie, detraction, and pardon, were never heard of amongst them."

Montaigne learned of Indians ("They spend the whole day in dancing") through reading the travel books of his time, talking with returned explorers, and questioning (through a highly unsatisfactory interpreter) three Indians who visited France in the time of Charles IX (1560–1574).

These last were able to explain to him something of the common Indian custom of dividing the people of a town into moieties, two groups or societies with special and separate duties, such as the Summer and Winter people of various North American tribes; and the Indians were struck by the two opposing moieties they seemed to see in the towns of Europe: "They had perceived, there were men amongst us full gorged with all sorts of commodities, and others which hunger-starved, and bare with need and povertie, begged at their gates: and found it strange, these moyties so needy could endure such an injustice, and that they tooke not the others by the throte, or set fire on their house. . . . "

Shakespeare, in writing *The Tempest*, took for the play's framework the Bermuda shipwreck of some Virginia-bound colonists in 1609; twisted the monster Caliban's name for an anagram of *canibal*; and in Act II, scene 1, gave the honest old

**This idyllic *Danse de Mariage chez les Canadiens* by an eighteenth-century French romanticist typifies the European tendency to idealize Indian life as the simple, happy existence of unspoiled children in a state of nature.**

Counsellor Gonzalo this celebrated speech on the ideal commonwealth:

*I' the commonwealth I would by contraries*
*Execute all things; for no kind of traffic*
*Would I admit; no name of magistrate;*
*Letters should not be known; riches, poverty,*
*And use of service, none; contract, succession,*
*Bourn, bound of land, tilth, vineyard, none;*
*No use of metal, corn, or wine, or oil;*
*No occupation; all men idle, all;*
*And women too, but innocent and pure;*
*No sovereignty...*
*All things in common nature should produce*
*Without sweat or endeavour: treason, felony,*
*Sword, pike, knife, gun, or need of any engine,*
*Would I not have; but nature should bring forth,*
*Of its own kind, all foison, all abundance,*
*To feed my innocent people...*
*I would with such perfection govern, sir,*
*To excel the golden age.*

Maybe Thucydides could be paraphrased to say words change the world, not kings nor empty wars. Anyway, these same thoughts, filtered through the centuries, were in 1750 distilled by Jean Jacques Rousseau into his vision of the blessed state of the natural man, the noble savage, pure, simple, and above all free. "Man is born free, and everywhere he is in chains"—and the words almost literally undermined the thrones of Europe and sent them crashing into chaos with the French Revolution and the powder train of subsequent convulsions.

Rousseau's spiritual heirs pursued the glorious vision of natural freedom, idealistic liberty pure and simple, in the face of such worthy defenders of the traditional European faith as Goethe, who said in 1827: "Freedom is an odd thing, and every man has enough of it, if he can only satisfy himself.... The citizen is as free as the nobleman, when he restrains himself within the limits which God appointed by placing him in that rank.... Freedom consists not in refusing to recognize anything above us, but in respecting something which is above us.... " Hegel took his stand on the same dictum; but the dictum went the way of the thrones and it too was overthrown in the leveling sweep of the idea of liberty pure and simple, a sweep in which, as has been seen, the image of the American Indian was not entirely absent.

A divergent line of European thought gradually turned to the problem of property and, clearly not altogether unaware of the ghosts of Montaigne's philosophical Indian tourists, proceeded to take some of the propertied moiety by the throte and set fire on their house.

A pioneer American anthropologist, Lewis Henry Morgan, was an authoritative student of the Iroquois and unbefuddled with naïve notions of an Indian golden world, but the peculiar character of Indian society, the propertyless society of the "ancient gentes," nevertheless gave him a message he felt was important. He wrote in his most ambitious book, *Ancient Society*: "Since the advent of civilization, the outgrowth of property has been so immense... that it has become, on the part of the people, an unmanageable power. The human mind stands bewildered in the presence of its own creation.... A mere property career is not the final destiny of mankind, if progress is to be the law of the future as it has been of the past.... The dissolution of society bids fair to become the termination of a career of which property is the end and aim; because such a career contains the elements of self-destruction. Democracy in government, brotherhood in society, equality in rights and privileges, and universal education, foreshadow the next higher plane of society to which experience, intelligence, and knowledge are steadily tending. It will be a revival, in a higher form, of the liberty, equality and fraternity of the ancient gentes...."

This was published in 1877, in time to be of use to Karl Marx and Friedrich Engels in writing the second and third volumes of *Das Kapital*. Marx made notes for a book on Morgan's researches but did not live to write it. Engels did so, in his *The Origin of the Family, Private Property and the State*, published in 1884, in which he described the notion he had gathered of the Indian way of life with a restatement of the old familiar pattern: "And a wonderful constitution it is... in all its childlike simplicity! No soldiers, no gendarmes or police, no nobles, kings, regents, prefects, or judges, no prisons, no lawsuits.... There cannot be any poor or needy—the communal household and the gens [related family groups] know their responsibilities towards the old, the sick, and those disabled in war. All are equal and free—the women included.... And what men and women such a society breeds is proved by the admiration inspired in all white people who have come into contact with unspoiled Indians, by the personal dignity, uprightness, strength of character, and courage of these barbarians...."

The Indian image operative on the European soul was often a far cry from Indian reality. The European soul thus altered often achieved an even farther cry from its expressed aim. But the fact remains that an undeniable reality, the peculiar character of the American Indians, was the kernel of this process, and, for good or otherwise, it did have its effect on the changing world of Europe. Those Europeans who came to the New World by 1600 and later were already subtly different people from the firstcomers of a century before, and at least some of their subtle differences were due to influences from the Indians they were coming to displace.

The Indian image that touched Europe with its shadow was of course more directly influential still in helping to shape the new countries and peoples that came into being in the Americas. Mention has already been made of the important and sometimes decisive Indian participation in colonial history, and in the action and reaction that set white frontiers in motion.

Not surprisingly, the leveling sweep of the idea of liberty pure and simple ran first through America before making its tour of Europe and then the world. In America this idea sometimes manifested itself in outright Indian costume, such as in the various pseudo-Indian political, military, and fraternal societies organized from the time of the French and Indian War onward. The most famous of these was the Tammany Society, taking its name from the great Delaware councilor Tamenend and calling its different lodges "tribes," its officers "sachems," and its meeting place the "wigwam." It came into prominence shortly after the Revolution, dedicated to promoting "the independence, the popular liberty, and the federal union of the country," in particular opposition to the powerful elements working to make the new country a kingdom or an oligarchy. The Tammany Society earned a fair share of credit for the eventual triumph of libertarian ideals in the United States; it also eventually managed to force through universal manhood suffrage in New

York State in 1826, and abolish imprisonment for debt in New York City in 1831. It was also principally responsible for securing the 1790 treaty with the Creek Indians that was so useful at the time in ensuring the peace and safety of the southern borders of the new United States. In later years, after the Civil War, the Tammany Society degenerated into the New York City political machine familiar to our own day.

Mention has also been made of the possible influence of Indian confederations on the conversion of European colonies into new American states. But there may be still other less apparent traits in the makeup of modern American nations that perhaps owe something to the peculiar character of Indian society. The policy of free immigration, for example, among the countries of the Americas, is scarcely in the European tradition. The free land of the frontier contributed to this policy, certainly, but what then of Australia, with vast free frontier lands but never a policy of free immigration? Could the common Indian tradition of free access into the tribe be at work here? The speculation seems permissible.

There may be a number of other such permissible speculations. Again and again Indian tribes sent food to starving European colonists; again and again early European writers remarked on the fact that among the Indians if one starved they all starved. Could this have anything to do with American traditions of charity on a mass scale, even an international scale? Are there clearer European sources for such traditions?

At any rate, it seems clear that the peculiar character of the American Indian constituted a force in history deserving of serious consideration.

The question of what that peculiar character was, what made the Indians behave as they did, is involved with the total picture of Indian life and thought, and lends historical importance to that study. The question *in toto* is exceedingly complex. But a speculation may be permitted here as to the essence of it, the essential peculiarity of the Indian character, the basic difference between the Indian world and the Old World.

The European culture that invaded the New World was infinitely superior to the culture of the Indians in the broad field of mechanics. In concepts of virtue, ethics, justice, and wisdom the two cultures frequently differed, but seldom widely.

The one great Indian difference appears to have been rooted in the matter of property: the general Indian view (with exceptions) of cooperation in the use of property in common as against the general European view (with exceptions too) of competition for the acquisition of private property.

This encouraged an appearance of classless freedom in Indian society, encouraged a strong group identity, and encouraged a prevailing interest in matters other than work. The bohemian, impractical attitudes that resulted acted against material progress but Indian life, in its preoccupation with rituals, games, the beauty of soft spring rain, the making of pretty gewgaws to wear in the hair, or other such folderol, may have been quite a bit of fun.

During the colonial Indian wars Dutch, French, and English captives often refused to part from their captors and return to civilization when they had the chance. This was a subject of indignant remark by generations of uncaptured Europeans. Said the historian of an Ohio Valley Indian campaign in 1764, when a number of white captives had to be forcibly repatriated:" For the honour of humanity, we would suppose those persons to have been of the lowest rank, either bred up in ignorance and distressing penury, or who had lived so long with the Indians as to forget all their former connections. For easy and unconstrained as the savage life is, certainly it could never be put in competition with the blessings of improved life and the light of religion, by any persons who have had the happiness of enjoying, and the capacity of discerning, them." But a surprising lot of white captives opted for it, nevertheless. What did it profit a man to work the fat off his back for the blessings of improved life, when the twinkling stars were equally bright for everyone lost in the dark? Indian life may have had an edge in the pursuit of happiness precisely because it would not race.

In a word, the Indian world was devoted to living, the European world to getting.

This, the essence of the peculiar character of the American Indian, was the essence of the force that, hidden in the image of the noble savage, helped change the course of history. It was also the essence of the weakness that destroyed the Indian nations. It was also, as has been mentioned before, the unbridgeable gulf separating whites and Indians from direct communication and understanding.

Thomas Jefferson, among many others, proposed a bridge for this abyss and described it quite accurately in a Washington speech to certain Indian chiefs: "Temperance, peace, and agriculture... will prepare you to possess property...." It seemed so simple, this bridge, but it invariably collapsed in an inextricable tangle.

Bishop Landa admired the idyllic sheen of the Maya world, their women nursing fawns, their "good habit of helping each other in all their labors," but like other missionaries and civilizers for the next 400 years he was frustrated by their indolence. "Indolence" is probably the most used word in all the reports about Indians from the Discovery to the present day. It is the key word for the white point of view. Why wouldn't they work? Why didn't they want to labor to acquire things? The European simply could not comprehend a view of life (at least for respectable men) in which this objective was not paramount.

The gulf between the Indian and white view of life was at its most unbridgeable in the region that became the United States, colonized by a people to whom diligent labor, thrift, Benjamin Franklin's admonition to "Remember, that time is money," became the highest virtues, and work was literally man's sacred calling. The colonies of Catholic Spain to the south and Catholic France to the north, while by no means less interested in reaping golden pesos or gross sous, were less devoted to the principle of absolute utilitarianism—measuring fields, woods, streams, people, and above all time, only by the yardstick of potential profit. In Protestant America this principle emerged as a ruling ethic. The *summum bonum* of this ethic, in the words of the great economist Max Weber, was "the earning of more and more money, combined with the strict avoidance of all spontaneous enjoyment of life," leading to gain, profit, acquisition, that was thought of "purely as an end in itself." In the light of this ethic the Indian attitude was more than troublesome, it was downright sacrilegious.

This basic conflict in points of view helps explain some otherwise puzzling matters: why, for example, Indians were so seldom used as settlers or even as laborers in the Atlantic seaboard

**This scalping scene was painted by Peter Rindisbacher, a Swiss artist who studied and painted on the plains and in the Red River country from 1821 until his death in 1834. Like so many others, this painting perpetuated the image of the Indian as the savage redskin.**

colonies. Colonizers ransacked central Europe and the savage backwoods of Scotland and Ireland to find and transport colonists, sometimes at considerable expense, instead of making any serious attempt to transform the Indians, who were already on the scene and who are often described as being superior physical and mental types, into supplemental colonists.

Sometimes the heterogeneous colonists quarreled bitterly among themselves, Catholics versus Puritans in Maryland, Scotch-Irish versus German Pietists in Pennsylvania, but in the last analysis they could understand each other and make common cause since in the last analysis they were all after the very same thing.

Frontiersmen became more Indian than white in many respects, and in many deeper respects than simply borrowing such gadgets as snowshoes or canoes, but they never forgot the basic objective of their life—property—so different from the basic Indian objective that the two could never hope to be members of the same club.

Spain, in general, was far more tolerant in making use of the Indian peoples, who were absorbed in large numbers into the population of Spanish colonies, to such a degree that what is today called Spanish America could almost equally well, with a few regional exceptions, be called Indian America. In Protestant North America the Indian nations were deliberately stamped out to the point that a nineteenth-century synonym for the Indian race became the Vanishing American, and it was generally believed that some inscrutable natural laws were at work by which the Indians automatically perished under the withering touch of civilization (ignoring the millions of unwithered Indians in Spanish America).

The inscrutable natural laws at work were the aforementioned ultimate conflict in points of view, at its sharpest in the United States, and the various Indian images created under the fire of this conflict in the white mind.

The noble savage gave way to the bloodthirsty savage, reeking with gore. Says an 1837 volume entitled "Indian Anecdotes and Barbarities... Being a description of their customs and deeds of cruelty, with an account of the captivity, sufferings and heroic conduct of many who have fallen into their hands, or who have defended themselves from savage vengeance; all illustrating the general traits of Indian Character. . ." in describing a massacre at Schenectady in 1690: "They ravished, rifled, murdered and mutilated the inhabitants, without distinction of age or sex, without any other provocation or excitement than brutal lust and wantonness of barbarity! Pregnant women were ripped open and their infants cast into the flames or dashed against the posts of the doors!!"

The insensate barbarian gave way to the Red Brother Asking for Guidance of the missionaries, the Return of the Son of Noble Savage of the sentimentalists, the whisky-begging, beetle-eating derelict of the realist, the culture-index cipher of the scientists. There were infinite varieties of the Indian image. Some left a pronounced impression on the American character (the psychiatrist Jung has said he could detect an Indian streak in all his American patients). Most had an even more pronounced effect on the fate of the Indians.

Town-dwelling Indians, rich in culture and cornfields, were transfigured in the popular mind into nomadic hunters, rather dirtier and less desirable than gypsies—which of course made it easier to drive them away, or shoot them if they became dangerous. Well-meaning citizens—good people—had to keep reminding themselves that the dispossessed Creeks or the dispossessed Sauk and Foxes of the particularly synthetic Black Hawk "War" were savages.

But at the same time sizable sections of public opinion magnified the Creeks and their neighbors into romantic heroes. The indignation of idealists in the North to the methods of Indian removal in the South may be supposed to have added fuel to the various heated reform movements of the time, among them the militant American Antislavery Society, the Abolitionist movement, formally launched in Boston in 1833. To be sure, the North also had its full share of practical men, but while Illinois militiamen were shooting Sauk and Foxes to persuade them to stay west of the Mississippi in accordance with the terms of a dubious treaty ("It was a horrid sight to witness little children, wounded and suffering the most excruciating pain, although they were of the savage enemy"), the Sauk and Fox leader Black Hawk was becoming a national celebrity. After his capture at the end of the "war" in 1832, he was taken on what can only be described as a triumphal tour of the cities of the East (and after his death in 1838, his bones were stolen for exhibition). In an epic poem written in his honor he was compared, "As soldier, patriot, soul magnanimous," with Napoleon and Wellington:

*And sure they had no better cause,*
*Than fight for country, kindred, laws!*

The mid-nineteenth century found its Indian heroes in fact as well as in Fenimore Cooper fiction, in the past as well as the present, in biographies, novels, dramas dealing not only with such superstars as Tecumseh, Pontiac, King Philip, Moctezuma, but with relatively obscure Indian sages of long before, such as Big Mouth the Onondaga.

A look at minor Indian luminaries of the age may be revealing. One such, a sensation in Washington during his visit there in 1821, was the young, dashing, and intrepid Petalesharo, a hereditary chief of the Skidi (Wolf) Pawnee. The Pawnee, an important confederation of Caddoan peoples that in recent centuries had moved up the west bank of the Mississippi and the Missouri to Nebraska and beyond, retained a showy collection of (seemingly) temple-mound religious practices, splendid with symbolism and poetry and culminating, at least among the Skidi Pawnee, in a splendidly gruesome human sacrifice at the time of the summer solstice. Petalesharo put a stop to the practice, so it was reported, by rescuing an intended victim, a Comanche girl, in the best last-minute tradition, and dramatically defying priests and thunderbolts in forbidding any more such sacrifices in the future. A figure of the Washington social season of 1826 and 1827 was an Ojibwa confidence woman, Tshusick, who ran a sanctimonious racket on high government officials and their ladies, including the lady of President John Quincy Adams. A contemporary, Eleazar Williams, a Christianized Oneida called by a biographer "the most perfect adept at fraud, deceit, and intrigue that the world ever produced," was alleged to have looted the Oneida and several missionary societies of thousands of dollars during the 1820s (while moving most of the Oneida against their will from New York to Green Bay, Wisconsin, into the bargain), and turned up in the 1850s as the pretended Lost Dauphin of France, son of Louis XVI, immediately gaining a large claque of white followers.

Obviously, in areas mystical and romantic a certain cachet attached to being an Indian, and it is not surprising that Indian-model mumbo jumbo played a part in the founding of various religious sects during the period. The Book of Mormon, stating that the Indians were descendants of the tribe of Joseph, one of Israel's twelve tribes, dubbed them Lamanites, and offered a history for their movements from 600 B.C. until after the Resurrection, when Christ appeared to them here and there under the guise of Viracocha, Kukulcan, or Quetzalcoatl. The sects of the Shakers and the Spiritualists gave quite a bit of attention to Indians, generally regarding them as virtuous and mystically powerful simply because they were Indians, in contrast to the wicked Lamanites of the Mormons. A natural counterpart to the virtuous Indian mystic was the Indian herb doctor (sometimes a very good doctor indeed), forerunner of the Kickapoo Medicine Show of a generation or two later.

In the various images the Indian was sometimes wondrous wise, and a virtue attached itself to Indian wit as well as to Indian yarbs and roots: when a Jesuit priest reproached an Algonkin priest with the immorality of his people, saying, "You don't even know which of the children around you are your own," the old Indian replied, "I will never understand you Frenchmen—you love only your own children, but we love all children." When a Dutch pastor told some Iroquois that in his sermons he reminded the Christians each week "that they must not steal, nor commit lewdness, nor get drunk, nor commit murder," the Iroquois (puffing on their long tobacco pipes) said he did well but asked in pretended amazement, "Why do so many Christians do these things?" A Seneca sachem, objecting to Christian missionaries among his people, said he had been to Buffalo and seen how the white people lived, and they needed missionaries more than the Seneca did. These and other bright sayings from the past were given wider than usual circulation in the mid-nineteenth century, almost for a time threatening to replace the dominant but spurious wooden image of the dour and humorless Indian with one a little nearer to reality; although in reality the favorite ironic wit of the Indian was not always either so virtuous or so printable.

In the various images a romantic virtue sometimes attached

**Chief Payouska, leader of the Great Osages, is shown here in an 1804 crayon sketch by C.B.J.F. Saint-Mémin. Payouska was a member of an Indian delegation to Washington whose visit preceded the cession of a greater part of the Osages' land, which today constitutes much of Missouri and Arkansas. The powerful, well-organized Osages were once respected universally as formidable foes.**

even to Indian savagery, so that London street brawlers of the eighteenth century proudly called themselves "Mohocks," as Parisian toughs of a later period were given the name Apaches. And a real honorary Mohawk, the English Duke of Northumberland who had been adopted into the Mohawks as a warrior during the Revolutionary War, wrote in 1806 from England to the Mohawk leader Joseph Brant: "There are a number of well meaning persons here, who are very desirous of forming a society to better (as they call it) the condition of our nation, by converting us from warriors and hunters into husbandmen. Let me strongly recommend it to you, and the rest of our chiefs, not to listen to such a proposition."

In the various images a certain scientific virtue even attached to strong-stomached primitivism (the long fingernails of an old Montagnais woman scraping a greasy pot, and the professionally long fingernails of the official Choctaw bonepickers, who cleaned the bones of the dead for burial; and the Creek Honored Men vomiting with punctilio the black drink), for the age was intellectually elevated as well as refined.

Intellectual curiosity probed Indian mythology, legend, and folk history, and a scholarly treatise accidentally transferred the name of the great Iroquois political reformer Hiawatha to the story of the Ojibwa demigod Manabozho, and the accident was sealed in marbled meter for posterity in Longfellow's poem (would it have been as deathless under its right name of Manabozho?).

As the Vanishing American vanished from the Eastern states, he became a figure bathed in nostalgic fable and the rush of poignant affection that one feels for the dying. Sang Lydia Sigourney ("The Sweet Singer of Hartford"), America's most popular poetess of the first half of the nineteenth century:

*Ye say that all have passed away,*
*The noble race and brave*
*That their light canoes have vanished*
*From off the crested wave;*
*That 'mid the forests where they roamed,*
*There rings no hunter's shout;*
*But their name is on your waters,*
*Ye may not wash it out....*

*Ye say their cone-like cabins*
*That cluster o'er the vale,*
*Have disappeared as withered leaves*
*Before the autumn gale:*
*But their memory liveth on your hills...*

Mid-nineteenth-century images of the Indian in history emphasized tribes melting away at a touch, or skulking savages being eradicated like other agricultural pests. The war was over, the conquest won, and a curious blindness blacked out the long and important Indian role in the American story, relegating it to a minor, if colorful, bit of business. The central mystery of the Iroquois, for example, their tremendous staying power that had been so influential in the course of American events, was obscured by the noisy side show of Joseph Brant's howling desolating band. The similar staying power and historical importance of the Chickasaw and Creek Indians were lost in the emotional sideshow of their removal.

The tumbling phantoms of the jumbled Indian images occupied the popular fancy to an amazing degree in literature, laws, and the practice of the comfortable nineteenth-century morality. In the official image the Indian problem was an economic matter to be handled as economically as possible; the starched missionary image saved the Indian child and killed the Indian poet and created pious, if rather childish and indolent, Christians of the second class; academicians, always correct and seldom right, created rattle-shaking taboo-conditioned automatons who had nothing whatever to do with the stagey ghosts of Those Who Have Gone to whom the sentimentalists strewed grateful garlands, using thank as the past tense of think.

But all the tumbled phantoms of all the jumbled images could not bridge the gulf to a comprehension of the Indians as people to be taken seriously, as people who were part of the national history and the national life. Admirable as the images were, the public could comprehend the practical necessity of the removal of the Civilized Tribes, tragic and not quite legal though it might be. Practical men, at least, could comprehend the necessity and condone the conspiracy, as practical men were later to condone further instances of rapacious exploitation of

America's natural resources; the curious schism in the American character between private right and public wrong was not born with the dirty business of the Great Removal, but it received a resoundingly helpful whack therefrom. The tragedy of the exiled Civilized Tribes brought sympathy, and the long and heroic resistance by the Creeks and Cherokee to a persecution that should have crushed an ordinary people in six months brought admiration; but even the most indignant idealists could not perceive the other side of the tragedy—the costly loss to the states of Georgia, Alabama, and Mississippi of such potentially superior citizens.

"Why should you take by force from us that which you can obtain by love?" Old Powhatan asked. "Because thou believest in it, I think myself obliged to kill it," Old Nils said to his Indian companion.

But the old men were long gone, while wild roved an Indian girl, bright Alfarata, where sweep the waters of the blue Juniata, and she was swift as an antelope through the forests going and loose were her jetty locks in wavy tresses flowing and it would be a safe bet she had never pounded hominy. But what difference? Phantoms live on memories, not food. Phantoms looked from the Alabama hill that broke Menewa's heart, and danced a solemn step or two in the busy streets of Plymouth, among the phantom lodges of Patuxet, and phantoms grinned at phantom jokes in a thousand phantom councils. Phantoms settled down to live in the names of the land, as the Sweet Singer said, but also, perhaps more than most Americans suspected, in the heritage of their past and the dream of their future.

In the meantime the real Indians, most of them, were jumbled west of the Mississippi. The exiles came to start life over, and brought with them the tumultuous winds of change; and from Texas to the high plains of the Missouri to the blue snowscape of the Arctic the story began again, declining in force and influence as a voice in major history, but this time to produce the most stirring images of all.

The nations beyond the Mississippi thus invaded were, most of them, made up of peoples who lived a life similar in some respects to that of the Eastern woodlands, similar in other respects to that of the great plains farther west. The Caddoan tribes of east Texas and adjacent country were farmers, villagers, mound-builders, and guarded sacred fire in their temples, but their dome-shaped houses were usually of grass. Such westward representatives of the group as the Wichita confederacy were practically transformed into buffalo-chasing people of the plains—these were the people of Quivira (Kansas) found by Coronado in 1541.

The Siouan Quapaw (also known as the Arkansa) were prairie Sioux who nevertheless built forest-style stockades around their towns. The Siouan Osage of present Missouri, one of the most powerful of the trans-Mississippi nations, lived in a country of prairie and cross-timber woodland and were prairie Sioux in their clan divisions but Southeastern woodland in their arrangment of peace and war moieties. Both the Osage and Quapaw were famous for the bow wood of Osage Orange that came from their country: the name Ozark is an Americanization of the French, *Aux Arcs*, meaning "at the (place of the) bows."

The Kansa, relatives of the Osage and the Quapaw, as well as of the Omaha and Ponca to their north, were prairie villagers, familiar during the mid-nineteenth century to travelers along the eastern stretches of the Santa Fe Trail, the men always recognizable by their distinctive haircut—the head shaved or plucked except for a lock at the back. The Pawnee, village people living at the borderline of prairie (tall grass and islets of woods) and plains (short grass and treeless), have been previously mentioned. Three related Siouan groups ranged northward of the Kansa: the Missouri, Oto, and Iowa (this last name supposed to be from the Dakota term *Ayuhwa* meaning "Sleepy People"), all three small tribes of, probably, fewer than 1,000 souls each in their best days. The Missouri were almost destroyed in a war with the Sauk and Foxes in 1798, and in the early 1800s suffered another disastrous defeat from the Osage which ended the tribe as an independent unit, survivors going to live with the Oto and Iowa.

North and west up the Missouri River began the country of the Sioux par excellence, the various divisions of the Dakota. But far up the Missouri, deep in the short-grass plains of modern North Dakota and environs, were three tribes of village people stubbornly clinging to many of their village ways, farming and living in earth houses. These were the Caddoan Arikara, an emigrant group from the Skidi Pawnee, and the Siouan Hidatsa and Mandan. Very well known to early fur trappers, traders, and exporers along the upper Missouri, these three nations were almost wiped out by the terrible smallpox epidemic that swept across the plains in 1837. In the figures of one account, there were only thirty-one people left alive in the two Mandan towns out of a population of 1,600.

To the west of all these nations there were still others, seemingly endless ranks of tribes, each with its own territory and its own way of life, stretching across the seemingly endless Western plains and mountains; when Lewis and Clark made their flea-plagued three-year trip to the Sea of the West from 1804 to 1806, they met these differing peoples all the way. They were in fact guided by one of those distant people, a Shoshoni girl from the Rocky Mountains named Sacagawea, who left an enduring image in a very literal sense: there are said to be more statues erected to her honor than to any other woman in American history.

# X

# Kayakers and Cannibal Dancers

**The Northwest Coast Indians lavished great artistic care upon their dress and art, as seen in the flamboyant costumes of these Tlingits, fully arrayed for a potlatch.**

Westering exploration and trade by sea outstripped that by land, and the strange faraway tribes of the Pacific coast were generally known to eastern America while the nations of the plains and mountains in between were still no more than shadowy half-realities. New England deep-water sailors of 1800 knew the outlandish whale-hunting Indians of Nootka Sound better, no doubt, than they knew the Indians of New England. Whalers, fur traders, and missionaries had known the fur-clad peoples of the far North for more than 200 years when in 1848 the vanishment of Sir John Franklin's great Arctic expedition turned the eyes of the world on the land of the Eskimos. Thirty-eight relief expeditions were sent out in the next ten years (it was at last discovered that Franklin's large party had perished to a man, of starvation); 7,000 miles of new Arctic coastline were incidentally explored; and the Eskimos were solidly implanted in the consciousness of America and Europe.

Due to their distinctiveness the Eskimos probably remain the most widely known of all America's native peoples. European provincials who may never have heard of the Iroquois or the Aztecs are likely to know about Eskimo igloos and dog sleds. Nevertheless, in spite of the exhaustive ethnologizing and publicizing they have received, the Eskimos remain, in a sense, semiconcealed, hidden by the fearsome unfamiliarity of their country. One can picture the people but not the life, the life of long dark winters and incredible cold, hardships, and dangers. It is especially difficult to conceive of this bitter, anxious life bringing forth a people usually described as placid and rather jolly and who created, within the limits imposed by their harsh if vivid world, a culture of spectacular richness.

One further uniqueness, as far as European views of the Eskimo are concerned: long before the early Greenland whale fisheries, long before the first voyage of Columbus, Eskimos and Europeans commingled in an association that lasted for centuries. The Norse, Irish, and Vikings who settled in Iceland from circa A.D. 850 to 1100 planted colonies in Greenland, the far eastern frontier of the New World and the Eskimo world. In contrast to their brief and dreamlike excursions to the coast of North America, Norsemen established settlements in Greenland and lived in some contact with the Eskimos there for several centuries. These settlements were eventually either wiped out by the Eskimos or abandoned, but until the mid-1300s, if not somewhat later, they remain in fairly frequent contact with Europe.

But the two peoples met, so to speak, incognito, neither realizing that the other was from a different world. Europe was unaware, and the Eskimos were unimpressed. A few words of Old Norse or Old Icelandic origin found their way into Greenland Eskimo dialects, a few hammers were made of church-bell metal, a few tubs were coopered (with hoops made of the corset whalebone known as baleen), and a few Greenland Eskimos of the time learned to write a few lines in medieval runic rhyme.

Otherwise the kayaking life of summer and the snow-goggled life of winter went on as always, and to the New World people of Greenland the generations of intruding Europeans were as if they had never been. This long and bootless contact reveals something of the difficulty of transferring elements from one culture to another, and something of the difficulty of discovering a New World before the discoverer is ripe for the event.

The Eskimo are generally reckoned to be relatively recent arrivals among the American peoples. There had been previous inhabitants of the Far North, long before, but whether these were distinct and separate predecessors or remote Eskimo ancestors is not known; the ancient relics of these earliest people constitute the so-called Denbigh Flint Complex, centering in Alaska and environs, tentatively dated from 5,000 to 8,000 years ago, and featuring the minute, exquisitely tooled microblades that are also found in some of the first Eskimo cultures. Even so (pointing up once more the stupendous scale of time in the Indian story), the established antiquity of the Eskimos themselves is fairly respectable, since they must have been in their present Arctic homeland at least 2,500 years ago if not considerably earlier; in other words roughly as long as the Romans have been in Rome, and considerably longer than the French have been in France.

They have an Asiatic look, but are a physical type unto themselves (average in height, plump, massive-faced, narrow-nosed, long-headed) and are not usually classified by anthropologists as Indians, nor do they regard themselves as Indians. Anthropologists classify them as Eskimo, and the Eskimos regard themselves as the race of Inuit, which is to say The People. (The name Eskimo may come from an Algonquian word meaning "raw-meat-eaters" or then again from a term applied by early French missionaries meaning "the excommunicated"; the Norsemen called them *skraelingar*, meaning "little people"; most of their Indian neighbors to the south speak of them by the usual Indian appellation for foreigners, some term or other meaning "snakes" or "enemies"; the central Eskimo retaliate by calling the Cree and Chipewyans south of them *itqilit*, meaning "lousy.")

Their language is believed to be unrelated to any other language on earth. Occasional loan-word parallels hint at contacts in bygone ages with such languages as Finnish, Lapp, Pequot, and even the Aztecs' Nahuatl, among others, but no real kinship has been demonstrated. One eminent authority has discerned possible deeper connections with Indo-European and suggests a very tentative but tantalizing possibility that the Eskimos might be descendants of a people originally from inner Asia still speaking a form of proto-Indo-European, parent language of Sanskrit, Greek, Latin, German, English, and a galaxy of other more or less cultured tongues. Thus the English world "ignite," for example, from the Latin *ignis* meaning "fire," may stem ultimately from the Eskimo *ingneq* meaning "to make fire by twirling a stick in a block of wood." But the hypothesis is only suggested, and Eskimo is still officially listed as unrelated to any other language. This is a reasonably good place to mention, by the way, that "primitive" languages are usually far from primitive in structure or capability, being often more complex and a fitter instrument for abstract thought and poetry than the streamlined and busier languages of technologically advanced peoples.

For a swing of 5,000 miles across the Arctic and sub-Arctic seacoast, islands, tundra, and forest, from Siberia across Alaska and the vast reaches of the north of Canada to Greenland, the isolated villages of the Eskimo were the only sign of man. Their total population in this immense country probably never exceeded 100,000, and more probably seldom exceeded 50,000. There were no tribal governments, no real village governments, and consequently no war and no law, other than observance of custom and taboo. (Murder was punished by the victim's relatives, if they felt up to it.) The real unit of government was the family. And yet there was a remarkable uniformity among the people—with a few exceptions, notably the Aleuts (pronounced Alley-oots) of the Aleutian Islands. There was a remarkable basic similarity among the various dialects of the language, Aleut again excepted. And there was a remarkable similarity in the way of life, allowing for differences necessitated by variations in the food supply.

More, there is a remarkable similarity down through the centuries—the rise and fall of Eskimo culture follows a curve so slow as to be almost imperceptible unless it is measured from stations a thousand years apart. In some regions it has been difficult for archaeologists to detect much change at all: Aleut culture of 2000 B.C. was very similar to that of A.D. 1700. In other regions periods of gradual cultural development have been distinguished, reaching a high point (and a brilliant one) not long after the time of Christ.

Investigators divide the Eskimo into geographic groups for purposes of identification, but the basic Eskimo division is between the whale and walrus and seal hunters of the coasts and the caribou hunters of the interior (some groups hunt both in different seasons, still today as 2,000 years ago). And the basic question in Eskimo ancient history is which came first—the coastal or the inland way of life. The answer is not yet known. Further unanswered questions concern how much of the Eskimo way of life came from Asia and spread eastward over the Eskimo empire, and how much was originated in America and spread back to Asia. The famous vaulted snow house, for example, never observed in Asia, would seem to be one of the definite Eskimo inventions. Some experts trace lines of cultural influence to and from the south, involving such ancients as the Great Lakes Old Copper people of more than 5,000 years ago.

In the earliest Eskimo cultures so far identified most of the familiar Eskimo elements are already present: boats made of skins sewed over wooden frames, the decked one-man kayak and the larger, open umiak; sleds with runners of bone or ivory, probably for use with dogs (according to observed custom of later times, the dogs were hitched tandem in the west, fanwise in the east); ivory snow goggles, at first with round holes, later with slits; hobnails of bone or ivory for lashing to your boot soles in working your way over ice, very similar to the crampons of the modern mountaineer; ice scoops and ice picks; plugs to stop up the wounds of animals and save the precious blood; specialized fishing gear, specialized harpooning gear for use with floats of inflated bladders, specialized bird-catching gear; bows and arrows for hunting musk ox, caribou, and other big game; and usually the seal-oil lamp, the center of the Eskimo household from time immemorial. This, the only lamp known in the Americas, a saucer of oil floating a wick of moss, was at first used only for light, later for heat and cooking. Traditionally its small, smokeless (if properly trimmed) flame was the only heat in Eskimo homes of woodless areas—where the temperature could settle down and stay for a while at 50 or 60 below.

In the centuries between A.D. 1 and 1000 Eskimo art reached its climax. The best known of the cultures believed to have been roughly contemporary during that time are known as Ipiutak and Old Bering Sea in northern Alaska; pre-Koniag and Kachemak Bay in Kodiak Island and southern Alaska; late Dorset and early Thule in the Hudson Bay country, the eastern Arctic, and Greenland. All produced decorative work in bone and ivory, sometimes of a high order; perhaps the finest of all Eskimo carving and engraving is found in the exquisite ivories of Ipiutak, where the dead in their log tombs were furnished with artificial eyes of inlaid ivory, mouth covers and nose plugs of carved ivory, and accompanied by elaborate ivory masks, fantastic carved animal figurines, carved ivory spirals and chains. These last are believed to represent imitations of the metal chains and swivels hung as magic gadgets to the gowns of shamans far to the west in Siberia. The artificial eyes are thought to resemble jade eye amulets of Han dynasty times in ancient China. The mysterious ivory winged figure (looking a little like a butterfly) prominent in the art of the Old Bering Sea people is reminiscent of nothing plausible, and no one can guess what it meant.

During this time pottery appears to have been introduced; and—probably the one great revolutionary event in coastal Arctic history—the virtuoso profession of whaling from an open boat was developed.

During this time, so the central Eskimo say, another race lived among them, a mighty race with mighty ancestors, men so powerful one of them alone could haul a walrus across the ice as easily as an Eskimo could drag a seal, people known as the Tunit. For some reason they went away, but "so greatly did they love their country, that when they were leaving... there was a

**An Eskimo of the central Canadian Arctic prepares for the hunt, as painted in 1832 by John Halkett, a Hudson's Bay Company official. Until the twentieth century, Eskimos were little touched by the outside world, perhaps because they lived on land no one else coveted.**

man who, out of desperate love for his village, harpooned the rocks with his harpoon and made the stones fly about like bits of ice." There are indications that the Tunit are not mythical but historical (perhaps the bearers of the Thule culture), but who they were or where they went is not known.

Possibly there were other non-Eskimo groups in the Arctic past of this period: some features of the Dorset culture are thought to hint at the now extinct pale-skinned Beothuk Indians of Newfoundland. Possibly among the Eskimos there were varying peoples: possibly the inland and the coastal tribes were then distinct in physical type; and the Aleuts are so different from other Eskimos, possibly due to Asiatic immigrations from the Kamchatka peninsula, that they almost (but not quite) seem to represent a separate people.

In many respects the ancient way of life changed in the centuries after A.D. 1000. The quality of art declined. Tools and weapons became more specialized. There were a few further innovations—such as pipes and tobacco—that traveled around the world after the discovery of America to reach at last the Eskimos via Siberia in the 1700s and 1800s. But essentially the pattern of living remained the same. Depending on what was available, winter houses were built (usually over a dug-out floor) of driftwood, whalebones, sod, stone, or snow. The domed snow house (rare in Alaska) is most typical of Canada, where modern explorers have visited vaulted halls of snow roomy enough for dancing parties of sixty people, and noted that the roaring sheet-iron heating stoves in use today—their rusty chimneys elbowing out through the domed snow ceilings—did not melt the well-built walls or roofs. Skylights were paned with stretched walrus gut. The principal piece of furniture was the drying frame, for drying the constantly wet clothes. The great winter amusement (next to sex, in which the Eskimos by report have always taken a frank and enthusiastic interest) was gymnastics performed on stretched ropes of sealskin.

Summer dwellings were usually skin tents, conical in the western regions, ridged in the east. Winter clothes were commonly tailored from caribou skins, boots from sealskin. Sea-mammal gut was also used for waterproof coats—a man hooded with it and lashed watertight in his kayak might drown but he would not get very wet.

In the winter, seals were hunted at the ice edge or breathing holes (a freezing job, waiting motionless for hours with harpoon ready); in the spring they were hunted as they basked on the shores; in the summer they were harpooned from kayaks in the open sea. Kayakers became desperately expert at handling their fast and maneuverable craft, but even so Arctic waters are wild and dangerous, and it is not surprising that one of the Eskimo words to travel farthest among neighboring people is *pivoq*, meaning "he lost his life by upsetting in his kayak." In the summer the whalers put out in their umiaks (which were occasionally rigged with grass-mat sails), sometimes operating almost out of sight of land, and where there were no whales, whole villages moved inland to hunt the caribou:

*Glorious it is*
*To see long-haired winter caribou*
*Returning to the forests . . .*
*While the herd follows the ebb-mark of the sea*
*With a storm of clattering hooves.*
*Glorious it is*
*When wandering time is come.*

The song may be old, but no one is sure. It was sung for (and translated by) the late Knud Rasmussen, greatest of interpreters of the Eskimo mind and poetry, a poetry which in his hands, at least, shimmers and flames like the northern lights.

All activities were ringed with taboos. Illness, misfortune, lack of game, were certainly caused by some broken law that had thrown the world out of balance. A shaman would find out what had gone wrong and correct it. Had the sick woman's husband perhaps speared a salmon at a time when he was restricted? Then of course the salmon were indignant and would not let themselves be caught. Or perhaps a sin had floated down to the bottom of the sea, to fall like dirt in the hair of the great goddess known as "She Down There." Then of course she was indignant and was keeping the fat creatures of the sea out of reach of those on land, and the shaman would have to make a spirit journey down to her and square things. The shaman, common among many Indians as well as among Siberians, was particularly popular among the Eskimos. Shamans could be women as well as men, maybe better. They performed magic, secured revenge, cured illness, sometimes by a method very widely known among the peoples of both North and South America—sucking out the illness and spitting forth a pebble or some such object to prove it.

The ages passed, and the Eskimos moved with the same age-old acts and gestures, through the summers as swift and brilliant as flights of ravens and wild geese, through the winters of interminable night, when they harnessed their sled dogs by the green light of the aurora. Perhaps the ancient life of men in caves still lived in their names for constellations: the Caribou and the Wolf (in the Big Dipper region of the sky). The Pleiades were "Branches on Antlers." And a magic song ran:

*I will take care not to go towards the dark.*
*I will go towards the day . . .*

Among the Eskimos of the seacoast, as among nearly all people who live from the bounty of the sea, there was little tradition of famine. Among the comparatively few Eskimos who lived permanently inland, particularly among the caribou hunters of the Barren Grounds, winter was only another name for hunger.

The inland Indians of the great black forests bordering the treeless tundra on the south also knew seasonal starving times, although the season varied with the pattern of game migration—it will bear repeating that Eskimos are regarded as distinct from Indians, and that Indians also inhabited some regions of the Far North. These tribes were the Naskapi in Labrador, the (Algonquian-speaking) Cree and (Athapascan-speaking) Chipewyan around the south and west shores of Hudson Bay (with a long history of border wars with each other), and various wandering Athapascan groups stretching across the broad interior or northwest Canada from Hudson Bay almost to the Pacific.

The Athapascan language family derives its name from a Chipewyan band, the Athabaska, who lived in the area of the lake of the same name; the Athapascans of northwestern Canada, still today the least-known Indians of North America, are divided by ethnologists into twenty-one main tribes, some of them bearing such traders' names as Yellowknives, Dog-ribs, Slaves (so called by the Cree), Beavers, and Carriers—this last from a tribal custom demanding that a widow carry the ashes of her dead husband for three years in a basket.

The northern Athapascan hunters may have been the last important body of people to drift into America by way of the Bering Strait and become American Indians. Since the Athapascan language family is the most widely distributed of all Indian language families in North America, this entrance could hardly have been really recent. But some students believe Athapascan-speaking people may have been entering America as late as the middle of the first millennium A.D., or about the time the Angles and Saxons were entering England.

Among those people men sometimes wrestled for wives (winners got harems and losers slept forlorn); and a slain bear was propitiated with solemn ceremony, as among some Eskimos and some other Indians, as among the Ainu of Japan, and as among Old World paleolithic men more than 50,000 years ago.

The foggy, raw, and windy climate of the Aleutians and the southwestern coast of Alaska, while often defined by its denizens as miserable, is much less rugged than that of the rest of Eskimo country. ("It doesn't rain in the Aleutians, it rains in Asia and blows over," said the GIs of World War II.) The Eskimos here have certain marked differences in dialects and styles of life (with the Aleuts the most extreme variants, as already noted), so much so that two general Eskimo divisions have been suggested: Arctic Ocean Eskimo and Pacific Coast Eskimo, with the breaking point in the vicinity of Norton Sound in Alaska.

Coastal Eskimos below this point are still kayakers, of course, and some are whalers, using poisoned harpoons, but the principal food for some villages becomes salmon and birds; an un-Eskimo interest in social status appears; hats and ceremonial masks are elaborately carved in wood.

All these things reflect the ways of the people living next door south, the Indians who developed the remarkable culture of the Northwest Coast.

The Northwest Coast people are marvelous on several counts. They produced a genuinely high culture (ranking with that of the Pueblos of the Southwest or the temple-mound people of the Southeast) without benefit of either agriculture or pottery, usually the chiefest handmaidens of cultural progress. Alone among such high cultures in the New World, it was uninfluenced by the ancient civilizations of Mexico and points south;

**A war chief of the Chilkats is shown in European clothes in this 1885 photograph; he stands with his wife and child beside a stylized carving that probably served as the family symbol. The Chilkats were a subgroup of the Tlingits and part of a long chain of coast-dwelling Indian nations running south from present-day Alaska.**

its ultimate affinities were more with northeastern Asia, although the Northwest Coast people vigorously disguised borrowed elements into their own highly individual patterns.

Almost alone among such high cultures in the New World, it seemingly reached its zenith after contact with Europeans, rather than some centuries before (possibly with an assist from the steel wood-carving tools the Europeans brought).

And almost alone among American Indians, various peoples of the Northwest Coast area placed an inordinate value on the acquisition of private property, the purpose being a bizarre and inordinately pompous display of personal munificence.

In its purest form the Northwest Coast way of life was seagoing and fishing (salmon, cod, halibut). Roots and berries in the tall, lush coastal forests furnished variety: camas root first of all, and cranberries and blueberries, and the Saskatoon berry that contains three times as much iron and copper as prunes and raisins. Food was plenty, and easy to come by. Work in the spring and summer laid up enough for a year. The mild, idle winters were for luxury, a luxury that created fantastically intricate systems of ceremonials; of clans and the groups of clans known to the anthropological trade as phratries; of secret societies; a wealth of decorated blankets, baskets, and boxes; an outpouring of fantastic wood carving; and a fantastic elaboration of social climbing.

Related families lived together in gabled plank houses, with the house posts and door poles carved and painted with the family crest—from which developed the wooden memorial monuments known as totem poles (the word is from central Algonquian and means literally "family" or "clan" or the armorial bearings thereof). Trees were hollowed out by fire and adze into great sixty-foot canoes of admirable workmanship, bounteously adorned with carving, "carved in grotesque figures and remarkably well handled," in the expert testimony of a British sea dog, Captain Sir Edward Belcher, R.N., C.B., referring to some Tlingit crews he saw in action in 1837.

A few of these people, notably the Nootka of Vancouver Island, used their barbaric longboats for harpoon whaling, the real McCoy, in which the whale was harpooned again and again and finally killed with a thrusted lance and then towed to shore. Slat armor was worn in warfare, and wooden helments, and (maybe) terrorizing carved masks. Mustaches and occasional beards were in fashion among some tribes, as among some Eskimos. Slave raids and the resultant slaves were common; in ultra-rich villages slaves were said to make up nearly a third of the population; a Nootka chief of the early 1800s had "nearly fifty male and female slaves," reported an American captive. Social classes (above the slaves) were divided into commoners and nobles, with here and there, as among the exceptionally powerful chiefs of the Haida of the Queen Charlotte Islands, a sort of embryonic royalty.

These were an emotional people (like many Indians), much given to weeping, melodrama, and soaring imagination. Mighty spirits, beings of boundless power, walked the earth—at least in the stories told in the winter, when the North wind smoothed the sea: "Something wonderful came in and stood there. His large eyelids were too powerful to look at. Where he placed his foot he stood for a while. When he took another step the earth and the house shook. . . . "

The nations of the Northwest Coast culture area extended from the Tlingit in the north, along the southernmost islands and coastal reaches of Alaska (its center about at the present Sitka, which is the name of a Tlingit subgroup), down through the Haida, Tsimshian, Kwakiutl, Bella Coola, Nootka, and Coast Salish of the coast and islands of British Columbia, the Salish and Chinook of Puget Sound and the lower Columbia River, to the Yurok, Karok, and Hupa of northern California.

Ways of doing things of course varied considerably throughout this long strip. The heart and high point of the Northwest Coast spirit was toward the north, with the Tlingit and Haida its best representatives for certain aspects, the Kwakiutl or Tsimshian or Nootka for others. Among other front-ranking activities, Tlingit and Tsimshian people made the famous Chilkat blanket, woven from cedar bark and the hair of the wild mountain goat into a mystic design that was imbued, so they say, with the power of speech. The Haida and Kwakiutl were the premier wood carvers. The Tsimshian were the great traders, dealing in copper from the north and captured Salishan slaves from the south, otter skins from the Haida, dentalium shells (a kind of West Coast wampum) and candlefish oil from anywhere. The Kwakiutl apparently originated the secret societies, each paying dramatic ceremonial homage to its protective supernatural being, that spread throughout the Northwest Coast.

Most of these national names meant, as usual, "people," and the Northwest Coast styles spread over many varying peoples speaking varying languages. These language groups, large and small, became more complex and tangled toward the south, approaching the Babel of tongues that was California.

The Columbia River region was another great aboriginal crossroads, similar to the lower Mississippi, and the language of the Chinook people there was used as the basis of a trading jargon spoken far and wide over the Northwest. It was eventually spoken from California to Alaska—but oddly enough the Chinook themselves merged with another tribe (the Chehalis) in the mid-nineteenth century and dropped their own language entirely. But the Chinook jargon continued in use. One of its later words, *hootchenoo*, meaning homemade liquor, was the origin of the slang term "hootch."

It was the Chinook jargon that changed the Nootka word *patshatl*, meaning "giving," into "potlatch," the best known feature of the world of the Northwest Coast. The potlatch was a feast given to celebrate any sort of an occasion (often a coming-out party for a debutante daughter); extravagant gifts were distributed—blankets, cedar chests, sea-otter furs; wealth was wasted with the greatest ostentation possible, all of which redounded to the prestige of the potlatch giver. Potlatches became contests of squandering between rival clan chiefs. Precious oil would be thrown on the fire at a "grease feast" until guests were singed by the flames, and perhaps an opulent chief would kill a valuable slave with the special club known as a "slave killer" and contemptuously fling the slave's scalp to his opponent, or break and destroy an even more valuable "copper" (plates of wrought copper, used as very high-priced currency), an act roughly equivalent to lighting a cigar with a $1,000 bill. All the gift giving and destruction was carried out with immense formality, and the rival clan leaders sang songs of insult to each other:

"What will my rival say again—that 'spider woman,' what will he pretend to do next?... Will he not brag that he is going to give away canoes, that he is going to break coppers?... Do you know what you will be like? You will be like an old dog, and you will spread your legs before me when I get excited. You did so when I broke the great coppers 'Cloud' and 'Making

Ashamed,' my great property. . . . This I throw into your face. . . ."

The humiliated loser sometimes sailed off to war and deliberately threw away his life, out of sheer chagrin. More importantly, the entire clan of the chief won or lost face as a result of these contests, and the whole clan more or less participated to make the really grand potlatches possible, a spur to industry that may have played its part in the growth of the Northwest Coast culture.

The Kwakiutl complicated the potlatch system with an interest rate of 100 percent—gifts had to be repaid double at the return potlatch. This interest rate (possibly picked up from Hudson's Bay Company practices) saturated all Kwakiutl business customs, producing involved deals that would try the acumen of a Hollywood agent.

The notion of property extended to intangibles so that titles, society memberships, professions such as carving or boatbuilding, ownership of certain songs or dances, could be handed down from the mother or the father, depending on the custom of reckoning descent—or, among the northern Kwakiutl villages, in a hybrid arrangement that passed inheritance from the father to his son-in-law, then to the son-in-law's son, and so on, descent progressing like a flight of stairs.

Young men and women of many Indian nations went alone into the forest to fast and pray and seek a guiding vision, but on the Northwest Coast the right to do so and sometimes the blessing of the vision as well (transformed into the ritual of a secret society) became an item of property to be inherited. Membership in a secret society brought as much high prestige as high drama, and the drama was the keen clear note of life itself, life unchanged from ancient ages: for here again the cult of the Bear appeared, and the cult of the Cannibal, echoes from the dawn of man.

Sang the people, while the Bear dancer danced and juggled glowing coals and threw them among the onlookers, sometimes setting fire to their cedar-bark clothes, and while the Bears of the Bear Society, wrapped in their great black bearskins, angrily clawed the earth:

*How shall we hide from the bear that is moving*
*all around the world? . . .*
*Let us cover our backs*

**This Tlingit totem near Ketchikan, Alaska, is called the Sun and Raven Pole. Like most totem poles it has a story to tell, not a religious meaning to express. This one tells of the great flood and how Raven helped man to survive it. The Alaskan Indians are considered to be the best of the totemic carvers.**

*with dirt that the terrible great bear from*
*the north of the world may not find us . . .*

The initiate of the Kwakiutl Cannibal Society fasted in the woods until, emaciated and hysterical, he appeared for the frenzied dance of initiation. He was lured into the house of the Society by a naked woman, dancing backward, enticingly, holding in her outstretched arms a corpse. The Cannibal dancer followed her step for step, trembling, drawn on as if against his will, and in the house was seized with wildness and bit flesh from the arms of the communicants around him, and in ecstasy he danced, while the people sang for him:

*Now I am about to eat,*
*My face is ghastly pale.*
*I am about to eat what was given me by Cannibal*
*at the North End of the World.*

The ceremony ended with a ritual feast of dog, stand-in for man in mock-cannibal performances among a number of Indian peoples.

But anyone could see spirits in secret dreams, and the spirits could be prayed to. Toward the southern periphery of the Northwest Coast world, below the present Canada–United States boundary, this spirit dreaming was of much moment; and reverent young dreamers deep in the cathedral forests of douglas fir or towering redwood prayed, with all the devotion of their being, "I want to be rich."

The fur trade was the great bringer of civilization to the people of the North, Indians and Eskimos alike. Its chief apostles were the agents of the "Governor and Company of Adventurers of England Trading into Hudson's baye," organized in 1670 to compete with French *coureurs de bois* for the prime "oiled beaver" (skins worn next to the body, for a season, hair side in) of the Cree and their northern neighbors. The other great English-backed fur combine, the North West Company, began to get under way in the 1770s; in 1796 it split temporarily into rival factions that spent no less than 195,000 gallons of liquor on the Indians during a two-year trade war. The inevitable conflict between the North West Company and the Hudson's Bay Company reached a bloody climax in 1816, with a veritable war on the Red River of Canada; the two companies merged five years later.

The usual new diseases took their toll, consuming the people of the northern forests "as the fire consumes the dry grass of the fields" (in the words of the first European to cross the continent from coast to coast, the North West Company's Alexander Mackenzie in 1793). Among the Eskimos, tuberculosis became the high-scoring killer. The usual inter-Indian disruptions ran their course. But the deepest changes were wrought on the people of northern Canada by H.B.C. (Canada's name for the Hudson's Bay Company), which transformed the Indians and Eskimos it touched from a hunting economy to a fur-trapping economy, and their supply of winter food from caribou or seal meat to flapjacks from the trading post's supplies—caribou, butchered by the herd for their hides in the nineteenth century, virtually disappeared from some parts of their range.

Missionaries and whalers contributed to the European infiltration of the north country. The Moravian United Brethren, after much difficulty and some loss of life, established in 1764 their influential mission among the Labrador Eskimos. Danish missionizing in Greenland, begun in 1721, developed a series of trading posts and Danish colonization and the world's first relief fund, set up in Greenland in 1783 for the support of the aged and poor. Nineteenth-century whalers summered so reguarly with the Polar Eskimos that their local nickname was *upernagdlit*, "harbingers of spring." New Bedford whalers plowing the waters of Hudson Bay were frequently crewed by Aivilik Eskimos of the bay's far northwestern shores.

In the west, in the Aleutians and Alaska, the fur trade came from Russia, led by the freebooting Siberian frontiersmen called the *promyshleniki*, who killed with true frontier abandon whatever they found on the beaches—seals, the six-foot Bering Sea king crabs, or the artistic, "mild, polite, and hospitable" Aleuts.

Freebooting was brought under organized restraint when the Russian American Company was given a fur monopoly by Russian imperial decree in 1799. By that time the Aleuts were said to have been reduced to one tenth of their pre-*promyshleniki* population.

The survivors were put to work as sea-otter hunters and voyaged under Russian command as far south as Santa Barbara in southern California; and eighty Aleut sea-otter hunters helped colonize the Russian post of Fort Ross in northern California in the 1820s. The Eskimos of Alaska's Pacific coast got off easier, only having to pay a tax in furs.

The Tlingit fought the Russian fur company for many years, although a Russian fort was established at Sitka, at great expense in powder and ball.

The Russian company made some real effort to look after the welfare of the remaining Aleuts, and in the years following 1824 Russian missionaries converted them to the Greek Orthodox Church: tradition records that the Aleuts said to each other, "Any religion which can save the Russians must be very strong," and they joined the church to a man.

The Russian advance into the New World brought a hurried response from the Spanish in a voyage up the Northwest Coast to Alaska in 1773 and 1774. Thereafter Spanish, English, and, later, American ships called with increasing frequency at Nootka Sound on Vancouver Island; fast and loose trade with the Nootka resulted in several savage massacres—a Yankee vessel, the *Boston*, was attacked and destroyed in 1803, and another, the *Tonquin*, in 1811—and earned for the whale-hunting Nootka a reputation for toughness which they richly deserved. But it was this trade that brought the previously mentioned steel tools, sending the art of the Northwest Coast into a most glorious sunburst.

But it came at sunset. The Russian advance also brought a response in Alexander Mackenzie's transcontinental journey, and in the arrival of Lewis and Clark at the Pacific twelve years later, in 1805, and in the subsequent establishment of English and American trading posts roundabout the lower Columbia River. In the 1830s American and Canadian missionaries appeared in Oregon, and in the 1840s settlers; and the world of the Northwest Coast, its potlatches and its arrogant nobles, entered upon the days of its decline.

The Crimean War (raising justifiable fears that Great Britain would lay hands on Russian possessions in America) set Russia to dickering with the United States for the sale of Alaska. The sale was finally made at a price of $7,200,000, one ninety-fourth of the amount since taken out of Alaska in gold alone.

Transfer officially took place on Friday, October 18, 1867, at Sitka, when American officials and troops arrived by a steamer which also brought one Hayward Hutchinson, a Baltimore businessman who did a little business that day with representatives of the Russian sealing monopoly. Back in San Francisco he helped organize the Alaska Commercial Company, which obtained from the Grant administration in 1870 a monopoly lease of the Pribilof Islands with their priceless seal fisheries.

During the twenty years of its lease the Alaska Commercial Company netted many millions of dollars for its few stockholders and left the seal herds generously depleted. It claimed, however, to have improved the lot of the Aleuts who lived on the Pribilof Islands. Missionaries claimed otherwise. The company was the subject in 1876 of a Congressional investigation which got nowhere; a United States Treasury agent stationed in Alaska to guard the public weal against overexploitation happened also to be the company's Superintendent of Seal Fisheries. Would-be competitors kept the company under fairly constant fire for years, charging in effect that Alaska was kept as its private pork barrel and subjected to merciless plundering. Since the company controlled Alaskan trading posts and shipping, and thus exerted a certain amount of control over travel in those parts, the charges were difficult to investigate.

But it was in this same epoch (1884) that an American Presbyterian missionary, Dr. Sheldon Jackson, set up shop in Alaska as Superintendent of Education. He found that whisky, prostitution, and disease, liberated from the more rigid controls of Russian times, had drastically reduced the Eskimo population. The thousands of Eskimos that in the 1820s had inhabited the Alaskan north and northwest coasts were only hundreds in the 1880s.

Disease had probably done the greatest damage, but the most dramatic destroyer was the new institution of the summer drunk. Summer was the time of preparation for winter, and really not a time to gambol. But Eskimos, swapping their furs and ivory for whisky with the summer traders, would go on a mighty drunk during the short, vital hunting season, and wake up to find winter at hand and nothing in the meat pit. They would then starve. In 1888 a revenue ship visiting St. Lawrence Island, at the southern entrance of the Bering Strait, found the entire populations of three neighboring villages—400 men, women, and children—dead from these causes.

Even for a sober man, meat was hard to come by. In many areas the rifle had all but done in the walrus and the whale, the seal and caribou. Dr. Jackson set about to replace the vanished caribou with tame reindeer, change the Eskimos from hunters to herdsmen, and bring to them some education, some medical care, and some legal protection.

Hercules never faced a task more beset with discouragements and opposition—passive from the Eskimos, violent from frontier whites who could not see any earthly reason for helping the dirty and wretched natives to survive. But in 1892 the United States government brought in the first sizable herd of reindeer, and hired Lapps from Norway to teach their care and breeding; and to everyone's amazement except Dr. Jackson's the experiment began to work.

No doubt it is an oversimplification to say, as some do, that Sheldon Jackson (an eyeglassed, diminutive, Teddy Roosevelt sort of man but "by inside measurement a giant," as a contemporary wrote) saved the Eskimos in Alaska. But since his time, anyway, the United States has hung up a generally excellent record in its dealings with the Alaskan Eskimos—at least the Danes and Canadians in the Arctic think so, with praise that is rarer than rubies, examples for it being exceedingly scarce.

# XI

# Beulah Land

Gustavus Sohon painted these Indians at an 1855 peace meeting between the Blackfeet and the Nez Perce and Flathead tribes, one of the largest such gatherings ever held.

The land ran down in golden hills from the mountains to the sea, with green groves of oaks in the folds between and poppies red on the slopes in their season. A little river, dry for half the year, curled along the bottom of the valley. This was the site of the present Los Angeles, and in the year 1602 there were probably several villages scattered here and there over its area, impermanent-looking clusters of mat-made huts and trash and tumbled baskets. People speaking the same language (a Shoshonean tongue) also lived on a couple of islands off the coast, the nearer now known as Santa Catalina or, in song and tourist promotion, as Avalon.

Three Spanish ships, commanded by a Basque navigator named Sebastian Vizcaino, put in at the nearer island on Santa Catalina's day (November 25th) of the year 1602, and the recorder of the expedition wrote of the people who lived there: "*The women are very beautiful* and virtuous, the children are fair and blonde and very merry."

Some days later the same three ships anchored in an "excellent harbor" 325 miles up the coast; Vizcaino named this bay after the Count of Monte Rey, the viceroy of New Spain who had sent out the expedition. The crews of these three ships were riddled with scurvy, and sixteen men had already died since their departure from Acapulco, Mexico, seven months before; the explorers were scarcely in a condition to look at this particular new world (perfumed by a dead whale washed ashore, upon which bears fed by night) through rose-colored glasses. Nevertheless, the Carmelite friar who was keeping the journal of the expedition wrote that the people of Monterey Bay were "affable, generous Indians, friendly to the point of giving whatever they had; they much regretted the Spaniards' departure, because they had so much affection."

The people of the California coast had been encountered now and then by other Europeans—English pirates, Manila galleoneers, previous Spanish explorers—for at least sixty years before the time of Vizcaino, and in general had been described as friendly, frank, handsome, light-skinned, of good stature and extraordinary strength. They could stride along for a mile carrying a weight an Englishman could scarcely lift, wrote a companion of Francis Drake's in speaking of the people north of San Francisco Bay; and he added that they were marvelous runners.

Vizcaino in a letter to the Spanish king spoke of the plank canoes used by some of the southern California coastal and island people "in which they go to sea with fourteen paddle-men of a side, with great dexterity—even in very stormy weather," darting over the water with such speed "that they seemed to fly."

The life described by these first foreign observers—the nearly naked men occasionally dressed in skins and the women in "aprons" of rushes, the fishing and acorn gathering, the multitudes of baskets (and the little round basketry hats of the women), the dancer with a belt of deer-hoof rattles, the sweathouses in which the men sweltered of an evening before plunging into a cold stream for a bath—had been going on basically unchanged for a very long time.

In many material respects this life of most of the California people was exceedingly primitive, more primitive than that of any other region in the area of the United States with the exception of the Great Basin—the Nevada-Utah deserts—next door east. With a few exceptions, there was no agriculture and only scarce, crude pottery; no wealth of art, except in basketry; no elaborate dance costumes, no carved and painted masks; no leagues and confederacies and formally organized governing councils.

And yet California was, as a whole, more densely populated than any other region north of Mexico, with a bewildering variety of peoples, and with a remarkable stability as to their location—each little group usually inhabiting a tiny country marked out with some precision and regarded as having been forever theirs. There were very few migration legends among the Californians—most believed they had sprung from the earth where they had always lived.

Food was abundant, in profuse variety, and easily obtained. The staff of life was acorn flour, made by a fairly intricate process of pounding the acorns and then leeching out the tannic acid. Fish and mollusks came next; then every kind of game, reptile, and bird; then various kinds of nuts, clovers, berries, grasses, cactus fruit, yucca, and sage.

The living was easy, and this made for leisure. Leisure and dense population are supposed to make for material progress.

But here there was an almost inconceivable sameness century after century, penetrating enormous deeps of time. As in the case of Eskimo history, it is necessary to set up stakes 1,000 years apart to catch the slow motion of change.

There is a feeling among some experts that the California life remained relatively primitive and changeless because it had reached a comfortable state of balance with what the pleasant environment had to offer. The lotus-eaters may have spent part of their free time in contemplation of spiritual matters—then as now California seems to have been a spawning ground of religions. But mostly they appear to have been content with drifting and dreaming on their sunny oceans of time. Maybe the principal occupation was being very merry.

The oldest inhabitants of California had probably been there a long time indeed, very possibly being descendants of some of the earliest people to inhabit the hemisphere so many thousands of years ago. Likely candidates as the most ancient ancients were peoples speaking the dozens of various languages now gathered into the language family called Hokan. Among these widely scattered groups were the Chumash of the coast and islands around Santa Barbara (Vizcaino passed by there on Santa Barbara's day); the Shasta, in the neighborhood of the present Oregon line, north of the mountain of the same name; the Salinans, who ranged the highest coastline in the world, the coastal mountains south of Monterey now known as the Santa Lucia mountains (Vizcaino passed by there on Santa Lucia's day).

Perhaps equally ancient were other groups speaking the dozens of various languages now classified in the language family called Penutian, such as the many tribelets (each with a distinct dialect) of the related Wintu, Wintun, and Patwin in the Sacramento Valley; the forty or fifty distinct tribes of the Yokuts of the San Joaquin Valley; or the many villages of the Costanoans along the coast from San Francisco Bay to below Monterey.

It is thought that newcomers spread into California, from the north and from the southeast, in the 1,000 years between 500 B.C. and A.D. 500. In the north some of these may have been such Athapascan-speaking tribes as the Hupa, of the picture-post-card Hoopa Valley on the Trinity River, and in the south numerous groups such as the Cahuilla of the mountains and deserts east of modern Riverside, and the aforementioned people of the region of present Los Angeles, these speaking various Shoshonean tongues.

Along the lower Colorado River the Yumas were farmers—the only farmers in the California area—and produced crops that outrivaled those of Mexico, said an early Spanish explorer, who added that these people "are the tallest and the most robust that I have seen in all the provinces, and their nakedness the most complete." Related people speaking Yuman dialects lived in the Mojave Desert of California, in the region of San Diego, and down most of the peninsula of Lower California.

All these different people and many, many more had become solidly settled, by about A.D. 1200, in their diverse little homelands. During the same long epoch, from about A.D. 500 onward, other broad, gradual changes took place. The Northwest Coast culture reached down from the north to embrace a few river and coastal groups below the present Oregon boundary, and perhaps to communicate the worship of the raven to the Santa Barbara country, where it became the worship of the giant California condor; and from someplace the Chumash seamen there learned to make their remarkable plank boats—the pine planks joined with lashing of sinew, and calked with asphaltum. These plank canoes were unique in North America, and only known elsewhere in the hemisphere at a spot on the coast of Chile.

Among such people as the Pomo north of San Francisco Bay the art of basket making reached a phenomenally high point, producing extravagant work dripping with feathers and beads. At Drake's Bay in 1578 these people showed Drake one of their famous feathered baskets "so well wrought as to hold water"; and virtuoso examples exist of tiny baskets the size of a pinhead, made with stitches too minute to be counted with the naked eye.

Everywhere, the ancient fears and placations—fear of speaking the name of the dead, fear of the shaman's magic power, fear of the mysterious force that touched adolescent girls—were overlaid with refinements and new religious ideas.

Most of these new cults were highly localized. Feather-veiled Kuksu dancers, so important to the Patwin, Pomo, and Maidu, were practically unknown to their next-door neighbors, both north and south. Stylized deer dancers were limited to the Yurok, Karok, and Hupa, who had most fully absorbed the Northwest Coast ways of splendor and display. Annual rites to renew the world (with sometimes a New Fire ceremony) were limited to the northwest, and periodic rites of public mourning for the dead were limited to the central and southern regions. Singing protectively over the adolescent girl and forcing her to hide her dangerous eyes so she would not wither trees or drive away the game were alone universal, as these customs were practically universal over all of western North America. Otherwise, the threads of the different California religions are difficult to untangle.

Shamans held contests in which they tried to outwizard each other, and perhaps from these came group ceremonies that became sacred dances, repeated each year in dance cycles that went on all winter. Some of the dance cycles were based on voluminous, dreamlike creation and animal myths possibly composed by unknown Homers among the mystical, myth-making peoples of southern California. The *toloache* initiation ritual, a religious system involving holy visions induced by the narcotic Jimson weed, is believed to have originated on Santa Catalina Island—although ground-painting ceremonies connected with it doubtless came from the Southwest of the Pueblos. But on the whole, imported ideas were not very prominent. In a very general sense the California religious ideas were growths from the California soil.

Spain left the upper California coast more or less unattended for 166 years after the voyage of Vizcaino in 1602 and 1603. During that time the Spanish frontier of missions and mines, Indian vaqueros and leather-jacketed border solders, crept laboriously up through northern Mexico to New Mexico, eastward into the "kingdom of the Texas," westward into southern Arizona and the desolate peninsula of Lower California. As swollen Spain grew older and more tired, the movements of such expansion became more and more reflex responses to alarms real or imaginary: to the menace of the French in Louisiana, or of the Illinois French working their way westward to the Rocky Mountains, or of the Canada English working their way westward to the Pacific. In the middle of the eighteenth century a new threat appeared—the Russians in the Aleutians and Alaska, and seemingly ready to swallow up the whole Pacific coast. This coincided with the Spanish colonial renaissance under Charles III, when for a brief generation new vigor surged through the veins of the Spanish empire. The Spanish occupation of Upper California resulted.

In the spring of 1769 Spanish frontiersmen, priests, soldiers, and Indian allies were at San Diego, and in the spring of 1770, after many difficulties, a Spanish expedition was at Monterey "to occupy and defend the port from the atrocities of the Russians. . . . " During the next fifty years or so, twenty-one mission stations were planted from San Diego to San Francisco Bay, accompanied by a half dozen garrisoned presidios and settlements of colonists.

The missions gained their sustenance from Indian lands and Indian labor, and in return undertook to educate the Indians in the ways of Christianity and civilization and thus prepare them to become responsible citizens. The "Mission Indians," the people of about 700 miles of coastal country, were only a fraction of California's total Indian population. Converts numbered 21,100 at the most, in the missions' best year, 1820. They lived in large pueblos at the missions, laboring at every trade from adobe making to soap making, from sheepherding to pigeon tending. They were restrained by force from going back to the "monte" (back to their old free life), although groups would now and then be given a few weeks off to gather wild fruit in the woods and the hills, both literally and figuratively—figuratively in proselytizing for new converts or coaxing runaway neophytes to return.

Of course discipline was difficult. It was maintained by punishment of shackles, hobbles, stocks, imprisonment, or flogging—although no more than twenty-five lashes a day; and women, says a report of 1800, were very rarely flogged. Runaways were a constant problem, and the terrible death rate among the mission populations was a greater problem still.

But in the main the myth-shrouded world of the California coast people, idle and merry, collapsed almost at the first toll of a mission bell; there were a few armed revolts; but none of any consequence—these people were hopelessly simple when it came to making war. Resistance, where it occurred, tended to emphasize such passive measures as the persistent abortions practiced by the sullen women of a mission district near Santa Barbara, as noted in a report of 1810.

It would seem that the collapse of their world changed the

very look of the people. Travelers during mission times describe Indians markedly different in appearance from the tall, candid, handsome natives seen by the early voyagers 200 years before: the Mission Indians are usually pictured as short rather than tall, dark rather than fair, and above all dirty and spiritless. The Shoshonean people of part of the coast undoubtedly were short and dark, but the Chumash and Yuman people of other coastal regions were undoubtedly not. Possibly crowded living, heavy new clothes, and the suppression of the cleansing sweathouse helped make the people dirtier, and possibly suppression of such pagan (but incidentally bleaching) cosmetic aids as washing the hair with urine, or plastering the hair and face with clay or mud for several hours—to give gloss to the hair and kill vermin—made the people darker. Possibly shrinkage of the spirit made them shorter.

A European artist writing of San Francisco Mission Indians in 1816 said the mission Fathers characterized their native charges as "lazy, stupid, jealous, gluttonous, timorous," and he added, "I have never seen any of them laugh, I have never seen a single one look anyone in the face. They have the air of taking no interest in anything."

The missions flourished mightily, however, with commodity prosperity. Thousands of horses and hundreds of thousands of cattle and sheep grazed on the millions of acres of mission lands, and crops of wheat, corn, and beans ran to 120,000 annual bushels; mission storerooms were treasure houses of wine, leather, wool, oil, and other such riches. Given time enough such going concerns might still have transformed the California Indians, shrunken spirits notwithstanding, into the solid basis of a native population in the typical Spanish colonial pattern. But time ran out for Spain while the colony of California was still a raw, unassimilated frontier. The missions were in business, on the average, only a bare half century.

In the early years of the nineteenth century a wind of revolt, born of the American and French Revolutions, ran round the world. Rather suddenly, the 300-year-old Spanish empire was blown apart. Between 1811 and 1825 most of Spain's New World colonies fought for and won their independence; Mexico became an independent kingdom in 1821, and a republic only three years later.

In California, for the moment remaining a possession of Mex-

**Native dancers at this San Francisco mission were painted in 1816 by a visiting Russian artist, Louis Choris. Although such ceremonies were based on pagan ritual, the friars, viewing them as a form of innocent Indian amusement, often allowed their native converts to continue them.**

ico, revolution first made itself felt in the destruction of the wealthy missions, which were secularized in 1834. Theoretically this secularization was supposed to give the mission lands back to the Indians, thus making the Mission Indians a self-sustaining people. In practice, the missions were carved up to form the great California ranchos, and the Mission Indians were scattered like quail.

The distribution of the immense mission spoils was only being completed at the time of the American conquest of California in 1846, during the Mexican War. The discovery of gold came two years later, the stampede of the California gold rush followed, and by the autumn of 1850 California had become a full-fledged state. The non-Indian population jumped from about 15,000 in 1848 to nearly 93,000 in 1850, according to the federal census of that year—or to some 260,000 according to a doubtless exaggerated claim by the state government after a census of its own in 1852.

Indians in pre-gold-rush days numbered something more than 100,000 by conservative estimates. They were killed off in what seems to have been the biggest single spree of massacring in American history. Some guesses say 30,000 were left by 1859. These had dwindled to roughly 15,000 by the end of the century.

The thousands of newcomers to California brought with them the Indian policy of the American frontier—clear the Redskins out. The California Indians obligingly furnished depredations, occasionally killing or robbing the bearded miners, or driving off livestock. The California Indians were, as a whole, even more obliging in another respect—they were far from formidable in a fight. Whooping bands of the new California citizens formed companies of Indian fighters and butchered Indians with abandon in a long series of Indian "wars" that are all regarded as illegitimate by modern California historians. However, the Indian fighters asked and received pay and expenses from the government, a point that became increasingly important as the diggings played out and times grew hard. The United States government reimbursed the state of California $924,259 for this sort of semi-pro Indian killing between 1850 and 1859, exclusive of the expenses of the United States Army in policing California Indian country, and suppressing uprisings.

Prostitution and venereal diseases ran rampant among gold-country Indians, and gang rapes of Indian women became so flagrant that even the white press took cognizance. Kidnaping of Indian children to be sold as servants or laborers was common—one recent authority, in a careful calculation from such records as exist, has estimated that between 3,000 and 4,000 Indian children were stolen in the years from 1852 to 1867, "not including women taken for concubinage or adults for field labor."

It was not good to be a California Indian in the 1850s. And yet, in the discussions of the time as to the propriety or necessity of extermination there were many who spoke for the Indians, both on grounds of humanity and economy. An official report to Congress in 1850 stated that it was "*cheaper* to feed the whole flock for a *year* than to *fight* them for one week." Said Benjamin D. (Don Benito) Wilson, ex-Rocky Mountain trapper who had become a prosperous rancher in southern California, "None here but see and lament their sad condition.... Humanity, not war is the true policy for them."

Southern California, relatively untouched by the swarms of immigrants hot-footing it for the northern gold fields, was inclined to be less bloodthirsty about extinguishing all the Indians in sight; there were troublesome, half-wild Indians in the deserts not far distant from Los Angeles, but a reasonable peace was enforced by such peacemakers as Don Benito Wilson and Juan Antonio, noted chief of the still consequential Cahuillas. The debauched ex-Mission Indians of Los Angeles furnished a revolving slave-labor force for years, regularly arrested for drunkenness on Saturday night and bailed out on Monday morning for $2 or $3 a head by anyone who could use an Indian for a week's work.

The *aguardiente* sold to the Indians was real firewater, being sometimes mixed with corrosive acids, and gave rise to wild weekly jamborees in which Indian men, women, and children brawled tooth and nail. "Those thousands of honest, useful people," wrote a Los Angeles resident of the 1850s, speaking of the local Mission Indians, "were absolutely destroyed in this way."

Eventually, most of the surviving California Indians were placed on tatterdemalion little reservations that grew steadily littler, there to finish dwindling away in comparative peace. They didn't quite, although many once populous stocks became extinct. They were sacrifices, said a government inspector in 1858, for the "great cause of civilization, which, in the natural course of things, must exterminate Indians." But mass extermination by the gun still went on, here and there, into the 1870s. An old-timer with a Mark Twain touch recalled years later an incident of 1871, when some ranchers in the Sacramento Valley found a steer wounded by Indians, trailed the Indians with dogs, cornered them in a cave, and killed "about thirty. . . . In the cave... were some Indian children. Kingsley could not bear to kill these children with his 56-calibre Spencer rifle. 'It tore them up so bad.' So he did it with his 38-calibre Smith and Wesson revolver."

The entire frontier process was so accelerated in California that the California people seem scarcely to emerge from their aforesaid deeps of time before they vanish in an instant. It was quite possible for an aged Indian to have encompassed the whole story, from the coming of the Spanish colonizers to the destruction of the Fifties, in a single lifetime.

One island woman from San Nicolas, farthest offshore of the Santa Barbara Islands, did even better in living the full circle of the drama. In her time she had seen the Russian and Aleut sea-otter hunters bring death and carnage to the island, and press gangs from the missions had rounded up and taken away all those who could be caught. In 1835 Mexican authorities removed the last of the natives still living on the island. The woman was left behind when she ran back from the boat to find her child, who had been overlooked. Apparently no one missed her, or if so no one cared. The boat did not come back. The child soon died, and the woman was alone and forgotten on the island for eighteen years.

She had the houses of her people to live in, houses made of the ribs or jawbones of whales, walled with skins. There were seals, birds, fish, shellfish, and roots, and the island's ancient gods belonged to her alone. The island is wrapped in incessant winds and fogs, at their worst in the summers when the young hair seals cry like babies; and the woman dressed herself in warm but delicate gowns of bird skins.

She was found by accident, and taken into a Santa Barbara that had become an American town, and efforts were made to locate some of the remnants of the thousands of Chumash and Pepimaros who had inhabited the other offshore islands not so many years before. A number were turned up and brought to see her, but no one could understand her language. She died within a few months, although she was given the very best of care.

East of the great wall of the Sierra Nevada that separates California from the ordinary world there roamed numberless bands of primitive people, picking an arduous living from the pastel-colored deserts and the brilliant, flowery, barren desert mountains. Their manner of life—gathering wild seeds and grasshoppers, digging roots, hooking lizards out of their holes, making baskets and brush huts, circulating forever over a given territory around a recognized village site—apparently preserved the beginning ways of long, long ago on which had been built the somewhat more developed cultures of California.

It is usually assumed these people of the Great Basin were too busy finding food to build much of anything, cultural or otherwise. Their ceremonies were slight family affairs—there was not enough to eat in any one place for large gatherings. They sang their dreams, and sometimes performed a public mourning for the dead. In common with many other people of the Americas and elsewhere they believed that illness came from theft or loss of the soul—a belief curiously missing, by the way, from much of California.

As in the case of California, the various unorganized bands are customarily grouped on the artificial basis of language. All those within the Basin country proper spoke some Shoshonean tongue, and most had a Shoshonean look—short-legged and dark-skinned. The people known specifically as the Shoshoni occupied a great arc of country all the way from the Panamint Mountains and Death Valley in California through a wide swath in Nevada and contiguous belts in Utah and Idaho into the heart of the Rocky Mountains in Wyoming. Some of the desert Shoshoni, such as the Gosiute of the shores of the Great Salt Lake, were abysmally poor; some of the Rocky Mountain Shoshoni were gorgeously rich and showy, as befitted people living in some of the most gorgeous and showy mountain country on earth, that of the Grand Tetons and Wind Rivers.

The Utes ranged up and down Utah and eastward into the Colorado Rockies. The people known as the Paiute (sometimes said to mean "true Utes") inhabited most of those parts of Nevada and its borderlands not occupied by the Shoshoni; a mountain branch of the Paiute, in Idaho and Wyoming, were known as the Bannocks.

Around the edges of the Great Basin there were some people of non-Shoshonean language who nevertheless seemed to be Basin types in their manner of life. Such were the Washo, of the region between Reno and Lake Tahoe; and the conspicuously fierce Klamaths and Modocs of the California-Oregon border. The Klamaths made the most beautiful and warlike arrows that he had ever seen, said Kit Carson; and their bows could send arrows, said a veracious missionary, clear through a horse.

Most of the dwellers in the limitless mid-Basin deserts were desperately poor and correspondingly weak. They made a little trouble, but not much, when miners and ranchers moved into their country. In the end they usually attached themselves to ranches or towns as casual laborers or beggars, and thus remained on the sunburned native soil where they had lived for unnumbered thousands of years. Whites called them Digger Indians and generally regarded them as scarcely worth kicking out of the way.

To many of the perennially hungry mid-Basin people a horse was only something else to eat. But in the far western reaches, in the 1850s and 1860s, Paiutes and friends raided California ranchos in great horse-rustling expeditions, fought a pair of formal little battles with the whites at Pyramid Lake in 1860, and gained signal remark by making elegant horse-race pursuits of such desert interlopers as Pony Express riders and stage coaches. On the eastern and northern periphery a number of tribes acquired the use of horses and became rather splendid horse Indians, most notably some of the Northern Shoshoni of the slopes of the Rockies—one migrating branch of these people, known as the Comanche, were ranked as the finest horsemen and the most redoubtable warriors in America by quite a few experts who had had the hair-raising pleasure of their acquaintance.

Lewis and Clark's providential and beloved girl guide, Sacagawea, came from the Shoshoni of the Rocky Mountains, being captured in 1800 by Minnetarees (a name applied to both Atsinas and Hidatsas) in Atsina country on the plains and winding up, by a set of curious chances, at the Hidatsa towns on the Missouri far to the east three years later, at the moment Lewis and Clark were in the neighborhood preparing to head west.

The historical importance of this happy accident can be overestimated: maybe the Lewis and Clark expedition could have made it to the coast anyway, without her services as interpreter, and without the horses she was able to get from her people when they reached the Shoshoni, and maybe Clark's party could have extricated itself anyway from the Montana mountain passes on the way back without her help, and maybe subsequent constant friendship of the mountain Shoshoni for Americans, with its effect on far-western colonization and American possession of the Oregon country, would all have come to pass anyway. On the other hand, maybe not.

It is certain that Sacagawea had no sense of directing destiny. Meriwether Lewis wrote of her, "If she has enough to eat and a few trinkets to wear I believe she would be perfectly content anywhere."

The destiny of western America received a few other nudges from people around the Great Basin who were quite innocent of any such intention, as so often seems to be the case in the making of history.

The tall and naked Yumas of the lower Colorado River became great friends of the Spaniards and contributed to the success of overland colonizing expeditions that marched from Sonora, Mexico, to California in the 1770s. These expeditions were under the leadership of Juan Bautista de Anza, first-class desert expert, son and grandson of desert frontiersmen, tough, honest, likeable, and a friend of the important Yuma chief whom the Spaniards called Salvador Palma. The greatest of these expeditions, made up of 240 people (more than half of them children) and a long train of animals, colonized San Francisco in 1776. The continued good will of the Yuma people was vital to California's land connections with Mexico; and missions and a few settlers were planted among them to cement that good will. But trouble came between the Yumas and the settlers; the Yumas slew all the Spaniards at hand in 1781 and closed the trail, and it was never reopened during Spanish times. Cut-off California was left to some degree weaker and more remote, perhaps to fall the more easily into American hands in 1846.

In 1805 the Spanish governor of New Mexico sent his top scout, a Frenchman named Pierre Vial who had a twenty-year string of superb feats of frontier exploration to his credit, to raise the northern Indians against Lewis and Clark and thus

**This 1873 photograph shows an encampment of the Paiute tribe near St. George, Utah. The Paiutes were one of a number of tribes who eked out a meager existence in the Great Basin of Nevada and Utah, subsisting primarily upon roots dug from the barren and desolate landscape.**

parry the thrust of the United States toward the Far West. But Vial was attacked on the Arkansas River (probably by Pawnees) and turned back. He tried again in the spring of 1806, and again the experienced Vial failed—while the greenhorns Lewis and Clark had already, by that time, won through to the Pacific.

Westward of the mountain Shoshoni, ranging over much of central Idaho and the eastern sections of Washington and Oregon, there lived a number of neighboring tribes speaking various related languages now known collectively as Shahaptian. These included among others the Nez Perce, most easterly of the group, centering in Idaho and the Snake River country where Idaho, Oregon, and Washington come together; and the Palouse, the Walla Walla, and the Yakima, the latter among the most westerly of these peoples, living along the Yakima River westward of the great bend of the Columbia. All these had been river people, living pretty much on salmon, camas bulbs, and roots, but they took enthusiastically to horses when they became available. This was probably in the very early 1700s; the horses probably came from the Spanish settlements of New Mexico and were probably passed along to this upper country by the Northern Shoshoni. By the early 1800s the Nez Perces were more skillful than Virginia hostlers at handling horses (so said Americans who had seen both), and had already become identified with a famous breed earlier developed in the region, the Appaloosa horse—the name coming, of course, from the neighboring Palouse. A small, distantly related tribe living south of the Yakimas, known as the Cayuse, built up such a trade reputation as horsedealers that "cayuse" became another name for horse among early Oregon settlers.

These were proud, warlike people, and of them all the Nez Perce were the most numerous (Lewis and Clark guessed their population at 6,000) and most powerful. But like the Shoshoni, they were friendly and hospitable and helpful not only to Lewis and Clark in 1805 and 1806 but also to the other Americans who passed through their country during the next fifty years, and whose name in that time became legion. The stubborn, although sometimes sorely tried, Nez Perce friendship for Americans—through all those fifty years, and more, not one American lost his life at Nez Perce hands—was of considerable influence, due to their position of leadership in the region.

The Nez Perce were minor instruments of history in still another manner, which came about in the following way. In 1825 Canadian fur traders arranged to have two deserving Spokan and Kutenai youths sent to the Red River of Canada for schooling. The Kutenai and Spokan were neighbors living to the north of the Nez Perce. Later three Nez Perce youths also attended the Red River Mission School. Apparently the Nez Perces became increasingly interested in obtaining the advantages of formal education for their young men, and some Nez Perces visiting St. Louis in 1831 asked this boon of General William Clark (of Lewis and), then governor there.

Somehow the story of their request got a little twisted in the telling, and the deputation of distant Indians was represented as coming all this way to seek the white man's religion. As a matter of fact there had been Christianized individuals here and there among the Nez Perce and their neighbors since before 1820, due to the amateur missionary work of Christianized Canadian Indians (particularly Iroquois from Caughnawaga, a settlement of Catholic Iroquois in Quebec) brought to the Far West in fur-trapping brigades.

On the other hand, a request for teachers and a request for missionaries were one and the same thing, there being no other kind of white teacher known to trans-frontier Indians anyplace in the hemisphere.

In any case, the tale of the "Four Wise Men of the West" journeying so far to deliver their appeal for "The Book" of the white man was widely reprinted, and the eastern religious press became much exercised.

The missions to Oregon of Rev. Jason W. Lee (1834), Dr. Marcus Whitman and Rev. H. H. Spalding (1836–1837), and others, followed, with some effect on the opening of heavy American emigration to Oregon during the next ten years. This in turn, by installing the nucleus of a settled American population in Oregon, had its effect on the boundary question then in dispute between England and the United States as to which was to have possession of the Oregon country. The boundary issue was settled in 1846, and the Oregon country—embracing the entire region that had been the real bone of contention, that between the Columbia River and the Forty-ninth Parallel—was turned over to the United States.

Among most of the people of the far Northwest, fishing was usually the mainstay of life—Lewis and Clark in October of 1805 found the broad Columbia almost continuously lined with fish racks and bands of salmon fishers. But toward the east, toward the sweeping Rockies and the sweeping winds of the Great Plains, the coming of the horse brought changes: hunting became more important, especially the annual buffalo hunt; and clothes and customs took on some of the dash and flamboyance of the wild horsemen beyond the mountains. A house became a tipi, full-dress fringed skins and feathered war bonnets came into fashion, and flowered bead designs blossomed on anything that would hold still to be stitched.

Such were the Nez Perce and their neighbors, such as the Bannocks to their south, and the Flatheads to their northeast, centering around Flathead Lake in present Montana. The Flatheads were, in their own name, the Salish; the name was later applied to one of the largest language families of the Northwest—Salishan. The Flatheads did not flatten their heads but left them as nature made them. However, an undeformed head appeared flat on top compared to the tapered skulls of various Salishan and Chinookan people farther west who did practice ornamental skull deformation. Hence the misnomer, applied to the Flatheads by these more richly cultured neighbors who thought of a pointedly deformed skull as a mark of proper upbringing, of having been "well-cradled."

Most of all these tribes of the Northwest plateau country—Lewis and Clark counted twenty-five along their route through the area—were unfailingly friendly to the first American settlers. The Nez Perce and the Northern Shoshoni, as mentioned, were particularly distinguished in this regard—Washakie, the illustrious war chief of the Eastern Band of the Wyoming Shoshoni, was given a memorial of gratitude signed by some 9,000 emigrants, having helped them cross difficult fords or recover strayed stock, and having kept his people out of quarrels even when an occasional unruly emigrant seemed bent on same.

But the first settlers to the Oregon country were not looking for trouble with anyone (unless it might be with the British); they were looking for a Promised Land of corn and wine, green grass and fertile loam—Beulah Land they called it in their hymns, after the land of heavenly joy described by Pilgrim in his Progress. They were for the most part earnest, honest, pious people, and they met the Indians' friendship with a friendship no less genuine in return.

Perhaps as many as 10,000 came to settle in the Oregon country in the early 1840s, mostly in the Willamette Valley, with a few in the valleys of the Columbia and the Cowlitz and on Puget Sound. If the river tribes restrained themselves from any grave objections to this invasion of "Bostons" as they called the settlers, the Americans likewise invoked patience when a Klickitat passerby stopped at a farmhouse to demand a prepared meal, or a few roistering Smackshop Chulluckittequaws requisitioned an ox or a horse, or a drunken Chinook stopped respectable people to shout in the jargon, "Nah, six, potlatch blue lu!" ("Hey, friend, give me whisky!")

The first real trouble came in 1847, with the destruction of the Whitman mission among the Cayuse (near modern Walla Walla, Washington), and the murder of twelve Americans there, including Dr. Whitman and his wife. The subsequent deaths from measles of two little girls among the surviving women and children—Mrs. Whitman was the only woman killed—are usually added to the total. The immediate causes of the Whitman massacre are not clear. The Cayuse are said to have been increasingly resentful of the missionaries as more and more Bostons swarmed into the country, believing that the missionaries were in league with the Bostons to dispossess the Indians entirely. Bitter competition between Protestant and Catholic missions caused angry controversies among the Indians themselves, making for quarrels, grudges, and high feelings. A measles epidemic just before the murders—killing a couple of hundred Cayuses in a few weeks—helped to overheat the atmosphere.

Settlers formed a volunteer army and exacted preliminary revenge, and Congress was importuned for military protection. To make peace the Cayuse eventually (in 1850) turned over to the Oregon authorities five of the Whitman murderers, or five Cayuses who at any rate played the part for the sake of saving the rest of their people. They were duly tried and hanged in Oregon City.

The early 1850s brought a surge of new population to Oregon, much of it consisting of ex-gold-rushers from the California diggings looking for a fresh bonanza. The political

**In 1872 and 1873 the Modocs waged a fanatic, last-ditch fight in northern California's lava beds, as sketched here by William Simpson for the London *Illustrated News*. The battle marked a final phase in the decay of the Northwest tribes, although the Modocs, led by Kintpuash, or Captain Jack as whites called him, fought so fiercely that field guns were finally required to shell them from the lava beds. Kintpuash was hanged.**

machinery of organized territorial government got into high gear—Washington was split off and established as a territory unto itself in 1853, under the governorship of Isaac I. Stevens, regarded as a strong anti-Indian man. United States Army troops were on hand by 1850, as a result of the alarms of the Cayuse War, and were regularly augmented thereafter.

These circumstances set the frontier process of Indian disposal in operation more or less automatically. For the next ten years it clattered with remarkable celerity through its familiar routine.

There were the usual councils large and small, the usual treaty chiefs of doubtful authority, the usual stubborn bands who did not want to obey the treaty chiefs' treaties, the usual hostilities to force them to do so. There was the usual reluctance on the part of some tribes to make any land-ceding treaties at all, and the consequent overrunning of their country by unauthorized immigrants and the consequent hostile incidents and the consequent wars.

There were numerous sizable operations involving the military, as well as countless volunteer "wars" on the California model, with attendant bills to the government. One of the least illegitimate of these volunteer activities was the brief foray against the Rogue River Indians of southern Oregon in 1853, resulting in the "purchase" of the entire Rogue River Valley, more than 2,000,000 acres, for a price of $60,000; $15,000 to go to settlers for claims of war damages, $45,000 to the Indians, to be paid in annuities of approximately $2.75 per Indian for sixteen years. There was also an added bill to the government of $258,000 for the five weeks' services of the 200 to 500 volunteers involved. The Rogue River country was left far from pacified by this expense; an outbreak in 1856 cost the lives of many innocent settlers and officials, extensive military operations, and the near extermination of a number of the various tribes known as the Rogue River Indians.

As the Indians were increasingly cowed there was the usual increase of lawlessness on the part of opportunistic whites, which goaded new wars into being. Military commanders, sent to Oregon to protect American settlers, found that they had to spend much of their effort vainly trying to protect the Indians from outrages by white men.

These outrages were sometimes deliberately intended to keep the hostilities burning, due to a quite sincere belief in many quarters (and an eye on profit in others) that the Indians should be wholly exterminated. "Let our motto be extermination, and death to all opposers," said a newspaper in Yreka, a trading town in the California-Oregon border country—whose merchants, incidentally, sold goods to a volunteer Indian-chasing expedition in 1854 at such exorbitant prices that the commanding general on the Pacific Coast sent a protest to Washington against paying the expedition's expenses, alleging that the expedition was unnecessary and had only been drummed up as a speculation to benefit the suppliers.

The exterminators were noisy and given to ever more violent visions—saloon orators as well as the official newspaper of the Know-Nothing Party in Oregon called for the extermination of all Catholics as soon as the Indians were finished off. They also committed quite a bit of exterminating in their small way—three unauthorized squads in one sector of Oregon killed between twelve and eighteen Indians per squad in less than a week in 1853, in each case by inducing them to lay down their arms under pledges of peace and then shooting them.

But it should be pointed out that a reasonable proportion of the Oregon and Washington settlers seems to have felt sympathy toward the Indians, sometimes when such an attitude was so unpopular as to be dangerous. There were members of volunteer companies who denounced with considerable fervor the killing of Indian women and children. There were farmers who hid Indian friends in their houses when the troops or the volunteers were on the warpath—and Indians who did vice versa when the Indians were uprising. However, the anti-Indian people were more actively interested in removing the Indians than the just and peaceful people were interested in peace and justice. As a result, the peaceable part of the public was not as a rule very effective.

A great treaty-making council was held in the rainy spring of 1855 with the tribes east of the Cascades. Kamaiakan, a leader of the Yakimas, headed the opposition against confinement on a reservation, even though the United States commissioners offered to make him supreme chief of all the tribes gathered there. But at last each band of the fourteen present was permitted to select its own favorite home valley as a reservation, and on these terms the treaties were signed.

Charges and countercharges of duress, deceit, and plotted

treachery in connection with the treaties came in later years, but they were academic—for within three months after the council war broke out, the major and decisive conflict in the Northwest. Miners and settlers did not wait for the ratification of the treaties by Congress before streaming into the treaty lands (gold strikes in the Colville and Coeur d'Alène countries spurred them on), and the Yakima and a half dozen neighboring tribes decided almost unanimously that they did not want to ratify the treaties at all. White squatters were attacked, an Indian agent was killed, and Governor Stevens called out the troops.

The war lasted for three years, spreading to engulf tribes as far away as the Haida of British Columbia and some member peoples of the Duwamish League of Puget Sound—although Chief Seattle of the Duwamish League remained a strong American ally. It featured innumerable actions by irregulars of both sides, two Indian victories over regular Army troops, two naval engagements—an attack of Yakimas and their allies on river steamers, and a hot assault on the town of Seattle fought off by a naval force then in the harbor—and ended with the defeat of the Indian allies by an Army force of more than 700 artillery, cavalry, and infantry troops. Two or three dozen of the Indian leaders were hanged. Kamaiakan, wounded, escaped to Canada.

Wars continued, official and otherwise, and raids and retaliations, but for most of the tribes of the Northwest there remained only the final phase of decay and dissolution.

Sometimes, though, they decayed hard, as in the case of Captain Jack and his band of Modocs. By 1870 this was a degraded band that hung around Yreka getting drunk and selling children when it wasn't out in the country terrorizing honest farmers, according to some accounts; according to other accounts, Jack carried letters from prominent Yreka citizens testifying to his good conduct and good faith with the whites.

Captain Jack, as he was known to the whites—his Modoc name was Kintpuash—preferred the Lost River country south of Upper Klamath Lake to the Klamath reservation on the lake where all the Modocs were supposed to go, and where about half the tribe was already installed. The Lost River country was his home, Kintpuash said, and besides that he didn't like the Klamaths and couldn't live with them. But settlers wanted the Lost River country too, and they didn't want Kintpuash and his people as neighbors.

When troops came in 1872 to remove him by force to the reservation, Kintpuash and his band killed as many soldiers and settlers as they could manage and then took up a position in the lava beds (now a national monument) south of what is today called Tule Lake, just below the California line. More troops were summoned, and still more, and were joined by Indian scouts and allies—some of them Modocs from the Klamath agency—until after seven months, more than 1,000 men were in action against Kintpuash and his handful of followers. The Modoc band consisted of perhaps 250 men, women, and children, with perhaps seventy or eighty men of warrior age—most of the men were well-known to the whites, under such monikers as Humpy Jerry, Shacknasty Jim, or Curly-headed Doctor.

Attack after attack was trapped and shot to pieces in the nightmare lava beds, total Army casualties running to over 100 killed and wounded. A peace conference was arranged, and Kintpuash broke up the proceedings by killing out of hand the president of the peace commissioners, and Army commander of the Department of the Columbia, the noted General E. R. S. Canby—Kintpuash wore General Canby's uniform in later engagements. A Methodist minister was also murdered, and the other peace commissioners barely escaped with their lives. The nation was shocked by this cold-blooded treachery; President Grant demanded commensurate action from his commander of the Army, and his commander of the Army, General William Tecumseh Sherman, replied, "You will be fully justified in their utter extermination." Field guns were finally brought up and the Modocs were shelled out of their lava beds and at last, in scattered groups, hunted down and forced to surrender. Kintpuash and three of his lieutenants were hanged, and that was the end of Captain Jack; but the rest of his band drew a harder fate, being sent to the Quapaw agency in the malarial southeastern corner of Indian Territory, where in the next thirty years they quietly decayed and diminished in numbers to less than a third of the 170 men, women, and children who had surrendered.

Among the Nez Perce, so constant in their American friendship, there lived a man of importance named Joseph, the name having been given to him by Reverend Spalding, whose school Joseph had attended. Joseph was the son of a Cayuse father but his wife was a Nez Perce, and he had been at the great

Walla Walla council of 1855 as one of the Nez Perce spokesmen. The treaty he signed there reserved for his Nez Perce band what it claimed as its ancient home, the Wallowa Valley along the Snake River at the mouth of the Grande Ronde, crossroads of the present boundaries of the states of Oregon, Washington, and Idaho.

After 1855 the Nez Perces stuck to peace and American alliance while all Oregon was on fire with war, rescued a body of American troops in 1858, and refused entanglement in trouble-making plots at the start of the Civil War.

In 1863 a new treaty was negotiated, in which Joseph's band did not participate, and which ceded the Wallowa Valley to the government for settlement. Joseph protested that the other Nez Perces who had made this cession had acted without authority, and in violation of the previous treaty of 1855. He and his band stayed on in the valley, although white settlers started moving in and the usual unavoidable hostile incidents occurred.

In 1871 Joseph died and the leadership of his band went to a son named Hin-mah-too-yah-laht-ket (Thunder Rolling in the Mountains), who was known to the Americans as Young Joseph, and later as Chief Joseph.

The Nez Perces are so often described as noble, handsome, brave, truehearted, and in general excellent in all respects, that it seems likely they may have been, J. Fenimore Cooperesque though the assumption may be. When it comes to Young Joseph, the paean reaches crescendo. He was, so they say, of wisdom, eloquence, goodness, and mercy unmeasurable, and in his pictures as a young man he is obviously no mountain Indian, but a figment of Sir Walter Scott's imagination, or more likely George Sand's.

In the spring of 1876 a man of Young Joseph's own band was killed by a settler in the course of one of the unavoidable hostile incidents—all of which the Nez Perces had so far endured without retaliation. Young Joseph said of this murder: "As to the murderer I have made up my mind. I have come to the conclusion to let him escape and enjoy health and not take his life for the one he took. I am speaking as though I spoke to the man himself. . . . I pronounce the sentence that he shall live."

Young Joseph and his people did not want to leave their valley not only because it was their home but because they were horsemen, with wealth that they very much cherished in their thou-

On the way to Oklahoma exile after his surrender, Chief Joseph of the Nez Perces sat for this portrait in Dakota Territory, where local citizens hailed his "bravery and humanity." Long friendly to white settlers, the Nez Perces were finally harassed into war, and the peace-loving Chief Joseph gained a reputation for extraordinary military prowess.

sands of horses, many of them the blue Appaloosas with five-finger-spotted rumps, that had become traditional Nez Perce war and hunting horses. The twenty acres allotted to each head of a family on a reservation was far from enough for a stockman. But to avoid a hopeless clash with the American authorities, Young Joseph at last agreed to take his people out of their valley and settle on the Lapwai Reservation, where the government wanted them to go. This was in the spring of 1877.

Unfortunately some white neighbors took the opportunity to make away with several hundred of the Indians' horses while the Nez Perces were preparing to move. The departing people, already heartsick, homesick, and enraged, counted their multiplied grievances until at last a moment came when they could be restrained no longer. In a night and a day of vengeance a mutinous party of a few young men murdered eighteen settlers, and out came the troops. After seventy-two years of peace, the Nez Perces were at war. Joseph, who had said, "rather than have war I would give up my country . . . I would give up everything . . . ," no longer had any choice.

It happened that among the troops there was a twenty-five-year-old West Pointer, one Lieutenant Wood, who later, under the name of Charles Erskine Scott Wood, became one of the finest writers in America. The picture of Indian fighting scribbled in his journal might be dull but is probably real. "Hot stifling march across a dry prairie. No breakfast no water, men fainting and falling by the wayside." But, the next day: "The afternoon march and camp on the prairie, grass to our knees, rolling hills. . . . "

And his first Indian battle: "The advance, more rains, Indians speckling the hills like ants. Firing. Sudden feeling of intoxication on hearing the shots nervous eagerness for the fight. . . . " But the fight was over. The ants speckling the hills and the distant slam of shots was an Indian battle.

In a series of such fights the American commander, General O. O. Howard, found himself consistently outmaneuvered, suffering heavy losses, and unable to gain an advantage although superior in numbers, firepower, and mobility—Joseph being burdened with all of his refugee people and their belongings. It began to appear that young Chief Joseph might be a military prodigy. He was, according to the Army officers who fought against him. For he decided to lead his band—400 to 500 people, with at the most something between 100 and 200 effective warriors—to safety in Canada, and for four months he fought his way through and around Army units (with their Indian scouts) that were rushed in from all sides to head him off, fought a running campaign of over 1,000 mountain miles that has been compared to the *Anabasis* of Xenophon's Ten Thousand Greeks, conducted with a magnificent generalship that has been compared to Napoleon's best.

The question has been raised in recent studies as to how much of the credit for his campaign should go to Joseph and how much to the leaders of smaller bands or other chief men present during the march—the lean Looking Glass, famous warrior, who joined along with his band after Joseph's first startling victory had been achieved; or Too-hul-hul-sute, the aged and influential Dreamer priest; or White Bird, who at the last moment did succeed in reaching Canada with about 100 followers; or Joseph's brother, Ollokot, leader of the warriors in Joseph's band, "he who led the young men," as Joseph spoke of him; or others among the ranking men.

In the absence of written records from the Nez Perce headquarters it will never be possible to assign exact credit for the various battle plans—even in the presence of written records the same sort of question is raised among Napoleon buffs, wondering about the real contribution of such gentry as Marshal Ney.

Nor is it possible to assign exact commands to the various principal men. Indian rank and authority are slippery matters at best, when it comes to defining them in traditional European military terms. The custom of separate peace and war chiefs, common among some Indian peoples, was not followed by the Nez Perces and the neighboring people of the Columbia River plateau region, or by the people of the neighboring Great Basin area and the California region. Authority was instead likely to be rather informal. The contemporary evidence, at the time of the epic adventure of his fighting Nez Perces, associates the aura of principal authority with Joseph. He may thus be regarded as the inspired tactician of the march of his people, or, if one wishes, simply as the symbol of their inspired spirit.

He fought over a dozen engagements with four different Army columns, cut off pursuit by a daring night raid that left the pursuers without transport animals, or by an adroit feint that turned the pursuing columns around to run into each other, or simply fought and outfought the enemy with his handful of dazzling Nez Perce cavalrymen. "They rode at full gallop along the mountain side in a steady formation by fours; formed twos, at a given signal, with perfect precision, to cross a narrow bridge; then galloped into line, reined in to a sudden halt, and dismounted with as much system as regulars," said an Army general. The Nez Perces were hurt several times by casualties—eighty-nine killed in one engagement, fifty of these being women and children. But they continued to march, and they continued to fight. They practiced one further novelty, novel for either red or white warriors, in the warfare of the time and region: Joseph had reportedly ordered no scalping in the battles that he was to command, and there was none.

The war they fought, said General William Tecumseh Sherman, was "one of the most extraordinary Indian wars of which there is any record. The Indians throughout displayed a courage and skill that elicited universal praise; they abstained from scalping, let captive women go free, did not commit indiscriminate murder of peaceful families, which is usual. . . . " General Nelson A. Miles, whose column finally cut off Joseph's retreat, was quoted as saying, "In this skillful campaign they have spared hundreds of lives and thousands of dollars worth of property that they might have destroyed . . . ," and was moved to add gratuitously that Joseph's Nez Perces "have, in my opinion, been grossly wronged in years past."

Joseph "led his tribe—men, women and children, sick, wounded, maimed and blind—through the Bitterroot Mountains, twice across the Rocky Mountains, through the Yellowstone National Park, across the Missouri River, to the Bear Paw Mountains, where, on Eagle Creek, within thirty miles of the Canadian line, he finally surrendered, Oct. 5, 1877," wrote young Lieutenant Wood some years later, in a letter recounting the saga and its conclusion. Lieutenant Wood had been made General Howard's aide-de-camp and so was in at the finish. His letter, which it would be presumptuous to paraphrase, continues: "He was stopped in his retreat by Gen. Miles, on notification sent out by Gen. Howard, but stood at bay for two days, refusing to surrender, until on the third day, Gen. Howard arrived on the scene, when, on the evening of a wintry day, the prairie powdered with snow, and a red and stormy sun almost at the horizon, Joseph surrendered, his people coming out of the burrows they had made in the hills, and where they had been living without fires, subsisting on the flesh of the dead horses....

"In the final attack, a surprise by Gen. Miles, Joseph's little girl, about eight or nine years old, and of whom he was very fond, fled in terror out on the prairie, and at the time of his surrender she was supposed to have perished from cold and starvation. As a matter of fact, she was afterwards found among the Sioux as a prisoner or slave, and was restored to Joseph; but with little effect, as his express condition of surrender—that he should be allowed to go back to the reservation which had been provided for him—was broken by the government, and he and his people were sent to the malarial bottoms of the Indian Territory, where all of his own children (six) and most of his band died.

"At the time of the surrender, the able bodied warriors were surprisingly few, in contrast to the number of sick, aged and decrepit men and women: blind people, children, babies and wounded that poured out of their burrows in the earth as soon as it was known that they could do so with safety.

"Joseph came up to the crest of the hill, upon which stood Gen. Howard, Gen. Miles, an interpreter, and myself. Joseph was the only one mounted, but five of his principal men clung about his knees and pressed close to the horse, looking up at him, and talking earnestly in low tones. Joseph rode with bowed head, listening attentively, apparently, but with perfectly immobile face. As he approached the spot where we were standing, he said something, and the five men who were with him halted. Joseph rode forward alone, leaped from his horse, and, leaving it standing, strode toward us. He opened the blanket which was wrapped around him, and handed his rifle to Gen. Howard, who motioned him to deliver it to Gen. Miles, which Joseph did. Standing back, he folded his blanket again across his chest, leaving one arm free, somewhat in the manner of a Roman senator with his toga, and, half turning toward the interpreter, said:

"'Tell General Howard I know his heart. What he told me before, in Idaho, I have it in my heart. I am tired of fighting.... My people ask me for food, and I have none to give. It is cold, and we have no blankets, no wood. My people are starving to death. Where is my little daughter? I do not know. Perhaps, even now, she is freezing to death. Hear me, my chiefs. I have fought; but from where the sun now stands, Joseph will fight no more forever.'

"And he drew his blanket across his face, after the fashion of Indians when mourning or humiliated, and, instead of walking towards his own camp, walked directly into ours, as a prisoner.

"After long delay, and when his band was reduced to a comparatively small number of people, he was [in 1885], with the remnant of his tribe, allowed to come north from the Indian Territory—not to his old ground in Idaho, but to Northern Washington. No supplies were provided for them. They marched from the Indian Territory to their new home, and arrived on the edge of winter in a destitute condition, experiencing great suffering. . . .

"I think that, in his long career, Joseph cannot accuse the Government of the United States of one single act of justice. . . . "

The above version of Joseph's surrender speech was written from memory, although it was Lieutenant Wood who took down the original at the time, in his capacity as General Howard's aide. The speech has become one of the most famous in Indian literature and has been many times quoted, in almost as many different versions.

# XII

# The People of Dreams

**A Blackfoot medicine-pipe carrier wears the distinctive coiled hairdo of his station.**

Beyond the Spanish frontier in northern Mexico, in the year 1594, the chief of a village of Laguneros Indians rode out on horseback to welcome a venturesome Jesuit, the first missionary in those parts. The exploring padre duly reported his cordial reception, in no wise making anything remarkable of the mounted chief. Obviously there was nothing extraordinary about wild Indians owning and riding horses. And yet this was only seventy-five years after Cortes had landed the ten stallions, five mares, and a foal who were the first Spanish horses to appear in horseless North America.

The prehistoric horse was born in the Americas, many millions of years ago, but for some reason became extinct in the New World at the close of the Ice Age. However, horses had long before spread to the Old World, no doubt across the occasional Siberian land bridge. Thus the horses brought by the Spaniards to the New World were, fairly literally, coming back home. Perhaps they knew it. In any case, they went forth and multiplied at an astonishing rate.

For horseless South America the principal early center of distribution was Peru, where horses arrived in 1532. By 1535 they had entered the horse heaven that is modern Argentina. By 1600 they were streaming over the Argentine pampas in herds too vast to count. The varying peoples there, and in the rolling, scrub-covered country adjoining on the north, known as the Chaco, became intense horsemen and utterly revolutionized the ways of their world in the process.

In North America the horse frontier jumped to northern New Mexico, to the heel of the Rockies, when Oñate's colonists drove up thousands of head of assorted livestock in 1598. The Santa Fe country remained for generations the chief dispersal point for the American horse. Spanish officials now and then made efforts to enforce security regulations against letting Indians learn the use of horses, but the *mayordomos* at ranches and missions had to reply that there were only Indians available to work as vaqueros. The Indians learned.

The secret plans of the manipulation of that ultimate weapon, the horse, must have been stolen many times over by amateur Indian secret agents. And having learned, Indians stole horses by the bunch, by the herd, by the multitude, from the huge ranches of Chihuahua and New Mexico.

The Pueblo revolt of 1680 threw all the horses in New Mexico on the open Indian market for a dozen years, and from this point on the horse frontier left the white frontier years behind. Bartered or stolen from band to band, ridden on terrorizing raids that covered 500 miles or more, galloped into hitherto unknown lands on wonderfully lucrative hunting trips, driven in herds to distant nations by Indian merchants, horses fanned out over the West, their hoofbeats a flourish of drums announcing a marvelous new life. The sun-cracked wastes of Utah and Nevada were too poor in graze and water for a man to keep a horse, but the Ute people of the Rockies' western slopes took to horses and passed them along (unintentionally, of course), and by the 1690s horses were being introduced among the Northern Shoshoni of Wyoming by someone, spies or tradesmen or exiles from horse-owning tribes, who could teach the mysteries of their management. And now, with Shoshoni war feathers tied in their flying tails and with Shoshoni bowmen on their backs, horses trotted eastward out of the mountains to sweep across the high plains, the seemingly endless plains that stretch from the Rockies to the Mississippi River Valley prairies, in pursuit of the antelope, the buffalo, and the constant Shoshoni foes, the bold-hearted people of the northern plains known as the Blackfeet.

Intrepid or not, the trudging foot people of the plains were thrown into panic by enemies transformed into centaurs nine feet tall who could dash upon their victims with the speed of the screaming wind. Mounted Shoshonis were attacking the Blackfeet by 1730, according to the best recollection of an aged Blackfoot more than half a century later; the Blackfeet asked for help from Crees and Assiniboins to their east, who came and defeated a Shoshoni war party with the aid of another fantastic new weapon—the gun.

The horse frontier, moving in from south and west, and the gun frontier, advancing from the east, met on the Great Plains in a spectacular clash and created the figure that has obsessed the world ever since as the archetype of the American Indian: the feather-streaming, buffalo-chasing, wild-riding, recklessly fighting Indian of the plains.

This figure, shaped by the European's horse and gun, decorated from war-bonnet band to moccasins with the European's beads, only reached full glory when the real Indian world was all but a memory. The Plains Indian was a late, last flowering of the ancient culture already vanished or in ruins over most of the hemisphere. He was less sheer Indian than almost any of his predecessors down through the ages of Indian history, from the proto-Olmecs and the Mayas to the Creeks and Iroquois.

But in some other respects the Plains Indian is an excellent happenchance choice as an Indian symbol. In his exaggerated world he intensified a whole palette of more specialized Indian colors common to some previous Indian societies although by no means to all: warrior societies and elaborate codes of combat, fear of sex and grief for the dead and emotional excesses deriving from both, sacred objects and sacred rites deriving from dreams and inspired visions, and the omnipresent sacred power to be sought in dreams and inspired visions. In all these respects and many more the Plains Indian was the Indian carried to extremes. Finally, the boundless land in which he lived, confined only by the wide and starry sky, gave obvious emphasis to the pervasive notion of Indian freedom.

These modern Plains Indians sprang from several different roots, from farmers and hunters who had lived on the plains and their margins for untold centuries as well as from the diverse tribes and nations who poured into the plains with the storm fronts of the horse and the gun.

There had been buffalo hunters on the plains at least since Folsom times, possibly 10,000 years ago. Eventually villages of farmers appeared along the river courses; the typical plainsmen for many hundreds of years seem to have been not hunters but pottery-making farmers who hunted as a sideline. Some were clearly connected with the great Hopewell culture centering in the Ohio Valley far to the east, and there centering some 2,000 years ago in time. Later earth-lodge villages, but dating back to at least more than 400 years ago, are identifiable as Pawnee, carrying associations from the Temple Mound people of the Southeast. In more recent times farming gave way to a return to nomadic hunting over most of the plains country, and some people who had once grown corn and made pottery forgot how to do both, and devoted their lives to hunting the inexhaustible buffalo.

Among the historic peoples of known location the Blackfeet

are regarded as the ancients of the northern plains, although how long they may have been there no one can guess. Their language, a much-altered Algonquian variant, had obviously been separated for a long period from other Algonquian languages to the east. In the vague but not too distant past they expanded southward from the Alberta-Saskatchewan plains and took over much of Montana, thrusting out a people then living in the plains in the region of the present Canadian boundary; these were the Kutenai, a tall, estimable race speaking a language unrelated to any other, who gradually moved westward across the Rockies and became northern neighbors of the Flatheads and Nez Perces. These slow changes of homeland were still going on in the eighteenth century. On the eve of the coming of the horse, the Blackfeet dwelt along the eastern base of the Rockies throughout Montana and far up into Alberta, to the edge of the black northern forests that begin beyond the North Saskatchewan River.

Known collectively as the Blackfeet, or the Blackfoot confederacy, they were a numerous (estimated 15,000 in 1780) people divided into three tribes of common descent, common language, and, sometimes, a common front against a common enemy. These divisions were, in the farthest north, the Blackfeet proper (from their own name, Siksika, meaning black-footed people and possibly referring to black-dyed moccasins); next, to the south, the Bloods (possibly from their sacred face paint of red earth); and farthest south, the Piegans (pronounced Payganns, meaning "poor robes"). On the north a small Athapascan-speaking tribe, the Sarcee (Blackfoot for "no-goods"), allied itself to the Blackfeet in later years for protection.

East of the Piegans another group speaking a highly aberrant Algonquian language roamed the plains of Montana and Canada between the Missouri and the Saskatchewan. These were the Atsina, brothers of the Arapaho of the Wyoming plains from whom they had separated perhaps as late as the seventeenth century; they may have been in the plains country—somewhere—well before that, possibly as long as the Blackfeet. Misreading the sign talk, early traders often called the Atsina by the various names of Minnetarees or Gros Ventres (French for "big bellies"). The same names were applied to a totally unrelated tribe speaking a Siouan tongue, the Hidatsa, who as village farmers along the Missouri River in what is now North Dakota may have been survivors of the plains farmers of an earlier time, and so also old residents of the plains at the time of the arrival of the horse. The Hidatsa were bordered on the north and south by a few other villages of plains farmers, the Siouan-speaking Mandans upriver from them and the Arikara, an offshoot of the Pawnee, down the Missouri to the south.

A part of the Hidatsa who called themselves the Absaroke, meaning Crow-people or Bird-people, left the Hidatsa towns and traveled westward to settle in the country of the Yellowstone and its southern branches of the Powder and Big Horn rivers. This evidently happened several centuries ago. They stopped farming, building earth lodges, and making pottery, and became hunters living in skin tipis, and are known historically as the Crows. Their country ran so much to mountains that they are sometimes spoken of in the two divisions of Mountain Crows and River Crows.

These, then, were the principal known inhabitants of the northern plains before the coming of the horse and the gun. The gun frontier drove in new peoples from the east, who seized on the horse and became thoroughgoing plainsmen seemingly almost overnight.

In the northeast a part of the Cree, snowshoe and canoe people when they were at home in their Canadian forests, pressed into the prairies and then the plains with Hudson's Bay Company guns, looking for beaver, and became the Plains Cree. They drew along friends from southern Ontario, the Assiniboin, a sizable tribe that had separated not long before from the great Siouan-speaking nation known as the Dakota.

The Ojibwa, triumphant with trade guns, drove the rest of the Dakota and the Algonquian-speaking Cheyenne out of the forests of the Upper Mississippi country in Wisconsin and eastern Minnesota. Both the Dakota and the Cheyenne were farming people as well as hunters, decorous and yet valorous, and were clearly of a high order in character, intellect, and ability. They became some of the most notable of the Plains Indians.

The Cheyenne crossed the wide Missouri into the short-grass plains and in the space of perhaps fifty years or so roundabout the last quarter of the eighteenth century and the first quarter of the nineteenth transformed themselves into horsemen, constant hunters, magnificent warriors, in short into Plains Indians of the first class. They divided, after much wandering, into two

**Plains life had a savage beauty. In his painting of a buffalo chase, Montana's cowboy artist Charles Russell captured the rhythm that made horse and rider one. By 1880 white encroachment onto western lands brought about the virtual extermination of the buffalo.**

groups, the Northern Cheyenne around the headwaters of the North Platte and the Yellowstone, and the Southern Cheyenne headquartering along the plains of the Arkansas within sight of the southern Colorado Rockies.

The Dakota, who formed a true confederacy (the word means "allies"), were made up of seven tribes—their own name for themselves was *Ocheti shakowin*, "the seven council fires." Some of these tribes, such as several known collectively as the Santee, remained on the edge of the eastern forests and adjoining high-grass prairies and remained semiagricultural. Others, such as the tribe known as the Teton, moved into the plains in the late 1700s and within a century or less were known the world over as the very embodiment of Plains Indianism—the famous Sioux. The French coined the name Sioux from an Algonquian term meaning "enemies"—in fact, referring as usual to "serpents" in its full original form. Out of all the different Siouan peoples the Dakota have usually been designated specifically as the Sioux, somewhat as the Five Nations Iroquois became the specific Iroquois.

For all these people of the plains, newcomers and old residents alike, the horse brought a miraculously changed life.

Before the horse, families moved their possessions with the help of dogs, dogs bearing little packs or dogs dragging the A-shaped frames of trailing sticks across which baggage was lashed, the contraption named by French Canadians a travois. Possessions, therefore, could be neither many nor heavy.

After the horse, lodge poles could be as long as thirty feet, tipis (a Sioux word) could be made of as many as eighteen or even twenty dressed buffalo hides, enclosing a room some fifteen spacious feet across crammed with furnishings, riches, and relations.

After the horse, buffalo could be found miles away, surrounded at a gallop, chased down if they stampeded—although the formal hunt was still strictly regulated, as was the camp life, by a police society.

After the horse, dried meat and the everlasting pemmican (dried meat pounded up with suet, marrow, and wild cherries) could be kept and moved by the ton. There was a wealth of tools, new clothes, spare time, and new delights.

Better still, there was time for war, and horses gave it method as well as purpose. A man's fortune was counted in horses, a young man's future depended on horses, and so horses became the common goal of war, and the capture of horses the prime reality of war. War's other aspects, fighting and the danger of death, were gradually bound around with as much ceremony as a Japanese tea party. Elite soldier societies multiplied, each with special costumes, special grades, special manners, special sacred rites, and special taboos.

Wars called for fancy tricks, fancy riding, fancy fighting, as war songs called for fancy drumming. Two of the three finest feats of war were to capture by stealth an enemy's best horses, the valued stallion or fleet hunters he kept picketed close beside his lodge, or to touch an enemy's body in battle—this last, called via the French "counting coup," gave rise to rigid, complicated, and jealously administered systems of war honors. Coup systems and soldier societies were brought to the plains from the Indian world of the forested East, but in the plains they reached their most elaborate development. The taking of scalps was not important—the Crees and the Teton Dakotas alone regarded a scalp as a first-class trophy. The Dakotas, if they had time, would take all the skin of the head and face, possibly similar to the "skins of five men's heads" shown to Jacques Cartier in Canada in 1535. Scalping was apparently very limited in extent before the coming of Europeans; scalp bounties undoubtedly helped spread it far and wide over the Indian world.

Above all, the new world of the horse brought time and temptation to dream. The plains are afloat in mysterious space, and the winds come straight from heaven. Anyone alone in the plains turns into a mystic. The plains had always been a place for dreams, but with horses they were more so. Something happens to a man when he gets on a horse, in a country where he can ride at a run forever; it is quite easy to ascend to an impression of living in a myth. He either feels like a god or feels closer to God. There seems never to have been a race of plains horsemen that was not either fanatically proud or fanatically religious. The Plains Indians were both.

A man dreamed of the horse he would capture, and of what sort of feathers to wear in his hair, and the paint to put on his face, and the foe he would kill, and the girls he would marry, and the pattern to put on his shield, and the way he would die.

With horse prosperity entire tribes could gather every year or two or three for observances of the greatest solemnity, when the tribe was reunited and renewed. Such observances took a variety of forms with different peoples, but the principal appeal to dreams and visions, the Sun Dance, was common to nearly all the people of the plains. For days and nights (usually four) the dedicated participants went without food or water and stared fixedly at the top of a central pole, where a red-painted buffalo skull or some other symbolic object represented the sun. The Sun Dance was scarcely a dance; the celebrants stood more or less in one place, rising up and down on their toes or shuffling a little backward and forward. They held eagle-bone whistles in their mouths, to sound with each breath. For those who lasted long enough, a vision might be granted. Some, in fulfillment of a vow or to wring pity from the gods, tortured themselves by running skewers through the muscles in their chests or backs and swinging from thongs until the skewers were torn loose.

The Creator, the Old Person, God by whatever name, spoke through dreams and visions over much of the Indian world; it was merely typical of the plains people to go to extremes in this conversation. These were people of emotional excesses. Death was a matter of magnificent emotion. Mourning brought wild displays of grief. The third great feat of war was bravery in rescuing a dead body from the enemy, so it could not be mutilated.

In general there was a considerable sameness among the people of the plains, in spite of the diversity of their origins; and all, too, lived in the same dream-haunted atmosphere. Many whites found the Plains Indians remarkably alike, all as natural and colorful as tigers. But within the general pattern there were also considerable gulfs of difference, extending far deeper than the differences in ceremonies, moccasins, arrow-feathering, or styles of decoration—rich and varied as these last are. These deeper differences might be represented at one end of the spectrum by the relatively earnest and austere Cheyennes, very much concerned with living up to an ideal of high-minded and responsible behavior, and at the other end of the spectrum by the relatively free and easy Blackfeet. A trader among the Blackfeet in the era around 1800 wrote that they were the "most independent and happy people of all the tribes of the Rocky mountains. War, women, horses and buffalo are their delights, and all these they have at command."

By 1800 French fur traders had been in the Great Plains for 100 years. In the early 1700s the Illinois country was an important district of New France, producing grain, tobacco, and Indian traders—a party of Illinois traders made a try at crossing the plains to New Mexico sometime before 1703, and five years later Illinois Frenchmen were reported to have explored the Missouri for 1,000 miles. Lead mines were opened in the country of the lower Missouri in the 1720s—200 French miners and 500 Santo Domingo blacks were imported to work them—and by the 1730s French traders were established among the Pawnees, Arikaras, and Mandans. In the 1740s a trading post was founded on the Saskatchewan, and traders were among the first immigrant Cheyennes and the old resident Crows on the North Platte, within view of the Rocky Mountains; by the 1750s French traders had reached the Rockies by nearly every important river between the Saskatchewan and the Red. Within the next few years the great Pawnee trade in Santa Fe horses made itself felt all the way east to the Atlantic seaboard: Governor Patrick Henry of Virginia was one of the purchasers of thoroughbred Spanish horses.

In the later 1700s English traders were working their way up the Missouri and the Arkansas. The French fur-trading organization had been destroyed by the defeat of France in the French and Indian War, but the French wilderness mechanics, the *voyageurs* and *coureurs de bois*, remained; they, and the Indians they had such a knack of getting along with, hired out their talents to English and Scottish masters and were the muscles of the English fur-hunting combines.

Six veteran Frenchmen and two Indians accompanied Alexander Mackenzie on his trail-breaking journey to the Canadian Pacific in 1793, and five Frenchmen crossed the plains with the Lewis and Clark expedition in 1805—not counting the infant Jean-Baptiste Charbonneau, born to the Shoshoni girl guide, Sacagawea, two months before the start of the trip.

Lewis and Clark opened the way for a new specimen of foreigner in the plains and the "Shineing Mountains," as Captain Meriwether Lewis referred to the Rockies. This was the American trapper, the "free" trapper, the mountain man. The mountain men became a byword for knowledge of the wild Far West and how to survive therein; a few who survived gained fame in specialized circles as guides for later western explorers. One of the most remarkable, so much so that some students have thought of him as wholly legendary, was Sacagawea's son

Baptiste Charbonneau, who was educated at the court of a European prince and returned to the Rockies to whack out a monumental mountain-man career, packed with the history of westward-rolling America, and at last went home to his mother's people, the Northern Shoshonis, to die in their Wyoming country of the Wind River Mountains.

The mountain men lived and worked with the Indians and constituted, in effect, a small, scattered tribe of their own, in some respects more Indian than the Indians themselves, so far from the civilization of "the States" they were scarcely recognizable as Americans. With one implacable exception the Indians usually dealt them more hospitality than hostility, the friendliest being the Northern Shoshonis, or Snakes, as the mountain men called them, using the name given them by the Sioux and the French.

The one implacable enemy of the American trappers in the early days was the Blackfoot confederacy. The source of the savage Blackfoot hostility was to be found, more than likely, among the Canadian companies on the Saskatchewan, where the Blackfoot people traded. It was considered a legitimate business tactic, in the fur trade, to urge one's Indians to kill off the competition. The Blackfeet did so with joyous abandon, and their very name was enough to make a mountain man swallow hard and think serious thoughts of his hair. Since they constituted the most powerful nation north of the Missouri, they effectively deflected American penetration to the north.

Finally, in the 1830s, American traders made some progress at winning Piegan trade from the Hudson's Bay Company, and some progress at making peace (with a great flow of rum), although trapper killing still went on. Most of the trade of the Piegans and their Atsina allies, controlling the country that is now northern Montana east of the Rockies, was in American hands by the late 1840s.

The mountain men, by this time, had vanished from the trapped-out beaver streams; their place, in the plains and the Rockies, was being taken by trains of West Coast–bound overland emigrants. The frontier stole in from the East like dusk, and before the 1840s the nations of the plains had already felt its touch, in the form of whisky, plagues, syphilis, and a bewildering increase of war.

Throughout the 1830s the Southern Cheyennes and Arapahoes fought the Comanches and Kiowas along the Arkansas River; to the north, above the Platte, the Sioux and the Northern Cheyennes were at war with the Crows; most of the people of the farther plains were hostile to the Shoshonis, who ranged down from the mountains, and to the Pawnees, who ranged westward from the eastward reaches of the plains. Eastern Indians, Delawares and Shawnees and Potawatomis and many others, driven across the Mississippi, were fearful adversaries, expert with firearms at a time when the plains people had few guns, when they "would pay a good price for a barrel hoop to convert into knives and daggers," as a mountain man remarked of the early 1840s.

Some of these wars were conducted with propriety and a regard for the laws of tradition, but some were not. Such Cheyenne warriors as Little Wolf, chief of the Bow String soldier society, and White Antelope, one of the chiefs of the Crooked Lance society, won great fame fighting the Comanches and Pawnees in the most honorable and decent manner, but in 1838 a group of Bow String men whipped with their quirts the aged and respected keeper of the Medicine Arrows, the Cheyennes' most sacred possession, in order to force him to perform the requisite ceremonies so they could go to war. This was an unheard-of thing. The chief of the Dog Soldiers, the principal Cheyenne soldier and police society, killed another Cheyenne in a drunken brawl. This was an unheard-of thing. He had to go into exile along with all his relations. As a result of these things the Cheyennes suffered bitter defeats at the hands of the Kiowas and Comanches, until a peace was made between them in 1840. Thereafter the Arapahoes and Cheyennes made the Utes, westward across the Rockies, their grade-A enemies.

The wars were bad for trade and travel. In the early 1840s five Blackfoot chiefs took a three-year trip to see the world, traveling from the Alberta plains down the eastern curb of the Rockies all the way to Taos, along the Old North Trail—the very, very old North Trail, the probable main route of the first people to enter North America so many thousands of years ago. Less than a century ago stretches of it were still rutted by travois and marked by countless generations of travelers, in particular by the circles of stones that sometimes represented lodge burial: the practice of honoring a great and brave man by leaving his body propped up in his lodge to receive death alone, and the tipi

**To the white man, they were enemies to be feared and destroyed; to their own people, leaders like Wolf Robe of the Cheyenne, photographed here, were heroes patriotically committed to the defense of the Indian nations. Following the Civil War white settlement expanded increasingly into the Indian country of the Great Plains, where tribes like the Cheyenne fought with great valor to maintain their culture.**

weighted with stones around the edges to resist as long as possible the whipping wind of the plains. The five Blackfeet may have been the last Indian tourists to travel the Old North Trail in peace.

Especially, wars bothered the trade and travel of Americans, filling the country with excitable war parties that menaced and frightened emigrants and sometimes stole their stock. American troops were marched up and down the plains several times in the 1830s and 1840s, to the delight of the Indians, who admired the show of color and guns and, most of all, the soldiers' swords. "Big Knives" was the polite name for white Americans among the plains people, as it was among most other Indians over the United States, and a saber was much valued by Plains Indians as a weapon. In 1849 two military posts were established along the Platte, and in 1851 the peerless mountain man Tom Fitzpatrick, appointed United States Indian Agent, held a great council near the farther west of these, Fort Laramie, a converted fur trading post at the mouth of the Laramie River on the North Platte.

The council encampment was at Horse Creek, thirty-seven miles east of the fort, and was the scene of the greatest assembly of Indians in plains history, the number present estimated at from 8,000 to 12,000 persons, representing Assiniboins, Atsinas, Arikaras, Crows, Shoshonis, Sioux, Cheyennes, and Arapahoes, some of these nations never having met before within their memory except in battle.

All agreed on a general peace (Pawnees tacitly excepted, no Pawnees being present), and promised to be more considerate of emigrants, whose covered-wagon trains had by then been familiar along the Oregon Trail for ten years, and during the previous two summers had filled all the westward trails to overflowing, rushing to the gold in California. The United States promised to keep troops in the plains to protect the Indians from white depredations.

Three years later, ten miles or so from the scene of this great peace council, the wars of the United States against the Plains Indians were opened.

The immediate cause was a dilapidated cow, allegedly abandoned, killed by a Minneconjou Sioux for the hide. The emigrant who owned the cow put in a claim at Fort Laramie for damages; spokesmen from the Sioux camp offered $10, the emigrant demanded $25, the Sioux could not meet his price, and a lieutenant who fancied himself a fire-eater took thirty-two men and two howitzers and went to the Sioux camp to drag out the cow killer. There were many lodges of Oglala and Brulé people, and among the Brulés a few lodges of Minneconjous, summer visitors from the Missouri; all these were subtribes of the Teton Dakota. An argument developed, and the lieutenant had the Brulé chief shot down on the spot. In the fight that followed, the lieutenant and all his men were killed.

This was not the first blood spilled between the plains people and the soldiers who had come to protect them. The summer before, a detachment of Fort Laramie troops had killed three or four Sioux in a regrettable misunderstanding, which the Sioux had recognized as such. But this was the first blood of American soldiers.

The American public clamored for retaliation, which was provided the following summer, in 1855, when an army of 1,300 men marched into the plains from Fort Leavenworth and destroyed a Brulé village near the forks of the Platte, killing eighty-six persons. At a conference in the spring of 1856 the properly humbled Brulés promised to turn over the man who killed the cow.

In the same spring of 1856 a controversy with a band of Cheyennes over one of several stray horses led to an attack by troops on a Cheyenne family that had had nothing to do with the controversy. Other Cheyennes then killed a stray trapper who had had nothing to do with the military attack. Troops from Fort Kearny then attacked a group of unsuspecting Cheyennes who had had nothing to do with any of the foregoing, killing a half dozen of them and seizing all their horses and property. Cheyennes then plundered two wagon trains, killing seven innocent persons, including a woman and two children.

The tragicomedy dragged along until the summer of 1857, when Colonel E. V. Sumner set out with a strong force to put a stop to it. On a July day in a handsome plains setting along the Solomon River, in present Kansas, he met the flower of the Southern Cheyennes in one of the few real picture-book battle scenes in all Indian history. Everything was as it should be: some 300 mounted warriors drawn up in battle line singing their war song, all in their full war costumes, colorful as fireworks; and they had all had time for all the necessary prebattle ceremonies. Their great medicine man, Ice, had picked the battleground for them, and seemed to be certain that he had been granted the spiritual power to render the soldiers' bullets harmless. Accordingly, the Cheyennes were confident of victory. But Colonel Sumner charged with cavalry, and curiously enough decided to make the charge with the saber, possibly the only instance of a full-fledged saber charge in all the plains wars.

No medicine had been made against sabers. The Cheyennes fired a panicky flight of arrows, and fled. Losses on both sides were small, but there was no question as to who had won. A peace was made the following spring.

But war had settled down to stay. Peace, from now on, would only be intervals that could not last, like sunny days in winter. Everyone believed, each time—at least they said they did—that peace this time was forever. The whites congratulated each other on having settled the Redskin problem at last, and held foot-stomping jamborees to celebrate. The Indians rejoiced in their lodges and invited each other to company dinners; high-spirited social dances abounded, and young warriors became young dandies, dripping rich habiliments and waving turkey-feather fans, and contriving elaborate strategies to get a word with their girls by the light of the moon. But then the whirlwind of hostility would suddenly spring up again, spin to a climax and stop with a jolt at still another peace. As the frontier reached out to envelop the plains, the intervals of peace grew briefer and more clouded, the rings of war more distended and more violent.

Some Cherokee gold-rushers had seen placer deposits in the Rockies on their way west in 1849; in 1858 they returned with other prospectors and discovered gold in Cherry Creek at the foot of the Rockies, near present Denver, Colorado. The Pike's Peak gold rush got under way the following summer, pouring an estimated 80,000 Pike's-Peak-or-Busters into the plains during the next three years. Other mining strikes followed; many of the Plains Indians seriously thought the crowds of would-be prospectors rushing hither and yon to new strikes real and fanciful were people who had gone insane by the bunch. Town founders and real-estate promoters appeared in the wake of the mining camps, with settlers following after, and within less than a decade railroads were being driven across the buffalo plains.

The frontier wrapped its coils around the Indians of the plains and in due time swallowed them up. Basically the story is no different from the penetration and destruction of Indian nations elsewhere. There were the treaties, the dissensions and factions within the Indian nations, the enforced new treaties, the quarrels, the wars, the clarion call for extermination and piecemeal attempts at same, and the long, agonizingly long, diminuendo ending.

The wars were founded on very much the same elements as in the Indian wars that had gone before. At the bottom there was pressure for property—time after time agreements on reservations were upset by mining, railroad, or land-speculation interests that were able to bring sufficient influence to bear on the government. Orders went out to persuade the Indians to accept revised treaties and revised reservations. The Indians often had to be persuaded by force. Each of these occasions broke a solemn promise of the United States and led to a thorough Indian distrust of anything American. General George Crook, the most experienced of western Indian-fighters, summed up this process: "Greed and avarice on the part of the whites—in other words, the almighty dollar, is at the bottom of nine-tenths of all our Indian troubles."

There were the usual subsidiary causes, such as the refractory bands, sometimes making up the majority of a tribe, that denied the authority of treaty chiefs; wild warriors who would not be controlled; gangs of bootleg traders, buffalo hunters, prospectors, or amateur Indian killers who would not be controlled either, and overran Indian lands in defiance of government orders to stay out and keep the peace. Said the Superintendent of Indian Affairs for Montana in 1868: "Nothing can be done to insure peace and order till there is a military force here strong enough to clear out the roughs and whisky-sellers in the country." Five years later the Canadian North West Mounted Police were organized specifically to put down this whisky trade north of the border; 150 "Mounties" ended it in less than three months, to the indignant howls of its Montana proprietors.

There were also some trouble spots that attained new prominence in the plains wars. The Bureau of Indian Affairs was transferred to the Interior Department from the War Department in 1849; conflict between its agents and the Army became frequent and sometimes serious, an occasional consequence being the dishonoring of Indian peace or surrender terms when

**These Sioux warrior chiefs on horseback evoke one of the most haunting images from the last years of Indian conflict with the white man. It was the Sioux and the Cheyenne, whose victory over Custer at the Little Big Horn brought final disaster to the Indians. United States troops retaliated mercilessly, permanently fragmenting Indian resistance.**

one department triumphantly succeeded in overruling the other. "Indian Rings" of crooked officials and crooked suppliers made graft a big business, while Indian families imprisoned on reservations suffered concentration-camp privations, ate their gaunt horses or the bark of trees, and sometimes starved to death by the hundreds.

The disappearance of the buffalo is generally emphasized as a cause of war on the plains, perhaps too much so. As early as the close of the 1850s, when the buffalo could still darken the earth and their gigantic mirages fill the sky, numbers of Indian leaders foresaw the finish of buffalo hunting. The question was not if the buffalo would vanish, but when. Some thought soon; some thought not for 100 years. It was the former who usually associated themselves with the treaty factions, anxious to make a deal for the sale of land and mineral rights that would subsist their people through the coming time of change.

But the buffalo motive is further diminished by the fact that the Blackfeet, Bloods, Crees, and Assiniboins of Canada, buffalo people from horns to hocks, made no war to save the buffalo. The only major Indian war in British Canada's history, in fact, was not primarily an Indian war at all, but was styled by Canada a rebellion, and had strong overtones of religious war: Protestant Ontario against the Catholic Métis of the Red River of the North. The Métis were mixed-blood French-Indian plainsmen, mostly French-Cree and French-Assiniboin; under the mystical Louis Riel they made a noble effort (in 1870, with an epilogue in 1885) to set up an independent semi-Indian state in Canada's great plains, and lost.

So much for the prosaic reality behind the Indian wars of the plains. In reality, like so many other Indian wars, they were dismal, dirty, and needless. But their reality has been largely forgotten, if it was ever noticed to begin with. The wars of the plains entered immediately into our folklore, and there they will remain, no doubt, until the end of time.

In our folklore they are all Indians and all Indian wars in one gaudy package. As the Plains Indians were amalgamations of other Indians of the eastern forests and the western mountains, and, with their horses and guns, were in part the white man's creation, so the folklore of their wars is an amalgamation of all such folklore from every point of the continent.

In western tradition, for example, the Plains Indians are great torturers of captives (save the last bullet for yourself, pardner). However, the researches of ethnology have shown that captive torture was not traditional among the people of the plains, as it was among so many people of the eastern forest. Of course sadistic morons, both Indian and white, indulged in torture when they got the chance, as the wars worked up to a really savage lather. But the authentic records of official torture, so to speak, among the Plains Indians seem to be extremely rare. On the other hand, Indians regarded hanging, a custom generously practiced by the military, as the most barbarous sort of death; a refugee who had been brought by his people into Canada was said to have cut off his own feet and one of his hands to escape from the shackles in which he had been chained, fearing that he was going to be hanged.

But it is the Plains Indian as hyper-Indian, as the Indian carried to extremes, that folklore of the plains wars reveals best. Never were such brave knights, such reckless horsemanship, never such tragic nobility, and when a general said, as a general did, that they were good shots, good riders, and the best fighters the sun ever shined on, one can see the mist of emotion in his eyes, and he'll shoot the man who doesn't bare his head. And above all, never was there such rainbow color brought to combat—the painted shields and war horses, the painted eyes and bodies, the buffalo hats, the lynx-skin headdresses with an eagle feather for each slain foe, the rippling war bonnets, sometimes trailing down to the heels, the jewel-work of beads and porcupine quills, arrow quivers furred with the magic skin of the otter, hearts made strong by dreams that always came in the form of songs.

The wars of the plains are America's *Iliad*. It is sung in the jagged rhythm of a wild Sioux charge. It is all poetry, for poetry is really made of blood and not of daffodils. It will outlive sober history and never quite die, as poetry never quite does. Red Cloud and Roman Nose will, very likely, still touch a light to the spirit as long as America is remembered.

The Minnesota Sioux, the four Dakota subtribes known as the Santee, had signed a treaty in 1851. They felt cheated by the treaty and were cheated in their reservation life, and in the summer of 1862 they tried to kill all the whites in their country, under the leadership of one of their chiefs, sixty-year-old Little

Crow. They murdered some 700 settlers and killed 100 soldiers before they were driven out of Minnesota to join the other Dakotas on the plains. Several dozen Santee chiefs and warriors were hanged. Fugitive Little Crow, foraging for berries, was shot by a farm youth.

The Sioux of the plains were asked to sign a treaty in 1865 to permit passage from Fort Laramie along the Powder River to the gold fields of Montana. Red Cloud, greatest of Oglala warriors, refused to sign and refused to cede. When the troops built forts along the trail, Red Cloud with his followers and Cheyenne allies closed the trail to supplies and held the troops under a virtual siege for two years at Fort Phil Kearny, at the foot of the Bighorn Mountains in what is now northern Wyoming.

There was a famous fight on a December day in 1866 when one Captain William J. Fetterman, who was reported to have said, "Give me 80 men and I'll ride through the whole Sioux nation," rode forth with not eighty but eighty-one and was decoyed by a daring party of ten picked warriors—two Cheyennes, two Arapahoes, and two from the three Sioux tribes present—into ambush and annihilation. There was another famous fight the next summer when Red Cloud's finest cavalry stormed down to make meat of a wood-chopping detail from the fort—thirty-six men. Thirty-two managed to reach the shelter of a wagon-box corral and, armed with new breech-loading rifles, fought off repeated and suicidal charges throughout the day; twenty-nine were still alive and fighting when relief arrived from the fort.

But Red Cloud could not be pushed aside, the trail could not be used, and in 1868 the government at last surrendered. The forts were dismantled, the troops moved out, and the Powder River country, including the Black Hills, reserved for the Dakotas forever. Red Cloud signed the treaty, and, true to his word, never again made war on the whites; he only tried to avoid them, and counseled his people to do the same. If you wished to possess the white man's things, he said, "You must begin anew and put away the wisdom of your fathers. You must lay up food and forget the hungry. When your house is built, your storeroom filled, then look around for a neighbor whom you can take advantage of and seize all he has." He was one of the foremost of Sioux patriots, and when he recited his war deeds it took a long time, because he had counted the incredible total of eighty coups; and once had returned from the wars with a Crow arrow driven entirely through his body, projecting front and back.

Peace had lasted very pleasantly through the early days of Denver, for the Southern Cheyennes and Arapahoes. A large village of Arapahoes camped in the heart of Denver during the town's first couple of years around the turn of 1860, and left the women and children there while they went to make war against the Utes, for all the world like pioneers. And then a treaty was made in 1861—only a few chief men could be induced, with great difficulty, to sign, and some of those later claimed they had been misled as to what they were signing. The treaty ceded most of Southern Cheyenne and Arapaho territory, but worse than this contained a clause that government officials later construed as permitting a railroad through what Indian lands were left. A railroad meant white settlements, and this meant an end to the last of their country, and the Cheyenne and Arapaho general public at length forced a number of the treaty chiefs to repudiate the treaty, under pain of death. White politicians regarded this as hostility, and the refusal of some bands and soldier societies to sign the treaty at all was regarded as hostility. Buffalo hunters followed herds into the Indian country whenever the herds went that way, and this too brought hard feelings.

But peace dwindled along until the spring of 1864, when the Reverend J. M. Chivington, colonel of Colorado volunteers, reported that Cheyennes had stolen some cattle from a government contractor's herd. The report was suspect at the time and later—old mountain men said that whenever a greenhorn lost a stray he blamed the Indians—but Colonel Chivington took stern and instant measures, troops attacked families of the astounded Cheyennes, the Cheyennes attacked families of unsuspecting settlers, and another war was on.

Using the most eloquent persuasion, Colorado's governor managed by autumn to get some of the alarmed Cheyennes to come to Denver for peace talks. The peace party of the Cheyennes was headed by Black Kettle and the distinguished war chief White Antelope; they talked to the governor and, on the advice of the military commandant of Fort Lyon, established their village on Sand Creek, thirty miles from the fort. The village was then destroyed in a stealthy, sudden attack by Colonel Chivington and a force of something between 600 and 1,000 troops, mostly volunteers. Colonel Chivington had said, "Kill and scalp all big and little; nits make lice." The boys, as his reports refer to his soldiers, did so with enthusiasm.

Black Kettle ran up both an American flag and a white flag, but the boys were having too much fun. They butchered any Indian in sight (except for some Cheyenne men who managed to fort up on the creek bank, and who had rifles). Black Kettle's wife was shot down, and passing soldiers fired seven more bullets into her body; she had nine wounds, but lived. Black Kettle managed to escape. White Antelope refused to run. He stood in front of his lodge and folded his arms and sang his death song. It was a good death song, and has been remembered. It went: "Nothing lives long, except the earth and mountains." He sang until he was cut down by bullets and died. He was some years past seventy at the time.

Perhaps 200 Cheyenne women and children were killed at Sand Creek, and perhaps seventy men, and an estimated forty or more Arapaho people who were with the Cheyennes; but there was a great deal of dispute among the boys as to the number of dead, and the figures are not accurate. The boys went back to Denver and exhibited scalps and severed arms and legs in a theater. The boys had reason to be proud. This was probably the greatest victory, measured by Indians killed, the whites were to record in the Indian wars of the plains.

Not all Americans were proud of the boys. One named Kit Carson spoke of them as cowards and dogs. Nor were all the settlers jubilant. The Cheyenne plains went up in flames during the next three years; in two summer months alone 117 settlers were killed and their women and children dragged away as captives, in dozens of widely separated raids. And a government commission reported, four years after Colonel Chivington's victory: "It scarcely has its parallel in the records of Indian barbarity. . . . No one will be astonished that a war ensued which cost the government $30,000,000 and carried conflagration and death to the border settlements. . . ."

There were many men of valor among the valorous Cheyennes, including such leaders of exalted rank as Little Wolf and White Antelope. But none, surely, was more famous at the time to the ordinary public both Cheyenne and American than a hook-nosed six-foot, three-inch warrior named Bat. The

**The massacre of Lieutenant Colonel George A. Custer and more than 250 men of the Seventh Cavalry on June 25, 1876, shocked the nation just as it celebrated its centennial. Around 1898, Kicking Bear, an aging veteran of the battle, was asked by the artist Frederic Remington to paint the fight. A detail of his pictographic work is shown here.**

Americans called him Roman Nose. Roman Nose was famous because he was invulnerable in battle. He had a magic headdress, made for him by Ice, the medicine man, and while he wore it bullets and arrows could not touch him. He proved this time after time, riding at a leisurely lope up and down in front of the enemy, while all the enemy shot at him and missed. This always inspired the other Cheyenne warriors. There was only one catch—Roman Nose could never eat anything taken from the pot with an iron instrument: fork or knife. If he broke this taboo he broke the war bonnet's medicine, and long rites of purification would be necessary to restore it.

It happened that in the summer of 1868 a company of fifty experienced plainsmen, enlisted in the Army as scouts, was trapped by a large number of Cheyenne, Sioux, and Arapaho warriors, possibly as many as 600. On the night before this battle started, Roman Nose was a guest in a Sioux lodge and the hostess, unaware of his taboo, took the fried bread from the skillet with a fork. Roman Nose did not notice this until he had already eaten some of the bread. The next day when the fight started he did not go to it. But the chiefs came to him and told him he was needed to inspire the warriors. A chief said, "All those people fighting out there feel that they belong to you." Roman Nose explained about his broken taboo. He said, "I know that I shall be killed today." Then he painted himself and shook out his war bonnet and put it on, and mounted his horse and rode very fast at the enemy. He was shot from his horse, but lived to be carried back to the tents, where he died at sunset.

The Indians made two more desultory attacks during the next two days, principally to recover the bodies of their dead, and then went away. The company of scouts fought from an island in the dry bed of the Arickaree River, and the island has been called Beecher Island ever since, after the name of the company's lieutenant, who was killed there.

Occupation forces fighting guerrilla terrorists are at a disadvantage, since they cannot often lay hands on the terrorists. If their government, or the spirit of the public back home, will stand for it they prefer the hostage system—executing all the people of a hostage town, in reprisal for acts of guerrilla resistance. When the War Department gained the ascendancy in its incessant conflict with the Indian Bureau, it sometimes used this method. Unfortunately the village chosen for destruction, in the case of the wars of the plains, was more than likely to be a stronghold of pro-American peace party Indians endeavoring to be friendly since such a village was likely to be the nearest one available.

Black Kettle had made unceasing and increasingly successful efforts for peace since the Sand Creek massacre, believing there was no other hope of survival for his people. In the winter of 1868 his village, then camped on the Washita River in Oklahoma, was treated to its second stealthy and totally unexpected attack by troops, who were under orders to destroy a village and hang all the men and take all the women and children prisoner. Something between thirty-eight men, women, and children (Cheyenne figures) and 103 warriors (Army figures) were killed, and this time Black Kettle was killed too. But men from nearby Arapaho, Kiowa, and Comanche villages came to the rescue, and the American commander withdrew, prudently leaving behind a detachment of nineteen troopers who had gone prisoner-catching—all nineteen were slain. The American commander was Lieutenant Colonel George A. Custer, and this was his first major engagement with Indians. It might be called Custer's first stand.

The wars reached their climax in the 1870s, after the discovery of gold in the Black Hills in 1874. The Sioux had to be persuaded to sell out, the Black Hills having been guaranteed to them by the last treaty. The persuasion was a difficult job. It required many columns of troops and many scouts—Pawnees and Crows and Shoshonis who joined the white soldiers to fight their old enemies of the plains.

In this war Red Cloud remained apart. The Sioux and their allies came gradually under the general command of two powerful and very different personalities. One was Crazy Horse, an Oglala warrior famed for his recklessness, who had led the decoy party that had beckoned Captain Fetterman and his eighty-one men into the hereafter.

The other was Tatanka Yotanka, Sitting Buffalo, known to the Americans as Sitting Bull. There was a fashion for some years among western historians of belittling Sitting Bull's importance; recent scholarship seems to have restored him to the place of eminence he held in his own day. He was a dreamer of visions, a seer of the future, and war chief of the Hunkpapa division of the Teton Dakotas. He was also one of the most able, honest, and idealistic statesmen in Indian history.

In June of 1876 the main body of unpersuaded Sioux was found by General George Crook, leading 1,000 or so soldiers. A more or less equal number of warriors attacked him, but the ground kept growing Indians, and Crook at length limped back to his base of supplies to await reinforcements. The battle was fought among wild-plum and crab-apple blossoms in the valley of Rosebud Creek, in southern Montana.

The Indians moved across the ridge to the next river west, the Little Big Horn, and established a large camp, made up of Crazy Horse's people and Sitting Bull's people and allies from the other Sioux divisions and the Cheyenne. Eight days after the battle with Crook, this camp was attacked on a Sunday afternoon by a regiment of cavalry. The attack was defeated. Crazy Horse himself, shouting, "Today is a good day to fight, today is a good day to die," led a rush that cut off half the attacking forces. Every man in this surrounded group of cavalrymen was killed in a desperate, blazing fight that lasted less than half an hour.

The attacking force had been the elite Seventh Cavalry, organized for the specific purpose of whipping the Plains Indians, destroyers of Black Kettle's camp on the Washita. It had been led by Lieutenant Colonel Custer, who died in the battle along with more than 260 of his men.

This battle was the sensational moment of truth in the wars of the plains, at least for the Americans. It was the kind of humiliating defeat that simply could not be handed to a modern nation of forty million people by a few scarecrow savages. Especially not in the very middle of the great centennial celebration—the first report appeared in eastern newspapers on the morning of July 5, 1876, and caught the country smack in the act of congratulating itself on its first 100 years. The Custer defeat was, in effect, the end of the wars of the plains, and Crazy Horse and Sitting Bull lost by winning. Troops harried them without mercy, and the Indians had no means of keeping a standing army in the field indefinitely. Separated into small bands they were hunted down or driven into Canada.

The ending went on and on, like the dying wail of a death song. It went on for years, while the poetry and the romance evaporated, and these were seen to be not knights and paladins after all but only bedraggled scurrying creatures rather like fugitive convicts. So they were turned over to jailers who knew how to handle tough prisoners; the greatest of warriors is nothing more than any other weak-stomached man when he has nothing to do but crouch under guard and watch his people starve.

But it was at this time, when the glitter and nobility were vanished, that the greatest feats of gallantry occurred, all the greater in that they were utterly hopeless. There were more of them than there were battles in all the wars put together. Some became famous, some did not.

In an obscure little police action a young Sioux, wearing a trailing war bonnet that is somehow comical, like his father's hat, paraded up and down and said to the soldiers, "I am a soldier walking on my own land. I will give up my gun to no man." A moment later he treacherously fired into a truce party of the soldiers. His uncle said sadly, "My friend is young." Then the uncle too fired treacherously into the soldiers. They were both dead in three minutes. Someone knelt and took careful aim and shot the young Sioux through the forehead, the bullet cutting the war bonnet's brow band. They were scalped and left to stay forever in their land. It was all so obscure the name of the young Sioux is not even certain. He might have been called Big Ankle.

Well, it all ended. Through the years it wavered away and ended. The New York *Herald* was still calling for extermination in 1879, saying editorially, "The continent is getting too crowded." But no one really took that seriously anymore. Starvation, disease, and tough prison wardens were just as good anyway; and there were the noisy sentimentalists who kept insisting that sooner or later some of the Red Men could be saved by being civilized. And there was whisky. That Indian trade whisky, said Charles M. Russell, the old Montana cowboy turned world-famous painter—you could be shot and killed and you wouldn't die until you sobered up. So if you never sobered up you were bound to be all right.

At the very end the messiahs appeared, as they always do. One was a Nevada Paiute named Wovoka; his father (or it might have been his uncle) had been a messiah before him. His religion was called the Ghost Dance by the whites, because it preached that the ghosts of dead Indians were on hand to help living Indians in their hour of extremity. A great revival spread among the emotional people of the plains, and the authorities feared the excitement might lead to riot and violence. Sitting Bull was killed in the process of being placed under precautionary arrest.

Three days after Christmas in 1890 a unit of the Seventh Cavalry arrested a band of 250 or 350 Hunkpapa Sioux that an officer thought might be suspect, two thirds of them women and children. The Indians were held overnight, camped in the center of a ring of 500 cavalrymen. Four Hotchkiss guns were set up and carefully sighted in on the Sioux camp. In the morning the troops formed a hollow square with the Indian camp in the middle and disarmed the Sioux men, who were called out from the others to form a line. Somehow, a disturbance began. It is said that someone fired a shot. In any case, the troops quite suddenly opened an intensive fire at point-blank range into the Sioux camp. The Sioux men seem to have been shot down first, and most of them finished off at once or in a few minutes, although enough people attacked the soldiers with their bare hands or what weapons they still had or could seize to kill twenty-nine soldiers. But the shooting went on as long as anyone, woman or child, remained to be shot at. The rapid-firing Hotchkiss guns may have terrified the people more than the simple fact of death. Some of the women were pursued as far as three miles over the plains before they were caught and killed. A few are said to have escaped.

There has been dispute about the total number of Sioux dead. The military commander of the department reported there were no fewer than 200. But it was at least the second greatest victory for American arms in the wars of the plains. The event took place on Wounded Knee Creek in South Dakota.

Stephen Vincent Benét wrote a poem in which he mentioned Wounded Knee, although there is no reason to suppose he was thinking of this incident. The last lines go:

*I shall not rest quiet in Montparnasse. . . .*
*I shall not be there. I shall rise and pass.*
*Bury my heart in Wounded Knee.*

They gathered up the frozen dead in wagons at Wounded Knee, and buried them all together in a communal pit.

# XIII

# The Last Arrow

**The enduring image of the Indian warrior, complete with war whoop and scalp, was painted by Carl Hassman in 1907.**

On the 4th of July, 1776, a Spanish priest sat beside his saddle in the plaza of ancient Oraibi, the principal Hopi pueblo. He had been sitting there for two days but no one had spoken to him except three traveling salesmen from Zuñi, and they had been fearful about it. The Walapai guides who had brought him had taken fright and disappeared. The Hopis were patient and peaceful people but they had not wanted Spaniards among them since they had killed their missionary priests nearly a century before. The priest was patient too, and he wanted very much to make peace with the Moquis, as he called them, using the name most other people in the Southwest gave to the Hopis.

During the day on the 4th of July the people in town stopped ignoring the priest and gathered in a crowd and watched him. Then four chief men came and told him to go away instantly. His mule was brought and he went away. He had expected to be killed when the crowd gathered. But the Hopis, who were connoisseurs of endurance, may have been impressed by his two long days of sitting there, in silence, beside his saddle.

The priest was Fray Francisco Garcés, a Franciscan, one of the foremost of North American explorers. Sometimes alone, but most often with a single companion, a Lower California Indian named Tarabal, he had opened "roads" across the deserts and the mountains and the canyons to nearly everyplace a New Spain citizen of the 1770s might want to go in the Southwest. Said another priest of him, "Father Garcés... appears to be but an Indian himself.... He sits with them in the circle, or at night around the fire, with his legs crossed... talking with them with much serenity and deliberation. And although the foods of the Indians are as nasty and dirty as those outlandish people themselves, the father eats them with great gusto and says that they are good for the stomach and very fine.... "

The road he had wanted to open this time was a road from Santa Fe to Upper California via some route north of the Gila River. Such a road would be more direct than the Gila, and it would be out from under the constant menace of Apaches.

For the Apache, by 1776, were already an old and familiar menace.

The Spanish mission frontier, laboriously pushing northward

from Sonora toward what is now Arizona, had been stopped in the 1650s by a loose alliance of unconvertible wild tribes dominated by the Apaches. Garcés's illustrious Jesuit predecessor, Padre Eusebio Kino, had managed to move into the area in the 1680s, and for nearly twenty-five years had explored the Gila-Colorado River country, founding missions and ranches among the Pimas—the Apaches' most obdurate enemies. The Pimas themselves had later given this new frontier a considerable amount of rebellion trouble, apparently for good and sufficient cause, and the Apaches had remained predominantly hostile, a constant hindrance. A silver strike in the late 1730s in the region known as Arizonac had seemed for a time to ameliorate the Apache problem by establishing a strong bulwark of mining towns. This was in the Altar valley below the present Mexican border, southwest of modern Nogales; giant nuggets of almost pure silver were found lying on the ground, some up to two tons in weight. But no important lodes were discovered, and the surface workings played out within five years. Apacheria—the Apache country—continued to be the perilous end of the world.

By the 1850s various Apache bands had dwelt on the frontier of European settlement for 200 years and throughout all that time had stayed completely independent. This seems to be a record unequaled by any other Indian people on the continent.

The impression should not be given that the Apaches were unremittingly hostile to whites during those long generations of living, so to speak, on the edge of town. There were intervals of peace and even alliance; eastern Apaches in what is now Texas were even missionized—briefly—in the eighteenth century, and on a number of occasions allied themselves with Spanish troops against the Louisiana French or against other enemies of the southern plains. The Apache record of hostility was perhaps no more constant than that of some of the Yaquis of southern Sonora. But the Yaquis, a farming people speaking a Piman language, had been beguiled into a general peace treaty in 1610 and thereafter had been pierced, disintegrated, and divided, and their outbreaks of serious hostility, continuing into the 1900s, had been the convulsions of isolated groups that simply refused to be subdued.

The Apaches remained generally unbeguiled—wild and untamed, in the usual sense of the words, which is to say independent. Since they were regarded as a lost cause anyway, Spanish and Mexican administrators had no compunction about playing them false in negotiations or promises, if anything was to be gained thereby. The Apaches responded to such perfidy, naturally, with renewed hostility. Each side raided the other now and then for slaves and stock, in which industry the Apaches, being past masters of the art of the raid, unquestionably kept the score more than even.

The important point is that the Apaches, after these two centuries, were by no means strange mountain hawks wide-eyed at the wonders of a town, and savagely simple in their dealings with white men. They had had long experience in dealing with white men—while still managing to keep themselves apart and free. They had had even longer experience at occupying a frontier of civilization, the frontier of the prehistoric Pueblo civilization. With the Pueblos, too, there had sometimes been friendship and active alliance, traditionally more so with certain of the Pueblo towns than others; a long history of trade; and a frequent history of raids and enmity, traditionally more so with certain towns than with others.

The Apaches of the region of southern Arizona found their one irreconcilable foe in the Pima, this being Pima country which the Apaches had invaded. The Apaches centering in northeastern Arizona were on terms of basic hostility with such nearby people as those of Zuñi and the later pueblo of Laguna (founded 1699), for the same basic reason: invasion or trespass. The word Apache, from a Zuñi word meaning enemy, was first given as a name, it seems, to the specific invaders who took over the lands of an abandoned Tewa pueblo called Navahú. These invaders were called the Apaches de Navahú, or at least so it sounded to the ears of the early Spaniards. Eventually the name Apache was applied by extension to other related people all over the Southwest. The Apaches of Navahú, however, came to be known as the Navaho, or as the Spanish spelled it, Navajo, and in time were reckoned as an entirely distinct tribe, no longer included among the Apaches in general. The Navahos, indeed, did become a distinct tribe, gathering in new peoples and new customs until their ways, race, and language were considerably changed.

In the beginning all these, Apaches and Navahos, were Athapascan-speaking people who must have drifted down from the great Athapascan hive in the far northwest of Canada. It is assumed they made their way, over the course of generations if not centuries, down the eastern flank of the Rockies, some of them spreading gradually westward as they reached the latitudes of New Mexico. This may have taken place from 1,000 to 700 years ago. The epoch during which the Navahos and Apaches at last settled in their permanent homes in the Southwest is uncertain—it can only be placed sometime between A.D. 1000 and 1500 or thereabouts. Without doubt it was a very slow process, attended by much misery, prayer, and mayhem.

By the time Americans were beginning to get acquainted with the Southwest, in the early 1800s, most of these people had been long established in their desert and mountain fastnesses, and were as familiar with each rock and beast and useful plant as if they had been there forever. In a very broad view, the Apache tribes formed a rough ring around the country of the upper Rio Grande that was the center of the Pueblo world, and of the early Spanish settlements. Nomadic in the sense of moving about quite a bit within vaguely localized ranges, the various groups of Apaches have been given at different times almost as many different names as there were Apaches. A recent classification reduces all this to some three dozen separate bands, exclusive, of course, of the Navaho.

Southward from the Navaho country, in and about the mountain chains of central and eastern Arizona and the upper waters of the Gila and Salt Rivers, was the domain of a number of bands or tribal groups, some of the best known, under their best known names, being the so-called Tontos between modern Flagstaff and Roosevelt Lake, and the White Mountain bands roundabout the White Mountains and the midsection of the present Arizona–New Mexico line. Southward still, in southeastern Arizona and southwestern New Mexico, were a number of other groups, most notably the Chiricahuas of the mountains of the same name in southeastern Arizona, and the Mimbreños, of the Mimbres Mountains in southwestern New Mexico. In the mountains and plains of southern and eastern New Mexico were the Mescaleros, in several divisions; their name came from the custom common to most Apaches of roasting mescal (agave) to make a highly nutritious and much admired dessert—some Apaches carried on a trade in roasted mescal with underprivileged town-dwelling Pueblo people who didn't have mescal to roast.

The Apaches centering in Arizona, excluding the Navahos, are usually regarded as more or less alike. They got perhaps a fourth or a fifth of their food from farming, and the rest from hunting and an intensive use of wild foods: mescal and acorns first, and nearly innumerable others led by piñon, prickly pear, yucca, sunflower, mesquite, and saguaro. The Apaches east of the Rio Grande, such as the Mescaleros, placed more dependence on the chase of the buffalo. They are sometimes considered as forming a grand division separate from the Western Apaches.

To the north of the Mescaleros, in northeastern New Mexico and the mountains of southern Colorado, were a number of Apache bands considered a somewhat more separate group still, the Jicarillas (pronounced Hee-ka-ree-yas, being a Spanish word, referring to little baskets which they made with great skill). The Jicarillas were in much contact with the pueblo of Taos, and through the centuries became as close as brothers with the Taos people, each making a point of attending the other's ceremonies—this in spite of the fact that the original Taos name for the Jicarillas was an uncomplimentary word meaning "filthy people."

The country of the Jicarillas extended on the west toward the country of the Navahos, and on the north, above the present Colorado line, bordered the ancient people of the southern Rockies, the mountain Utes.

The total population of all the Apache tribes—always excluding the Navahos—has been estimated at between 5,000 and 6,000, including both prehistoric and historic times.

For centuries during their slow migration southward, the Apaches and Navahos were among the most important occupants of the Great Plains—at various periods in the old pre-horse times, from the 1300s to the 1700s, they may have been the strongest force in the southern plains. They were sometimes enemies, sometimes allies, of the terrible Tonkawas of Texas, a ferocious plains people (cannibals, it was said) who were dreaded by all, and who were assiduously wooed by both the Spanish and the French. An Apache captured and adopted by the Tonkawas became their most noted chief, and in 1782 brought about a great Apache-Tonkawa council for the purpose of unifying the two peoples to fight the Spanish. More than 4,000 Tonkawas and Apaches gathered for this meeting—and to trade stolen horses for French guns. The pact of unity failed to go through, and a couple of years later the Spanish managed to seize the Tonkawa chief by treachery and assassinate him. They called him El Mocho (the cropped one), due to the fact that he had lost his right ear in a fight with the Osage.

This was one of the last high points of Apache power on the southern plains. By the 1700s new people were invading from the north: these were the Comanches and Kiowas. The old name of Padoucas, prominent in the literature of the southern plains until the late 1700s, is associated by some authorities with the Comanches, by others with the Apaches, attesting the duration and confusion of their war.

At last the Apaches of the plains, most of them, withdrew to the plains' western margins. This marginal country had probably been the center of gravity of the wide-ranging Apache people since their first appearance, with extensions eastward across the southern plains and westward into the Arizona country. A string of towns within this marginal area, the Tano pueblos, southernmost of the Rio Grande pueblos, had been devastated in 1525 by a war of hurricane pitch, believed to have been made by Apaches.

One Apache group stayed on the plains—the people known as Lipan, close relatives of the Jicarillas. They remained in west Texas, ranging westward to the Staked Plains of New Mexico, and went on fighting the Comanches the rest of their lives. They were also the only Apache unit of any importance to be really beguiled by the frontier of civilization. They accepted Spanish missions repeatedly (the missions were repeatedly destroyed by Comanches) and played politics with the whites rather eagerly, possibly because their anti-Comanche position left them perilously exposed.

An Athapascan-speaking band that entered the southern plains with the Kiowa came to be known as Apache because of their language, and were called the Kiowa Apache. People of alien speech, they were nevertheless a fully accredited band of the Kiowa nation, and had a designated place in the camp circle.

The Comanches, as remarked earlier, were an offshoot of the mountain Shoshoni who came down into the plain with the acquisition of the horse. Short-legged, ungraceful people when on the ground, they turned themselves into some of the showiest horsemen the world has ever seen. Mystically certain of their superiority, in the way of born riders, the Comanches regarded other people, white and red, as inferior beings. This helped to make them tremendously successful in trade and war. With an estimated seventeenth-century population of 7,000 the Comanches must have considerably outnumbered the Apache families on the plains, and were more than three times the strength of their constant allies, the Kiowas.

The Kiowas present something of a puzzle in their early history. Their traditions—and historical evidence—place their origin in the Montana mountains at the headwaters of the Missouri River. They were friends of the Crows in that area during the 1700s, and at the end of that century drifted southward to the Arkansas River, where they effected their alliance with the Comanches and thereafter occupied the plains eastward of northern New Mexico. Many students, however, feel sure that the Kiowas had originally come from the southern plains long before, so long ago that the memory has been erased from their traditions. This belief is based in part on the kinship of the Kiowa language with that of the Tano pueblo people—a kinship deformed and wasted away by age, but nevertheless definite, according to recent studies. For many years the Kiowa language was thought to be unrelated to any other, and, according to an old mountain man famed as an Indian linguist, harder to learn than any other. It sounded like chunking stones in the water, he said.

The Kiowas were generally acknowledged as among the most eloquent in the sign language, the international language of the plains, by which Plains Indians from different tribes could converse with remarkable precision. A similar sort of communication with signs made by the hands existed here and there elsewhere in the Indian world, but it reached by far its most elaborate form on the plains.

There may have been a connection between the perfection of this sign language and the very ancient use of signals on the plains: signals of smoke, fire, or signals made by waving blankets or by moving in a circle or back and forth. On the level high plains, where objects can be seen many miles away in the crystal-clear air, such signals would be a natural development.

This battle scene on hide is believed to show the defeat in 1720 of Spaniards and Pueblo Indians by French troops with Pawnee and Oto allies in what is now Nebraska. The painting, perhaps by a Spanish-trained Indian, was sent by a priest to his brother in Switzerland, where it was recently found.

Their use was noted by the first white men to enter the Southwest, in the 1540s. In later years the Sioux worked out a system of signaling with mirrors, and troops were often only aware of the presence of Sioux around them by the flickering of this mysterious heliograph on distant bluffs and ridges. The Sioux are also said to have signaled at night with fire arrows. Much of the paraphernalia of Plains Indian signaling, but principally the heliograph, was adopted by the Army of the United States and the British Army, and used in early operations of the Signal Corps.

The Comanches and Kiowas took over the southern plains in parlous times. The dust raised in the Southeast by the French and Indian War rolled across the Mississippi and far out on the plains during the late 1700s. Spanish Louisiana, wanting buffers against the mighty Osage, coaxed Indian colonists westward from the lower Mississippi into the Caddo country on the eastern edge of the great plains; such strong Caddoan people as the Pawnee, Wichita, and the Kadohadacho confederacy welcomed the immigrants more or less peacefully, but the mighty Osage took alarm and fought and formed war-making alliances.

A band of Cherokees moved west of the Mississippi in 1794, after killing a number of white men, to announce the reason why. The band was headed by a leader named Bowl, a war lord of great repute; refugees from several other tribes later joined, and in the 1820s the augmented band went to Texas. There the Mexican government gave Bowl and his people a grant of land between present Dallas and Houston. After Texas was seized from Mexico by its American colonists in 1835, Sam Houston made every effort to protect Bowl's Cherokee band. But most of the new owners of Texas were opposed to leaving any part of the country in the possession of any Indians. Sam Houston's successor as president of Texas was the ex-private secretary of Governor Troup of Georgia, of Creek and Cherokee expulsion notoriety, and the policy makers of Texas thereafter were generally dedicated, in the highest degree, to the proposition of exterminating or clearing out the Indians.

Several regiments of Texas troops attacked and destroyed Bowl's town on the Angelina River in 1839; Bowl and many others were killed, and survivors were driven across the border. In the same year the Lipan Apaches happily sided with the Texans in fighting the Comanches; a few years later, however, Texas settlers drove the Lipan Apaches themselves into Mexico, where Mexican troops, aided by expatriate Kickapoos, annihilated the remnants of the tribe. Years afterward the Lipan survivors, fewer than two dozen persons, finally found a home among the Mescaleros in New Mexico. The miserably primitive people of the Texas coast, the Karankawan tribes among whom Cabeza de Vaca and his companions were shipwrecked in 1528, were hunted into complete extinction, the last of them being killed off some time before the Civil War.

But it was in these parlous times, from the late 1700s to the middle 1800s, that the Kiowas and Comanches, like the other tribes of the great plains, reached their peak of power, wealth, and brilliance. Situated as they were, in contact with the Spanish settlements, some of them became practiced and prosperous middlemen. The trade relations of the Comanches were especially complex, due to the widely separated range of the various important bands. The southern division known as the Penatekas (Honey-eaters) and the Nokoni (Wanderer) band did some trading with the Spanish settlements in Texas, but outlaw American traders and filibusters trickling into the country before 1812 encouraged them in enmity and insolence toward the settlements, an attitude of hostility that carried over into later times. The Kwahadi (Antelope) Comanches of New Mexico's Staked Plains kept pretty much out of touch with whites until the very end of the free era, in the middle 1800s. A number of bands toward the northern frontier of Comanche country, along the Arkansas, became first great raiders and then great traders among the settlements and pueblos of New Mexico. The Yamparikas (Root-eaters) was one of the principal groups in this area; the western division of the Kotsotekas (Buffalo-eaters) was also important.

Ordinarily these bands did not constitute an Indian nation, with a unified council or other machinery of overall government. Some of the important bands were so far apart—700 miles or even more—that they may have hardly been aware of each other's existence. However, there were occasions when a man of extraordinary ability and ambition became head chief of several great bands temporarily confederated. One such seems to have been the famed Cuerno Verde (Greenhorn), killed in a battle with the Spanish in 1779 near the mountain in the southern Colorado Rockies that bears his name. The leader of the 600 Spanish troops in this battle (259 of them were Indians) was the New Mexico frontiersman Don Juan Bautista de Anza, who encouraged the idea of a head-chiefship and gave Spanish support to Ecueracapa, Cuerno Verde's successor. Only with a genuinely authoritative chief, able to control his people, could peace be lasting, as Anza knew.

Ecueracapa was said to represent 600 Comanche rancherias, or villages, which means that either he padded the voting lists or later estimates of the Comanche population figures are much too low, since this very large figure of 600 rancherias would only have represented the western Comanches, exclusive of the Texas Comanches in the east and south. Ecueracapa succeeded in overcoming the leaders of the anti-Spanish party, killing one of them with his own hands, and a Comanche-Spanish peace was made in 1786 that was fairly real in the New Mexico region for many years to come. Not that all the Comanches stopped raiding, or even that the Spaniards wanted them to stop all raiding. One of the Spanish objectives in this alliance was to make use of the Comanches in fighting Apaches. The Comanches obliged with an excess of zeal, continuing their traditional attacks on even the Jicarilla Apaches whom the Spaniards regarded as friendly; it appears that a shattering Comanche raid during this period on the once populous pueblo of Pecos may have been made because Pecos was known to be harboring some fugitive Jicarillas.

Comanches had been admitted to the great Taos trading fair as early as 1749. They occasionally enlivened business by early-summer raids on pueblos or settlements—not excepting Taos itself—to collect captives who were then brought into the Taos fair to be ransomed, to the furious indignation of Spanish officials. After the peace of 1786, Comanches and their Kiowa friends were naturally much more in evidence as traders—another Spanish objective in making the peace. Competition in better-made English trade goods was coming to the plains by this time, and the Spanish needed all the trade-jobbers they could find. The Taos trading fiesta, biggest doings in all the West, helped to hold the customers and keep them coming back. One of the most wanted items, strangely enough, was a large-size silver cross hopefully offered by the missionaries. The Comanches and Kiowas had no interest in Christianity, but the crosses were traded for high prices over the plains, as emblems of military rank to be hung around the necks of soldier-society chiefs.

Horses were always the basic goods of trade. Some, probably the best blooded animals, were obtained by legitimate purchase from the Spanish settlements, and many more were stolen, particularly in raids on the Texas settlements. Comanches and Kiowas then went into winter camp on the upper Arkansas River with Cheyennes and Arapahoes and did a thriving business in horses and other trade articles, including captive slaves both red and white. A party of American traders camped with an enormous village—700 lodges—at a plains rendezvous of this kind in November of 1821. Crows were camped two days' journey away, on the Platte, and nearly every night brave young Crows would creep into the very center of this immense camp and steal some of the extra-fine horses that were kept there, under the most stringent security, in log pens.

A band of western Comanches known as the Jupes even tried settling down as farmers under Spanish guidance, early in the time of Anza's great peace. Spanish authorities financed the building of a model pueblo for them in what is now southern Colorado; the town was named San Carlos de los Jupes and was the envy of the mountain Utes, who began clamoring that they wanted pueblos too. But the project was a failure. Everyone had overlooked the fact that people of the plains moved their camp after the death of an important person. At the first such death the Comanches packed up and moved away, leaving the neat little adobe houses of San Carlos de los Jupes to melt into ruins.

Texas Comanches asked several times for a formal peace, after Texas had won independence from Mexico, but the Comanches insisted on a definite boundary line reserving their territory from settlement, and this the Texas politicians refused to consider. Texas land offices were open, settlers were pouring in by the thousand, and Texas's official position was that any Texas citizen could be settled on any land not already occupied by a white owner; Indians must withdraw and keep away from these settlements, wherever they were.

One early border settlement was established east of modern Waco by Elder John Parker and his numerous children and relatives, totaling nearly three dozen people. In the spring of 1836 Kiowas and Nokoni Comanches swept down from the north on the stockaded "Parker's Fort," killed several of its defenders, and took five captives. The tales of barbarities told by some of these captive women after their ransomed return were widely circulated and of considerable moment in making the name Comanche a byword for cruelty on the Texas frontier. One of the captives was not recovered for many years. This was Cynthia Ann Parker, variously reported between nine and thirteen years old at the time of her capture. She eventually became a wife of Nokoni, chief of the important Nokoni Comanches, and bore him several children. Her brother visited her "in her Indian home" after some years but could not persuade her to return to civilization. Finally, in 1860, she was forcibly repatriated, together with an infant child, although both died soon afterward. A son named Quanah, about fifteen at that time, stayed with his father, who had extended his influence over other Comanche bands to become the most important of Comanche leaders. After Nokoni's death, Quanah, usually known as Quanah Parker, rose to become head chief of the Comanches, apparently by virtue of his own extraordinary ability rather than hereditary rights, there being no other instance of an inherited chieftainship in Comanche history.

In 1839, the Texas legislature having appropriated more than a million dollars for militia expenses, a number of citizen companies took the field against the Comanches, sometimes traveling several hundred miles to find and attack Comanche rancherias. In March 1840, a small band of Comanches, invited to a peace conference in the San Antonio council house, was surreptitiously surrounded by troops and captured, several dozen of the Comanches and a few of the militiamen being killed in the process. This brought an outraged response from Isomania, one of the best known of the Penateka Comanche leaders of the time, who a week or so later rode into San Antonio with a single companion, like a medieval knight with his squire, lambasted the Texans for their treachery, and roared challenges to the troops to come forth and fight the army of warriors he had left parked outside of the town. No fight was forthcoming, the Texas citizen-soldiers explaining that a truce was in effect, and as usual the scattered frontier settlers, sitting ducks for any handful of angry young men, suffered the most in the long run.

Later in the summer Texas troops defeated a Comanche force in a pitched battle at Plum Creek, midway between Austin and San Antonio. But Comanche fighting remained a recognized profession on the west Texas plains for a generation longer. Officially, most of the Comanches kept peace with the United States, with only rare lapses, but it was a peace that did not include Texas, even after Texas's admission as a state in 1845; Comanches distinguished between Texans and other Americans. Murderous raids on settlers and travelers within the sphere of the Texas frontier became part of the standard way of life.

Essentially, such raiding parties were of two types: those maddened by attacks of the whites and seeking revenge, and those looking for loot. As the attrition of years of white military operations took its toll, both types naturally increased. The ever increasing poverty of the Plains Indians has perhaps not been given its due in this connection; at each destruction of a village there went up in smoke not only the immediate food supply of jerked meat and pemmican but the product of years of hunting and work. Buffalo robes, beaded clothes, thousands of arrows, tipis and their hard-to-get poles, painstakingly manufactured articles of all kinds, were burned by the museum-load. Horses, the real treasure, were stolen by the herd or killed on the spot, sometimes in vast numbers. A U.S. Army column reportedly killed 1,400 captured horses and mules after a raid on a Kiowa Camp in the Texas Panhandle in 1874. Early reports from the plains speak of the wealth and prosperity of the people; later reports indicate, decade by decade, the advancing tide of poverty.

It was this long attrition that at last smothered the resistance of the Plains Indians, who had no other source of supply than what they carried with them. But it was also this long attrition that drove more and more men and boys to the business of looting, especially since the business of looting became constantly easier and more tempting as the plains filled up with green pilgrims and settlers.

There was, of course, no shortage of excuses for hostility. The cavalier Kiowas were given ample offense in difficulties with tradesmen along the Santa Fe Trail, and for years the shout of "Kioway!" was the most dreaded of the Trail's alarms. Some footloose parties, however, were quite honestly out for loot, an employment as old and honorable as humanity. One such, made up apparently of a few Comanche youths, was idling along the Cimarron cutoff of the Santa Fe Trail in the summer of 1831, and there met the Galahad of mountain men, Jedediah Strong

Smith. They told someone later, it seems, that they joked with him while they casually used the mirrors hanging in their hair to blind Jed's horse, causing him to spook, and while Jed was busy trying to manage the horse they ran him through with lances. Jed Smith was far and away the greatest explorer among the mountain men, with an unequaled map of the whole wide West etched in his brain; but he was always unlucky with Indians. His pistols turned up for sale in Taos.

In the middle 1850s the United States government set up several Indian reservations in Texas, for some of the Comanches and Kiowas as well as other peoples of the region, including the Tonkawas. The once terrible Tonkawas, much reduced by disease and evil times, had turned humble, and Tonkawa men had served the Texans faithfully as scouts in forays against Comanches and other Texas Indians. But Texas extremists reacted so violently against the reservations that the reservees, Tonkawas and all, had to be moved. The Tonkawas were established of the Washita River in Indian Territory, where in 1862 neighboring refugees from east Texas who had suffered at the hands of the Tonkawa-guided militia massacred more than 100 of them, leaving only 100 or so survivors.

The Comanches and Kiowas signed a treaty with the United States in 1865 reserving for them the Panhandle of Texas and sundry other lands. But Texas, which had pleaded from the outset of statehood the "perfectly irresistible" spread of settlement, insisted on the complete expulsion of all Indians, and the Comanches and Kiowas were persuaded to accept a revised treaty two years later and settled in Indian Territory. It was in the Texas Panhandle, shortly after the expulsion of the Comanches and Kiowas that Chicago investors formed the largest single cattle ranch in the history of the West, the XIT Ranch, bigger than the state of Connecticut. Eight hundred miles of barbed-wire fencing were required to enclose this great domain.

Not all of the Comanches and Kiowas went to live at the Indian Agency, and not all of those who went there stayed there. One who was still there in 1869 was an otherwise obscure Comanche chief named Tochoway (Turtle Dove), who stepped briefly into the limelight to play straight man for an immortal phrase. The time was six weeks after Custer's destruction of Black Kettle's Cheyenne village on the Washita, and the place was Fort Cobb, Indian Territory (where Black Kettle had gone in vain to ask for official camping instructions, just before the troops descended on his village). General Phil Sheridan, Custer's boss and patron since Civil War days, was on tour, testing the temper of the shaken tribes. Tochoway, introducing himself, explained that he was a "good Indian." Said General Sheridan, "The only good Indians I ever saw were dead." It was by no means the first expression of this staunch old frontier notion, but it was the one the general public took to its heart and made part of the language; it was the extermination philosophy in a nutshell, and given the sanction of high rank.

Quanah Parker, on the way to becoming the most influential of all the Comanche chiefs, refused to sign the reservation treaty of 1867 and remained on the buffalo plains, although within the area reserved for Indian use. His Nokoni band changed its name after the death of Chief Nokoni, since a man's name could not be spoken after his death; it was called the Detsanayuka, which referred to its hasty camps made in a life of constant movement. Apparently the Kwahadi Comanches also associated themselves with young Quanah Parker's leadership. When buffalo-hide hunters illegally invaded the Indian country by the hundreds in the early 1870s, these two important Comanche bands seem to have spearheaded a desperate effort to drive them out. Hostilities began in 1874 and spread over five states, harmless settlers and travelers furnishing more victims than the guilty but tough hide-hunters. Troops immediately poured into the Indian country to put down the hostiles and ended most of the fighting after a year. Quanah Parker surrendered with his band a couple of years later. His real career, and a long and distinguished one, began at this point, as the industrious, able, and devoted savior of the remnant of his people under the hardships of agency life.

The first two signers of the 1867 treaty were Setangya, known to the Americans as Satank, principal chief of the Kiowas, and Satanta, a noted orator, warrior, and Kiowa patriot, some twenty years younger than Setangya, and regarded as the second chief of the Kiowas. However, both continued to lead raids into Texas—one story has it that Satanta went raiding for vengeance after a practical-joking army officer gave him a swig of an emetic in place of whisky. Setangya's son was killed on one such raid, and the grief-stricken old man thereafter bore his son's bones along with him on a lead horse wherever he went. Both

**The Kiowa chief Satanta is shown in a photograph taken by W. S. Soulé about 1870. The Kiowas of Oklahoma and the Texas Panhandle were sorely harried by U.S. troops in the 1870s, and their brutal retaliatory raids made the cry of "Kioway" for years one of the most chilling alarms on the Santa Fe Trail.**

chiefs were arrested for their part in a raid of 1871; Setangya wrenched off his manacles, taking the flesh of his hands with them, and attacked his guards until he was shot to death—he meant the act for suicide, and sang his death song first. Satanta was given a conditional release from prison but was imprisoned again, for life, when the Kiowas joined in the war against the invading buffalo hunters of 1874. He too killed himself, four years later, in the Texas state prison. Their deaths may have been meant to inspire the Kiowas with an iron will to survive during the iron subjugation facing them; this was what the Kiowas thought, at any rate.

The 1870s brought a number of despairing outbreaks from normally peaceful people, such as from some of the Utes of Colorado or the Bannocks of Idaho, as reservations were whittled away by "rings" of local developers and county officials, or Indian agents sprang a little too lustily at the task of civilizing their charges, or reservation inmates became discontented with enforced starvation—the Bannocks were being rationed at a cost of 2 1/2 cents per day per person.

In Arizona and New Mexico, however, the same period saw permanent peace envelop a people—the Navaho—who had been constantly warlike, by reputation at least, throughout all known history.

Navahos had long before created a unique society, in their country of magic mesas, vermilion cliffs, and painted deserts. Captives and immigrants made them a truly composite people and triggered a vigorous, thriving growth that had increased their numbers to perhaps 10,000 by 1860—far more than the population of all the other Apache tribes together. The only heritage they continued to share with their original Apache brothers was the Athapascan basis of their language, but even that was much changed by accessions from new tongues. One accession the language never picked up was the letter "v"—most Navahos, in consequence, found the word "Navaho" unpronounceable. Many Navahos, in fact, scarcely knew of the word until fairly recent times. Their name for themselves was and is Diné, meaning, as usual, the Folks, the People. All of the nearly four dozen Athapascan languages use some variation of this word as a tribal name.

At some time after the arrival of the Spaniards in the Southwest, the Navahos took to the raising of sheep and became herders and stockmen. Their women learned weaving and made the Navaho blanket world famous. They learned silversmithing and produced work of high excellence, for which Pueblo importers came to trade, bargaining in sign language.

They adopted the altars of the Pueblos—the much admired "sand paintings" that the Navahos have made their own. They never adopted the formal, community-wide religious ceremonies of the Pueblos, although religious feeling sifted into every nook and cranny of the Navaho way of life. Religion, very simply, was living the Right Way, and entreating the world, by means of inspired poems led by priestly Singers, to behave in the Right Way. Sang the Singer, in one of the Songs of Talking God:

*Now I walk with Talking God...*
*With goodness and beauty in all things around me I go;*
*With goodness and beauty I follow immortality.*
*Thus being I, I go.*

They farmed a little: peach trees and corn patches, Hopi style, wherever a touch of moisture in the earth permitted. But they never formed villages. Their hogans—crude earth lodges—were sometimes gathered in family clusters, houses of a mother and her married daughters, but otherwise were anywhere; and the brush shelters of summer were as scattered as their flocks.

A house was customarily abandoned upon the death of an occupant; usually the people would not touch a dead body, from fear of the dead and of witchcraft. By custom they would not touch even the body of a slain enemy; the Navahos, like many other Indians, had not practiced scalping in original times and, unlike many other tribes, never did pick up the practice.

The keeping of family-owned flocks may have helped bring about a sharper distinction between rich and poor than was usual among most Indians; the Navahos, too, were much noted for an industriousness uncommon to seminomadic Indians. These are touches that blend well with the faintly Old World, almost Old Testament, atmosphere that hangs about the early Navahos, as the only pastoral non-village people in the Americas. But there was certainly no Old Testament ring to their character—"Wit, merriment and practical jokes enliven all their gatherings," wrote one nineteenth-century observer, in an observation typical of most. And in the testimony of generations of town-dwelling neighbors—Pueblo Indians, Spanish colonials, and Mexicans alike—the Navahos were raiders and warriors first and gentle shepherds a distant second, finding far more joy in coming down like wolves on a fold than in patiently tending one.

It may be significant that the great majority of Navaho war names—war names being the only formal personal names—made some use of the verb "to raid." This was true for girls' names as well as boys', although a very common girl's name was simply Warrior Girl.

But it is possible that the Navahos—and the Apaches also—were as much sinned against as sinning, in the matter of raids. The Spanish pronunciamentos picture New Mexico a martyr for centuries to the rapacious Navahos, the "Lords of the Soil," who reportedly boasted that they only tolerated the Spaniards' presence because the Spanish ranchos were so pleasant to plunder. Unquestionably Navaho raiders removed much movable property, including children and women, from the Spaniards and the Pueblos.

There must have been some plunderers from the other side, though, to capture the thousands of Navaho and Apache women and children who were commonly the slaves of the New Mexico settlements. Said a New Mexico resident in the 1860s, "I think the Navajos have been the most abused people on the continent, and that in all hostilities the Mexicans have always taken the initiative with but one exception that I know of." Kit Carson spoke of the way some Mexicans were accustomed to "prey on" the Navahos, but also mentioned the "continuing thieving carried on between the Navajoes and the Mexicans," which is probably the most accurate general summation.

Official American acquaintance with the Navahos came in the autumn of 1849, three years after the American conquest of New Mexico during the Mexican War. New Mexico was a land of uneasiness at this time. Early in 1847 an insurrection of Taos Indians, urged on by Mexicans who wished to overthrow the conquest, cost the lives of a number of Americans, including the acting governor, and was only put down with a hard-fought battle at Taos and the subsequent hanging of the *insurrecto* leaders. By the summer of 1849 new American arrivals, some of them emigrants on their way to California, were causing much anxiety by robbing and outraging the Indians, particularly the patient Pueblos. The Pueblos—"a more upright and useful people are no where to be found," said the Indian agent at Santa Fe—entreated the government for compensation and protection, but in vain, there being no way to control these lawless elements or make restitution for their misdeeds.

There were also endless complaints of Navaho raids and thefts, and to settle these the governor of New Mexico marched a body of troops westward from the Rio Grande to the Navaho country and made a treaty. Nothing like an authorized chief existed among the Navahos, each band operating with complete independence under an informally chosen head man. However, a local patriarch of considerable repute, known as Narbona, came with several hundred of his followers to meet with the Americans.

Narbona explained that lawless men were everywhere and that "their utmost vigilance had not rendered it possible for the Chiefs and good men to apprehend the guilty, or to restrain the wicked." But he offered to make every possible restitution for Navaho thefts, and as an earnest of this intention turned over 130 sheep and four or five horses and mules.

A treaty of "perpetual peace and friendship" was signed, but then a Mexican with the American command demanded still another horse, the Navahos objected, the governor threatened, the Navahos wheeled their horses and "scampered off at the top of their speed," and the governor ordered his troops to fire on them. Six or seven Navahos didn't get out of range in time and were killed, including the patriarch, Narbona. Possibly his age, about eighty, slowed him up, or possibly the business of signing the treaty of perpetual peace and friendship had left him in an unhandy getaway position. The rest of the Navahos, "three to four hundred, all mounted and armed, and their arms in their hands," fled without offering any resistance. The artillery with the troops, noted a young army officer in his report, "also threw in among them, very handsomely—much to their terror, when they were afar off, and thought they could with safety relax their flight—a couple of round shot.... These people evidently gave signs of being tricky and unreliable.... "

This diplomacy did not stop Navaho marauding, and a fort,

Fort Defiance, was established in the Navaho country in 1851. Thereafter reasonable quiet prevailed until 1858, when an altercation between a Navaho subchief and an army officer's black slave blew up a war. It featured a massed Navaho attack on Fort Defiance; and the country was strewn anew with garlands of wild-blooming violent deaths and disasters.

Exigencies of the Civil War intervened, and it was not until the winter of 1863 and 1864 that Colonel Kit Carson was sent to round up the Navahos and did so. In the impregnable Navaho stronghold of the Canyon de Chelly the troops cut down 2,000 to 3,000 peach trees and found, among other plantings, one field of corn that took 300 men the better part of a day to destroy. Flocks and herds were seized or butchered. Most of the Navahos were starved into submission and were removed to the Bosque Redondo, a reservation near Fort Sumner in eastern New Mexico, to be reformed from the incurable brigands everyone said they were. The idea was to turn them into peaceful farmers.

The idea was given up after four years of much Navaho misery, and the Navahos were allowed to return to their own country, or rather to a part of it which was made the basis of a permanent reservation. The government gave them 35,000 sheep and goats to put them back in the pastoral business. There were difficulties and hardships in getting started again, but in the main the tribe waxed greater year by year, sometimes prospered, and was at peace.

There was no peace for the Apaches. Spanish authorities had at times drawn up rather grandiose battle plans for complete extermination of the Apaches, and the Mexican states of Chihuahua and Sonora occasionally paid very generous bounties for Apache scalps, as did some communities north of the border—in 1866 an Arizona county was still offering $250 for each Apache scalp. It was in a bounty boom year, 1837, that a party of American trappers invited a band of Mimbres Apaches to a fiesta at the Santa Rita copper mines, in southwestern New Mexico, and then massacred the guests, procuring many scalps. The Mimbreños had until then been friendly to Americans but were not trustworthy thereafter, and killed a number of trappers in their country. The Mexican village at the Santa Rita mines was made untenable and the mines abandoned for several years.

South of the Gila River the peaceful Pimas had fought Apaches for generations, apparently always winning, by the traditions of both sides. The Maricopas, a tall Yuman people from the lower Colorado River, emigrated to the Pima country over a long period of time ending in the early 1800s, moving up the Gila to escape the attacks of their kinsmen, the Yumas. It is said the Pimas made them promise to fight no wars except defensively, to which the Maricopas agreed; the two peoples thereupon lived together in perfect friendship, although neither spoke the other's language, and ran up frequent high scores in their defensive wars against the Apaches to the east and the Yumas to the west—of a war party of ninety-three Yumas that invaded Pimeria in 1857, for one example, only three lived to get home.

The other Yuman tribes living above the Yumas on the Colorado—the numerous and valiant Mohaves, who "talk rapidly and with great haughtiness," meanwhile giving "smart slaps with the palms on the thighs," as Fray Francisco Garcés sketched them; and the smaller groups of Yuman peoples such as the Walapai, Havasupai, and Yavapai, living in western Arizona from the Grand Canyon to the Gila, were the only sizable bloc in the Southwest whose hands were not raised against the Apache. The Yavapais, in fact, mingled with the Tonto Apaches to such a degree that both were called Tontos indiscriminately; the Yavapais were also sometimes known as Apache Mohaves. It may well have been a gang of Yavapai hoodlums who in 1851 committed a famous massacre usually credited to the Tonto Apaches: the killing of the Oatman family of emigrants along the Gila, at what has been known since as Oatman Flat. Olive Oatman, twelve-year-old daughter of the family, was sold into slavery to the Mohaves. She was rescued by a Yuma five years later and returned to civilization, which made a sensation of her story and her Mohave tattooing.

More than anything else, it was probably the incessant kidnaping and enslavement of their women and children that gave Apaches their mad-dog enmity toward the whites, from earliest Spanish times onward. It was officially estimated that 2,000 Indian slaves were held by the white people of New Mexico and Arizona in 1866, after twenty years of American rule—unofficial estimates placed the figure several times higher. More enslaved Apaches still were in Sonora and Chihuahua. "Get them back for us," Apaches begged of an army officer in 1871, referring to twenty-nine children just stolen by citizens of Arizona; "our lit-

General George Crook's Apache scouts, described as a "turbulent, desperate, disreputable band" by General Nelson Miles, helped Americans track down Geronimo. Despite their loyal services they, too, as Crook noted, were "rewarded . . . by captivity in a strange land."

tle boys will grow up slaves, and our girls, as soon as they are large enough, will be diseased prostitutes, to get money for whoever owns them. Our women work hard and are good women, and they and our children have no diseases." Prostitution of captured Apache girls, of which much mention is made in the 1860s and 1870s, seemed to trouble the Apaches exceedingly. It was during this period—the 1860s—that Apaches are supposed to have taken generally to the custom of mutilating enemy dead.

Demure overtures of friendship characterized the usual Apache approach to the first Yankees who appeared in their country. The newcomers were very different from Mexicans—a common Apache name for Americans was White-eyes—and might prove to be allies against the constant Mexican foe. But the wonted hostile collisions were not long in occurring. Apaches, with their wild-flying hair (the usual custom was to shampoo it daily, which might make for cleanliness but not for neatness), their raggle-taggle bands sometimes consisting of only a few families, their dusty brush-hut rancherias in the dusty brush, looked miserably primitive. They had little of the finery of the Plains Indians. There was not much about them, at a glance, to command respect.

Furthermore, there was a great deal to create suspicion. They came and went with exceeding softness. They were often genial and talkative but without quite saying anything. The wandering American, everybody's buddy, could usually pick up a working knowledge of a strange tribe's customs in a week, but until the 1930s the Apaches remained the least known important Indian people in the United States—while "Apache" had been a world-wide household word for generations. In brief, Apaches were watchful. They were some of the most watchful people who ever lived, and that was the reason they had been able to go on living through centuries of playing dangerous big game for hunters with guns. To blunt White-eyes in heavy shoes their sly, grinning watchfulness had an air of menace and guilt.

Americans mining for gold in western New Mexico in the early 1850s were annoyed, or unnerved, by an Apache who persisted in hanging around their camp. He was an unusual Apache, a massive-headed giant of a man, comically bowlegged. The miners tied him up and lashed his bull back to ribbons, as a warning to keep away. He was an important man of the

Mimbreños, a survivor of the Santa Rita scalp bounty massacre of 1837, related by marriage to chiefs of the White Mountain and Chiricahua bands who lived next door west. His name in Spanish was Mangas Coloradas (Red Sleeves). He was probably close to sixty years old at the time of his flogging, and he lived to be about seventy; and for the rest of his life he warred against white men, Mexicans and White-eyes alike, without mercy.

In 1861 the Chiricahua people were not only friendly to Americans but were employed in cutting wood for a stage station in Apache Pass, on the stage line through the Chiricahua mountains. An impetuous young lieutenant leading a military detachment searching for depredators summoned the leading Chiricahua men to a conference in his tent, above which the lieutenant flew a white flag of truce, and during the conference attempted to make prisoners of the Apache conferees. The Chiricahua chief and several others escaped, and battle began; the troops withdrew from the pass after each side had executed its prisoners—the Apaches by torture, the Americans by hanging. The Chiricahua chief was named Cochise; he escaped from the conference tent, so they say, with three bullets in his body. For the next ten years he warred against the white men without mercy.

Together, Mangas Coloradas and Cochise laid waste the white settlements and promoted hatred of Americans throughout all Apacheria. At the opening of the Civil War, when garrisons were recalled from most of the forts in Arizona and New Mexico, Arizona was swept virtually clean of whites by triumphant Apaches. Only old Tucson, in Pimeria, remained as a settled place of any importance, its population having shrunk to no more than 200.

The White-eyes were occupied with menacing each other in the Southwest, as a brief and distant part of the early Civil War, until the close of 1862. General James H. Carleton, who had come with 3,000 California volunteers to take command in New Mexico, then set on foot a campaign of Apache extermination. This campaign got under way in 1863, reached all-out proportions in 1864, and continued, although gradually declining in energy, until 1871. In the first flush of enthusiasm, the cooperation of Sonora and Chihuahua was obtained; miners were encouraged to return to Arizona and were offered expenses, California style, for informal Apache-killing expeditions; Pimas, Papagos, and Maricopas were furnished with guns and American leadership; troops, at a wartime high, were employed to the full. Many of the troops were Californians, and California methods were adopted, which meant that any means whatever were acceptable as long as Apaches were killed. Thus there was no official objection if Apaches were coaxed to appear for "treaty" talks and were then shot—old Mangas Coloradas was one of the first to fall for this, dying in 1863.

Some officers, such as Colonel Kit Carson and Colonel John C. Cremony, who had known the Apaches for years, simply ignored the orders to kill all men and take the women and children prisoner, and accepted Apache surrenders. But in general the forces combined for the great extermination program went to their work with enthusiasm, and the peak year of 1864 recorded hundreds of armed encounters. However, the official score of a total of 216 Apaches killed in this big year was not terribly encouraging—and the rest of the score, 3,000 sheep captured by Indians as against 175 captured back, and 146 horses captured by Indians as against 54 recovered, was even less so. There was also a definite feeling in the territories that the official white loss of sixteen was incomplete.

Mines were reopened in Arizona, settlements were reestablished, and the Apaches were driven deep into their mountains and made destitute by ceaseless destruction of their rancherias. But no Apache band was conquered—most of the Apache casualties were noncombatants—the life of a traveler was not safe in Apacheria, nor the lives of small groups of prospectors or settlers, and even settlements of some size lived in fear of bloodcurdling Apache raids. In effect, the old conditions of the Spanish frontier were restored, with the difference that there were more whites to be raided, and the methods of the war brought bitterness and cruelty to new highs. Some of the milder frontier tales of Apache atrocities spoke of captured women whose bodies had been literally torn apart, and of prisoners hung head downward over small fires, their uncontrollable jackknifing affording amusement for hours while their brains slowly roasted until they died.

We do not have, of course, the tales of white atrocities that Apaches may have told each other. Arizona in the 1860s and 1870s had the reputation of being the toughest territory in the West, filled with gentry who had departed other climes a quick jump ahead of the vigilantes. There is no reason to suppose they dealt gently with an Apache, when they could get hold of one. The 1871 massacre by a Tucson mob of some eighty-five Aravaipa Apache people who had put themselves under the protection of the military at a nearby fort, Camp Grant, caused national indignation, but was generally defended by the Arizona press—100 Americans, Mexicans, and Papagos were indicted and tried for these murders and declared not guilty by a jury after less than a half hour's deliberation. A plenary representative of the President, sent to Arizona to take over Indian affairs after this incident, reported that "acts of inhuman treachery and cruelty" had made the Apaches "our implacable foes," after they had tried to be friends of the Americans in the beginning.

"How is it?" asked Cochise, chief of the Chiricahuas. "Why is it that the Apaches want to die—that they carry their lives on their fingernails?"

The Camp Grant massacre ended the war of Apache extermination—a war of almost ten years that had cost 1,000 American lives and more than $40,000,000 and resulted in complete failure. The special report of the President's representative concluded that the country was no quieter nor the Apaches any nearer extermination than they were when it all began.

And so the policy of extermination was replaced by a policy of conciliation, while the frontier seethed with resentment. Fortunately, the command of the military department of Arizona was given in that same summer of 1871 to General George Crook. General Crook was an Indian fighter of skill and wisdom, and what was still more extraordinary, of an honesty as stubborn as one of his treasured pack mules. He would no more break his word to the leader of a pack of ragged Apaches than he would break his word to a field marshal of England. Fighting was his profession but people were his business. He realized that Apaches were not the hell hounds the frontier pictured them, and they were not the saintly martyrs pictured by the sentimental friends of the Red Man in the East. They were frightened people who were tremendously experienced at being the subjects of extermination, an experience that had made them the most polished masters of ruthless guerrilla fighting in the history of the United States.

Captain John G. Bourke, General Crook's adjutant for many years, became extremely well acquainted with Apaches, and wrote, "No Indian has more virtues and none has been more truly ferocious when aroused.... For centuries he has been preëminent over the more peaceful nations about him for courage, skill, and daring in war; cunning in deceiving and evading his enemies; ferocity in attack when skillfully planned ambuscades have led an unwary foe into his clutches; cruelty and brutality to captives; patient endurance and fortitude under the greatest privations. . . . In peace he has commanded respect for keen-sighted intelligence, good fellowship, warmth of feeling for his friends, and impatience of wrong.... "

The Apache could cover forty miles in a day on foot, shambling along in his sloppy legging-like moccasins, or could reel off seventy-five miles a day on horseback, caring nothing about running his horse into the ground since his remount station was the nearest ranch. He could live off the country, "hilarious and jovial" while a civilized pursuer was perishing of hunger, thirst, and sunstroke. He could travel as invisibly as a ghost, appear or disappear as silently as a shadow. The soldier on his trail only knew of his presence when the lethal Apache bow or Winchester announced itself from a concealed and highly defendable position.

The dusty warrior, with a dash of color at the headband or in the Pima-like turban, was seldom seen, and if seen was seldom hit, and if hit was seldom knocked down to stay. Apaches were terribly hard to kill.

There being no solidarity among Apaches in general, Crook employed the warriors of conciliated bands to fight the bands that insisted on remaining hostile. Crook's Apache scouts became famous, and by the end of summer, 1874, all important hostile bands had been either conciliated or relentlessly rounded up, and were settled on reservations, peaceful and reportedly happy. There was "almost a certainty," said the governor of Arizona in 1875, "that no general Indian war will ever occur again." This was the first phase of Crook's program. The second phase was not as easy. It consisted in protecting these peaceful Apaches from white troublemakers, well-meaning or otherwise.

General Crook said in 1879, "During the twenty-seven years of my experience with the Indian question I have never known a band of Indians to make peace with our government and then break it, or leave their reservation, without some ground or complaint; but until their complaints are examined and adjusted, they will constantly give annoyance and trouble."

The greatest cause of later trouble, among the Apaches, was the arbitrary removal of bands from their homeland reservations to new reservations where they did not want to go. This was done by the Indian Bureau for reasons of operational efficiency, or to throw the business of an agency to some go-getting community that was pulling strings to get it, or for similar humanitarian motives. The second greatest cause of trouble was the activity of crooked "rings" that supplied supplies Indians never received, stole reservation land by shady manipulation, or practiced other such arts and crafts. Captain Bourke summed this up by saying that the wicked Indians labored under a delusion that a ration was enough food to keep the recipient from starving to death, while the agent issued supplies by throwing them through the rungs of a ladder—the Indians getting whatever stuck to the rungs, and the agent getting what fell to the ground. Finally, there were the seamy whisky wagoners and petty thieves who were not averse to stirring the Indians up for a profit of two bits.

General Crook again, on the subject of bad Indians: "I have never yet seen one so demoralized that he was not an example in honor and nobility compared to the wretches who plunder him of the little our government appropriates for him."

In New Mexico and Arizona these causes brought trouble from a number of Apache bands but most of all from the Chiricahuas, whose furious outbreaks of protest added considerable size to the Apache legend. The great Cochise died in peace on the Chiricahua reservation in the summer of 1874, but within eighteen months some of the Chiricahuas were rampaging into Sonora, killing innocent bystanders right and left along the way, to resist removal to another reservation.

For a fair share of the next ten years various Chiricahua groups, generally accompanied by some families of Mogollon, Mimbres, and Coyotero in-laws, were breaking loose to storm up and down the border country, performing ghostly raids and elusive campaigns that make the staid military reports read like fiction. Such leaders as Victorio and Geronimo (pronounced and in his day sometimes spelled Heronimo), entered the ranks of the West's top celebrities. Both these men were Mimbreños by birth; Victorio had been a lieutenant of Mangas Coloradas. After Victorio was killed by Mexican troops in 1880, a rheumatic old gentleman named Nana stepped up to take a turn stage center, and for a wild, incredible couple of months in 1881 led a handful of warriors, perhaps fifteen Chiricahuas, later joined by a couple of dozen Mescaleros, on the champion raid and running campaign of them all, fighting and winning a battle a week against 1,000 U.S. troops, Texas Rangers, armies of frantic civilians, and the military and police establishments of northern Mexico. Nana was some seventy or eighty years old at the time, and so stove up with aches and pains he had to walk with a cane. He liked to wear gold watch chains in his ears.

General Crook had been sent away to fight the Sioux in 1875, when Arizona was quiet and there was never again going to be an Indian war. He was brought back in 1882, and for four years patiently rounded up hostile Apaches and then patiently tried to pacify hostile elements on the home front, and then rounded up his Apaches again when they were prodded into another break. Geronimo, half clown and half monster, came to the fore during this period and made his name a matter of dread on both sides of the border.

There came a time when Crook's superiors had had enough of his patience and his insistence on honorable behavior, and replaced him with General Nelson A. Miles. When Apache scouts were able to talk Geronimo into surrendering again, he and his band were packed off to Florida as prisoners, and for good measure Miles sent along Crook's old Apache scouts as prisoners too, and just to make sure he had everyone, sent along all the other Chiricahuas he could lay hands on, including hundreds of those who had remained quietly on the reservation from the first.

This happened in 1886, and Crook was still waging a campaign in the halls of Congress to get his Apaches moved back west (as far as Oklahoma) when he died of a heart attack in 1890. A few months before his death he visited the largest group of exiled Chiricahuas, who had been temporarily settled at Mount Vernon Barracks, near Mobile, Alabama. They crowded around him, his old scouts and his ancient enemies—and a number were both—and there was quite a reunion, and this is as good a place as any other to declare a final, formal end of the Indian wars.

Old Geronimo was in the schoolroom at the time of General Crook's visit, threatening with a stick any children who misbehaved.

# XIV

# Reservations

**Photographed in 1891, this tipi settlement was part of the Pine Ridge Reservation in South Dakota, the largest U.S. camp of the then aimless and defeated Indian peoples.**

From end to end of the two continents the American Indians lived, and they still do. Disease, conquest, mass exterminations, oppression, and decay had by about 1900 reduced the number of Indians in the United States to an estimated 237,000. Since that time the number of Indians has increased, at a rate higher than the increase in the general population, to more than a half million in 1960, and to more than a million and a half at the beginning of the 1990s.

The Inuit (Eskimos), Aleuts, and Indians in Alaska are now estimated at some 85,000. Canada counts more than a half million Inuit and Indians. Inuit communities make up four fifths of Greenland's 50,000 people.

But it is necessary to remember that all this area north of Mexico was peripheral to the central Indian world. Where the modern Indians of the United States equal less than one percent of the total population, the modern Indians of Guatemala, Bolivia, and Peru make up 45 to 60 per cent of the total population, or even more. Many more millions who are to a lesser degree Indian in blood and heritage enhance the Indian character of the populations from Mexico southward. In Peru, for example, where the Indian population increased mightily during the 1800s due to the reduction of mining and a return to agriculture, the population of mestizos—people of mixed European and Indian descent—increased more mightily still. When in the 1890s Mexico finally surpassed with some twelve million people the estimated population of Aztec times, only a million or so were whites, the rest rather evenly divided, at that time, between pure Indians and mestizos.

In some broad terms, Indian history throughout much of the rest of the hemisphere paralleled the Indian story in the United States. The colonial culture of the 1700s in general provided a sort of shadow protection for Indians, if only as natural resources or Crown possessions. The egalitarian winds of the 1800s swept away this protection and left Indian groups and their remaining community holdings at the mercy of whatever bloc controlled local legislation.

Indian lands were broken up, Indians were transformed into peons, wars of resistance were fought, sometimes for decades—as in the case of the Mayas in the Mexican state of Quintana Roo on the Yucatan peninsula, who fought a full-scale rebellion from 1847 to 1850, and continued resisting in some degree until the 1940s. The effort to break up community lands was now and then given up in the face of Indian opposition. And here and there, when an Indian struggle became hopeless, messiahs appeared. The talking cross of Chan Santa Cruz inspired the above-mentioned Mayas of Quintana Roo; and at the very time that the dreamer and prophet Wovoka was originating the Ghost Dance that swept the western United States, in the late 1880s, a messiah was calling the Chiriguanos to arms in Bolivia, saying the guns of the soldiers would only spit water.

But in Latin America generally, Indian culture had mingled inextricably with European, and in regions of heavy Negro slavery, with African. It had not so much resisted this mingling as it had retained, with remarkable tenacity, certain Indian traits. In recent years there has been a growing recognition of Indian elements in the Latin American character, with a tendency to glorify Indian history and individual Indians, such as Juarez, who have been of moment in national history. This so-called Indianist feeling is strongest in Mexico, where it was a factor in the "Revolutionary" school of art that reached its climax in the 1930s, one of the few American art movements ever to be taken seriously by Europe.

"Indianism" has also led to somewhat revised policies toward the masses of pure Indians, sometimes even in areas where caste distinctions continue to relegate Indians to second-class status. A tendency toward genuine protection and encouragement of surviving Indians began to appear in various American countries in the early 1900s. Brazil founded in 1910 the Service for the Protection of the Indian, to bring education and modern techniques in medicine and agriculture to the many tribes of Amazonia, and gradually to make these tribes a part of the national life and culture. One of the directors of the Service, speaking of the Indian's strength of personality, courage, staying power, "affection and devotion to the family, and generous hospitality to the stranger," said, "these are attributes sufficient to constitute the strongest and most progressive race in the world, if they had been properly encouraged... by the first colonists."

Slowly and by no means steadily the notion began to get around that the Indian heritage might still contain values more subtle than those so far found in silver and gold and cheap labor. In the 1930s an inter-American group sponsored a study which demonstrated that the Indians were not a vanishing race but a rapidly growing race; this gave rise to the Inter-American Institute of the Indian organized in 1940 by nineteen American republics. Some of the results have been a partial eradication of remnants of Indian slavery or forced labor; an occasional shot at bilingual education—encouraging learning and even literacy in an Indian as well as a European language; and an inclination toward encouraging or sustaining the tribe or Indian community rather than shattering it. In Peru and Bolivia the ancient clan division of the ayllu owns and regulates the land in thousands of Indian villages, and in some cases such a community buys or builds such neo-Inca contraptions as hydroelectric plants—perhaps in much the same manner as an ayllu of olden times built a temple pyramid. Mexico began a program of restoring to Indian and mestizo communities the community lands, the *ejidos*, that had been seized for great estates during the turbulent, greedy years of early independence in the nineteenth century.

In the United States repeated and rigorous attempts were made over many years to demolish tribal ties and structures. The ideal was to chew the Indian up in the social machine and assimilate him. The problem was complicated by many special aspects, among them the fact that most tribes still owned some property that various interested citizens never gave up trying to get. A constant, overriding handicap was the depressing fact that any Indian program was subject to complete change at each change of political administration.

In the Indians' darkest hour—the couple of generations from the 1870s to the 1920s—there was no doubt much more silent suffering than will ever be related. On the spiritual side, religious activities were proscribed, children were taught to feel shame and contempt for their "blanket Indian" parents and all their ways; life, in the case of many agency Indians, was made aimless and hopeless by the pervasive concentration camp air. On the physical side, hunger was the big reality for those confined peoples who could only secure their dinners out of promised government subsistence. The Bureau of Indian Affairs labored for years under charges of crookedness that no amount of reform could seem to hush; President Grant even tried the expedient of appointing only church-nominated agents, who too often turned out to be mainly interested in proselytizing for their sects, and the heathen—especially the heathen—still went hungry.

A glimpse of the dark ages of reservation life comes from the report of an army surgeon in the early days of the Crow Creek, South Dakota, Agency: "Some time about the middle of the winter a large vat was constructed of cotton-wood lumber, about six feet square and six feet deep in connection with the steam sawmill, with a pipe leading from the boiler into the vat. Into this vat was thrown beef, beef heads, entrails of beeves, some beans, flour and pork. I think there was put into the vat two barrels of flour each time, which was not oftener than once in twenty-four hours. This mass was then cooked by the steam from the boiler passing through the vat. When that was done, all the Indians were ordered to come there with their pails and get it.... The Santees and Winnebagos were fed from this vat; some of the Indians refused to eat it, saying they could not eat it, it made them sick.... The Indians reported several deaths from starvation.... "

Some individuals, particularly from dispersed or transplanted eastern nations, made progress in coming to terms with the white world on the outside. The articles of surrender that Lee signed at Appomattox were penned by Grant's secretary, Brigadier General Eli Samuel Parker, a Seneca sachem and grandson of the famous orator Red Jacket. Quite a few Sioux warriors found their way eased into the outside world via tours with Buffalo Bill's Wild West Show. One of the first to reach the scene of the Wounded Knee massacre was Dr. Charles Eastman, Santee Sioux graduate of Dartmouth and the Boston University medical school, then serving as government physician to the Pine Ridge, South Dakota, Agency. He described, quite dispassionately, the way young girls had knelt, and covered their faces with their shawls so they would not see the troopers come up to shoot them. Even some organized tribal groups, such as the Five Civilized Tribes and affiliated Shawnee and Delaware communities, persisted with marvelous stubbornness, through Job's plagues of setbacks, in trying to reach full adjustment with the new scale of the world being built around them.

But the more typical adjustments were those of the thousands of dispirited people who merely killed time in the institutionalized slums of their reservations, becoming adept in the skills of wise old boys who have lived a long time in the orphanage. They learned how to wheedle and hoodwink the agency staff for the nickels and dimes in scraps of supplies that trickled down through the budget to their level, and how to give some point to a pointless existence by finding delight in unutterable trivia. And the friendly agents said in a fond way, "They're children." Unfriendly agents said, "Indolent, insolent, and uncivilizable," and usually resigned.

The Railroad Enabling Act of 1866 sliced some choice cuts off a number of reservations. This act gave to railroad builders alternate sections of public lands forty miles deep on either side of a projected right of way, as an inducement to railroad building. The forty-mile depth was later extended to fifty miles to offset losses from prior claims of white settlers; but for the purposes of the Act, reservations were considered public lands, and unlucky Indian communities found themselves being evicted from railroad property.

Reservations, as previously noted, existed under the authority of acts of Congress or treaties between organized groups of Indian people and the President of the United States, with ratification by the Senate. Reservations were established in payment for huge land cessions and other tribal acts of cooperation; the treaty commissioners who established them usually felt they were making excellent bargains. The United States was perfectly willing to promise that the reservations would be permanently Indian land, protected by the federal government from interference by neighboring white residents, including state and county governments. More often than not, particularly when the comparatively small reservation area left a hunting people without range enough for livelihood, the commissioners also promised lagniappe in the form of goods, tools, subsistence, or annuities; and the treaty commissioners still felt they were making excellent bargains.

After 1871, "treaties" with Indian nations and tribes were replaced by less stately "agreements," and reservations were enlarged or diminished, within limits, by executive order of the President. Reservation lands were still supposed to be inalienable, as the language of the treaties and agreements customarily stated. But later Congresses were under no obligation, of course, to keep the nation's promise, there being no power, at least not here below, to compel them to do so. The reservations began to look bigger and shinier every day, as land in the West picked up in value. And even friends of the Red Man had to admit that reservations fostered tribal unity, which was a bar, everyone said, to civilizing the savages.

Thus in 1887, after much strenuous politicking, the so-called Allotment Act became law, a rope trick designed to make all Indians and their problems disappear and place the broad reservations in the more appreciative hands of white owners. Under this law tribes were to surrender their reservations, fragments of which were to be allotted to individual Indians as small, family-sized farms—from 10 to 640 acres each. The immense reservation acreage left over was to be declared "surplus" and, after a token payment to the tribes involved, opened to white ownership.

Obviously the Allotment Act would break up the tribes and change all Indians instantly into God-fearing, industrious small farmers indistinguishable from anybody else. In this belief many sincere Indian friends backed the measure, and even General Crook lent his presence to the task of dragooning the plains tribes into going through the motions of accepting it. Since it would also give a massive shot in the arm to the land-office business, land speculation interests promoted the bill with an equal or even greater sincerity.

In this last objective the law succeeded magnificently. More than 100 reservations were allotted, principally on the plains, the Pacific coast, and in the Lakes states. Of the approximately 150 million acres owned by the Indians in 1880, most of it guaranteed by treaties made less than thirty or forty years before, over 90 million acres—an area more than twice the size of Oklahoma—were abstracted from the Indians' pocket. The process lost steam after some of the big plains reservations, the principal targets, were carved up and sold, but it went along in a desultory way for many years.

In its ostensible objective of civilizing Indians, the Allotment Act was a failure. If Indians were children just learning to walk, as *fin-de-siècle* unction expressed it, the Allotment Act helped this along by cutting their legs off at the knees. Allottees did not turn instantly into sturdy small farmers. It wouldn't have

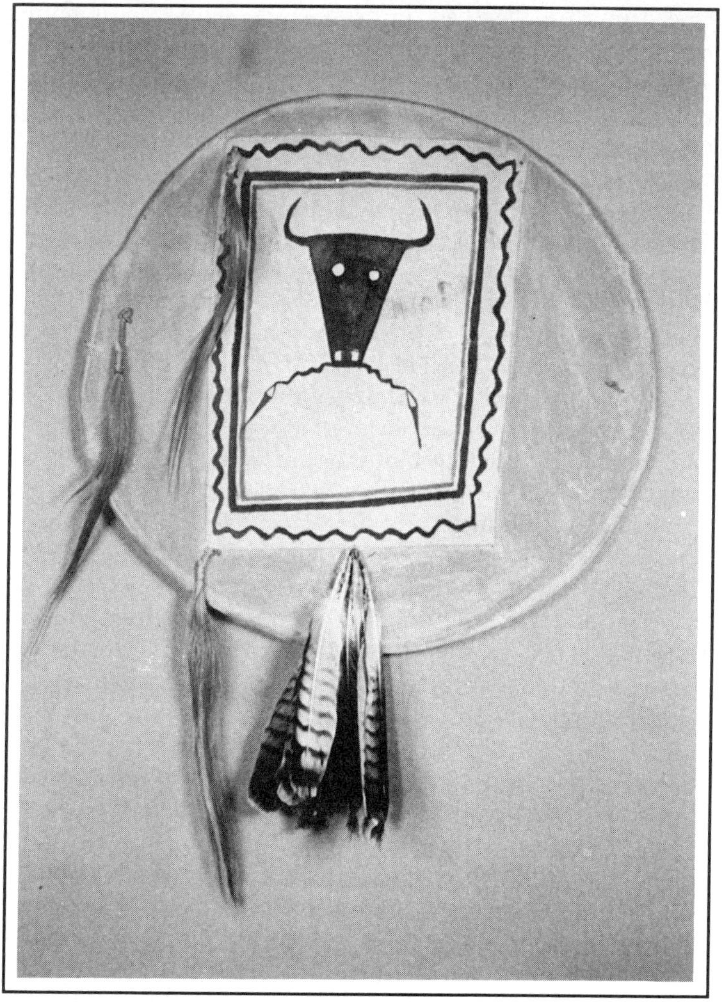

In the 1890s Ghost Dance cults swept across the West, inspired by the vision of a Paiute Indian named Wovoka. According to him, a messiah would call to life the Indian dead and even restore the buffalo to the plains; the white man would vanish and the Indian regain control of the land. Trancelike dances were performed to hasten these events, and Ghost Dance shields like this one were fashioned for the rite.

helped much if they had, in many cases, since even imported Russian peasants went gaunt trying to work small claims on the northern plains. Instead, by one means or another, allottees frequently lost their ragtag and bobtail patches of ground to white ownership, or leased the land for messes of pottage to larger operators. Some were thus utterly dispossessed, and congregated in junkyard squatter communities here and there, or piled in by wagonloads to "visit" with any relations who still had the wherewithal for a square meal of tough beef and fried bread. Hundreds of families collapsed into a permanent pauperdom. The Sioux centering in South Dakota were the hardest hit; their economic wreckage is evident yet.

The law provided that the government hold allotted land in trust for twenty-five years before making the allottee the outright owner by granting him a patent in fee simple. (The fee simple titles had the effect of putting the land on tax rolls and also made the land subject to alienation.) As the pattern of allottee ruination came clear, the government adopted (in the 1920s) a policy of automatically renewing the trust periods. Much Indian land today is held under government trusteeship in this fashion; other reservation lands, often in desert or otherwise unproductive areas, have never been allotted. But the drastic reduction of reservations already accomplished had by the 1920s made Indian poverty chronic, and above all no room had been left for an expanding Indian population. When this totally unexpected event began to come to pass, overcrowding the reservations still further, poverty became widespread and acute.

A thorough, government-sponsored survey carried out in the late 1920s stated in its opening sentence, "An overwhelming majority of the Indians are poor, even extremely poor, and they are not adjusted to the economic and social system of the dominant white civilization." The same study also found Indian health and education remarkably poor. Perhaps most important, it found that the battered Indians of the United States were very definitely a living race. Clearly the impatient and repressive policies of the Allotment Act era had been in tragic error.

These policies were reversed in the Indian Reorganization Act of 1934, which put a stop to any more allotting of tribal lands, and tried to get back for the Indians any of the "surplus" reservation lands that had not yet been homesteaded. In keeping with the notions revolutionizing Indian affairs throughout the hemisphere at the time, this law endeavored to help the Indians get on their feet by encouraging group progress via a tribal approach.

A surprising amount of community spirit had survived the generations of attempts to break up the tribes. Not only did cohesive tribes and bands still exist, but a broader tendency toward pan-Indianism was becoming apparent, discernible in such items as the spread of the peyote religion. This cult, organized in 1918 under the name of the Native American Church, uses elements from various sources, including Christianity, and a vision-producing drug of ancient Mexican ancestry, peyote cactus buds; the church now has members in nearly all tribes, and represents the largest single Indian group in the United States today.

Government representatives went forth and talked with more than 250 tribes and bands, urging them to organize under the new law with constitutions and charters of incorporation, and offering loan funds for constructive community purposes from a revolving credit program. Most Indian groups cooperated with enthusiasm. For the first time in history Indian lands were increased, from about 47 million acres to about 50 million; tribe after tribe pulled itself up by its bootstraps, with the help of the new law, toward a solid foundation for solvency or even prosperity. Thousands of Indian families were restored to a life of some hope and independence. The repayment record for loans from the revolving credit fund was excellent; $20,000,000 was eventually available, including a portion furnished by various tribes from their own trust funds. Educational opportunities were greatly improved, with more Indian children attending public schools, tuition often being paid the school district by the federal government. An educated Indian was no longer a rarity, Indian college students no longer uncommon.

Native languages, crafts, ceremonies, traditions, were not only permitted but promoted, with a consequent reawakening of interest in what some Indians refer to as the old time religion. Venerable medicine men journeyed hundreds of miles in almost equally venerable cars or pickup trucks to teach the correct rituals to young people living in towns; factory workers came home from Detroit or San Francisco to take part in the Sun Dance or the Corn Dance.

By and large the people were still very poor, but there was a difference. Most communities showed some progress, and many made an astonishingly quick climb out of the slough of a century of despondency. The tribes, those that were left, had been in a desperate struggle during that century merely to survive: they demonstrated that they still had a power to help themselves, if they were encouraged to use it.

In World War II approximately 25,000 Indians served in the armed forces, somewhat more than one third of all able-bodied Indian men between eighteen and fifty; some first really learned English at this time, or a reasonable GI facsimile thereof, and thousands had their first real look at the outside world, and went back home full of new notions for their families and the tribal communities.

But in 1950 the government's Indian policy was reversed again. Efforts were made once more to reduce Indian land, and to chop back or break down the tribal societies. The revolving credit program ground to a virtual halt. The growth of Indian communities was no longer inspired and aided, but obstructed. Indians were not urged to work together, but emphasis was placed on individual emigration to large cities to find wage work and, in a word, get lost. An intensive "termination" program was put into effect, with the idea of removing all federal protection and services from the various Indian tribes as soon as possible, thus bringing about, presumably, their dissolution. The objective was to get the federal government out of the Indian business.

This reaction was the first ripple of the wave of political reaction in the early 1950s that took its name and fame from the leadership of Senator Joseph McCarthy. The reaction in Indian policy persisted until the decline of "McCarthyism" in the late 1950s, when a gradual return to the previous policy of honest helpfulness to the Indians took place. Said the principal government expert on Indian legal affairs, the late Felix S. Cohen: "Like the miner's canary, the Indian marks the shifts from fresh air to poison gas in our political atmosphere; and our treatment of Indians, even more than our treatment of other minorities, reflects the rise and fall of our democratic faith."

Only a few tribes were terminated by specific acts of Congress—the most important being the Menominees of Wisconsin and the Klamaths of southern Oregon, both owners of rich stands of timber. The drive to remove essential services from the Bureau of Indian Affairs brought, among other results, the transferal of Indian health programs to the Public Health Service, which under an increased budget made a considerable advance in the late 1950s in providing for Indians health services approaching those available to other citizens.

In preparation for expected wholesale termination, a special commission for Indian claims was established in 1947 to clear up all unpaid treaty claims, charges of past fraudulence, and the like. More than 800 claims were filed; in the first ten years 102 had been decided, recovery being granted in twenty-one claims; amounts totaling some $40,000,000 have been paid to date, reduced from a total of more than a billion claimed. Anthropologists and historians who serve as expert witnesses in these cases prepare extremely detailed documents dealing with the history of the tribes involved; it is expected that these documents will ultimately provide the first thorough history of the Indians of the United States, a side-effect of the work of this commission which may be of more lasting value than the money payments which it grants.

In 1960 a second major inquiry into present-day Indian matters, the first since the initial and epochal report of 1928, was begun by a group of experts under the sponsorship of the University of Chicago. The National Congress of American Indians, an organization of some eighty member tribes, and other Indian spokesmen were invited to a conference in Chicago in the summer of 1961 to help in shaping the course of this study and its subsequent statement of policy by offering some of the points of view of the Indian people. Substantial Indian participation in a work of this importance is regarded as the most significant event in the recent history of the Indians.

The number of Indian men and women in professional life, both in and out of the Indian world, has multiplied remarkably in the past generation. Movement back and forth from the Indian to the white world has become immeasurably freer. At the same time, the long-standing conviction that sooner or later all Indians would become totally assimilated into the standardized stream of American life has steadily lost ground. Most experts today feel that Indian tribes and communities will retain separate identities for a long, long time into the future—and most experts believe that is good, not bad. Habits of cooperation instead of competition are still pronounced among many Indians, affect-

Joseph Miller photographed these Navaho women of Monument Valley, Arizona, weaving the blankets for which their tribe is famous. The Navaho are also accomplished silversmiths and traded their unique handiwork around the pueblo communities of the Southwest.

ing schoolwork—where children may try not to "appear better" than each other—and all life. "Success is unpopular," said an official on an Apache reservation. The ascendant view at present, in the United States and throughout the Americas, is to accept and turn to account these inborn qualities. Wonders of achievement sometimes result; and the success of the tribe or community is never unpopular—although it may not always be the typical middle-class American concept of success.

Most Indians today are still very poor, their health is poor, and the general level of education is poor. They still own considerable property; the 949,000 people on the rolls of the Bureau of Indian Affairs in 1989 held assets in lands, timber and mineral resources, livestock and agricultural production, business enterprises, and so on, that can be calculated to a very substantial dollar value. Other assets, such as water rights, cannot be measured. These assets still attract the attention, now and then, of neighboring non-Indians who, in the old frontier phrase, have more gall than character. Thefts and attempted thefts, shady deals, and dirty political pool still make for scandals in the Indian business, and in much Indian opinion a fair share of the hard core feeling, still vocal, for breaking up the tribes is based on nothing more psychological than an itch for the last of the Indian loot. But more and more organizations and interested persons in and out of government are watchful of the Indians' interests, and the general public has considerably more gumption about demanding honesty and justice than it had in the tough, violent days of extermination. Even so, the shady operators sometimes accomplish their shady operations, simple zeal and persistence winning the day.

Those Indians who live on reservations or restricted trust land do not pay taxes on the land or the income therefrom. Those on the membership rolls of the various tribes are, in most matters, under federal jurisdiction rather than state and county jurisdiction. In these respects Indians are "wards" of the United States. The sense of the term, particularly in modern times, means protection: the United States, in return for value received, has guaranteed to protect various Indian peoples from local political discrimination or interference—such as the interference of Alabama, Mississippi, and Georgia that drove out the Five Civilized Tribes. For many reasons, most Indians feel they need this federal protection; state and local jurisdictions have too often shown a tendency to gnaw away at Indian holdings when they could get at them.

In all other respects Indians are full-fledged citizens, and have been since a law of 1924 extended citizenship to all Indians born in the United States. Some were legally citizens long before that by special legislation. They can come and go like any other citizen, vote like any other citizen, and pay takes like any other citizen—with the exemption of reservation land, as noted above. They can even, since a recent repeal of the ancient Indian prohibition law, buy liquor like any other citizen.

They are—those who retain reservation affiliations or property in trust status—federal citizens, so to speak, and their domain is, in a sense, an extra state scattered piecemeal over the face of the country. In this shadow state all services—roads, schools, police, hospitals, courts, public utilities—are furnished either by the federal government or by the tribal organizations themselves. In the aggregate this shadow state is somewhat larger in area than Nebraska or South Dakota, and considerably larger in population than Nevada or Alaska.

Administering this domain is what keeps the government in the Indian business. The cost of administration combines the costs that in an actual state would be shared among village, township, city, county, state, and federal expenses. This cost, counting total funding to the BIA, the Indian Health Service, and a hatful of other agencies dealing with everything from education and housing to welfare and urbanism, added up to $3.3 billion in 1988.

Unfortunately, not all of this trickles down to the Indian people, naturally, since it has to pay its way past many a desk. The Indian Self Determination Act of 1975, with amendments passed in 1988, may in time ameliorate some of this fiscal slippage, and even more important may provide the tribes with a greater control of their own affairs, as Indian leaders have been wearily requesting for many a long year.

Nearly 150,000 Indians live in eastern states, chiefly in North Carolina, Michigan, and New York. In 1960, the Six Nations Iroquois in New York lost a long court fight against condemnation of certain of their lands for a New York State project; in the course of this battle they proved the stubborn Iroquois spirit was far from dead by turning down cash offers for amounts well above the value of the land. Modern Mohawks have made something of a national reputation as structural steel workers.

Indian Territory fell under the axe of the Allotment Act and became Oklahoma in 1907—Congress refused the name of Sequoyah, desired by the state's residents. The creation of the state brought to an end a hopeless effort by the Five Civilized Tribes to keep the territory they had been promised would be theirs as long as water kept on running. "What about our people, who are, now, the legal owners?" wrote a Cherokee angrily in 1895. "Why the question is easy of answer. Crushed to earth under the hoofs of business gread, they would soon become a homeless throng, more scoffed at and abused than a Coxey's army." Pieces of the territory had been taken away at intervals ever since the arrival of the Civilized Tribes, for other groups of displaced Indians or for white settlement.

The Cherokee people, numbering more than 230,000, make up the largest tribe by far in the United States and, with about a third of this total resident in Oklahoma, comprise the most populous of the many Indian groups in that state, which also counts large Choctaw and Creek communities, sizeable numbers of Chickasaws and Seminoles, and smaller communities of numerous other Indian nations, such as a population of nearly 5,000 still on the Oklahoma Osage reservation. Many of these various peoples are more or less assimilated into the general population, and quite a few are doing quite well, although quite a few more are not.

In the early 1900s the Osage were reckoned among the wealthiest of tribes, with a per capita annual income of $265, most of it from pasturage leases on reservation land. Then oil was discovered, making each of the 2,229 "headrights" of the reservation land worth real money. Oil-rich Osages, surrounded by clouds of con artists, entered the national legend; and for years thereafter Indian oil scandals in eastern Oklahoma entered history.

The Navaho tribe, over 160,000 persons, nearly all concentrated on or about the vast Navaho reservation at the corner junctions of Arizona, New Mexico, and Utah (105,000 living on the reservation itself), is a reasonably representative example of a reasonably prosperous Indian community, prosperous as a community, as a business entity; but the 1980 census found more than half the Navaho people still below the poverty level, and nearly half their homes without indoor plumbing and electricity.

Heaviest populations of native people in the United States are today in California, Oklahoma, Arizona, and New Mexico. Largest present-day groups, after the Cherokee and Navaho, are the Sioux, Chippewa (Ojibwa), Inuit (Eskimos), Choctaw, Pueblo, Iroquois, Apache, Lumbee, and Creek, all with populations between 25,000 and 100,000.

Alaska would rank fifth in the above list. The reindeer introduced there by Dr. Sheldon Jackson did so well in later times that the business was pretty much taken over by white trading companies, the Eskimos being reduced from independent herd owners to employed herders. The depression of the 1930s ruined the industry, and with the help of government loans Eskimos got back the remnants of the reindeer herds.

Fighting men have come and gone but the people of peace, the Hopis, are still in their country, although a missionary stirred up a civil war among them some years ago over the occupation of their oldest town, Oraibi. They fought it out with a tug of war, and the losers moved. They have recently sued the Navahos, who have completely surrounded them. The peaceful Pimas are still along the Gila, as they have been for unnumbered thousands of years. They have been the intended victims of some extra-ingenious shady deals, due to those precious Gila waters; but they are still there. The great Spanish empire has long since vanished like castles in the air, but Zuñi, so easily conquered on that July day centuries ago, is still very real and very present.

The tourists who come by the thousands to the Hopi towns, to Zuñi, and to the other Pueblo villages, find a value clear apart from the earnest sociological matters that have been the burden of these last pages. They find what may be one of the most important of all the American Indian's contributions—a sense of permanence, the sense of an infinite past that implies an infinite future. The thought is comforting, and one for which the world seems hungry. It is good to feel that the history of the American Indian, any more than the history of America, is not finished.

# PICTURE CREDITS

Title Page: The New York Public Library
Table of Contents: New-York Historical Society
6: Museo Antropologico de la Universidad Veracruz
12: American Heritage Picture Collection
19: Arizona State Museum
24: Museo Nacional, Mexico
28: Peabody Museum
34: Bibliotheque Nationale, Paris
40: The Art Institute of Chicago
47: Thomas Gilcrease Institute of American History and Art, Tulsa
56: The American Museum of Natural History
62: Museum fur Volkerkunde, Vienna
68: Library of Congress
77: Library of Congress
84: Bibliotheque Nationale, Paris
92: Eastman House
98: Arizona State Museum
104: National Park Service
111: Chicago Natural History Museum
118: Smithsonian Institution, Bureau of American Ethnology
124: Library of Congress
130: The New York Public Library, Rare Book Division
138: University Museum, Philadelphia
144: (top and bottom) Smithsonian Institution, Bureau of Ethnology
150: National Gallery of Art
155: The New York Public Library, Rare Book Division
158: The New York Public Library
167: The New York Public Library, Stokes Collection
174: Schoolcraft, *Indian Tribes of the United States*, 1853
179: Historical Society of Pennsylvania
184: National Gallery of Canada, Ottawa
190: Missio Sancti Francisci Xaverii, Ottawa
197: National Gallery of Canada, Ottawa
204: Chicago Natural History Museum
212: Woolaroc Museum
220: American Heritage Picture Collection
227: The New York Public Library
234: The New York Public Library
242: Public Archives of Canada
248: Public Archives of Canada
255: West Point Museum Collection, U.S. Military Academy
260: New-York Historical Society
266: Bancroft Library, University of California
272: Hudson's Bay Company
277: Glenbow Foundation, Alberta
282: Alaska Department of Economic Development
288: Washington State Historical Society
296: Oakland Art Museum
303: Smithsonian Institution, Bureau of American Ethnology
308: Peabody Museum, Harvard
314: National Anthropological Archives, Smithsonian Institution
320: The New York Public Library, Rare Book Division
326: C. R. Smith Collection
333: Smithsonian Institution, Bureau of American Ethnology
338: The New York Public Library, Rare Book Division
344: Southwest Museum, Los Angeles
350: Lindley and Charles Eberstadt Collection of Western Art
358: Gottfried Hotz
367: Smithsonian Institution, Bureau of American Ethnology
374: American Heritage Picture Collection
382: National Archives
389: Museum of the American Indian
394: Arizona State Library

# INDEX

Italic page numbers refer to illustrations.

## A

# B

# C

# D



# E

# F



# G

# H

# I



# J

## K



## L

# M

# N

# O

# P

# Q



# R

# S

# T

## U



## V



## W

# X



# Y



# Z